Economic Issues, Problems and Perspectives

snova
New York

Economic Issues, Problems and Perspectives

Digital Challenges: What Is the Response of the Economy?
Igor Ilin, D.Sc (Editor)
Mariana Petrova, D.Sc (Editor)
2023. ISBN: 979-8-89113-168-2 (eBook)

Case Studies in Economic Survival: Experiences from Sri Lanka
Sumudu Senani Perera, PhD (Editor)
Prathap Kaluthanthri, PhD (Editor)
Janaka Fernando, PhD (Editor)
Ruwini Dharmawardene, PhD (Editor)
2023. ISBN: 979-8-88697-786-8 (Softcover)
2023. ISBN: 979-8-89113-139-2 (eBook)

The Theory of Qualitative Economic Growth: A New Framework for Economic Growth Theory
Sergio Focardi (Editor)
Frank J. Fabozzi (Editor)
2023. ISBN: 979-8-89113-029-6 (Softcover)
2023. ISBN: 979-8-89113-141-5 (eBook)

The Economy as a Complex System of Economic Actions: In Search of a New Paradigm
Paata Leiashvily (Editor)
2023. ISBN: 979-8-88697-909-1 (Hardcover)
2023. ISBN: 979-8-88697-952-7 (eBook)

More information about this series can be found at
https://novapublishers.com/product-category/series/economic-issues-problems-and-perspectives/

Olivier Bullock
Editor

Stablecoins

Background, Risks and Legislation

snova
New York

Library of Congress Cataloging-in-Publication Data

ISBN: 979-8-89113-502-4

Published by Nova Science Publishers, Inc. † New York

Contents

Preface

Over the last several years, the number of cryptocurrencies has exploded from the hundreds to the thousands. The use of cryptocurrency was supposed to democratize money or build a more inclusive economy, but none of these promises have materialized. Wild price swings and high transaction fees from cryptocurrencies make them useless for payments, the one thing they claim to be designed for. Stablecoins were supposed to solve this problem. Unlike other cryptocurrencies, their value is not just based on market enthusiasm; a stablecoin's value is supposed to be backed by real assets held by the company that issues the stablecoin.

Chapter 1

Stablecoins: How Do They Work, How Are They Used, and What Are Their Risks?*

Committee on Banking, Housing, and Urban Affairs

Tuesday, December 14, 2021
U.S. Senate,
Committee on Banking, Housing, and Urban Affairs,
Washington, DC.

The Committee met at 10:15 a.m., via Webex and in room 538, Dirksen Senate Office Building, Hon. Sherrod Brown, Chairman of the Committee, presiding.

Opening Statement of Chairman Sherrod Brown

Chairman BROWN. The Senate Committee on Banking, Housing, and Urban Affairs will come to order.

I welcome our witnesses. Today's hearing is in a hybrid format. Our witnesses, one is virtual; three are in person. Members have the option to appear either in person or virtually.

For those joining remotely, a few reminders: Members already know how to do this after many times. For our remote witness, just please try to minimize background noise, click the mute button until it is your turn to speak. You will

---

* This is an edited, reformatted and augmented version of Hearing before the Committee on Banking, Housing, and Urban Affairs, United States Senate, One Hundred Seventeenth Congress, First Session on Examining the Purposes and Risks of Stablecoins, S. HRG. 117–588, dated December 14, 2021.

In: Stablecoins
Editor: Olivier Bullock
ISBN: 979-8-89113-502-4

have one box on your screen labeled "clock" that will show how much time of your 5 minutes is remaining, or the questioner's 5 minutes. You will hear a bell ring when you have 30 seconds remaining. If there is a technology problem, we will move on to the next witness or Senator.

The speaking order is as usual, determined by seniority of the Members who have checked in before the gavel, either in person or remote. And then we go back and forth, Republican, Democrat, Republican, Democrat.

A few years ago, most people had never heard of cryptocurrency. Most people still did not know what all these terms mean, from stablecoins to nonfungible tokens. But they have become a hot topic in Washington, on Wall Street, online, among millions of Americans who, understandably, just do not trust big banks and are looking always for an opportunity to make money.

Over the last several years, the number of cryptocurrencies has exploded from the hundreds to the thousands. The supposed value of these digital assets in circulation recently passed $3 trillion, which is about the size of JPMorgan Chase's balance sheet, our Nation's largest bank. With that much money tied up, that is pretty much the definition of a systemic issue in our economy.

Those big numbers have come with big promises. We have been told that blockchain, the technology these coins are built upon, will democratize money or build a more inclusive economy, but none of these promises has materialized, likely never will. Instead, we have gotten wild financial speculation. As we have heard before in this Committee, the wild price swings and high transaction fees from any cryptocurrencies make them useless for payments, the one thing they claim to be designed for.

Stablecoins were supposed to solve this problem. Unlike other cryptocurrencies, their value is not just based on market enthusiasm; a stablecoin's value is supposed to be backed by real assets held by the company that issues the stablecoin. In other words, stablecoins are a particular type of cryptocurrency whose value is managed by a single company. These include, as you know, Tether, Circle, and Abracadabra, a fast growing scheme that makes "Magic Internet Money". That is their words, not mine. What could possibly go wrong with something that claims to make "magic" money? Cryptocurrency advocates argue that crypto assets are superior to real dollars because they are decentralized and transparent, but stablecoins are neither of those. Most of them, certainly the largest ones, rely on a single, centralized company to manage the reserve assets and their supply of coins. That sounds a lot like what traditional financial institutions do. It is not decentralized when one company controls when people can access their own money. It is certainly not transparent when critical information about stablecoins and the companies that issue them are not available to people who have their money tied up in those assets.

Last month I wrote to some of the biggest stablecoin issuers to get more information on how they manage their funds that back their coins and to ask what rights that their users have. Their responses were not particularly enlightening. They should lead us to—and should lead us to assume most ordinary customers do not have much in the way of rights at all.

So let us be clear about one thing. If you put your money in stablecoins, there is no guarantee you are going to get it back. They call it a currency, implying it is the same as having dollars in the bank and you can draw the money at any time. But many of these companies hide their terms and conditions, allowing them—in the fine print, allowing them to trap customers' money. There is no guarantee you will get your money back. That is not a currency with a fixed value; it is gambling.

And with this money tied up, it sure looks to me like a potential asset bubble. Stablecoins make it easier than ever to risk real dollars on cryptocurrencies that are, at best, volatile, at worst, outright fraudulent. Just a few weeks ago, we saw how quickly these tokens can crash with cryptomarkets diving by almost 30 percent in 1 day.

History tells us we should be concerned when any investment becomes so untethered from reality. Look at the 1929 stock market crash. Securities started out as a way for regular Americans to invest in new companies that wanted to bring new products to market to expand their operations. By the end of the decade, companies were invented out of thin air to create more stocks to satisfy wild demand. Banks allowed customers to borrow against one stock to buy another until the whole market collapsed.

And of course, many of us are old enough to remember, most of us are, the 2008 crash. Subprime mortgages were supposed to create—to give more families access to the American dream while derivatives were created to help financial companies reduce their risks. In reality, predatory mortgages were used to strip homeowners of their equity they had in their homes in order to create complex mortgage-backed securities and derivatives that ended up increasing risks at banks and financial companies. We know how that turned out for our country.

We cannot deny that betting on cryptocurrency has made a few people rich. That kind of action always does, just like some people became fabulously wealthy trading stocks in the 1920s or buying and selling derivatives 20 years ago. And we heard the stories about mortgage brokers and house flippers becoming millionaires more recently. But for most people, this kind of wild speculation ends in disaster. The only ones who tend to walk away unscathed are the big guys—it is always the big guys—the ones who call it innovation and then line their own pockets.

So far, what happens in the cryptomarkets has stayed in the cryptomarkets, so far, but stablecoins create a very real link between the real economy and this new fantasy economy. We saw this with Dogecoins, a satirical cryptocurrency that was all of a sudden worth billions when a tech billionaire tweeted about it. Think about that.

It is understandable a lot of people are looking for an alternative to our current financial system. Wall Street banks dominate this economy. They make record profits no matter what happens to workers and small businesses in Nevada, in South Dakota, in Ohio and Rhode Island. To a whole lot of people, that seems like a fantasy economy, too. But a big tech scheme that makes it easy for hardworking Americans to put their money at risk is not the answer. Stablecoins, cryptomarkets are not actually an alternative to our banking system; they are a mirror of the same broken system with even less accountability and no rules at all.

We will hear the same arguments today from this industry against regulation, the same arguments we hear from the financial industry, lobbyists so many times before: It harms innovation. The free market will solve all our problems. America needs to be globally competitive.

Of course, we do. What makes America, though, the strongest economy in the world is not wild betting in the financial sector. It is our workers. It is the dignity of work. It is their talent. It is their ingenuity, their dedication. That is what our economy is built on. You cannot fake that, but as we have seen so many times before you can put it all at risk. The rest of the world trusts the U.S. dollar when we have orderly, sane markets.

The real threat to our global competitiveness is regulators who ignore clear warning signs. We have reason to be encouraged this time around, though. The Biden administration is putting strong watchdogs in place, quite a change, strong watchdogs in place at the banking and market regulators. We are empowering workers. Wages are rising. Infrastructure investment is about to spur more job growth. We are fighting to bring down costs for families, for seniors, with prescription drugs, for the middle class with the Build Back Better plan.

We cannot put that potential at risk. I will continue to work with the financial watchdogs to ensure they have the tools they need to protect people's hard-earned money and our economic recovery from another bubble and another crash.

Senator Toomey.

Opening Statement of Senator Patrick J. Toomey

Senator TOOMEY. Thank you, Mr. Chairman. Stablecoins are a central component of the cryptocurrency ecosystem, which is itself at the vanguard of the tokenization of assets. Stablecoins can speed up payments, especially cross-border transfers. They can reduce costs, including remittances. And, they can help combat money laundering and terrorist financing through an immutable and transparent transaction record. Stablecoins can also be programmed and made interoperable with other currencies, creating efficiencies to improve access to financial services for more Americans.

But unlike volatile cryptocurrencies like Bitcoin, stablecoins do not fluctuate in their dollar price. In today's hearing, we will focus on stablecoins designed to maintain a one-to-one value relative to the U.S. dollar, meaning one stablecoin is meant to always equal one dollar.

Over the past year, the stablecoin market has exploded. As one of our witnesses, Dante Disparte, will explain, stablecoins are beginning to be used for small business payments and international remittances. While traditional payment systems can be expensive and take several days to settle, transferring funds via stablecoins is low cost and nearly instantaneous.

Given that stablecoins disrupt the status quo, they have naturally drawn skepticism from incumbent industries and regulators. Last month the President's Working Group on Financial Markets, or PWG, issued a report recommending that Congress pass legislation to establish a Federal regulatory framework for stablecoins. In their report, the Treasury Department and others expressed their worries about consumer protection and financial stability with stablecoins.

Although the report did little to highlight the potential benefits of stablecoins, I was encouraged that the report acknowledged that responsibility for clarifying whether, and to what extent, Federal agencies have jurisdictions over stablecoins is a question that rests with Congress. I am open to working with the Administration and my Democratic colleagues on this front. But whatever Congress does, let us be sure that we do not stifle innovation in an evolving digital economy or undermine our own country's competitiveness. Let us have the humility to recognize that many of our views about how financial services are delivered and how investments work are quickly becoming outdated.

This morning I am releasing a set of guiding principles that I think should influence our work on a stablecoin legislative framework. These principles recognize that stablecoins are a very important innovation and they introduce new capabilities into money that did not previously exist. In addition to their ease of use and reduced fees associated with their transfer, stablecoins can improve the privacy and the security of our transactions. They also introduce the concept of money programmability or smart contracts, which allow automated transactions based on a sequence of verifiable events. In recognition of the potential of these new capabilities, any regulation should be narrowly tailored and designed to do no harm. At the same time, sensible regulatory standards may help to protect against key risks such as redemption or run risk.

These principles take a different approach than the PWG report. For example, the PWG report recommends that all stablecoin issuers must be insured depository institutions. Well, there are three reasons that I disagree with that recommendation.

First, stablecoin issuers have different business models than banks. They do not provide the same services as banks and do not present the same risks. As one of today's witnesses, Ms. Massari, has observed, stablecoin providers do not engage in taking deposits and making loans in the manner that banks do. Because of these and other important differences, subjecting all stablecoin providers to the full suite of bank regulations and rules meant to address maturity transformation is not appropriately tailored to the potential risks.

Second, requiring all stablecoin issuers to become banks would stifle innovation. We know that a tremendous amount of innovation occurs outside of the banking system, including by technology companies. It is unlikely that much of this development could happen within the banking system because of the onerous regulations which create a difficult environment for innovation. Allowing entrepreneurs to innovate with digital assets like stablecoins will promote greater competition and deliver better results for consumers.

Finally, the regulation of payments activity should create an equal playing field. Great innovators like PayPal, Venmo, and Apple Pay are already subject to a State-by-State licensing regime as well as registration with a Federal regulator.

Recognizing the range of different business models, there should be at least three options available for a stablecoin provider. One would be to operate under a conventional bank charter if they chose. But, two, they could comply with, or acquire, a special purpose banking charter designed for stablecoin providers, which would be designed in accordance with legislation. Or, they could register as a money transmitter under the existing State regime and as a money service business with FinCEN at the Federal level. This optionality would match each stablecoin provider with the regulatory framework most appropriate to the business model.

Regardless of the charter or license they pursue, all stablecoin providers should meet certain minimum requirements. For example, they should clearly disclose what assets back the stablecoin as well as give clear redemption policies and subject themselves to periodic audits. These requirements would ensure that consumers have sufficient information about which stablecoins they use. It might also be appropriate to set minimum reserve requirements and attestations as well.

In addition, legislation should stipulate that non-interest bearing stablecoins are not necessarily securities and therefore should not automatically be regulated as such. This framework should protect the privacy, security, and confidentiality of individuals using stablecoins, allowing customers to opt out of sharing personal information with third parties.

Finally, antimoney laundering and other requirements regarding financial surveillance under the Bank Secrecy Act should really be modernized for all financial institutions subject to them, given the emergence of stablecoins, cryptocurrencies, and other new technologies, including artificial intelligence.

The emergence of stablecoins represents, to me, the latest development in the ongoing evolution of money. I stand ready to work on this issue and do so in a manner that does not discourage innovation or competition moving forward.

I look forward to hearing from our witnesses, and I yield back my time.

Chairman BROWN. Thank you, Senator Toomey.

I will now introduce the four witnesses today. First, we will hear from Alexis Goldstein, Director of Financial Policy at the Open Markets Institute; welcome. Jai Massari, a partner at Davis Polk & Wardwell, welcome. And, Chief Strategy Officer and Head of Global Policy at Circle and Professor Hilary Allen from the American—I am sorry. Dante Disparte I left out, I am sorry, Chief Strategy Officer and Head of Global Policy at Circle. And, Professor Hilary Allen, who is joining us from her home or office, from the American University Washington College of Law.

Ms. Goldstein, you begin. Five minutes, please. Thank you.

Statement of Alexis Goldstein, Director of Financial Policy, Open Markets Institute

Ms. GOLDSTEIN. Chairman Brown, Ranking Member Toomey, and Members of the Committee, thank you for inviting me to testify today. I am the Director of Financial Policy at the Open Markets Institute, where my work focuses on financial regulation and consumer and investor protection. My degree is in computer science, and I previously worked as a programmer for Morgan Stanley, building electronic trading systems, and as a business analyst at Merrill Lynch and Deutsche Bank, working with the over-the-counter equity derivatives trading desks.

I am a researcher, but I am also an investor. I invest in the equity markets, and I invest in the crypto asset markets. I have used large crypto exchanges. I have used DeFi to lend, to borrow, and to trade crypto. And I have bridged from one blockchain to another. In doing so, I have seen how stablecoins are used across the crypto ecosystem, and I agree with the Presidential working group's assessment that stablecoins are used today for speculation. Stablecoins essentially act as a waystation in between other speculative trades and as a way to avoid losses.

Stablecoins are often heralded for their potential. Maybe they are not used widely today to pay for goods and services, but they could be in the future. But the reality is that today U.S. retail investors across—sorry. Retail investors access stablecoins by trading them, not by using them to buy groceries at the corner store.

U.S. retail investors can neither purchase nor redeem the top two stablecoins directly from the issuer. Instead, they are reliant on exchanges to trade a stablecoin for a dollar. It is an awkward scenario and sort of a second step that we are not used to seeing with other kinds of digital payments. You do not need to also set up a stock brokerage account in order to send somebody money electronically.

There are a number of ways to earn interest and rewards on stablecoins. Many cryptolending platforms pay far higher rates for locking stablecoins into their platforms than they do for locking in non-stablecoins, and Coinbase pays its users a 1 percent reward for buying and holding the U.S. dollar coin by default without any action from the user other than purchasing USDC. Coinbase does not offer any rate of return for other stablecoins likely because the more USDC that Coinbase holds for its customers' accounts the more money they will make in a revenue sharing agreement that they have with Circle.

There are claims in the cryptocurrency industry and among some stablecoin issuers that they are fighting Wall Street or disrupting Wall Street, but they use the same forced arbitration agreements and class actions bans that Wall Street does, preventing their users from suing in a court of law should things go wrong.

There are also claims that regulations and Government oversight are not needed because the code is up there publicly available for anybody to read. But the moment a platform is hacked because an attacker has read the smart contract, found a bug, and exploited the bug, platforms tend to call for law enforcement to help chase down the stolen funds.

There are also promises that stablecoins could help drive financial inclusion outcomes, an admirable goal I think we can all agree is critical. A recent report from the World Economic Forum found that stablecoins have no benefit for financial inclusion as they are subject to the same or higher barriers as preexisting financial options, including the need for internet and for smartphones. I have also found this to be true as I have used stablecoins as fees begin to add up fast, especially when you want to send your stablecoin to your friend or to a different wallet off of the exchange.

The slice of the cryptocurrency markets with the least compliance with regulations, including checks for illicit finance, is what is called DeFi or decentralized finance. Put simply, DeFi does not work without stablecoins. Stablecoins help to facilitate trading on decentralized exchanges and access collateral in lending and borrowing protocols. The largest decentralized exchange is Uniswap, and as of yesterday eight out of nine of the top liquidity pools in Uniswap had at least one leg in a stablecoin. With only a few exceptions, the platforms on DeFi are not in compliance with Know Your Customer, antimoney laundering, and countering the financing of terrorism, nor does it seem that many of them are conducting a simple check to ensure that the cryptocurrency address making calls to the protocol are not on the sanctions list.

Today, the cryptocurrency market is not that entangled with the mainstream financial system, but if Wall Street and the cryptocurrency industry have their way it will be. I think the Committee is right to pay attention to stablecoins and crypto asset markets more broadly because absent your attention I do think that there is potential for crises, especially in the least regulated pieces of the ecosystem.

Thank you very much, and I look forward to your questions.

Chairman BROWN. Thank you, Ms. Goldstein.
Ms. Massari.

Statement of Jai Massari, Partner, Davis Polk & Wardwell, L.L.P.

Ms. MASSARI. Chairman Brown, Ranking Member Toomey, and Members of the Committee, thank you for inviting me here today to talk about this complex and interesting topic. I am Jai Massari, a partner in the Financial Institutions Group at Davis Polk. For the past several years, I have been advising stablecoin issuers, digital wallet providers, and financial institutions on the regulatory— the financial regulatory considerations for stablecoin activities. Today, I am presenting my own views, not those of any client or my firm. My remarks will focus on three key points.

First, stablecoins are an innovation in our understanding of money. This is particularly the case for true or payment stablecoins. These are non-interest bearing financial instruments designed to maintain a stable value against a reference fiat currency, say, one dollar. Today's stablecoins are used primarily for payments in connection with cryptocurrency transactions and decentralized finance, that is, DeFi applications. Stablecoin payments, though, could have broader uses, complementing existing payments such as cash, checks, credit and debit cards, and wire transfers, each of which has benefits and drawbacks.

Second, as stablecoins begin to find use in retail payments, we must seek to understand the risks they present along with the benefits. Like the innovations in money that preceded them, stablecoins squarely present the core regulatory concerns of consumer protection, systemic stability, safety and soundness, and combating illicit finance. And as described in the President's working group report, stablecoins give rise to more specific kinds of risks such as those related to the operation of blockchain platforms and risks arising from regulatory gaps.

And third, the regulation of stablecoins should address these risks while supporting their potential benefits.

My written statement goes into these points in more detail, but for now I will summarize my view of what regulation of stablecoins should look like. Stablecoins issuers should have restrictions on permissible types of reserve assets to ensure short-term liquid backing of those reserves. They should have auditing and transparency standards so regulators and the public can evaluate reserve composition. There should be restrictions that preclude maturity and liquidity transformation to shield reserve assets. They should have obligations to address illicit finance and sanctions considerations. And, there should be requirements to address operational risks from conducting transfers on blockchain networks.

But, requiring stablecoin issuers to be insured depository institutions, that is, insured banks, as suggested in the PWG report, is not necessary and, unless certain adjustments are made, is not workable. First, FDIC insurance is not necessary to address run risk where a stablecoin issuer, properly regulated, holds reserves of short-term liquid assets of at least 100 percent of the par value of outstanding stablecoins. Second, banks are subject to leverage ratios and risk-based capital ratios that assume relatively illiquid and riskier assets than cash and genuine cash equivalents. Unless Congress recalibrates these ratios, the stablecoin business model would be uneconomic.

Congress should instead consider an optional Federal charter for stablecoin issuers. At this time, U.S. stablecoin issuers and digital wallet providers are largely regulated by the States under money transmission regulators and State trust company authorities, but an expanded Federal law may well be appropriate and useful.

I would like to close by thanking the Committee for its focus on these important issues. While I do not believe that stablecoin issuers should be required to be insured banks, I strongly support commonsense regulation for stablecoins in a way that takes into account their risks and benefits. And I am optimistic that there is much common ground that can pave the way for a regulatory approach that safeguards consumers, the banking system, and the broader economy while continuing to promote innovation. I will be happy to answer any questions.

Chairman BROWN. Thank you, Ms. Massari.

Mr. Disparte, welcome.

Statement of Dante Disparte, Chief Strategy Officer and Head of Global Policy, Circle

Mr. DISPARTE. Chairman Brown, Ranking Member Toomey, Members of the Senate Committee on Banking, Housing, and Urban Affairs, thank you for the opportunity to share my testimony with you today. My name is Dante

Disparte, and I am the Chief Strategy Officer and Head of Global Policy for Circle, a leading digital financial services firm and the sole issuer of the U.S.D. Coin or USDC, a dollar digital currency supporting the extensibility of the U.S. dollar in a competitive, always-on global economy.

Having recently completed my 3-year term on the Federal Emergency Management Agency's National Advisory Council and being no stranger to disaster displacement and hardship, I want to acknowledge the communities affected by last week's devastating storms. Indeed, as this disaster and others have shown, with the movement of financial aid and disaster relief when speed matters most, friction stands in the way.

As a country, we have faced a Great Depression, a Great Deleveraging, and in 2020 with the onset of the COVID–19 pandemic, we faced nothing short of a Great Correction. In this correction, the centrality of technology for any semblance of political, business, economic, and household continuity was laid bare. What was also clear is that access to the internet and other digital public goods was unequal. How we engage with money and payments in digital form was clearly an area of prepandemic vulnerability in the U.S. and around the world.

The advent of stablecoins, or what we like to refer to as dollar digital currencies, like USDC, are an important innovation, enabling greater control over how we send, spend, save, and secure our money. To define a stablecoin, noting that like money itself not all of these innovations are created equal, is tantamount to the moment we converted our compact discs into MP3s. The CD and music is still yours but now enjoys the powers of programmability, user control, and a digitally native form factor that works anywhere, on any device, across the planet.

Stablecoins, in effect, are designed to reference and import the economic properties of an underlying asset, by circulation, the most successful of which all reference the dollar, with the economic aim of combating the buyer's and spender's remorse that plagued early cryptocurrencies. USDC is a now 3-year-old dollar digital currency standing at more than 40 billion in circulation and cumulatively supporting more than $1.4 trillion in on-chain transactions in a manner that enhances financial inclusion, responsible innovation, and integrity. Critically, the dollar-denominated assets backing USDC, which are strictly cash and short-duration treasuries of 90 days or less, are all held in the care, custody, and control of U.S. regulated financial institutions.

Indeed, as this internet native financial infrastructure continues to grow, we aim to do our part ensuring the future of payments and money is more inclusive than the past. Our recently announced Circle Impact Initiative has four core components, each of which are close to home for me, having growing up in poverty and being the first-generation high school and college graduate. These include:

Allocating a share of USDC dollar reserves to minority depository institutions and community banks across the country. We hope this will accrue to billions of dollars over time, strengthening the balance sheets of these banks and thereby strengthening their communities.

Embarking on digital financial literacy initiatives together with Historically Black Colleges and Universities and other partners supporting the development of essential learning and hands-on approaches to entrepreneurialism.

Leveraging our SeedInvest platform, which is one of the Nation's leading equity crowdfunding businesses, to catalyze targeted campaigns for women and minority entrepreneurs across the country.

And finally, assisting humanitarian interventions and coordinating public–private partnerships to mobilize blockchain based payments and USDC to deliver corruption resistant, real-time aid and relief.

Because nothing worth doing is worth doing alone, our hope is to catalyze uncommon coalitions on these initiatives, which are deeply connected to our mission of raising global economic prosperity through the frictionless exchange of financial value.

While some argue that the U.S. may lose the digital currency space race if it fails to issue a central bank digital currency, I argue that we are winning this race because of the sum of free market activity taking place inside the U.S. regulatory perimeter with digital currencies and blockchain based financial services. The sum of these activities are advancing broad U.S. economic competitiveness and national security interest.

Thank you, Chairman Brown and Ranking Member Toomey, for the opportunity to speak with you today. I look forward to addressing the Committee's questions.

Chairman BROWN. Thank you very much, Mr. Disparte.

We will now hear from Professor Hilary J. Allen from American University Washington College of Law, and she is joining us from a remote location.

Professor Allen, welcome.

Statement of Hilary J. Allen, Professor, American University Washington College of Law

Ms. ALLEN. Thank you, Chairman Brown, Ranking Member Toomey, and the Members of the Committee. Thank you for inviting me to testify at today's hearing. My name is Hilary Allen, and I am a professor of law at the American University Washington College of Law and the author of the book, *Driverless Finance: Fintech's Impact on Financial Stability*.

My area of expertise is financial stability regulation, and so I will focus my remarks today on risks relating to crypto, particularly stablecoins, and financial crises. I would also like to point out that, while not the primary focus of my testimony, stablecoins pose a threat to monetary policy as well, and I would be happy to take questions on that point.

Proponents of crypto often claim that it creates jobs and that it improves financial inclusion. But financial crises destroy jobs, and they disproportionately affect the most vulnerable members of our community, and so we should be extremely wary of the fragilities that crypto could create for our financial system.

Cryptotechnology introduces a number of new fragilities, including the ability for anyone with programming ability to create financial assets out of thin air, and more assets mean bigger bubbles and bigger busts. The distributed ledgers that crypto run on often have very complicated governance mechanisms, which make fixing problems caused by glitches and hacks extremely challenging. Fragilities also arise because the computer programs that operate on distributed ledgers, known as smart contracts, execute automatically even when the parties agree that forbearance is in their best interest and the interest of financial stability. Other fragilities include the possibility of runs on stablecoins if holders lose confidence in their ability to exchange stablecoins for fiat currency at the expected rate.

An important point to note about stablecoins, though, is that although it is hard to obtain concrete data on the cryptomarkets my understanding is that stablecoins are almost exclusively being used in DeFi apps rather than for everyday payments. DeFi stands for "decentralized finance," but DeFi is not particularly decentralized. Centralized governance and concentrated ownership proliferate in the DeFi ecosystem. Instead, what distinguishes DeFi from the established financial system is the technology that it relies upon, which I have already discussed, and what it is used for.

Our established financial system performs the important functions of channeling capital to people and businesses so that our economy can grow. That is why we have safety nets for the financial industry, like deposit insurance and finance—Federal Reserve emergency loans, that ensure that credit can keep flowing to the real economy. It becomes problematic, though, when the financial services being bailed out do not serve the real economy but exist primarily to make profits for industry leaders. This is already an issue in the established financial system, and DeFi has the potential to take this to the extreme.

DeFi has been described as an incorporeal casino, and that is why it is critical that DeFi not grow into something that the Government does feel compelled to bail out. A recent report from the Bank for International Settlements concluded that, given its self-contained nature, the potential for DeFi-driven disruptions in the broader financial system and the real economy seems limited for now, but allowing the integration of DeFi with the traditional banking system could change that. Congress or banking regulators should therefore prohibit insured depository institutions and their affiliates from participating in DeFi.

Insuring the issuers of the stablecoins that fuel DeFi would also encourage its growth in systemic importance, and so I disagree with the President's working group recommendation that Congress adopt legislation regulating stablecoin issuers as insured depository institutions. The run risk associated with stablecoins can be dealt with in other ways. One possibility is to ban stablecoins or to introduce a licensing regime that would only authorize the issuance of stablecoins if they can demonstrate a purpose outside of the DeFi ecosystem and that they do not pose any obvious threats to financial stability or monetary policy.

A ban or licensing regime would create some barriers to innovation, to be sure, but not all financial innovation is created equal. A recent World Economic Forum white paper concluded that stablecoins, as currently deployed, would not provide compelling new benefits for financial inclusion beyond those offered by preexisting options. Simpler mobile payments innovations may be a better and less risky way to promote financial inclusion than a system built on runnable stablecoins that operate on the distributed ledger with a convoluted governance structure that entails significant environmental cost to operate.

An alternative approach would be for stablecoins to remain regulated as they are currently, with the SEC and CFTC monitoring them from an investor protection perspective. The system risks associated with stablecoins and runs could be addressed by, first, prohibiting insured deposit-taking institutions from accepting any deposits from stablecoin issuers or from issuing their own stablecoins; second, the FSOC and the OFR monitoring the stablecoins for changes in usage; third, if necessary, the FSOC using its designation powers to designate a stablecoin as systemically important; and fourth, using antitrust regulation as well as the FSOC's designation power to prevent a large tech firm, like Meta or Facebook, from launching a stablecoin.

Thank you, and I look forward to your questions.

Chairman BROWN. Thank you, Professor Allen.

I will begin with Ms. Goldstein. I first just thought there were three votes beginning around 11, we think, and so meaning no disrespect to the four of you, but we will all be moving in and out but keeping the hearing going and asking questions.

Ms. Goldstein, even though—and please be brief on these because there is a lot of material to cover, of course. Stablecoins are mostly used for speculative betting. Some crypto advocates argue they have the potential to make the payment system faster and more efficient. Are they a better way to settle payments nationally or internationally than the traditional finance system?

Ms. GOLDSTEIN. Senator, thank you for the question. I think for that to be true you need four things. You need low fees. You need predictability. You need to be able to exchange them for goods and services. And, it needs to be consistently fast. And I do not think stablecoins meet all of those needed objectives.

As someone who has played around with sending them, both personally and sort of in my work, it often makes Western Union look cheap when you rack up all of the fees that you need in order to send it from one person to another, especially when the Ethereum blockchain gets congested. It can be very unpredictable. Fees can be very high.

And I think as you know, Senator, you know, people with low incomes cannot afford surprises, and unfortunately, transferring assets especially on the dominant Ethereum blockchain can be full of a lot of surprises and very high fees.

Chairman BROWN. Thank you, Ms. Goldstein.

Professor Allen, do you agree with her that stablecoins do not really show much promise as a payment system?

Ms. ALLEN. Yes, I think that is right. I think it is also important to think about the structure of the distributed ledgers. If there were problems, there is not someone you can go to if there is a problem, if it is run on a decentralized ledger with a lot of nodes managing its governance.

Chairman BROWN. And if stablecoins did in fact hold promise to provide faster, more inclusive payments, do you think it would make sense, Professor Allen, to bring them in the traditional finance system?

Ms. ALLEN. I think there are real concerns about bringing them into the traditional finance system primarily because of their relationship with DeFi. There is also the issue of their run risk, of course. So if they were to be brought—if they were to be used as payments and to be brought within the proper financial system, we would have to be very careful about monitoring their systemic risk, and I think that is a place where the FSOC and the OFR can play an important role.

Chairman BROWN. Thank you.

Speaking of, Mr. Disparte, bringing them into the financial system, at last week's hearing in the House your CEO agreed that stablecoins are still mostly used for trading in speculation, but your company is currently seeking a bank charter based on what you call USDC. Just be clear, interesting name to be sure, U.S. Dollar Coin is what it stands for, being a payment product. If Circle does become a bank, would you limit USDC, Mr. Disparte, to internet payments platforms, or would you allow—still allow USDC to be used to facilitate cryptocurrency speculation?

Mr. DISPARTE. Thank you for the question, Senator. The advent of a whole host of internet native capital market payments in an always-on economy that is built around these innovations in public blockchains is important. It is also important that the dollar fundamentally and dollar-referenced stablecoins ultimately win what that innovation represents.

And so Circle's counterparties, as a company, are other institutions and companies. We do not face the retail market as a retail payment system. And a lot of what that is supporting ultimately are payments, cryptocapital market trading, and other activities.

And we are also seeing—and I think this is a critical point we would like to highlight in this hearing. We are also seeing this increasingly becoming embedded as a mechanism of payment and settlement, including amongst traditional firms. Credit card companies, banks, and many others are increasingly using USDC as a settlement option on their networks, which makes the medium of exchange and payment argument quite strong.

Chairman BROWN. So if you are regulated, if you are inside the— if you have become—if you become bank, it would still be used for cryptocurrency speculation? Is that a "yes" or a "no"?

Mr. DISPARTE. Well, again, USDC and the end users of USDC have no expectation of a profit. It is ultimately a medium of exchange. A dollar goes in; a dollar comes out. And we have maintained price parity to the dollar with cash in short duration treasuries, Senator, inside the care, custody, and control of the U.S. regulated banking system.

Chairman BROWN. Let me ask a different way. If Circle were a traditional finance company, it would be a financial company. You understand it would be illegal for you to sell metal coins that said "U.S. Dollar Coin" on them, right?

Mr. DISPARTE. Senator, I think the question ultimately is as Circle has—

Chairman BROWN. Well, that is a pretty simple question. If you were a traditional finance company, could you sell metal, do you think you could sell metal coins that say "U.S. Dollar Coin" on them?

Mr. DISPARTE. No, Senator.

Chairman BROWN. OK. That is the answer. I mean, that is the law.

Do you think the name of your stablecoin, U.S. Dollar Coin, do you think it could mislead users to believe it is backed by the U.S. Government? I noticed you said throughout this hearing, USDC. You may have once at the beginning—I am not sure you ever did— said "U.S. Dollar Coin." I am sure you market it that way to some who may be less sophisticated than we pretend to be up here. But do you think that is misleading in any way, to call it "U.S. Dollar Coin?"

Mr. DISPARTE. No, Senator. The stablecoin innovation that we support is regulated consistently across the country according to electronic money and electronic money transfer and statutes as a payment innovation. We are on a level playing field with companies like PayPal and other major payments companies inside the U.S.

Chairman BROWN. OK. Fair enough. Let me ask a last question. So if the Fed moves forward the central bank digital currency, are you going to let them call theirs "U.S. Dollar Coin" or "U.S. Dollar?" Now that is meant with some irony.

Mr. DISPARTE. I appreciate the irony.

Chairman BROWN. I do not know if you have a copyright or a patent on "U.S. Dollar Coin," but I assume if there is, if we do a central bank digital currency, that they may have rights regardless of the Supreme Court or any financial regulators to "U.S. Dollar Coin," but just putting that out there. Last comment?

Mr. DISPARTE. Quickly, quickly, Senator. Thank you for that. Indeed, sovereign-issued currencies have three currency prefixes. So I am certain one day if a central bank digital currency is issued by the Fed they would enjoy total autonomy over that name choice. They would also, I think, enjoy the experience of stablecoins in circulation that all reference the dollar as important prototypes for what may one day be an opportunity in which we could upgrade this infrastructure to support a publicly issued digital currency as well.

Chairman BROWN. You are a good representative for USDC.

Mr. DISPARTE. Thank you, Senator.

Senator TOOMEY. Thank you, Mr. Chairman.

Mr. Disparte, some of our witnesses today seem to think that stablecoins are unlikely to ever serve any purpose other than facilitating cryptospeculation. They have cited the cost of transactions and various things although it seems to me this technology is moving very rapidly in the direction of facilitating and lowering the cost and increasing the volume and the throughput. Could you tell us what else is actually happening already with stablecoins outside of the facilitation of cryptotrading and what you think is imminent?

Mr. DISPARTE. Thank you, Senator. The blend of these types of innovations within the traditional payments and banking system, I think, is exactly where we are right now, that while we can, of course, acknowledge the original use case was to support cryptocapital markets and a host of activities in the trading domain, what we are seeing emerging however is integration of stablecoin-based settlements and payments across third-generation blockchains that are increasingly better, cheaper, faster than a lot of the analog alternatives for how we move money.

They increasingly also benefit from the immutable, permanent ledgering of financial transactions, which have enormous gains in terms of accounting and enormous gains in financial integrity.

Senator TOOMEY. So would it be—I am sorry to cut you off, but with the limited time, would it be fair to say that there are large, sophisticated, traditional financial institutions that are increasingly pursuing the use of these platforms for—as an alternative mechanism for settling payments, for instance?

Mr. DISPARTE. Indeed. And just to name a few of what would be traditional household name payments and money transmission companies and settlement networks, the Visa network has enabled USDC as a native settlement option across a network of 70 million merchants. Traditional companies in the remittance domain, like MoneyGram, have just announced a partnership with enabling USDC on the Stellar blockchain for remittances and solving for cash-in and cash-out across the world.

Senator TOOMEY. Visa probably knows something about settling payments. Let me ask you, it seemed to be suggested that one possible alternative we might consider would be to ban stablecoins. If Congress banned stablecoins, do you think that maybe people in other countries would develop stablecoins, and then if anybody who has access to a computer and the internet, wouldn't they be able to access those coins? In other words, wouldn't that be very unlikely to actually work at prohibiting the use of stablecoins?

Mr. DISPARTE. No question. I think it borrows then perhaps from early experiences with the advent of the internet, in which people creating websites was once upon a time considered a precluded activity or an activity that might warrant authorization. I think the same holds true here today with how the so-called internet of value is beginning to emerge.

I think it is profoundly in the American national interest and in our public interest that we have options for how people can move money in an always-on economy. Our financial needs do not take bank holidays, and our money should not either.

Senator TOOMEY. Let me move on to Ms. Massari. I think you have made it clear that you think that there should be a regulatory regime regarding stablecoins, but you point out that requiring them to be insured depository institutions does not make a lot of sense because their fundamental purpose is different from that of insured depository institutions. Could you just briefly elaborate on that a little bit, and then I have got one last question.

Ms. MASSARI. Sure, happy to. Thank you for the question, Senator Toomey. So I think the fundamental idea is that the business models and the risks raised by what I think of as well regulated stablecoins is quite different from that of traditional banks. Traditional banks take in deposits, and they make long-term loans and investments with those deposit proceeds. And so that activity, the maturity transformation and the liquidity transformation, that gives rise to run risks and is sort of the core of what traditional bank regulation is designed to address. This includes, for example, leverage ratios designed to address those core banking activities.

And so in my view, imposing regulation for insured depository institutions on stablecoins, which hold 100 percent short-term liquid reserves and are designed for payments, not lending, is the wrong approach.

Senator TOOMEY. Mr. Disparte, as Congress hopefully wrestles with the question of what should an appropriate regulatory regime look like, what are some of the principles that you think we should keep in mind?

Mr. DISPARTE. Well, first, if we—you know, I would argue do no harm and allow these innovations to continue thriving inside the U.S. regulatory perimeter. As a company, the State money transmission regulations have been the appropriate starting point. Again, if companies like PayPal and many of the other major American payments companies can exist and safely transmit trillions of dollars of transactions on their platforms under State money transmission statutes, I think that is a powerful starting point.

The concept of then having bank-like risks, managing bank like structures and supervision I think is similarly important. But it should be risk-adjusted, and it should be based on the type of activity. Technology neutrality and the type of activity should be what drives our policy.

Senator TOOMEY. Thank you. And then let me just say, Ms. Goldstein, I am going to submit to you a written question because we are out of time here. But I do think that the examples that you provide in the case where Western Union provides a lower-cost transfer is an unusually expensive transaction and that people who were interested in such a transaction and were concerned about lowering the cost could easily construct the transaction in alternative ways that would be much lower cost. But I will submit a question for the record to clarify that.

And with that, Mr. Chairman, I yield back.

Chairman BROWN. Thank you, Senator Toomey.

Senator Reed is recognized, from Rhode Island.

Senator REED. Thank you very much, Mr. Chairman.

Professor Allen, you, I believe, invited us to ask you about the monetary policy aspects of the stablecoin. We all understand that a critical part of our economy is the ability of the Federal Reserve to control money supply. So could you comment in whatever detail is appropriate about the impact of these stablecoins on monetary policy?

Ms. ALLEN. Thank you for the question, Senator. If you are dealing with a situation when there is high inflation or if you are dealing with a situation with deflation, the central—sorry, the central bank needs the ability to match the amount of money in the system to the needs in the economy. That is how monetary policy is carried out. If, however, the central bank loses control over some of the monetary supply, they lose their ability to put their hands on those levers. So this is something that central banks are extremely concerned about, and in fact, that is the impetus for a lot of interest in central bank digital currencies.

Interestingly, the same central banks that are worried about these issues are also worried about the financial stability issues that come with the introduction of a central bank digital currency, not to mention the privacy issues. So it is an interesting question that they feel the need to compete with stablecoins. Perhaps more interventionist policy is justified.

Senator REED. Well, thank you very much. And one other aspect is that this is a novel, or at least a fairly recent, phenomenon and it requires a great deal of thought, analysis, and projecting as to what we should do. And after the crisis in 2008–2009, we created the Office of Financial Research. Professor Allen, do you see a role for the Office of Financial Research here in terms of analyzing, structuring, and making recommendations to Congress with respect to the stablecoins?

Ms. ALLEN. Thank you, Senator. I very much do see a role for the Office of Financial Research here. The Office of Financial Research, as you know, was created to respond to the data gaps that we saw following the financial crisis of 2008. As finance has become more technologically informed, as finance, sorry, faces risks from climate change and things like that, we are now needing an interdisciplinary approach to financial regulation that includes computer scientists, data scientists, climate scientists. I think the OFR right now is underutilized and could really be built up with that interdisciplinary expertise, which would give regulators a more informed foundation to engage on issues of stablecoins amongst other things.

Senator REED. Well, thank you. I concur.

Ms. Goldstein, there are data gaps in the cryptocurrency markets. Could you highlight what you think are the most significant data gaps that we have?

Ms. GOLDSTEIN. Sure. Thank you for the question, Senator Reed. Unlike the stock market, where we can rely on things like the consolidated audit trail, where we know that all the quotes that go through every exchange are going to be reported back to a regulator at the end of the day, we are sort of at the mercy of what the cryptocurrency wants to self-report. And so we may get information about particular prices throughout the day, or trades, but we may not get quote information.

You also will see sort of arbitrage opportunities crop up, right? The price of Bitcoin on one exchange may be different than it is on another exchange, and I do not know that regulators currently have all of the data to truly understand why that might be.

And so there is a real sort of, I think, potential for Congress to look at is there a way to make sure that we do have standardized data reporting and a way that we make sure that all of the different exchanges are giving regulators all the information they need.

Senator REED. And, Ms. Goldstein, I presume that you would have some questions about the existing transparency, auditing, and disclosure requirements that are imposed on these entities. Is that correct?

Ms. GOLDSTEIN. Yes, Senator, that is correct.

Senator REED [presiding]. Thank you very much.

Senator Brown, Chairman Brown, asked me to recognize Senator Rounds at the conclusion of my questions. Senator Rounds, you are recognized.

Senator ROUNDS. Thank you, Mr. Chairman.

First of all, thank you to all of you for appearing before us today. As a consumer, I look at these and I say, OK, there has got to be an opportunity here or there is a reason why we have millions of people that are currently participating in these transactions, using the products and services that you provide. At the same time, it seems to me that we have a regulatory responsibility to make sure that the illicit uses of these types of services are limited. We are challenged because in the United States, as we regulate, certain organizations may very well simply move outside of the United States, move elsewhere.

If I am a consumer, why would I want—and I will direct this first of all to Mr. Disparte. If I am a consumer, why would I want to use your service as opposed to that of a Visa using dollars as the currency?

Mr. DISPARTE. Thank you, Senator for the question. So part of what Circle's innovations are providing—bearing in mind that our direct customers are typically businesses and we do not work with retail consumers. But nonetheless, part of the infrastructure that we are supporting today is enjoyed by more than 20 million people in the United States and 200 million people worldwide, for whom the price of access of the cost of access to things like international remittances, payments, money transfers both domestic and foreign, and then, candidly, access to the capital markets have been prohibited, right? On the one hand, if to be banked hinges on brick and mortar infrastructure, then there will be hundreds of millions of people around the world, if not billions, who will consistently be left in the margins.

Senator ROUNDS. So let me cut to the chase on this then. So what you are suggesting is that there is an economic benefit to someone because the costs of actually executing the transaction are less, I am going to say on average, for yours than what it would be for someone through the traditional brick and mortar processors. Is that the marketing that is being done?

Mr. DISPARTE. That is part of what the ultimate opportunity is. For example, in the remittance use cases, of which we can describe a number, there is companies like Tala, which is a woman-founded startup that is partnered with Visa to use USDC for remittances. The proposition ultimately is that sending digital currency payments is no different than sending data, of course subject to financial crime compliance and subject to the appropriate, you know, guardrails around protecting the financial system. But nonetheless, the value proposition is a fundamentally lower cost transfer of value on the internet.

Senator ROUNDS. Thank you.

Ms. Goldstein, I am curious. You indicated that the cost, the actual cost per transaction, was probably greater in this particular case. There seems to be a discrepancy here between your opinion on it and Mr. Disparte. Can you share with us why you think it is more expensive in this particular case?

Ms. GOLDSTEIN. Sure, Senator Rounds. I think it has to do with whether or not you are going to use the USDC coin to purchase other crypto. Are you going to keep it in this closed crypto ecosystem and just use it to buy something else?

My point is if you are using it for remittances, if you are sending it to another country, chances are you cannot go to your local grocery and use USDC to buy some milk. You are going to need to convert it to your local currency.

There is also a fee. When say I want to send something overseas, I need to send it to somebody else's wallet to do that. The USDC coin, it runs on lots of blockchains, but the predominant blockchain is the Ethereum one. There is an ERC–20 token standard that they use to do that. The Ethereum network fees are incredibly high. It can cost $10; it can cost $20; I have seen it as high as $40, just to send it from my wallet to somebody else's wallet.

And then once it gets to their wallet, if they are not going to use USDC to buy milk from the local grocery store, they need to convert it to the local currency. That involves putting it on an exchange. There may be a fee to trade it back to their local currency. And then they need to get it into their bank so they can pay for the milk at the grocery, and that may also include a fee.

So it has to do with do you need to bring it back to fiat or can you keep it within this closed crypto ecosystem. I think that is where you see the disparity.

Senator ROUNDS. Thank you.

Mr. Disparte, I am going to give you a chance to respond. What is your analysis of what you just heard?

Mr. DISPARTE. Yeah, so thank you for the opportunity, Senator. The quick version of this is early blockchains are a little bit akin to dial-up internet, and the argument to ban the stablecoin innovation because the current experience on certain early blockchains may be a little slower, a little cost prohibitive ignores the fact that the innovation is not standing still. There are late-generation blockchains, third generation blockchains that are approaching transaction throughput akin to major credit card networks and approaching cost structures on pennies on the dollar for value transfer.

Senator ROUNDS. Thank you.

My time is expired. Thank you, Mr. Chairman.

Senator REED. Thank you, Senator Rounds.

On behalf of Chairman Brown, let me recognize Senator Daines.

Senator DAINES. Senator Reed, thank you. Stablecoin policy is an area where I think there should be, and hopefully there will be, broad bipartisan agreement as well as compromise. Stablecoins are distinct from cryptocurrency in that there is a central entity that issues, and is responsible for, any individual token.

Personally, I believe that we should pursue a lighter touch approach to regulating the innovation taking place with cryptocurrencies and with stablecoins, but I do believe a bipartisan legislative framework that I hope this Committee would agree on is both possible for stablecoins and, frankly, necessary. I would urge my colleagues to avoid hyperpartisan solutions and instead seek consensus on something that is truly bipartisan that will provide certainty needed for the private industry to grow as well as to prosper. This, I believe, will help provide the best pathway forward for this technology to grow in a way that will benefit Montanans, the American people, as well as the global financial system.

Mr. Disparte, can you describe the current regulatory environment facing stablecoin users such as Circle?

Mr. DISPARTE. Thank you for the question, Senator Daines. And we agree with the spirit of appealing to a nonpartisan approach to how to regulate these innovations inside the United States.

Arguably, when I look at the experience of a company like Circle, we are licensed from sea to shining sea under State money transmission regulations and answerable through the examination process to the bank supervisors and the State money transmission supervisors across the country. We have also, as a company, helped contribute to creating a model law to try to make a more uniform operating environment. We are also a registered money transmission company with FinCEN and have worked over the years with law enforcement and other actors on protecting the integrity of the financial system, which is an important pillar.

When you think about this innovation outside of the United States, however, and what it means to compete on a global environment, this is where

I think the U.S. faces a gap. At the Bank for International Settlements, at the Financial Action Task Force, the Financial Stability Board, State regulators are not represented; it is the Federal and national regulators that are. And I think that is where the U.S. potentially faces a competitiveness gap at the moment, but broadly speaking, I think our current regimes for money transmission provide for a degree of sufficiency around the use of an electronic form of payment and a medium of exchange like a stablecoin.

Senator DAINES. Thank you. You touched on the issue, certainly on the global situation, and that really leads me to the question I have for Ms. Massari.

Can you describe how a U.S.D.-pegged stablecoin could advance the role of the U.S. dollar from an international viewpoint and how that might help preserve the dollar status as the world's foremost reserve currency?

Ms. MASSARI. Thank you for the question, Senator. To me, this is a very interesting line of thinking, about how stablecoins could affect monetary policy. To me, it is not entirely clear that they would be harmful to monetary policy where regulated in the manner that I described in my testimony, backed 100 percent, at least 100 percent by bank deposits, U.S. treasuries.

As some of my fellow witnesses have spoken about, you know, these stablecoins can be available for remittance transfers, for use outside the United States, just as other dollar-type accounts and payment instruments. And to my mind, just as those instruments help to bolster the standing of the U.S. dollar as the world's reserve currency, the argument should be the same for stablecoins.

Senator DAINES. So what do you think the future of stablecoin regulation would be if Congress does not act in a bipartisan fashion to foster safe and stable growth?

Ms. MASSARI. It is a great question, Senator. Thank you. My own view is that it would be useful for Congress to think about a Federal charter, an optional Federal charter for stablecoin issuers. I think this is a really important aspect of ensuring appropriate regulation at the Federal level to achieve all of the policy goals that I think we care about in a nonpartisan and bipartisan way. To my mind, the State regulatory regime that exists today has gone a long way to serve the interests of consumers in different States. I think a Federal framework would provide additional clarity if it is available.

Senator DAINES. Speaking of benefits perhaps, back to Mr. Disparte, what are some of the ways in which stablecoins lower costs within, and increase access to, financial systems?

Mr. DISPARTE. Indeed. Thank you for the question, Senator. On the one front, I get back to the question of if to be banked hinges on traditional brick and mortar infrastructure then many, many people will be unbanked or underbanked. And we saw that happening with the advent of the COVID–19 pandemic, and the inability to move money at scale across the internet was a vulnerability for the country and the world.

Stablecoins begin to solve for that by having a trusted medium of exchange that are dollar-referenced on the internet itself, and that allows for lower-cost transactions. It allows for a whole host of other financial services to blossom, where the fundamental trust in the dollar is protected and preserved.

Senator DAINES. Senator Reed—oh, Chairman Brown.

Chairman BROWN [presiding]. Thank you, Senator Daines.

Senator DAINES. All right.

Chairman BROWN. I just voted quickly. The senior Senator from Montana is recognized.

Senator TESTER. Yeah, thank you, Mr. Chairman. I want to thank you and the Ranking Member for having this meeting, this hearing, and I want to thank everybody for testifying.

So I have heard from a lot of folks in the cryptocurrency space. Their descriptions of their product reminds me of something, and it is not necessarily a good thing. It reminds me of the synthetic products that we saw leading up to the financial crisis of '08 because not in all cases, but in some, there is not anything real behind them.

Now I know stablecoin is backed by real assets, but that does not mean they cannot be manipulated, and it does not mean when you combine all these products together that there is not opportunity for some foul play. Let us put it that way.

So for you, Professor Allen, do you think that is a fair comparison I just made between cryptocurrency and the synthetic financial instruments?

Ms. ALLEN. Yes, I do. Thank you for that analogy, Senator. When we heard about the synthetic products in the lead-up to the financial crisis of 2008, we heard things like these will promote home ownership. And so you have to be wary, I think, of claims of financial inclusion because sometimes they are overblown, and you particularly have to be wary of them in circumstances where the means to providing that goal is unnecessarily complex. Complexity is a problem for financial stability. If we do not understand why things are the way they are, if they are too complicated, that primes the system for confusion, opacity, and then panics.

So when we have a product like the stablecoin that has been composed to solve financial inclusion, we have to ask ourselves: Why does it need to be so complex? Why does it need to run on a distributed ledger with decentralized governance mechanisms? You know, why do we need the environmental costs of that kind of process? Are there not innovations that are simpler, that could achieve the goal in a simpler way?

Senator TESTER. Ms. Goldstein, do you have anything you would like to add to that?

Ms. GOLDSTEIN. Senator, I would just add that I agree. I mean, I worked on Wall Street before, during, and after the financial crisis, and I do think that there are some important comparisons to the products that you raise. I do think that the secondary market where stablecoins participate, DeFi in particular, in some ways reminds me of the over-the-counter derivatives markets, but that was aimed at institutions. DeFi is very much retail and institutions.

Senator TESTER. Professor Allen, I want to go back to you for a second. I believe you were the one that stated that if you have problems there is no one to go to. Was that correct? That would have been in your opening statement?

Ms. ALLEN. Yes, that is correct.

Senator TESTER. So I have got to ask you. If I had a problem, if I was using these products, who would I go to?

Ms. ALLEN. Well, it depends——

Senator TESTER. Or, am I just out in the cold?

Ms. ALLEN. Thank you, Senator. I think it depends. If in fact the stablecoin has an issuer behind it that manages the reserve and there is a problem, you could go to that stablecoin issuer. But then that sort of highlights that these things are not as decentralized as anticipated. We are having new intermediaries coming into the system, and those intermediaries have profit motives like any established financial intermediary. And so the sense of democratizing finance, I think, falls apart.

If we are talking about a stablecoin that is being operated in a truly decentralized fashion, where it is operating on a ledger, where you need multiple nodes to agree to any change in how it operates, then that is something that could cause incredible problems. I mean, who would you go to? Which of those people would you be able to reach out to if you needed a transaction undone, for example, because there was a mistake made?

Senator TESTER. All right. Thank you.

Ms. Goldstein, you talked about that these—they have to meet four objectives. One of them was fees. What were the other three?

Ms. GOLDSTEIN. It needs to be predictable. You need to be able to exchange it for goods and services. And you mentioned fees. I forget what the third——

Senator TESTER. That is OK. That is all right.

Ms. GOLDSTEIN. My fourth.

Senator TESTER. You said it does not meet fees because fees are high.

Ms. GOLDSTEIN. Correct.

Senator TESTER. Does it meet the other three?

Ms. GOLDSTEIN. I think when you stay within the cryptocurrency ecosystem, it does meet the speed requirement. I do not think it meets the predictability requirement, and I do not think it meets the exchanging it for goods and services requirement, broadly.

Senator TESTER. Very quickly, because my time is slim, what kind of fees are we talking about compared to what we see in the industry today?

Ms. GOLDSTEIN. It depends on the exchange. It depends if you are moving back to fiat. But let us say you start at fiat. You move into stablecoins. You buy one on—by buying one on an exchange, right, because, as Mr. Disparte said, they do not service retail customers. You have got to go to an exchange. You send it to someone else. They put it on an exchange. You bring it back to fiat. It can be as high as $80 front to back or as low as $6. Western Union is about four or five.

Senator TESTER. OK. And what kind of amount? That is a flat fee regardless of how much money you are exchanging?

Ms. GOLDSTEIN. It is an accumulation of fees because you have to take several steps——

Senator TESTER. Gotcha.

Ms. GOLDSTEIN. ——throughout the whole system.

Senator TESTER. Thank you very much. Thank you all.

Chairman BROWN. Thank you, Senator Tester.

Senator Warner from Virginia is on from his office.

Senator WARNER. Well, thank you, Mr. Chairman. I appreciate you holding this hearing, and I am very concerned. I agree with the Ranking Member that there is a lot of innovation going on and we should not get rid of that.

I am very concerned, sitting from the intel standpoint, that a lot of this is being used for illegal and illicit purposes. We just had a major break-in to our State legislative system in Virginia. Everything is frozen. A ransomware effort has been—threat has been issued, and my fear is it will be paid off in some level of Bitcoin and potentially using a stablecoin as the ability to transfer it back to a fiat currency.

But let me ask the question that—and I will start with Ms. Goldstein, but I probably will take everybody. I think I understand some on distributed ledger, DeFi, and the notion of creating a different currency. Gold has no inherent value, so the idea if we as a society made Bitcoin or some other entity to have a value has some logic to me.

But the idea of a private-sector stablecoin, where you have a literally dollar-for-dollar or totally liquid security and no leverage at all, how do you make any money off this? I get it if you are Facebook and you have got a whole network effect and you become the default cryptowallet, then that means you are collecting a whole lot more information.

But, Ms. Goldstein, I will start with you. I get it now if they are making all these fees. But if Mr. Disparte is right and they are going to ultimately get down to a frictionless transaction, how do you make enough money just off the flow to have this kind of stablecoin become a viable financial investment?

Ms. GOLDSTEIN. I mean, Senator, I think that is a good question. I think that is why you see, for example, on Circle and some of the SEC filings have said they want to move potentially into a Circle DeFi and offer additional services that allow, you know, customers to access DeFi platforms like Aave and Compound with APIs that Circle talks in their investor presentation about building.

I also think, you know, they have a revenue sharing agreement with Coinbase. Perhaps they are making some profits from Coinbase.

I mean, I would direct the question to Mr. Disparte, but I imagine that it is not—if it is just treasuries and it is just cash, I think I understand why I see in the SEC investor materials that they do want to provide other services like Circle DeFi in the future.

Senator WARNER. I am going to get to Mr. Disparte, but I would like to hear from Ms. Massari first because, again, help me out here. One of the big name firms, they have got to be paying folks a lot of fees. If you have literally got no leverage at all and you have got a one-for-one exchange and you are going to bring down the transaction cost, how do you—and you do not have a network effect the way Facebook would from Libra or Diem or whatever they are calling it this week, how do you make money?

Ms. MASSARI. Thank you, Senator. It is a great question. And of course, I cannot speak about any of my clients or particular projects, but I think your observation is right. If we appropriately regulate stablecoin issuers, they should only be holding short-term liquid assets to back their stablecoin obligations. That likely is not the main source of revenues for them. They can provide payment services and other services adjacent to the issuance of the stablecoin, you know, the same kinds of payment services that I think we see today, whether it is remittances or peer-to-peer transfers or other kinds of services, and perhaps charge fees for those services.

Senator WARNER. But isn't it again—and I am going to get to Mr. Disparte. But just, you know, these other—PayPal I do not believe argues that it literally has a dollar backing every dollar that goes through the PayPal transaction system. I am going to let Ms. Allen answer as well, but I want to hear from Mr. Disparte. How are you going to make any money if we get to this frictionless system you claim to be heading toward?

Mr. DISPARTE. Thank you for the question, Senator. And for just a general matter, as a company, we are in the process of going public. So there is quite a lot of customer and market face and disclosure around the business' revenue model, but akin to a PayPal. PayPal holds an omnibus account that is held in the interest of customers to execute transactions. So we have a very similar business model and a very similar U.S. licensing platform.

And our current reserve structure is cash and short-term treasuries of 90 days or less. So there is a nominal degree of interest rate sensitivity on that reserve composition. That is part of our revenue model.

There is also a revenue model implied in terms of de minimis transaction fees for using Circle accounts and other services.

We also operate——

Senator WARNER. Let me get to Ms.—my time is running out. Let me get to Ms. Allen. I mean, again, stablecoins brags about the fact that you have a dollar-for-dollar exchange. Ms. Allen, my time is up, but if you want to add a comment I would appreciate it.

Ms. ALLEN. I will just say very briefly no one is going to offer this service if there is not a way for them to make money. If we are trying to promote financial inclusion, we want it to be a winwin. There are reasons to be skeptical when the actual money-making nature of the innovation is not fully disclosed.

Senator WARNER. Thank you, Mr. Chairman.

Chairman BROWN. Thank you, Senator Warner.

Senator Warren from Massachusetts is recognized for 5 minutes.

Senator WARREN. Thank you, Mr. Chairman. So unlike other cryptocurrencies like Bitcoin, stablecoins like Tether and USDC are supposedly pegged to the dollar, and the reason for this is to reassure people that stablecoins are as stable as using the dollars you have in your wallet or in your checking account. A stablecoin dollar, in other words, will supposedly be worth a real dollar. Now that would make it a lot easier and a lot safer to trade among different tokens, to put up collateral for a risky bet, or even to pay for a cup of coffee at your local bodega. But I want to examine whether or not the stablecoin talk matches the stablecoin reality. Ms. Goldstein, let us say that I own $10 worth of Tether or USDC, if I want to trade my $10 worth of these tokens, am I guaranteed to get $10 back?

Ms. GOLDSTEIN. No, Senator. You are sort of dependent on the exchange where you are trading it because as a U.S. retail customer I cannot go to Circle and say, please redeem my USDC, and Tether explicitly says no U.S. customer can redeem Tether. So I have to trade it on an exchange. Sometimes it fluctuates. Sometimes it is a little above the dollar; sometimes it is a little below. But if there were a run, the peg could collapse.

And we also do not really know necessarily what is backing all of these stablecoins, right? Tether is——

Senator WARREN. Hold on a sec. I want to get into that, OK? I promise. Because I want to just underscore this point, that if Tether's tokens were actually backed one to one it would be one of the 50 largest banks in the country, but we know that it is not. And that is because according to Tether's own report only about 10 percent of the assets backing its stablecoin are real dollars in the bank; 90 percent is something else, not real dollars.

And if that worries you—there is a little more news on this one— the report that 10 percent of Tether's stablecoins are backed up by dollars is not actually verified by a comprehensive, audited financial statement or verified by any Government regulator.

So, Professor Allen, let me ask you. Let us say I am not the only one who wants to redeem my $10 worth of Tether or USDC for dollars, and maybe there is bad news in the market and people rush to cash in their stablecoins. What would a run on the stablecoin market look like? Could it endanger our financial system?

Ms. ALLEN. Thank you for that question, Senator. So a number of the witnesses today have said that stablecoins do not engage in maturity transformation and therefore do not suffer the same fragilities as bank deposits and runs, and that is probably true to some degree. But a run on a stablecoin would look a lot like the runs that we have seen on money market mutual funds in 2008 and again in 2020, and it could also share dynamics with the foreign exchange crisis we have seen in the past, like the Mexican peso crisis.

So if holders of the stablecoins suddenly lose confidence in either the ability of the issuer of the stablecoin or the reserve of assets backing it to maintain a stable value, they could seek to redeem or exchange their stablecoin en masse. And if they have direct redemption rights, that would force the issuer to liquidate its reserve of assets.

So right now I do not think that would have systemic consequences. If stablecoin holders are only using them to speculate, they are not really going to expect stability, and so a run will be less likely. But if a run did occur right now, I think the impact would probably be felt in the DeFi ecosystem, and that is why it is critical that we not provide this Government support to the DeFi ecosystem and expect——

Senator WARREN. OK. So let me go there. Sorry to interrupt, but let me go there. We know that stablecoins are not always stable. In fact, it is worse than that. In troubled economic times, people are most likely to cash out of risky financial products and move into real dollars. Stablecoins will take a nosedive precisely when people most need stability, and that run on the bank mentality could ultimately crash our whole economy.

But there is another piece of the risk here, and you have headed in that direction, Professor Allen. DeFi is the most dangerous part of the cryptoworld. This is where the regulation is effectively absent and, no surprise, it is where the scammers and the cheats and the swindlers mix among part time investors and first-time cryptotraders. In DeFi, someone cannot even tell if they are dealing with a terrorist.

Stablecoins provide the lifeblood of the DeFi ecosystem. In DeFi, people need stablecoins to trade between different coins, to trade derivatives, to lend and borrow money, all outside the regulated banking system. Without stablecoins, DeFi comes to a halt.

So, Professor Allen, does DeFi threaten our financial stability, and can DeFi continue to grow without stablecoins?

Ms. ALLEN. I do not think DeFi can grow without stablecoins. I think it would struggle. Right now I think DeFi is contained to the point where it will not impact financial stability, but if it grows I think there is a real threat there, particularly if it becomes intertwined with our traditional financial system. And there is industry interest in pursuing this integration on both the traditional finance and the crypto side. So I think it is critical that stablecoins not be allowed to fuel that growth.

Senator WARREN. Well, I appreciate it. You know, this is risk to traders, risk to our economy. The time to act is before it all blows up. Stablecoins have no regulators, no independent auditors, no guarantors, nothing, and they are propping up one of the shadiest parts of the cryptoworld, the place where consumers are least protected from getting scammed. Our regulators need to get serious about clamping down on these risks before it is too late.

Thank you, Mr. Chairman.

Chairman BROWN. Thank you, Senator Warren.

Senator Smith from Minnesota is recognized.

Senator SMITH. Thank you, Chair Brown, and thank you to our panelists for being here today. I want to ask about this: So as businesses transition to cashless models, some businesses could adopt stablecoin or even crypto as an alternative or as the only method for a payment, and I am trying to figure out what impact that this could have on people, especially people of color who are so often left out of the financial system.

According to a report by the FDIC, approximately 7.1 million households are unbanked. That was in 2019. And so as we move to a cashless economy, what happens to people who are low-income or homeless or undocumented, and how do they pay for things that they would need in a stablecoins world? Does stablecoins actually give them more freedom and access, or does it become another barrier?

So, Ms. Goldstein and Professor Allen, could you help me answer this question? Advocates for stablecoin argue that they provide access for small businesses and unbanked people. What do you think about that argument, and how exactly does stablecoin work for someone who does not have a checking or a savings account?

Ms. GOLDSTEIN. If I may briefly and then give Professor Allen a chance to respond, again, because stablecoins are not widely accepted for goods and services, you need a bank. And not only do you need a bank, you need an account at a cryptocurrency exchange in order to buy stablecoins in the first place, at least the top two ones. And so I think this is why we saw the World Economic Forum find that there are not many financial inclusion benefits to stablecoins because it is essentially using the rails of the existing banking system.

So until, you know, and if—I think it is a big "if"—we see mass adoption of stablecoins as a way to accept things at the grocery store, to buy your groceries, I do not really see how this helps the unbanked because you need a bank and you need a cryptocurrency exchange.

Senator SMITH. Yeah. OK. Thank you.

Professor Allen.

Ms. ALLEN. So I agree with Ms. Goldstein's comments. I just want to add something further, which is financial literacy is already a huge problem for a lot of people. We expect a lot of consumers in terms of their ability to read complex financial documents and understand them. With the move to cryptorelated financial services, we are asking them as well often to understand computer code because disclosures do not always match the computer code, and so investors in these areas tend to go to the code themselves. So I think that it is just entirely unreasonable to expect people to be able to sense the risks in these types of products on their own by looking at the code.

Senator SMITH. Yeah. I mean, it is difficult enough for—you know. I mean, it is extremely difficult for anybody to understand. So I really agree with you.

Let me ask you another question about this. We, of course, need to make sure that workers can rely on their pensions, the pensions that they have earned. This is something that Chair Brown and I have worked on, focused on, since I first came to the Senate. So as stablecoins and cryptocurrencies become more prominent in the financial system, it seems like it is worth looking at what this could mean for retirement plan assets and figuring out whether it is a good idea for them to be offered as an investment options for pension plans or 401(k) plans.

So, Professor Allen, let me stay with you. For workers or teachers who are thinking about their retirement accounts or pensions, what do you think is the right role, or is there a role, for stablecoins in those plans?

Ms. ALLEN. I do not think that there is a role for them there. I appreciate that people are going through a really hard time right now. The search for yield in this environment, you know, is a very real pressure. But I feel it is very dangerous for people to gravitate toward highly volatile assets in that search for yield, and particularly when we are talking about long-term investments like retirement I think that is a recipe for disaster.

Senator SMITH. Ms. Goldstein, would you like to comment on that?

Ms. GOLDSTEIN. Yes. I will just add that I agree with Professor Allen. I do not really know that there is a retirement, you know, investor that wants the volatility and insolvency risk of Bitcoin that gives you, you know, very little yield if any at all.

Senator SMITH. Mm-hmm. Thank you. So we know that the stablecoin market is worth about $130 billion and a lot of this growth has happened really fast, in the last couple of years. And I personally do not think that regulators have kept up with this transition. The President's Working Group on Financial Markets recently released a report on stablecoins with suggestions for Congress as well as banking regulatory agencies on recommendations for what we should think about as we regulate stablecoin.

I just have a couple seconds left, but what—Ms. Goldstein, I will stay with you. What do you think we should be considering as policymakers as we think about a regulatory framework for stablecoins?

Ms. GOLDSTEIN. Senator Smith, I think we need to think about the secondary market and how stablecoins drive DeFi and make sure that there is not a gap between the protections that you receive as an investor in the equity markets and the protections that you may receive as an investor in the crypto asset markets. Whether it is best execution or making sure that the trades are not manipulated or being spoofed, wash tradings, you name it, I think we need to make sure that we are narrowing that gap as much as possible so that we can all enjoy the protections that we are used to seeing in the equity markets.

Senator SMITH. Thank you so much.

I know I am out of time, so I will yield back. Thank you, Mr. Chair.

Chairman BROWN. Thank you, Senator Smith.

Senator Sinema from Arizona is recognized from her office.

[No audible response.]

Chairman BROWN. I believe she is still getting on. She may be on the floor voting, but I would like to hold for a moment. And I will ask one question, if Senator Toomey wants to ask one, too.

Ms. Goldstein, is it true that cryptocurrency speculation on decentralized finance platforms would not work without stablecoins?

Ms. GOLDSTEIN. Yes, Senator, I think that is right or at least they would be a lot smaller.

Chairman BROWN. So could a company like Circle create a stablecoin that can be used for electronic payments but could not be used to gamble in cryptocurrencies like Dogecoins?

Ms. GOLDSTEIN. Yes, Chairman, I think you could. You could design the system however you would like, and there is nothing—yes, they absolutely could do that.

Chairman BROWN. So, Professor Allen, what are the risks of allowing stablecoins to be used both as a payment system and as a tool to allow gambling in DeFi markets?

Ms. ALLEN. In terms of allowing them to be used as a payment system, I think the biggest financial stability risk is if that is offered by a tech company like Meta, Facebook, or Amazon because then you have the potential for these to scale up really quickly to be used for everyday goods and services, and then we do potentially have both monetary policy and financial stability issues in the sense that the tech company would become too big to fail and essentially part of the Government safety net.

Unless one of those tech companies moves into this space, though, I do not see stablecoins becoming used for everyday goods and services payments absent some kind of Government support in the form of deposit insurance or the equivalent. So if that does happen, these could then be used potentially for payments, but also they would be used to a large extent in the DeFi ecosystem. And that is essentially, in my view, going to be Shadow Banking 2.0 in terms of the Government essentially having to bail out this entirely self-referential financial system that operates outside the boundaries of what we normally regulate.

Chairman BROWN. Thank you, Professor Allen.

So, Mr. Disparte, since the name of your company was invoked during this little discussion, when testifying in front of Congress, Circle—and in the President's working group, Circle—emphasized it is a payment platform that can help small businesses or enable cheap international payments, a concern also about which Senator Warner from Virginia was concerned, as you heard. But on their website, Circle highlights the DeFi protocols it is designed to work with. And your CEO recently bragged on Twitter that your U.S. Dollar Coin is the most used stablecoin for making bets in these unregulated markets.

So, Mr. Disparte, if Circle is a safe, stable banking product to facilitate payments to small businesses, why is your company also promoting its use to gamble on cryptocurrencies? How does that actually help small businesses or the economy?

Mr. DISPARTE. There—Senator, thank you for the question. There is, of course, a wide range of use cases for any payment infrastructure, any payment innovation. In the software intermediated capital markets, also known as DeFi, the use of stablecoins is an important innovation. But its fundamental function is exactly the same, and the expectation of the end user is that they only get a dollar out from the economic use of the stablecoin for any of these activities.

Chairman BROWN. Thank you.

Senator Toomey and then we will—after Senator Toomey, we will call on Senator Sinema if she is on. Otherwise, I think we will likely adjourn. So, go ahead.

Senator TOOMEY. Thank you, Mr. Chairman.

Ms. Massari, I have had a little back and forth with the SEC Chairman. Mr. Gensler has, I think, at times indicated that stablecoins, at least some stablecoins, may actually be securities even if they lack an inherent expectation of profits. But he has not explained to me exactly what the criteria he is using, what legal tests, what makes a stablecoin that has no expectation of profit a security. And it seems to me that some expectation of a gain on the part of an investor is fundamentally at the heart of what we consider to be securities.

So I want to ask you, if there is a non-interest bearing stablecoins—and most are not intrinsically bearing interest. And there is no explicit expectation of profits, and really the value proposition is there is a utility that is the reason people are interested in the stablecoin. But in such an example, do you think that it meets our definition of what is security and should be regulated as a security?

Ms. MASSARI. Senator Toomey, thank you for that question. As you might imagine, every practitioner in this area is extremely well versed in the Howey Test and the Reves Test, and I will not bore you with the technical details. But in short, in my view, a non-interest bearing stablecoin, fully reserved and regulated as many stablecoin issuers are today, as money transmitters, those stablecoins should not be viewed as securities. They are appropriately not viewed as securities under existing law.

Senator TOOMEY. Thank you.

And, Mr. Disparte, I was wondering if you could give us—you made a really interesting and I think important observation about how rapidly this space is evolving, how the capabilities are expanding, how speed and throughput are accelerating, and you made the analogy to back when the internet relied on dial-up modems. It is a little bit faster today.

And I suspect that the capabilities of these platforms to handle large volumes of transaction is also going to grow. And as it does, it seems to me there is very interesting potential for smart contracts. Could you give us an idea of how we should think about smart contracts and maybe even an example of a smart contract that would have a use case for an ordinary small business or consumer?

Mr. DISPARTE. Absolutely. Thank you for the question, Senator. Indeed, I would argue that the public infrastructure and this open-source technology wave that is happening—what many are likening to a Web 3, where Web 1 was read, Web 2 was read and write, and Web 3 is read, write, own—is an important innovation and has a lot of implications broadly for financial resilience and competitiveness.

An example of a smart contract innovation could be something really important and close to home for me, coming from the insurance world, for example. One of the most elusive aspects of the insurance world is this concept of a parametric claim. A homeowner's policy that could liquidate a claim based on a georeference where the disaster took place and there is no equivocation that it in fact was a total loss would be a game changer. The absence of being able to do that at scale and quickly and in real time is partly solved for by a trusted dollar digital currency, like USDC, but also partly solved for what the capability is of a smart contract.

So you have started to see some blockchain-based innovations taking place in that domain, in the insurance domain, but an open internet dollar functionally becomes one of the only missing links to enable that at scale.

Other examples, you know, are opportunities around zero default loans. Effectively, programmable money enables you to execute even micropayments, where by today's standards sending even small amounts of money, it often costs more than the sum of money sent. And so the ability to execute micropayments, I use an example in my written testimony about a journalist being able to accrue a penny for every like. By today's payment standards, it is not possible to execute that penny to the journalist, so the freelancer is effectively a starving artist or a starving writer or a starving journalist.

And then there is a whole host of other use cases that are enabled by this: cross-border payments, being able to have sanctions-compliant money movement, for example, corruption, bribery, and fraud internationally in a humanitarian context. Money is the honeypot, especially physical money because of its opacity. Stablecoin-based payments and blockchain-based payments, because of their transparency, their speed, and their auditability, can enable a whole host of applications. USDC was used, for example, to support doctors in Venezuela as one use case of moving humanitarian funds using these innovations.

So I think we are in the opening innings. And when people say we have failed the financial inclusion test, the presumption is the stablecoin has agency just as the dollar, and both are patently wrong.

Senator TOOMEY. Thank you, Mr. Chairman.

Chairman BROWN. Thank you, Senator Toomey.

Senator Sinema is recognized from her office.

Senator SINEMA. Thank you, Mr. Chairman, and thank you to Senator Toomey in particular for extending the questions so I was able to join today. I also want to thank our witnesses for being here today.

As you know, Mr. Chairman, I cochair the Senate's Financial Innovation Caucus alongside my friend, Senator Lummis of Wyoming. So I am glad that we are holding this hearing on stablecoins today.

As you know, stablecoins are cryptocurrencies that are pegged to other external reference assets like a fiat currency, another virtual currency, a commodity, or a combination of these assets. As more Americans choose to invest and hold and transact with digital assets, it is important for policymakers to consider the regulatory implications of this trend and the innovations happening in this ecosystem.

Ms. Massari, it is great to meet you and to discuss this important topic. If an Arizonan is looking at holding a stablecoin, how can he or she know for sure that it is truly backed by the asset that the issuer claims?

Ms. MASSARI. Thank you for the question, Senator Sinema. So today in the United States, stablecoin issuers, U.S. stablecoin issuers, are regulated by the States in which they offer their services and where they are located. This is regulation under State money transmission licensing regimes, which exist in every State but one. In addition, they are regulated for financial crimes purposes by FinCEN, a bureau of the U.S. Treasury Department, as money services businesses.

That being said, it is primarily the State regulators that are responsible for oversight and supervision of money transmitters, including stablecoin issuers. So we would look to those State regulators to ensure that the stablecoin issuers, like other payment service providers and stored value providers, are living up to their promises.

Senator SINEMA. Thank you. And as I understand it, currently, stablecoin issuers are generally subject to State level money transmitter laws. Do these State laws require a particular standardized way of disclosing how the stablecoin is backed?

Ms. MASSARI. It is a great question, Senator. So these laws generally require stablecoin issuers, like other payment providers and stored value providers, to maintain what are called "eligible assets" to back their obligations to customers. They are also required to provide financial reports to their regulators, and of course, any disclosures that they make about how they hold assets must be accurate.

Senator SINEMA. I see. Now in the event that a stablecoin is not truly backed, is there a risk that the Arizonan could try and redeem their token for cash and the issuer may not be able to provide it? Now that is a problem for the Arizonan in the near term, but what bigger problems could that cause in the long term?

Ms. MASSARI. It is a great question, Senator. I think the short answer is, yes, that could certainly be a problem. That is one reason why I support commonsense, strong regulation of stablecoin issuers. As I mentioned, the States are currently largely responsible for that regulation. In my view, a Federal option could also be explored to achieve the same goals.

Senator SINEMA. Thank you. Now, Ms. Massari, if the Arizonan holds $10,000 in a particular stablecoin and then there is a run on the issuer, how much of the $10,000 could the Arizonan lose if the backing on the coin is not credible?

Ms. MASSARI. That is a great question again, and I think these are really important questions to think about as we think about how to regulate stablecoins. Unfortunately, I am going to give you a lawyerly answer, which is it depends. It depends on the assets that are available in bankruptcy to redeem out the stablecoin holders, if the stablecoin goes into bankruptcy and, in general, how much money is left with the stablecoin holder that is available for the stablecoin holders to get in that kind of situation.

Senator SINEMA. Thank you. You know, this is an important issue for which consumers and investors deserve a clear answer. At the same time, though, we should not assume that simply overlaying every law and regulation we have for other issuers or depository institutions is automatically the correct issue here.

Now in the short time we have left, I would love to hear from Ms. Massari and Ms. Goldstein on my last question. Relative to banks or other issuers of digital currency, can you highlight the key differences, good and bad, that policymakers should continue when thinking about regulation of stablecoin issuers? So first, Ms. Massari.

Ms. MASSARI. Again, thank you for the question. To my mind, when thinking about stablecoin regulation, this regulation is really important. It is really important to protect consumers. It is really important to protect our financial system. But at its core, the most important thing is to make sure that the regulation fits the activity, right? Stablecoin issuance is different from traditional banking, and therefore, in my view, it does not make sense to overlay the same regulations that we have for traditional banks on top of stablecoin issuers.

Ms. GOLDSTEIN. And, Senator, I will just add very quickly that I think that stablecoin issuers, in particular when they go to raise funds or they are going to issue new tokens, we sort of have this uneven playing field. There are looser standards for fundraising for cryptotokens, including stablecoins, than say for a pharmaceutical company going in the public markets and raising money. And that is sort of like having a triathlon where you are asking—say 10 percent of the participants, they get to skip the swim, right?

And so I do not think that we should be——

Senator SINEMA. I would like to do that, personally, just to be clear.

Ms. GOLDSTEIN. Yeah, no. I think it would be a good trick, right? So I do not think we should be advantaging one industry over another when it comes to fundraising from the public markets.

Senator SINEMA. Thank you.

Thank you, Mr. Chairman and Ranking Member, for extending the hearing. I really appreciate the time today. And I thank our witnesses for appearing.

Chairman BROWN. Thank you, Senator Sinema.

This has been—and Senator Cramer is not on. OK. Thank you. This has been an important and eye-opening discussion. In the past, this Committee and financial regulators have failed to pay attention to these issues until it is too late. They have devastated— workers and families in too many cases have been devastated in this country, in the Ranking Member's State and my State, all over the country. We will continue to keep a close eye on stablecoins and cryptocurrency as well to ensure that this economic recovery that we have worked so hard to build is not destroyed by another crisis.

Thank you to the four witnesses today.

For Senators who wish to submit questions for the record, these questions are due 1 week from today, Tuesday, December 21st. Witnesses will have 45 days to respond to any questions.

Thank you again to the four of you.

The Committee is adjourned.

[Whereupon, at 11:57 a.m., the hearing was adjourned.] [Prepared statements, responses to written questions, and additional material supplied for the record follow:]

Prepared Statement of Chairman Sherrod Brown

A few years ago, most people had never heard of cryptocurrency—most people still don't know what all these terms mean, from stablecoins to nonfungible tokens.

But they've become a hot topic in Washington—and on Wall Street, and online, among millions of Americans who, understandably, don't trust big banks, and are looking for an opportunity to make money.

Over the last several years, the number of cryptocurrencies has exploded—from the hundreds to the thousands. The supposed value of all of these digital assets in circulation recently passed three trillion dollars.

That's about the size of JPMorgan Chase's balance sheet—the biggest bank in the country.

With that much money tied up, that's pretty much the definition of a systemic issue in our economy.

And those big numbers have come with big promises.

We've been told that blockchain—the technology these coins are built on—will "democratize" money, or build a more inclusive economy.

But none of those promises have materialized, and likely never will. Instead, we've gotten wild financial speculation.

As we've heard before in this Committee, the wild price swings and high transaction fees for many cryptocurrencies make them useless for payments—the one thing they claim to be designed for.

Stablecoins were supposed to solve this problem.

Unlike other cryptocurrencies, their value isn't just based on market enthusiasm—a stablecoin's value is supposed to be backed by real assets held by the company that issues the stablecoin.

In other words, stablecoins are a particular type of cryptocurrency whose value is managed by a single company. These include Tether, Circle, and Abracadabra— a fast-growing scheme that makes "Magic Internet Money". Their words, not mine— what could possibly go wrong with something that claims to be "magic money"?

Cryptocurrencies' advocates argue that crypto assets are superior to real dollars, because they are decentralized and transparent. But stablecoins are neither.

Most of them, and certainly the largest ones, rely on a single, centralized company to manage the reserve assets and their supply of coins. That sounds a lot like what traditional financial institutions do.

It's not decentralized when one company controls when people can access their own money. And it's certainly not transparent when critical information about stablecoins, and the companies that issue them, isn't available to people who have their money tied up in these assets.

Last month, I wrote to some of the biggest stablecoin issuers to get more information on how they manage the funds that back their coins, and to ask what rights their users have. Their responses were not very enlightening—and should lead us to assume most ordinary customers don't have much in the way of rights at all.

So let's be clear about one thing: if you put your money in stablecoins, there's no guarantee you're going to get it back.

They call it a currency, implying it's the same as having dollars in the bank, and you can withdraw the money at any time.

But many of these companies hide their terms and conditions in the fine print, allowing them to trap customers' money.

And if there's no guarantee you'll get your money back, that's not a currency with a fixed value—it's gambling. And with this much money tied up, it sure looks to me like a potential asset bubble.

Stablecoins make it easier than ever to risk real dollars on cryptocurrencies that are at best volatile, and at worst outright fraudulent.

Just a few weeks ago, we saw how quickly these tokens can crash, with cryptomarkets diving by almost 30 percent in one day. History tells us we should be very concerned when any investment becomes so untethered from reality.

Look at the 1929 stock market crash.

Securities started out as a way for regular Americans to invest in new companies that wanted to bring new products to market or expand their operations.

By the end of the decade, companies were invented out of thin air, to create more stocks to satisfy wild demand. Banks allowed customers to borrow against one stock to buy another, until the whole market collapsed.

And of course we should all remember the 2008 crash.

Subprime mortgages were supposedly created to give more families access to the American dream, while derivatives were created to help financial companies reduce their risks.

In reality, predatory mortgages were used to strip homeowners of the equity they had in their homes in order to create complex mortgage-backed securities and derivatives that ended up increasing risks at banks and financial companies.

We all know how that turned out.

We can't deny that betting on cryptocurrencies has made a few people rich—just like some people became fabulously wealthy trading stocks in the 1920s. And we all heard the stories about mortgage brokers and house-flippers becoming millionaires in the 2000s.

But for most people, this kind of wild speculation ends in disaster. And the only ones who tend to walk away unscathed are the big guys—it's always the big guys— the ones who call it "innovation" while lining their own pockets.

So far, what happens in the cryptomarkets has stayed in the cryptomarkets. But stablecoins create a very real link between the real economy and this new fantasy economy.

We saw this with "Dogecoins," a satirical cryptocurrency that was all of a sudden worth billions when a tech billionaire tweeted about it.

It's understandable that a lot of people are looking for an alternative to our current financial system. Wall Street banks dominate, and they make record profits no matter what's happening to workers and small businesses and the country at large.

To a whole lot of people, that seems like a fantasy economy too.

But a Big Tech scheme that makes it easy for hardworking Americans to put their money at risk isn't the answer.

Stablecoins and cryptomarkets aren't actually an alternative to our banking system. They're a mirror of the same broken system—with even less accountability, and no rules at all.

Today we'll hear the same arguments from this industry against regulation that we've heard from financial industry lobbyists so many times before—it harms innovation, the free market will solve all our problems, America needs to be globally competitive.

What makes America the strongest economy in the world isn't wild betting in the financial sector. It's our workers—their talent, their ingenuity, their dedication. That's what our economy is built on.

You can't fake that. But as we've seen so many times before, you can put it all at risk.

The rest of the world trusts the U.S. dollar when we have orderly, sane markets. The real threat to our global competitiveness is regulators who ignore clear warning signs.

We have reason to be encouraged this time around, though.

The Biden administration is putting strong watchdogs in place at the banking and market regulators. We're empowering workers. Wages are rising. Infrastructure investment is about to spur more job growth. And we're fighting to bring down costs with the Build Back Better plan.

We can't put all that potential at risk.

I will continue to work with the financial watchdogs to ensure they have all of the tools they need to protect people's hard-earned money and our economic recovery from another bubble, and another crash.

Prepared Statement of Senator Patrick J. Toomey

Thank you, Mr. Chairman.

Stablecoins are a central component of the cryptocurrency ecosystem, which is itself at the vanguard of the tokenization of assets.

Stablecoins can speed up payments, especially cross-border transfers, reduce costs, including remittances, and help combat money laundering and terrorist financing through an immutable and transparent transaction record.

Stablecoins can also be programmed and made interoperable with other currencies, creating efficiencies to improve access to financial services for more Americans.

But unlike volatile cryptocurrencies like Bitcoin, stablecoins don't fluctuate in their dollar price.

In today's hearing, we will focus on stablecoins designed to maintain a 1-to-1 value relative to the U.S. Dollar, meaning one stablecoin is meant to always equal one dollar.

Over the past year, the stablecoin market has exploded. As one of our witnesses, Dante Disparte, will explain, stablecoins are beginning to be used for small business payments and international remittances. While traditional payment systems can be expensive and take several days to settle, transferring funds via stablecoins is lowcost and nearly instantaneous.

Given that stablecoins disrupt the status quo, they've naturally drawn skepticism from incumbent industries and regulators. Last month, the President's Working Group on Financial Markets, or PWG, issued a report recommending that Congress pass legislation to establish a Federal regulatory framework for stablecoins. In their report, the Treasury Department and others expressed their worries about consumer protection and financial stability with stablecoins.

Although the report did little to highlight the potential benefits of stablecoins, I was encouraged the report acknowledged that responsibility for clarifying whether, and to what extent, Federal agencies have jurisdiction over stablecoins rests with Congress. I am open to working with the Administration and my Democrat colleagues on this front.

But whatever Congress does, let's be sure that we don't stifle innovation in an evolving digital economy or undermine our own country's competitiveness. Let's have the humility to recognize that many of our views about how financial services are delivered and how investments work are quickly becoming outdated.

This morning, I'm releasing a set of guiding principles that I think should influence our work on a stablecoin legislative framework.

Innovation

These principles recognize that stablecoins are a very important innovation, and they introduce new capabilities into money that did not previously exist. In addition to their ease of use and reduced fees associated with their transfer, stablecoins can improve the privacy and security of our transactions. They also introduce the concept of money programmability, or smart contracts, which allow automated transactions based on a sequence of verifiable events.

In recognition of the potential of these new capabilities, any regulation should be narrowly tailored and designed to do no harm. At the same time, sensible regulatory standards may help to protect against key risks, such as redemption or run risk. These principles take a different approach than the PWG report.

Options for Stablecoin Issuers

For example, the PWG report recommends that all stablecoin issuers must be insured depository institutions. There are three reasons I disagree with that recommendation.

First, stablecoin issuers have different business models than banks. They do not provide the same services as banks and do not present the same risks.

As one of today's witnesses, Jai Massari has observed, stablecoin providers do not engage in taking deposits and making loans like banks do. Because of these important differences, subjecting all stablecoin providers to the full suite of bank rules and regulations meant to address maturity transformation is not appropriately tailored to the potential risks.

Second, requiring all stablecoin issuers to become banks would stifle innovation. We know that a tremendous amount of innovation occurs outside of the banking system, including by technology companies. It is unlikely that much of this development could happen within the banking system because of onerous regulations, which create a difficult environment for innovation. Allowing entrepreneurs to innovate with digital assets like stablecoins will promote greater competition and deliver better results for consumers.

Finally, the regulation of payments activities should create an equal playing field. Great innovators like PayPal, Venmo, and Apple Pay are already subject to a State-by-State licensing regime, as well as registration with a Federal regulator.

Recognizing the range of different business models, there should be at least three options for stablecoin providers: operate under a conventional bank charter; comply with or acquire a special-purpose banking charter designed for stablecoin providers, which would be designed in accordance with legislation; or register as a money transmitter under the existing State regime and as a money services business with FinCEN at the Federal level.

This optionality would match each stablecoin provider with the regulatory framework most appropriate to the business model.

Requirements for All Stablecoin Issuers

Regardless of the charter or license they pursue, all stablecoin providers should meet certain minimum requirements. For example, they should clearly disclose what assets back the stablecoin, as well as give clear redemption policies and subject themselves to periodic audits.

These requirements would ensure that consumers have sufficient information about which stablecoin they use. It might also be appropriate to set minimum reserve requirements and attestations as well.

In addition, legislation should stipulate that non-interest bearing stablecoins are not necessarily securities and shouldn't automatically be regulated as such.

This framework should protect the privacy, security, and confidentiality of individuals using stablecoins, allowing customers to opt out of sharing personal informaion with third parties.

Finally, antimoney laundering and other requirements regarding financial surveillance under the Bank Secrecy Act should be modernized for all financial institutions subject to them, given the emergence of stablecoins, cryptocurrencies, and other new technologies, including artificial intelligence.

The emergence of stablecoins represents to me the latest development in the ongoing evolution of money. I stand ready to work on this issue and do so in a manner that doesn't discourage innovation or competition moving forward.

I look forward to hearing from your witnesses and yield back.

Written Testimony of Alexis Goldstein, Director of Financial Policy, Open Markets Institute, before the Committee on Banking, Housing, and Urban Affairs, United States Senate, "Stablecoins: How Do They Work, How Are They Used, and What Are Their Risks?" December 14, 2021

Chair Brown, Ranking Member Toomey, and Members of the Committee:

Thank you for the opportunity to testify today. I am Director of Financial Policy at the Open Markets Institute, where my work focuses on financial regulatory policy and investor and consumer protection. Previously, I worked as a programmer at Morgan Stanley in electronic trading, and as a business analyst at Merrill Lynch and Deutsche Bank focused on equity derivatives. There, I worked primarily as a product manager for the trading and risk management software used by the global equity options flow trading desks.

I want to start by thanking the Committee for holding today's hearing. I would like to highlight several areas that the Committee may wish to examine further as it relates to stablecoins, including their role in facilitating speculation in cryptocurrency markets, their centrality to decentralized finance, high cumulative fees as stablecoins move across the crypto ecosystem, and national security concerns.

Introduction

Stablecoins are crypto assets that attempt to maintain a stable value, either through a basket of reserve assets acting as collateral (asset-backed stablecoins), or through algorithms (algorithmic stablecoins). Often, stablecoins hold themselves out as being "pegged" to the U.S. dollar or to another currency. There are two major types of stablecoins: asset-backed stablecoins and algorithmic stablecoins.

Stablecoins are an integral part of speculative cryptocurrency trading, as nearly 75% of crypto asset trading involved a stablecoin.[1] Stablecoins are also central to the functioning of decentralized finance ("DeFi"), a section of the cryptocurrency markets largely out of compliance with Know Your Customer ("KYC"), Anti-Money Laundering ("AML"), Countering the Financing of Terrorism ("CFT"), and sanctions checks.

[1] Mitsutoshi Adachi, Alexandra Born, Isabella Gschossmann and Anton van der Kraaij.

Stablecoins play multiple roles in DeFi, including: simplifying the valuation of crypto assets that only trade on DeFi and acting as a store of value in between speculative trades. Recent research from the World Economic Forum found no financial inclusion value in stablecoins, but many increased risks due to potential hacks, insolvency, or technical failures.[2] Additionally, stablecoins and their usage across DeFi also have implications for national security and illicit finance.

Asset-Backed Stablecoins

While there is no universal nomenclature for stablecoins, asset-backed stablecoins are generally understood to be crypto assets whose value is collateralized by "a fiat currency, a basket of fiat currencies or other stable-value assets."[3] There are two main categories of asset-backed stablecoins:

1. Custodial stablecoins, collateralized by assets that are stored off the blockchain ("off-chain"). Examples include Tether, U.S. Dollar Coin, Pax Dollar, and Binance USD; and
2. Stablecoins collateralized by other crypto assets that are stored "on-chain": an example of this is MakerDAO's Dai token.

A brief discussion of four asset-backed stablecoins, Tether, U.S. Dollar Coin, Pax Dollar, and Binance USD, follows.

Tether (USDT)

Tether is an asset-backed stablecoin that has made its tokens available on several blockchains: Ethereum, EOS, Tron, Algorand, Solana and OMG.[4] Tether and the cryptocurrency exchange its executives co-runs it, Bitfinex,

---

[2] *What is the Value Proposition of Stablecoins for Financial Inclusion?*, WORLD ECONOMIC FORUMS (NOV. 2021), https://www3.weforum.org/docs/WEF_Value_Proposition_of_Stablecoins_for_Financial_Inclusion_2021.p df. ("stablecoins do not present features or capabilities that significantly reduce the specific barriers to financial inclusion in the scenarios studied – compared to pre-existing options, once accounting for consistent legal and compliance requirements. Stablecoins are subject to many of the same adoption and inclusion hurdles as other forms of retail finance, such as reliable internet and electricity, digital and financial literacy, and government identity documentation.")

[3] Wharton Blockchain and Digital Asset Project, "DeFi Beyond the Hype," THE WHARTON SCHOOL (2021), https://wifpr.wharton.upenn.edu/wp-content/uploads/2021/05/DeFi-Beyond-the-Hype.pdf.

[4] *FAQs*, TETHER, https://tether.to/faqs/.

paid $42.5 million in October to settle charges with the Commodity Futures Trading Commission of making untrue or misleading statements and omissions of material fact in connection with Tether.[5] Tether and Bitfinex have both been barred from doing business in New York state under the terms of a settlement reached with Attorney General Letiticia James.[6]

As a condition of the settlement with the Attorney General James, Tether must provide quarterly “documents substantiating Tether’s reserve account(s).”[7] Tether’s latest attestation, conducted by the Cayman Islands-based accounting firm Moore Cayman states that Tether is backed by a combination of commercial paper, cash and cash equivalents, corporate bonds, and “other investments” which include other cryptocurrencies.[8]

According to Tether’s website, the fee to redeem to fiat currency is $1,000 or 0.1% of the total redemption, whichever is larger.[9] Tether requires a minimum deposit of $100,000 in order to issue new Tether, and charges a fee of 0.1% of the deposit amount.

30 Day Transaction Value Sum Range‡	Fee per fiat Withdrawal	Fee per fiat Deposit	Fee per Tether tokens Deposit or Withdrawal
100,000† USD and over	The greater of $1,000 or 0.1%	0.1%	FREE

‡ Fees are calculated based on the sum of completed transactions over the previous 30 days.

† This represents the current minimum amount required for a fiat withdrawal or deposit.

Screenshot from Tether’s fee page (https://tether.to/fees/), accessed December 12, 2021.

As of January 1, 2018, Tether stopped allowing redemptions from U.S. residents, and also stopped issuing Tether to U.S. individual and corporate customers, though they allow for carve outs at Tether’s “sole discretion.”[10]

[5] “CFTC Orders Tether and Bitfinex to Pay Fines Totaling $42.5 Million,” COMMODITY FUTURES TRADING COMMISSION (Oct. 15, 2021), https://www.cftc.gov/PressRoom/PressReleases/8450-21.

[6] *NY Bans Tether, Bitfinex Over False Statements About Dollar Backing and Losses*, NBC NEW YORK (Feb. 23, 2021), https://www.nbcnewyork.com/news/business/ny-bans-tether-bitfinex-over-false-statements-about-dollar-backing-and-losses/2904206/.

[7] Attorney General of the State of New York, INVESTOR PROTECTION BUREAU (Feb. 17, 2021).

[8] *Consolidated Reserves Report*, TETHER HOLDINGS LIMITED (Sep. 30, 2021), https://tether.to/wp-content/uploads/2021/12/tether-assurance-sept-30-2021.pdf.

[9] *Fees*, TETHER, https://tether.to/fees/. (“Fee per fiat Withdrawal: The greater of $1,000 or 0.1%”) (last visited Dec. 12, 2021).

[10] *FAQs*, TETHER, https://tether.to/faqs/. (“Unfortunately, Tether has decided to stop serving U.S. individual and corporate customers altogether. As of January 1, 2018, no issuance or redeeming services will be available to these users. Exceptions to these provisions may be

Despite this, major cryptocurrency exchanges serving U.S. customers like Coinbase,[11] Binance.US,[12] Kraken[13] and FTX.US[14] still allow U.S. customers to purchase Tether.

Reporting by the cryptocurrency news site *Protos* has shown that the two biggest purchasers of Tether are the crypto market making giant Cumberland and the crypto trading fund Alameda Research.[15] In an interview with Bloomberg's *Odd Lots* podcast, the majority owner of Alameda Research[16] (and CEO of FTX) Sam Bankman-Fried was asked to explain the process of redeeming Tether. When answering, he stated four separate times that the process was "messy."[17]

Circle, Coinbase, and U.S. Dollar Coin (USDC)

U.S Dollar Coin ("USDC") is an asset-backed stablecoin issued by Circle. Circle has made its tokens available on several blockchains: Ethereum, Tron, Algorand, Solana and Hedera.[18]

According to the whitepaper for Centre (a stablecoin consortium co-founded by Circle and Coinbase) Circle's strategic investors include "IDG Capital, one of the largest venture capital firms in China," Breyer Capital, founded by Jim Breyer, the "first investor in Facebook," and others including "Goldman Sachs, CICC Alpha, Baidu, WanXiang, CreditEase and EverBright Bank."[19]

---

made by Tether, in its sole discretion, for entities that are: Established or organized outside of the United States or its territorial or insular possessions; and, Eligible Contract Participants pursuant to U.S. law.") (last visited Dec. 12, 2021).

[11] https://www.coinbase.com/price/tether.

[12] https://binance.us/en/trade/pro/USDT_USD.

[13] https://www.kraken.com/en-us/prices/usdt-tether-usd-price-chart.

[14] https://ftx.us/en/trade/USDT/USD.

[15] *Tether Papers: This is exactly who acquired 70% of all USDT ever issued*, PROTOS (Nov. 10, 2021), https://protos.com/tether-papers-crypto-stablecoin-usdt-investigation-analysis/.

[16] Roger Parloff, *Portrait of a 29-year-old billionaire: Can Sam Bankman-Fried make his risky crypto business work?*, YAHOO NEWS (Aug. 12, 2021), https://news.yahoo.com/ftx-ceo-sam-bankman-fried-profile-085444366.html. ("Bankman-Fried also still owns 90% of Alameda Research, he says. Alameda's digital wallet at FTX (which is not its only store of assets) contained over $10 billion in digital coins in mid-July, according to a screengrab he sent me. (More than $5 billion of that was "locked," however—not yet eligible for conversion to conventional money—and another $4 billion was in FTT, a digital coin issued by FTX.)").

[17] Joe Weisenthal and Tracy Alloway, *Transcript: Sam Bankman-Fried and Matt Levine on Crypto Market Structure*, BLOOMBERG (Aug. 6, 2021), https://www.bloomberg.com/news/articles/2021-08-06/transcript-sam-bankman-fried-and-matt-levine-on-crypto-market-structure.

[18] *Introducing USD Coin: A stablecoin brought to you by Circle and Coinbase*, CENTRE, https://www.centre.io/usdc.

[19] *Id.*

Circle maintains a revenue sharing agreement with Coinbase for USDC, allowing Coinbase to profit off the sale of USDC on its exchange.[20] These profits are likely substantial, as USDC has seen rapid growth in 2021 and Coinbase stated in a February SEC filing that they are the "principal reseller of the USD Coin."[21] This revenue share agreement is the likely reason that Coinbase does not charge users to purchase USDC, but does charge them for purchasing competing stablecoins like Tether (and other crypto assets), raising questions of price discrimination and steering of its customers towards USDC.

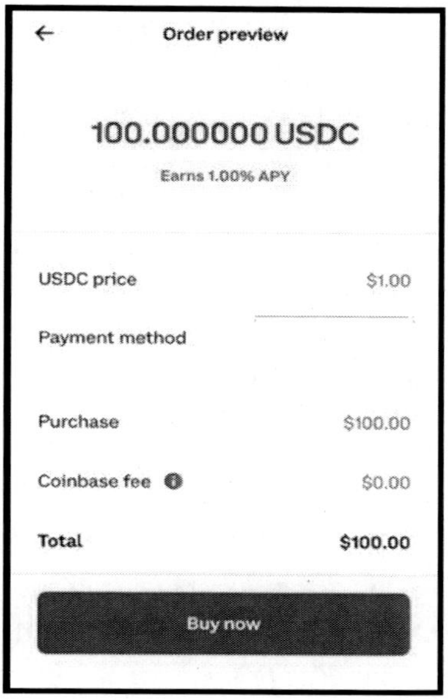

Screenshot of the Coinbase app, displaying an "Earns 1.00% APY" message in the Order Preview screen when attempting to purchase USDC, accessed December 7, 2021.

Currently, Coinbase pays a 1% APY on US Dollar Coin by default, with no action needed from the user apart from purchasing US Dollar Coin (The

---

20 *Amendment No. 1 to Form S-4*, CIRCLE (Oct. 4, 2021) https://www.sec.gov/Archives/edgar/data/1876042/000110465921122565/tm2124445-1_s4a.htm at 181. ("As part of our and Coinbase's investment in the development of the Centre Consortium, we entered into agreements with Coinbase, pursuant to which we share any revenue generated from USDC reserves pro rata based on (i) the amount of USDC originated by each respective party and (ii) the amount of USDC held on each respective party's platform (i.e., held in its customers' accounts) in relation to the total amount of USDC in circulation (the "Revenue Share Arrangement")").

21 *FORM S-1*, COINBASE (Feb. 25, 2021), https://www.sec.gov/Archives/edgar/data/1679788/000162828021003168/coinbaseglobalincs-1.htm at 23.

rate used to be 0.15% APY[22]). This appears to create an automatic expectation of profits for US Dollar Coin on Coinbase.

Circle and Coinbase Change Reserves, Website Terms Following Press Scrutiny

For many months during 2021, Coinbase stated that for every dollar offered to investors in U.S. Dollar Coin, there was one dollar "in a bank account" backing it. But a July disclosure from Circle showed their assets "actually include commercial paper, corporate bonds and other assets that could experience losses and are less liquid if customers ever tried to redeem the stablecoin en masse," as *Bloomberg*'s Joe Light reported.[23] Following the press scrutiny, the Centre consortium said it would shift its reserves into cash and short-term U.S. Treasuries.[24]

Circle's October attestation, conducted by the auditing firm Grant Thornton LLP, claims that Circle is backed by "cash and cash equivalents" which they define to be "include US dollar deposits at banks and short-term, highly liquid investments that are readily convertible to known amounts of cash and have a maturity of less than or equal to 90 days from purchase." It is unclear what percentage (if any) of these are U.S. Treasuries, and if so, what their maturities are.[25]

Paxos: Pax Dollar (USDP) and Binance USD (BUSD)

The Pax Dollar ("USDP") is an asset-backed stablecoin issued by Paxos. The Pax Dollar is built on the Ethereum blockchain and adheres to Ethereum's ERC20 token standard, according to the Pax Dollar white paper.[26]

Paxos' website states that they post monthly attestations for the Pax Dollar. The latest attestation posted is from October 2021, and states that the 981,753,175.81 million in Pax Dollar supply has a Reserve Account with

---

[22] *USD Coin rewards FAQ*, COINBASE, https://help.coinbase.com/en/coinbase/getting-started/crypto-education/usd-coin-rewards-faq. ("As of June 3rd, 2020, the APY for USDC Rewards is 0.15%.").

[23] Joe Light, *Coinbase Vowed Token's All-Cash Backing; That's Not True*, BLOOMBERG (Aug. 11, 2021) https://www.bloomberg.com/news/articles/2021-08-23/coinbase-circle-to-move-all-usdc-reserves-into-cash-treasuries.

[24] Joe Light and Vildana Hajric, *Coinbase, Circle Say USDC Reserves to Be In Cash, Treasuries,* BLOOMBERG (Aug. 23, 2021), https://www.bloomberg.com/news/articles/2021-08-23/coinbase-circle-to-move-all-usdc-reserves-into-cash-treasuries.

[25] https://www.centre.io/hubfs/pdfs/attestation/2021%20Circle%20Examination%20Report%20October%202 021%20Final.pdf?hsLang=en.

[26] Charles Cascarilla, *Whitepaper: Pax Dollar*, PAXOS (Aug. 24, 2021), https://insights.paxos.com/hubfs/USDP-whitepaper.pdf.

"U.S. dollars / amounts backed by U.S. treasuries."[27] The attestation does not specify which portion is in Treasuries versus U.S. dollars, nor does it specify the maturities of the Treasuries in their Reserve Account.

The majority of the current supply of Pax Dollar is locked into DeFi (over 65% of the Pax Dollar supply as of November 11, 2021[28]). Given that there virtually no KYC/AML checks in DeFi applications, there are risks that Pax Dollars may be utilized to convert ransomware payments from one crypto asset to another. (These risks are discussed further in the "National Security Concerns" section below).

Paxos also runs Binance's stablecoin BUSD. Binance has been subject to regulatory actions by Germany's BaFin,[29] Japan's Financial Services Agency,[30] Malaysia,[31] Hong Kong[32], and the UK's FCA.[33] The latest attestation posted by Paxos for BUSD is from October 2021, and states that 13,156,917,361.68 in BUSD supply has a Reserve Account with "U.S. dollars/amounts backed by U.S. government guaranteed instruments."[34] It is unclear from the attestation what these government guaranteed instruments are, and what maturities they have.

---

[27] *Examination of Management Assertions, Reserve Accounts Report – Pax Dollar Token (USDP)*, PAXOS TRUST COMPANY, LLC (Oct. 29, 2021) https://paxos.com/wp-content/uploads/2021/11/USDP-Examination-Report-October-2021.pdf.

[28] *Pax Dollar: Percent of Supply in Smart Contracts*, GLASSNODE, https://studio.glassnode.com/metrics?a=USDP&category=Supply&m=distribution.SupplyContracts&modal=loginForm (last visited Nov. 11, 2021) (Showing 65.89% of the Pax Dollar supply is locked into smart contracts).

[29] *Germany's Financial Watchdog Warns Crypto Exchange Binance Over 'Stock Tokens'*, REUTERS (April 29, 2021), https://www.reuters.com/technology/germanys-financial-watchdog-warns-crypto-exchange-binance-over-stock-tokens-2021-04-29/.

[30] FIN. SERVS. AGENCY, ABOUT THOSE WHO DO CRYPTO ASSET EXCHANGE BUSINESS WITHOUT REGISTRATION (BINANCE HOLDINGS LIMITED) (June 25, 2021).

[31] *Restricting of Product Offerings in Malaysia*, BINANCE (Aug. 13, 2021), https://www.binance.com/en/support/announcement/ab37eace9146494d990293d60423a34e.

[32] *Cryptoexchange Binance to Stop Hong Kong Users Trading Derivatives*, REUTERS (Aug. 6, 2021), https://www.reuters.com/technology/cryptoexchange-binance-stop-hong-kong-users-trading-derivatives-2021-08-06/.

[33] *Consumer Warning on Binance Markets Limited and the Binance Group*, FIN. CONDUCT AUTH. (June 26, 2021), https://www.fca.org.uk/news/news-stories/consumer-warning-binance-markets-limited-and-binance-group.

[34] *Examination of Management Assertions Reserve Accounts Report – BUSD Token*, PAXOS TRUST COMPANY, LLC (Oct. 29, 2021).

Asset-Backed Stablecoins Usage of Forced Arbitration Clauses and Class Action Bans

In traditional financial markets, consumers and investors are often subject to forced arbitration clauses and bans on class action lawsuits. These forced arbitration clauses prevent users from suing financial firms in a court of law, instead conducting dispute resolution in private arbitration, where the outcomes are typically secret and there is no right to appeal. Many asset-backed stablecoin issuers also include binding arbitration and class action bans in their terms of service.

A review of four major asset-backed stablecoins showed forced arbitration and class action bans present in every single one's terms of service:

Stablecoin	Issuer	Link to terms	Forced Arbitration?	Class Action Ban?
U.S. Dollar Coin	Circle	https://www.circle.com/en/legal/us-user-agreement	Yes	Yes
Tether	Tether	https://tether.to/legal/	Yes	Yes
Binance USD	Paxos	https://paxos.com/2019/03/29/general-terms-and-conditions/	Yes	Yes
Pax Dollar	Paxos	https://paxos.com/2019/03/29/general-terms-and-conditions/	Yes	Yes

I attempted to review the terms of service for the three algorithmic stablecoins discussed below, but I was not able to find any terms of service for the stablecoins or their platforms (OlympusDAO, Abracadabra Money, and Iron Finance).

Algorithmic Stablecoins

Algorithmic stablecoins are uncollateralized crypto assets that attempt to maintain a stable value through a variety of means, which can include: an ongoing rebalancing of a basket of other crypto assets or even just the mere expectation of future market value. Professor Ryan Clemens of the University of Calgary writes that algorithmic stablecoins operate in a "perpetually vulnerable state."[35]

[35] Dr. Ryan Clements, "Built to Fail: The Inherent Fragility of Algorithmic Stablecoins," 11 Wake Forest L. Rev. Online 131 (Nov. 2021), http://www.wakeforestlawreview.com/2021/10/built-to-fail-the-inherent-fragility-of-algorithmic-stablecoins/.

Below is a brief discussion of three algorithmic stablecoins: Olympus DAO, Magic Internet Money, and IRON.

OlympusDAO

OlympusDAO is an Ethereum-based project founded by a pseudonymous developer known as "Zeus" which issues a token called OHM. According to the Olympus DAO Frequently Asked Questions ("FAQ"), they "a free-floating reserve currency, OHM, that is backed by a basket of assets."[36] Strictly speaking OlympusDAO rejects being defined as a stablecoin in its documentation. However, it defines its project as aspiring to create "an algorithmic reserve currency backed by other decentralized assets."[37]

Olympus DAO claims to utilize a different stablecoin, DAI, as its backing, writing that "Each OHM is backed by 1 DAI, not pegged to it."[38] (DAI is a stablecoin issued by MakerDAO and collateralized with crypto assets.[39]) Cryptocurrency users can purchase OHM on decentralized exchanges or "mint" OHM at a discount by locking in other crypto assets to OlympusDAO.

OlympusDAO then uses these crypto assets to "accumulate its own liquidity."[40] The OHM a user receives in exchange is not delivered immediately: there is a vesting period.[41]

Once users obtain OHM tokens, Olympus DAO advertises an eye-popping, six-figure APY (over 439,000% APY as of December 13, 202) in exchange for locking their OHM tokens onto the platform:

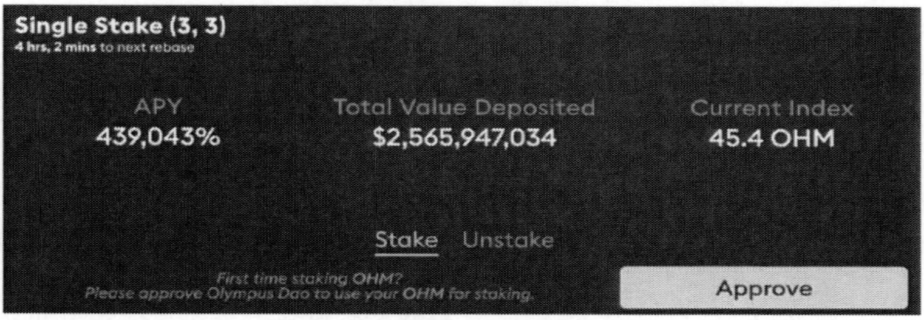

Screenshot from Olympus DAO, displaying a 439,043% APY for staking the crypto asset OHM, accessed December 13, 2021.

---

[36] *FAQ*, OLYMPUS DAO, https://docs.olympusdao.finance/main/basics/basics. (last visited Dec. 12, 2021).

[37] *Id.*

[38] *Id.*

[39] *What is Dai? (DAI)*, KRAKEN, https://www.kraken.com/en-us/learn/what-is-dai.

[40] *What is bonding?*, OLYMPUS DAO, https://docs.olympusdao.finance/main/basics/bonding.

[41] *Purchase A Bond (1, 1)*, OLYMPUS DAO, https://docs.olympusdao.finance/main/using-the-website/bonds.

Some in the Crypto Industry have Warned that Olympus DAO may be a Ponzi Scheme

Many in both the financial services and cryptocurrency industries have raised alarms about OlympusDAO and its stablecoin OHM. *Bloomberg*'s Matt Levine described OlympusDAO as having "Ponzi economics."[42] Scott Lewis, the founder of the cryptocurrency metrics site *DeFi Pulse* tweeted "ohm is a ponzi. it's clear as day"[43] And the cryptocurrency news publication *Coin Desk* wrote of OlympusDAO, "Yes, it's a Ponzi scheme. But who cares?"[44]

Despite multiple allegations that OlympusDAO is a Ponzi scheme, the project's popularity has led to dozens "forks" of the project[45] – a fork is when a software project's code is copied in order to be modified and adjusted for a new and different software project.

Magic Internet Money and Abracadabra Money

Magic Internet Money describes itself as a "pegged stable coin that is backed by interest bearing tokens." Its platform, called Abracadabra Money, states in its documentation that it always considers this [Magic Internet Money] token to be worth 1USD."[46]

Co-founded by pseudonymous developers[47], Magic Internet Money claims their peg to one U.S. dollar is maintained through arbitrage, conducted by trading bots: "a lot of the Market to Market arbitrage is done by automated bots that constantly monitor pools for opportunities to capitalize on these price differences."[48]

[42] Matt Levine, "What Does Payment for Order Flow Buy?," BLOOMBERG (Dec. 8, 2021), https://www.bloomberg.com/opinion/articles/2021-12-08/what-does-payment-for-order-flow-buy.

[43] Scott Lewis (@scott_lew_is), TWITTER (Oct. 12, 2021, 11:21 PM), https://twitter.com/scott_lew_is/status/1448126707903389701. ("been calling out scams for 4 years, no plans to stop now. ohm is a ponzi. it's clear as day, and delusional ad hominems won't change that.").

[44] Andrew Thurman, "Olympus DAO Might Be the Future of Money (or It Might Be a Ponzi)," COIN DESK (Dec 5, 2021), https://www.coindesk.com/policy/2021/12/05/olympus-dao-might-be-the-future-of-money-or-it-might-be-a-ponzi/.

[45] Owen Fernau, *OlympusDAO's Success Inspires Dozens of Forks*, YAHOO (Oct. 26, 2021).

[46] *Tokenomics*, ABRACADABRA MONERY, https://docs.abracadabra.money/tokens/tokenomics.

[47] https://www.bitcoininsider.org/article/129717/magic-internet-money-crosses-1b-race-occupy-defi.

[48] *Id.*

Screenshot from Abracadabra.Money (https://abracadabra.money/), stating "THE FORMULA IS STRAIGHT FORWARD. COLLATERAL IN - POOF - STABLE COIN OUT," accessed December 12, 2021.

Cryptocurrency investors that own certain crypto tokens can use them as collateral in order to borrow Magic Internet Money.[49] The collateral accepted by Abracadabra can change: for example, it recently added support for borrowing Magic Internet Money by using the Shiba Inu crypto token as collateral.[50]

The market cap of Magic Internet Money is estimated to be some $3.95 billion – higher than Pax Dollar's $1.14 billion market cap as of December 13, 2021.[51] In addition, the stablecoin has received some legitimacy from other crypto market platforms. For example, although Coinbase does not offer the ability to purchase Magic Internet Money, it has an entire section of its website dedicated to the stablecoin that explains where users can purchase it.[52]

---

[49] Abracadabra.Money, *Abracadabra, SPELL, and Magic Internet Money*, MEDIUM.COM (May 5, 2021), https://medium.com/abracadabra-money/abracadabra-spell-and-magic-internet-money-a563637ce92e.

[50] *#3 Add $SHIB as Collateral*, SNAPSHOT.ORG (Oct. 12, 2021).

[51] *Stablecoins by Market Capitalization*, COINGECKO, https://www.coingecko.com/en/categories/stablecoins (last visited Dec. 13, 2021).

[52] *How to buy Magic Internet Money*, COINBASE, https://www.coinbase.com/how-to-buy/magic-internet-money. ("Some cryptocurrencies are harder to obtain than others. Magic Internet Money is one of them. It's not available on the Coinbase app or Coinbase Wallet. But don't worry, we've provided some hints to help you find a way to buy Magic Internet Money that works for you.") (last visited Dec. 12, 2021).

IRON and the IRON/TITAN Collapse

In mid-June, the price of the cryptocurrency token TITAN collapsed from $60 to close to zero over just a few hours. The protocol that created the TITAN token, Iron.Finance, lost more than $2 billion in total value locked (TVL).[53] TITAN was linked to the algorithmic stablecoin IRON. IRON attempted to retain a dollar peg by relying on arbitrageurs. As Dr. Ryan Clemens writes, "If IRON lost its peg and traded below $1, an arbitrageur could purchase it on the secondary market and redeem it for $1 of combined USDC and TITAN."[54] But this worked better in theory than practice:

> "Iron Finance unraveled when the value of its unlimited supply governance token, TITAN, fell precipitously in the DeFi secondary market. Iron Finance reported that there was significant selling by certain 'whale' holders. The market for TITAN was already thin, and this large-value sale triggered a cascade selloff of TITAN and an IRON redemption 'negative feedback loop.' This caused the IRON token to lose its peg, which in turn 'triggered' the algorithmic minting mechanism for TITAN and an arbitrage opportunity in a resulting 'death spiral.'"[55]

Some theorized a design failure in IRON,[56] made by the largely anonymous development team, is what led to the collapse.[57] Billionaire investor Mark Cuban also lost money in this collapse, and in the wake of it, told Bloomberg that "There should be regulation to define what a stable coin is and what collateralization is acceptable."[58]

---

[53] *Analysis of the TITAN Token Collapse: Iron.Finance Rugpull or DeFi Bank Run?*, CIPHER TRACE (Jun. 21, 2021) https://ciphertrace.com/analysis-of-the-titan-token-collapse-iron-finance-rugpull-or-defi-bank-run/.

[54] Dr. Ryan Clements, "Built to Fail: The Inherent Fragility of Algorithmic Stablecoins," 11 Wake Forest L. Rev. Online 131 (Nov. 2021), http://www.wakeforestlawreview.com/2021/10/built-to-fail-the-inherent-fragility-of-algorithmic-stablecoins/.

[55] *Id.*

[56] Frances Coppola, "Crypto's Weimar," COPPOLA COMMENT (Jun. 2021), https://www.coppolacomment.com/2021/06/cryptos-weimar.html.

[57] *TITAN crypto-token does the opposite of zero to $60: Value plummets in hours*, THE REGISTER (Jun. 17, 2021), https://www.theregister.com/2021/06/17/iron_cryptocoin_titan/.

[58] Joe Weisenthal, *Mark Cuban Calls for Stablecoin Regulation After Trading Token That Crashed to Zero*, BLOOMBERG (Jun. 17, 2021), https://www.bloomberg.com/news/articles/2021-06-17/mark-cuban-defi-iron-finance-crashed-.

Stablecoins and Financial Inclusion

In a recent report, the World Economic Forum ("WEF") found that "where regulation is evenly applied, stablecoins are subject to the same adoption and inclusion hurdles as other forms of retail finance."[59] The WEF also found that stablecoins may introduce risks that include "financial failure at the stablecoin provider from illiquidity or insolvency, lost or stolen access to funds in digital wallets or exchanges, and technical failure at the underlying blockchain or smart contract levels."[60]

Because stablecoins largely cannot be exchanged for goods and services outside of the crypto ecosystem, stablecoin users still require a bank account to convert their stablecoins back to U.S. dollars. The details of Facebook's most recent cryptocurrency pilot, Novi, is an informative example, as they make it clear that Facebook understands the users of its pilot will need to have a bank, and will need to pay wire fees in some cases to withdraw their funds. The "Learn More" section of Novi's website states that users can "add money to their account with a debit card" and they can withdraw funds by "picking up cash at a nearby location or transferring it to their bank account."[61] This means that the Facebook pilot will not help the unbanked and underbanked, nor drive any new financial inclusion. Further, by utilizing banks as on- and off- ramps for the Pax Dollar, Facebook's pilot will be free riding off the banking system.

Fees to Send Stablecoins to Others Appear to Exceed Fees for Traditional Systems

Let's assume that Person A is in the United States, and wants to send $200 in the stablecoin Tether to Person B, who is in Europe. At the end of the process, Person B converts it back to Euros in order to withdraw it to their bank. ($200 was chosen because the minimum crypto withdrawal amount on Binance for stablecoins is $135). An examination of the total fees incurred by utilizing stablecoins and cryptocurrency exchanges is more expensive ($5.98 on the

---

[59] *What is the Value Proposition of Stablecoins for Financial Inclusion?*, WORLD ECONOMIC FORUMS (NOV. 2021), https://www3.weforum.org/docs/WEF_Value_Proposition_of_Stablecoins_for_Financial_Inclusion_2021.pdf.

[60] *Id.*

[61] David Marcus, *Pilot Version of Novi Now Available*, NOVI (Oct. 19, 2021), https://scontent-iad3-2.xx.fbcdn.net/v/t39.2365-6/245645778_229514682497390_5814575696636412345_n.pdf?_nc_cat=102&ccb=1-5&_nc_sid=ad8a9d&_nc_ohc=BHjkH4QpBuwAX87uHOs&_nc_ht=scontent-iad3-2.xx&oh=6e9445151d084b19c77eaf0d916fc56c&oe=619DCED6.

low end, and $86.44 in fees on the high end) than utilizing a payment system like Western Union ($4.88 in fees).[62]

Here is an estimation of the total fees buying, sending, and cashing out $200 worth of Tether would incur across exchanges:

	Western Union	Kraken	Coinbase	Binance.us to Binance.com	FTX.us to FTX.com
Fund account	Person A: $0 (ACH)[63]	Person A: $0 (ACH)[64]	Person A: $0 (ACH)[65]	Person A: $0 (ACH)	Person A: $0-$0.50 (ACH)
Convert USD to Stablecoins	n/a	0.26% or $0.52[66]	$2.99 (buy $200 Tether)[67]	0.1% or $0.20[68]	$0.20 - $0.80 (0.1% Maker fee - 0.4% Taker fee)[69]
Send to Person B	$0 (send to bank)	$20 (send to Person B on Kraken)[70]	0 - $3.60[71]	$65[72]	$5.00-$10.00[73]

---

[62] In this example, Person A uses ACH to initially move their $200 onto a cryptocurrency exchange, purchases a stablecoin, and sends ~$200 worth of stablecoins to Person B on the same exchange. Person B then trades the stablecoin for their local currency, and withdraws it.

[63] *Price Estimator*, WESTERN UNION, https://www.westernunion.com/us/en/send-money/app/price-estimator. (last visited Dec. 13, 2021).

[64] *Cash withdrawal options (fees, minimums and processing times)*, KRAKEN, https://support.kraken.com/hc/en-us/articles/360000423043-Cash-withdrawal-options-fees-minimums-and-processing-times-. (Withdrawal Minimum is 1 USD. The fee to use ACH for a withdrawal is free. The processing time is "1-2 business days (cutoff at 6pm EST)"). (last visited Dec. 13, 2021).

[65] *Funding your account with USD*, COINBASE, https://help.coinbase.com/en/exchange/trading-and-funding/funding-your-account-with-usd. (last visited Dec. 13, 2021).

[66] https://support.kraken.com/hc/en-us/articles/201893638-How-trading-fees-work-on-Kraken.

[67] $2.99 is the fee I was quoted on Coinbase when previewing the purchase of $200 worth of Tether on December 13, 2021.

[68] *Trading Fees: Maker/Taker*, BINANCE.US, https://www.binance.us/en/fee/schedule.

[69] *Trading fees*, FTX.US, https://help.ftx.us/hc/en-us/articles/360043579273-Fees. (Assuming a new user without trading volume in the past 30 days).

[70] *Cryptocurrency withdrawal fees and minimums*, KRAKEN, https://support.kraken.com/hc/en-us/articles/360000767986-Cryptocurrency-withdrawal-fees-and-minimums. (Tether USD (ERC-20 token) - Withdrawal fee: 20 USDT).

[71] $3.60 is the fee I was quoted on Coinbase when previewing the send of Tether to another cryptocurrency address on December 13, 2021.

[72] *Fee Structure: Deposit & Withdrawal Fees*, BINANCE.US, https://www.binance.us/en/fee/schedule. (Minimum withdrawal amount for the ERC20 token version of tether is $130. The fee to withdrawal is $65). (last visited Dec. 13, 2021).

[73] I was quoted both $5 and $10 fees on FTX.us when previewing the send of Tether to another cryptocurrency address on December 13, 2021. (FTX.us specifies that "FTX.US pays the withdrawal blockchain fees for all tokens except for ERC20/ETH & OMNI token withdrawals," but does not specify in writing what its ERC20 token withdrawals are.)

	Western Union	Kraken	Coinbase	Binance.us to Binance.com	FTX.us to FTX.com
			Fee depends on if it's an "off-chain"[74] or "on- chain" send.[75]		
Convert to EUR / Sell stablecoin s for EUR	n/a	0.26%[76] or $0.52	Person B: $2.99 (sell $200 Tether)	0.1% or $0.20[77]	$0.04 - $0.14
Person B sends to Bank	Person B: Receives €172.84 (1.00 USD: 0.8642 EUR)	Person B: €5-€35 (SWIFT)[78] (equiv to $5.64 - $39.50)	$0 (SEPA)[79]	Person B: (SEPA withdrawals for Binance are not available) There is a 0.05% fee to use an Etana custody account to withdraw[80]	Person B: $75 wire to withdraw to bank for amounts less than $10,000 (SEPA)[81]
Total Fees (to send $200)	$4.88 (Western Union)	$26.68 - $60.54 (Kraken)	$5.98 - $9.58 (Coinbase)	$66.40 (Binance)	$80.24 - $86.44 (FTX)

---

[74] *How to send and receive cryptocurrency*, COINBASE, https://help.coinbase.com/en/coinbase/trading-and-funding/cryptocurrency-trading-pairs/how-to-send-and-receive-cryptocurrency. ("If you're sending to a crypto address that belongs to another Coinbase user who has opted into Instant sends, you can use off-chain sends. Off-chain sends are instant and incur no transaction fees. On-chain sends will incur network fees.")

[75] *Id.* (On chain fees will be "based on [Coinbase's] estimate of the network transaction fees that we anticipate paying for each transaction").

[76] *How Trading Fees Work on Kraken*, KRAKEN, https://support.kraken.com/hc/en-us/articles/201893638-How-trading-fees-work-on-Kraken.

[77] Trading Fees: Maker/Taker, BINANCE.COM, https://www.binance.com/en/fee/schedule.

[78] *EUR (Euro) withdrawal options,* KRAKEN, https://support.kraken.com/hc/en-us/articles/360000423043-Cash-withdrawal-options-fees-minimums-and-processing-times-. (SWIFT (Bank Frick) costs 5 EUR with a 1-5 business days processing time.; SWIFT (Etana Custody) costs 35 EUR with 3-5 business days processing time.

[79] *Payment methods for European customers*, COINBASE, https://help.coinbase.com/en/coinbase/getting-started/add-a-payment-method/payment-methods-for-european-customers. ("SEPA transfers have no fees and can only be denominated in EUR. Please note that SEPA transfers only process on business days and can take up to 7 calendar days if sent over a weekend or bank holiday.") (last visited Dec. 13, 2021).

[80] *Deposit & Withdrawal Fees: Fiat*, BINANCE, https://www.binance.com/en/fee/fiatFee. (EUR withdrawal via Etana Account Balance Withdrawal Fee: 0.05%").

[81] *Depositing & Withdrawing Fiat* FTX.COM, https://help.ftx.com/hc/en-us/articles/360042050452-Depositing-Withdrawing-Fiat-. ("Fiat withdrawals below $10,000 in value will have a $75 fee. This is a fee our bank charges us. Otherwise, there are no fees.") (last visited December 13, 2021).

Stablecoins' Role in the Cryptocurrency Ecosystem

Stablecoins Are Dependent on the Existing Banking System

Because major retailers and vendors outside of the cryptocurrency ecosystem don't accept stablecoins as payments, cryptocurrency investors need a bank account to convert their stablecoins back to U.S. dollars to pay for goods and services. To obtain cryptocurrency in the first place also requires purchasing some on an exchange, and connecting that exchange to a bank, debit card, or another payment mechanism. Tim Swanson, the head of market intelligence at the blockchain firm Clearmatics, wrote that "it is clear that from trading activity and total-value-locked up (TVL), that the DeFi ecosystem (and all coin worlds really), are reliant on maintaining frictionless U.S. banking access."[82]

Stablecoins Are Integral to DeFi

Decentralized finance of "DeFi" is marketed as purely peer-to-peer programs that operate without intermediaries.[83] However, market participants, including crypto metrics providers, have raised questions as to whether or not DeFi is truly decentralized given factors such as protocol fees, governance token control, and platform treasuries.[84] Marketing oneself as "decentralized" may be opportune from regulatory, legal and marketing standpoints; however, when crises happen that warrant quick action, many DeFi platforms take actions with many indicia of centralized control. For example: the crypto borrowing and lending platform Compound threatened to report user's income to the IRS following a bug, and Curve Finance shut down a competitors' presence on their system via an "Emergency DAO."[85]

The true size of the DeFi market remains unclear, as metrics vary wildly: crypto metrics provider Glassnode estimates there is over $248 billion locked

---

[82] Tim Swanson, "Parasitic stablecoins," Great Wall of Numbers (Jan. 4, 2021), https://www.ofnumbers.com/2021/01/04/parasitic-stablecoins/.

[83] "DeFi vs. Traditional Finance," Ethereum Foundation, https://ethereum.org/en/defi/. (See: "One of the best ways to see the potential of DeFi is to understand the problems that exist today...There's a premium to financial services because intermediary institutions need their cut").

[84] Liesl Eichholz, "The UNI Token: Is Uniswap Really Decentralized?," Glassnode Insights, Sep 24, 2020.

[85] *Demystifying Crypto: Digital Assets and the Role of Government Before the U.S. Congress Joint Econ. Comm.* (2021) (written testimony of Alexis Goldstein), https://www.jec.senate.gov/public/cache/files/aa387917-9456-4b1f-a948-f086594c4d15/alexis-goldstein-jec-crypto-hearing-testimony.pdf.

into DeFi on the Ethereum blockchain,[86] while CoinGecko ranks it at $135.8 billion,[87] and DeFiPulse.com puts it at just shy of $100 billion.

As the President's Working Group wrote in their Stablecoin report, stablecoins "play a central role in facilitating trading, lending, and borrowing activity in DeFi." *DeFi Pulse* estimates that the total value of all stablecoins circulating on DeFi is $104.6 billions of December 12, 2021,[88] while the cryptocurrency research site *The Block* estimates the total supply of the top 8 stablecoins to be $148.45 billion.[89] This indicates that the percentage of the total stablecoin supply on DeFi is in the realm of 70 percent.

Eight out of nine of the top Liquidity Pools on Uniswap – the largest decentralized exchange – have at least one leg in a Stablecoin, as of December 13, 2021:

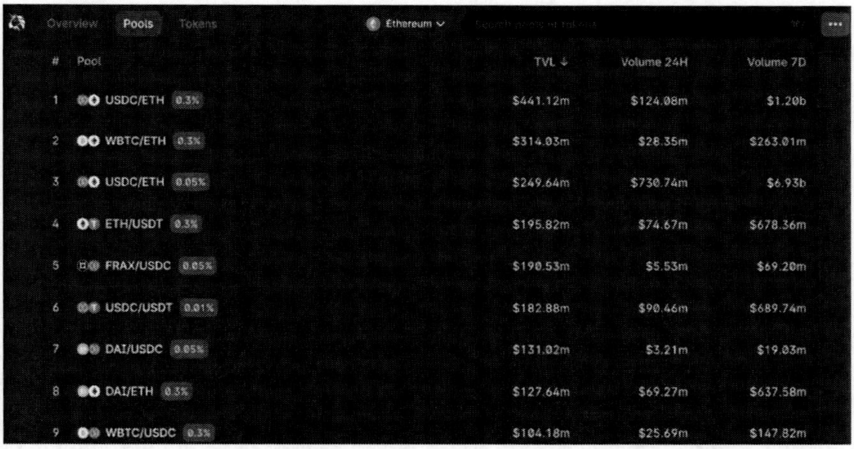

#	Pool	TVL ↓	Volume 24H	Volume 7D
1	USDC/ETH 0.3%	$441.12m	$124.08m	$1.20b
2	WBTC/ETH 0.3%	$314.03m	$28.35m	$263.01m
3	USDC/ETH 0.05%	$249.64m	$730.74m	$6.93b
4	ETH/USDT 0.3%	$195.82m	$74.67m	$678.36m
5	FRAX/USDC 0.05%	$190.53m	$5.53m	$69.20m
6	USDC/USDT 0.01%	$182.88m	$90.46m	$689.74m
7	DAI/USDC 0.05%	$131.02m	$3.21m	$19.03m
8	DAI/ETH 0.3%	$127.64m	$69.27m	$637.58m
9	WBTC/USDC 0.3%	$104.18m	$25.69m	$147.82m

Uniswap's top liquidity pools, sorted by Total Value Locked ("TVL"), https://info.uniswap.org/#/pools, accessed December 13, 2021.

---

[86] *ETHEthereum: Total Value Locked in DeFi (TVL)*, GLASSNODE, https://studio.glassnode.com/metrics?a=ETH&category=&m=defi.TotalValueLocked&modal=loginForm&s=1634640451&u=1639353600&zoom=. (last visited Dec. 13, 2021).

[87] *DeFi Market Cap*, COIN GECKO, https://www.coingecko.com/en/categories/decentralized-finance-defi. (last visited Dec. 13, 2021).

[88] *Total Value Circulating of Cryptodollars*, DEFI PULSE, https://defipulse.com/usd. ("This Cryptodollars page measures the amount of coins or tokens pegged to the US Dollar, commonly referred to as stablecoins, that are circulating and being utilized within the decentralized finance (DeFi) ecosystem. DeFi Pulse monitors these tokens on the Ethereum blockchain. Every hour, we refresh our charts by pulling the total balance held by these smart contracts") (last visited Dec. 13, 2021).

[89] https://www.theblockcrypto.com/data/decentralized-finance/stablecoins.

Finally, industry participants have noted the importance of stablecoins to DeFi. The head of policy for the Blockchain Association tweeted that "the point" of DeFi is to "let people get rid of their fiat" and that stablecoins ("a decentralized fiat instrument") are required to do so.[90]

For new tokens to gain ground, users need to be able to purchase them on DeFi. Token creators enable this by creating new Liquidity Pools on platforms like Uniswap. This involves taking two tokens: (1) the new token; and (2) another token (often a stablecoin), and calling a decentralized exchange's smart contract in order to issue a new "LP token" representing those two deposits. The assets supplied to the liquidity pool enables users to swap between them.

The Liquidity Provider earns a fee, but may also experience losses (which the industry calls "impermanent loss").

Investor Protection Concerns in DeFi

Given stablecoin's critical role in facilitating DeFi, it's worth briefly examining some of the investor protection concerns present in this section of crypto asset markets.

There are certain basic assumptions in traditional financial markets, including that, barring a serious liquidity crisis, you will be able to sell back a product that you buy. But in DeFi malicious actors can design tokens that can be bought, but not sold. One recent example of this phenomenon is the Squid Game token. The token gained considerable popularity following a series of uncritical headlines in the financial press, touting its 83,000% gains, all before the anonymous development team pulled all the liquidity out of the project – causing the price of Squid Coin to plummet to zero (a technique known as a "rug pull").[91]

Scams are prevalent enough that some DeFi websites include an explicit warning on their website if you attempt to import a custom token (by searching for the token by its alpha-numeric address). For example, the Avalanche blockchain-based exchange Trader Joe displays the following warning when you import a custom token[92]:

---

[90] Jake Chervinsky (@jchervinsky), TWITTER (Aug. 27, 2021, 3:09 PM).

[91] Matt Novak, "Squid Game Cryptocurrency Scammers Make Off With $3.3 Million," GIZMODO (Nov, 1, 2021), https://gizmodo.com/squid-game-cryptocurrency-scammers-make-off-with-2-1-m-1847972824.

[92] TraderJoe.xyz, accessed November 15, 2021.

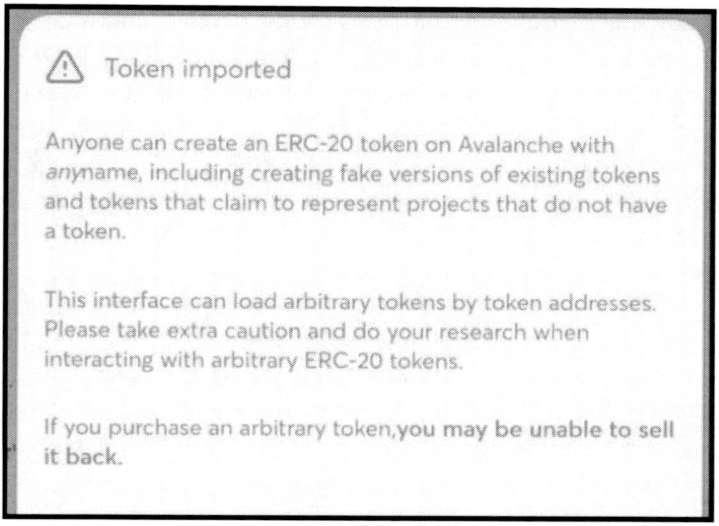

According to the website TokenSniffer.com, which scans for new token contracts and attempts to track known scams, there are nearly one million crypto tokens (999,546) trading on DeFi. Of those, 65,654 are known scams (more than 6.5% of all tokens TokenSniffer tracks).[93]

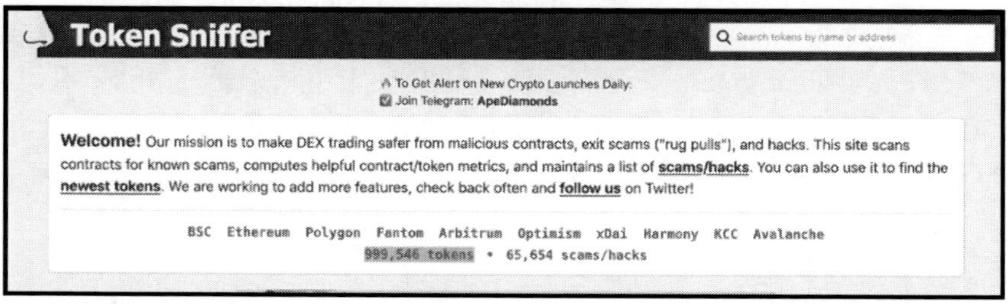

Image from TokenSniffer.com, noting 999,546 crypto tokens trading on DeFi, with 65,654 confirmed scams/hacks.[94]

National Security Concerns

A report by the cryptocurrency compliance firm Elliptic, "DeFi: Risk, Regulation, and the Rise of DeCrime" outlined two of the challenges that asset-backed stablecoin issuers face when it comes to AML compliance:

---

[93] TOKEN SNIFFER, https://tokensniffer.com/. (last visited Dec. 13, 2021).
[94] *Id.*

"First, they must ensure that the issuance of a coin is not used to directly facilitate money laundering activity. Such a situation could arise if, for example, a drug dealer were to obtain a virtual asset as a payment and then exchange that asset for a stablecoin. Likewise, the bad actor could convert fiat dollars into a gift card, and use that card to purchase stablecoins directly from the issuer…Secondly, They should seek to understand whether the stablecoin ecosystem that they facilitate is itself being used for bad activity."[95] One of the major challenges for stablecoin issuers to ensure their stablecoins aren't facilitating illicit finance is their importance to DeFi – which raises its own concerns for ransomware and money laundering.

An October report from ("FinCEN") found that DeFi was being used to convert ransomware-related payments to other types of cryptocurrency.[96] Elliptic's DeFi report found that "DeFi presents criminals with the opportunity to launder proceeds of crime by exchanging it for other assets or hiding the blockchain money trail."[97]

A large amount of many stablecoins' supply are locked into smart contracts on DeFi – either as one (or more) leg of a liquidity pool, that allows anyone to swap from their stablecoin to another asset; or locked into crypto borrowing and lending arrangements:

Smart contracts on DeFi exchanges typically do not compare the cryptocurrency addresses executing their code against the Specially Designated Nationals and Blocked Persons list ("SDN list"). Thus, stablecoins locked into Ethereum smart contracts could be helping to facilitate various forms of illicit finance, including the swapping of ransomware payments for other crypto assets.

---

[95] *DeFi: Risk, Regulation, and the Rise of DeCrime*, ELLIPTIC (Nov. 18, 2021), https://www.elliptic.co/resources/defi-risk-regulation-and-the-rise-of-decrime at 42.

[96] "FinCEN Issues Report on Ransomware Trends in Bank Secrecy Act Data," FinCEN, Oct 15, 2021, https://www.fincen.gov/news/news-releases/fincen-issues-report-ransomware-trends-bank-secrecy-act-data. ("Ransomware-related payments are being converted to other types of [Convertible Virtual Currencies] through decentralized exchanges or other DeFi applications. Some DeFi applications allow for automated peer-to-peer transactions without the need for an account or custodial relationship. FinCEN analysis of transactions on the BTC blockchain identified ransomware-related funds sent indirectly to addresses associated with open protocols for use on DeFi applications").

[97] *DeFi: Risk, Regulation, and the Rise of DeCrime*, ELLIPTIC (Nov. 18, 2021), https://www.elliptic.co/resources/defi-risk-regulation-and-the-rise-of-decrime at 21.

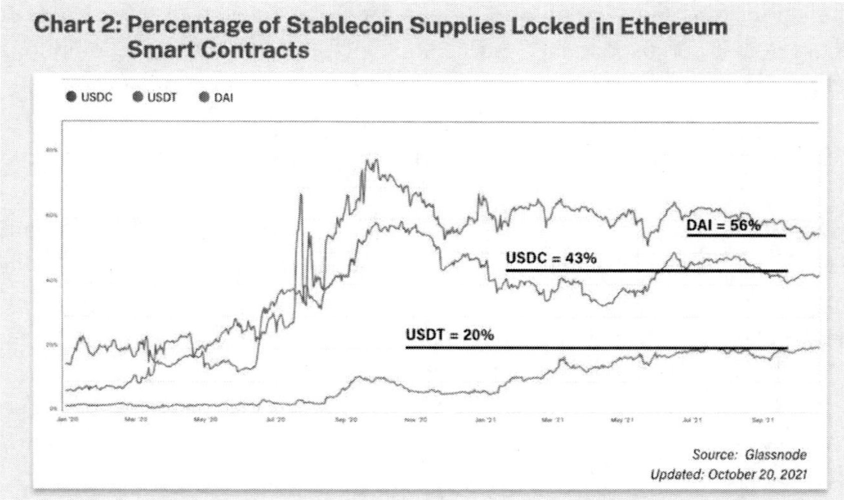

Image from the President's Working Group on Financial Markets report on Stablecoins.[98]

In October, the Treasury Department's Office of Foreign Assets Control (OFAC) clarified this October that all actors in crypto asset markets are expected to comply with sanctions.[99] OFAC's October guidance states that "[a]ll companies in the virtual currency industry, including technology companies, exchangers, administrators, miners, and wallet providers, as well as more traditional financial institutions that may have exposure to virtual currencies" should consider incorporating the controls outlined in OFAC's guidance into their sanctions compliance programs.[100] The secondary market for stablecoins, and the outsized portion of many stablecoin's supply in DeFi smart contracts, presents challenges for issuers for ensure full compliance with OFAC's October sanctions guidance and other illicit finance checks. Wherever possible, stablecoin issuers should proactively work to ensure that

---

[98] *Report on Stable Coins*, PRESIDENT'S WORKING GROUP ON FIN. MARKETS, THE FED. DEPOSIT INS. CORP. (FDIC), AND THE OFFICE OF THE COMPTROLLER OF THE CURRENCY (OCC) (2021), https://home.treasury.gov/system/files/136/StableCoinReport_Nov1_508.pdf.

[99] *Publication of Sanctions Compliance Guidance for the Virtual Currency Industry and Updated Frequently Asked Questions*, TREASURY DEPARTMENT (Oct. 15, 2021), https://home.treasury.gov/policy-issues/financial-sanctions/recent-actions/20211015.

[100] *Sanctions Compliance Guidance for the Virtual Currency Industry (Brochure)*, OFFICE OF FOREIGN ASSETS CONTROL (Oct. 2021), https://home.treasury.gov/system/files/126/virtual_currency_guidance_brochure.pdf.

the stablecoins they issued aren't used for illicit finance in any part of the ecosystem – not just conduct checks at the point of issuance or redemption.

High Fees to Move and Trade Stablecoins on Ethereum

Many stablecoins utilize the Ethereum blockchain and adheres to Ethereum's ERC20 token standard, including the Pax Dollar,[101] U.S. Dollar Coin, Tether, and Binance USD. The Ethereum blockchain remains the dominant blockchain for DeFi, with an estimated 70% of all decentralized finance ("DeFi") activity, according to an analysis by JPMorgan.[102]

As many reports[103] have made clear, the Ethereum blockchain faces challenges of scalability, congestion, and extremely high fees.[104] The mean Ethereum transaction fee was $56.45 on November 11, 2021, according to metrics provider Glassnode. Fees to merely transfer a crypto asset from one wallet to another were an estimated $22 on November 5, 2021 at 6 p.m., some $54 on November 11, 2021 at 9:45 p.m, according to Etherscan.[105]

As the Ethereum network can only process approximately 30 transactions a second,[106] fees often spike to extreme levels whenever there's increased congestion, as investors become increasingly willing to pay higher fees in order to get their transaction executed by an Ethereum miner. Ethereum blockchain fees are frequently prohibitively expensive for users with smaller holdings.[107] All of this creates heightened risks for stablecoin holders in the

[101] Charles Cascarilla, *Whitepaper: Pax Dollar*, PAXOS (Aug. 24, 2021), https://insights.paxos.com/hubfs/USDP-whitepaper.pdf.

[102] Joanna Ossinger, "JPMorgan Team Suggests Crypto's DeFi Boom Slower Than It Seems," BLOOMBERG (Nov. 12, 2021), https://www.bloomberg.com/news/articles/2021-11-12/jpmorgan-team-suggests-crypto-s-defi-boom-slower-than-it-seems ("The Ethereum network now has about a 70% share of DeFi activity, versus a near-total lock at the start of the year, the team added").

[103] Jeff Benson, *War Over Ethereum Gas Fees and Usability Continues*, DECRYPT (Nov. 22, 2021), https://decrypt.co/86640/war-ethereum-gas-fees-usability-continues.

[104] Will Gottsegen, *Ethereum's Fees Are Too Damn High*, COIN DESK (Nov. 22, 2021), https://www.coindesk.com/tech/2021/11/22/ethereums-fees-are-too-damn-high/.

[105] *Ethereum Gas Tracker*, ETHERSCAN, https://etherscan.io/gastracker (last visited Nov. 11, 2021, 6:00 PM).

[106] Luke Conway, *What Is Ethereum 2.0?*, STREET (Oct. 27, 2021), https://www.thestreet.com/crypto/ethereum/ethereum-2-upgrade-what-you-need-to-know.

[107] *See* Liesl Eichholz, *Avalanche: The New DeFi Blockchain Explained*, GLASSNODE (Feb. 10, 2021), https://insights.glassnode.com/avalanche-the-new-defi-blockchain-explained/ ("With the price of ETH on the rise, even basic token swaps on Ethereum are becoming prohibitively expensive for entry-level players, while interactions with more complex DeFi contracts can come attached with fees exceeding 0.1 ETH (over $170 at the time of writing).").

event of a run on a stablecoin, or the loss of its peg. It's likely that the fees to move stablecoins off DeFi (or to swap them for another crypto asset) would be highest, and most regressive, at moments of volatility and crisis.

Stablecoin's Ethereum Usage Raises Climate Concerns

Most major asset-backed stablecoins have a version of their token that runs on the Ethereum blockchain. Ethereum still uses "Proof of Work" to validate transactions, a type of cryptocurrency mining that creates a number of extensive climate harms, which include annual energy consumption akin to that of entire nations[108], 30,700 tons of electronic waste (computer hardware is notoriously difficult to recycle)[109] annually, higher electricity bills for residents of states with crypto mining[110], and quality of life issues[111]. More than 70 climate, economic, racial justice, business and local organizations recently wrote to Congress, asking them to mitigate the considerable contribution portions of the cryptocurrency markets are making to climate change.[112]

In addition, Proof of Work cryptocurrency mining has been exacerbating the shortages of semiconductors.[113] Senators Maggie Hassan and Joni Ernst recently introduced a bill calling on the Treasury Department to compile a report on how cryptocurrency mining operations are impacting semiconductor supply chains. It is unclear how stablecoin issuers plan to mitigate the increasing carbon footprint that follows the ongoing growth of their tokens.

See also Nivesh Rustgi, *Ethereum Miners Earn Record $110M Amid ETH Crash*, CRYPTO BRIEFING (May 21, 2021).

108 Cristina Criddle, *Bitcoin Consumes 'More Electricity Than Argentina'*, BBC (Feb. 10, 2021), https://www.bbc.com/news/technology-56012952.

109 *Global E-Waste Surging: Up 21% in 5 Years*, UNITED NATIONS U. (Jul. 2, 2020), https://unu.edu/media-relations/releases/global-e-waste-surging-up-21-in-5-years.html.

110 Laura Counts, *Power-Hungry Cryptominers Push Up Electricity Costs for Locals*, BERKLEY HAAS (Aug 3, 2021), https://newsroom.haas.berkeley.edu/research/power-hungry-cryptominers-push-up-electricity-costs-for-locals/.

111 Jeff Keeling, *Bitcoin Mine Spokesman Says Dealing With Noise Issue "Our Number One Priority,"* WJHL (Jul. 16, 2021), https://www.wjhl.com/news/local/noisy-bitcoin-mines-neighbors-hope-monday-meeting-yields-answers-from-power-provider/.

112 *Large Coalition of Public Interest and Environmental Groups Come Together to Urge Leaders to Address Climate Damages of Crypto*, OPEN MARKETS INST. (Oct. 7, 2021), https://www.openmarketsinstitute.org/publications/large-coalition-of-public-interest-and-environmental-groups-come-together-to-urge-leaders-to-address-climate-damages-of-crypto.

113 *Crypto-Miners are Probably to Blame for the Graphics-Chip Shortage*, ECONOMIST (June 19, 2021), https://www.economist.com/graphic-detail/2021/06/19/crypto-miners-are-probably-to-blame-for-the-graphics-chip-shortage.

Conclusion

There are many investor, national security, and usability concerns with both algorithmic and asset-backed stablecoins. Congress should continue to examine if there are regulatory gaps that require new legislation to ensure consumer and investor protection as it relates to stablecoins, and regulators should continue to monitor stablecoins and ensure compliance with existing laws.

Written Statement of Jai Massari, Partner, Davis Polk & Wardwell LLP, "Stablecoins: How Do They Work, How Are They Used, and What Are Their Risks?" Hearing before the United States Senate, Committee on Banking, Housing, and Urban Affairs, December 14, 2021

Jai Massari Biography

My name is Jai Massari, and I am a partner in the Financial Institutions Group of Davis Polk & Wardwell LLP, resident in its Washington, DC office. I began my legal career in 2007, just before the financial crisis, as a law firm associate learning about and advising on a wide range of complex financial regulatory topics, including Title VII derivatives regulation, the Volcker Rule, and other key Dodd-Frank regulatory reform matters.

As the boundaries of financial services have pushed into cryptocurrency, so has my practice. For the past several years, I have been advising financial institutions, cryptocurrency firms, and technology platforms—from two-person start-ups to the largest banking organizations—on financial regulatory considerations relating to cryptocurrency activities. This includes advising stablecoin issuers and wallet service providers on the financial regulatory aspects of stablecoin activities. Today, I am presenting my own views as a practicing financial regulatory lawyer, not those of any client or my firm.

Chairman Brown, Ranking Member Toomey, and members of the Committee, thank you for inviting me to speak today on this interesting and complex topic.

Since the earliest days of our nation, as our economy has grown and transformed, so too has our understanding of money. The dramatic changes we are all familiar with have seen purses of gold and silver coins eventually replaced by wallets holding state and later national bank notes, then Federal Reserve notes alongside checkbooks tied to demand deposits, followed by the proliferation of credit and debit cards, and more recently the swift rise of payment apps.

Like the innovations in public and private money that preceded them, stablecoins squarely present the same core regulatory concerns as earlier forms of money—those of consumer protection, systemic stability, safety and soundness, and combating illicit finance. But with thoughtful regulation, stablecoins can perhaps offer benefits over the technologies that came before, including lower costs, faster services, new services made possible by programmability, opportunities to expand financial inclusiveness, greater traceability, and the potential for enhanced operational resiliency through the use of distributed networks.

The Committee is today asking the key questions: how do stablecoins work; how are they used now and how will they be used in the future; and what are the resulting risks? To this, I would add: what are the potential benefits? The answers to these questions form the basis for understanding how stablecoin activities should be regulated.

U.S. regulators have made important progress in examining these questions. As you know, the President's Working Group on Financial Markets (PWG) published a policy statement on stablecoins in 2020.[114] Along with the FDIC and OCC, the PWG also published a report last month on federal regulation of the issuance of stablecoins and related stablecoin activities.[115] Indeed, regulators around the world have been thinking about these questions in earnest since 2019.[116]

---

[114] PRESIDENT'S WORKING GROUP ON FINANCIAL MARKETS, STATEMENT ON KEY REGULATORY AND SUPERVISORY ISSUES RELEVANT TO CERTAIN STABLECOINS (Dec. 2020), https://home.treasury.gov/system/files/136/PWG-Stablecoin-Statement-12-23-2020-CLEAN.pdf.

[115] PRESIDENT'S WORKING GROUP ON FINANCIAL MARKETS, THE FEDERAL DEPOSIT INSURANCE CORPORATION, AND THE OFFICE OF THE COMPTROLLER OF THE CURRENCY, REPORT ON STABLECOINS (Nov. 2021), https://home.treasury.gov/system/files/136/StableCoinReport_Nov1_508.pdf [hereinafter "PWG REPORT"].

[116] *E.g.*, BANK FOR INTERNATIONAL SETTLEMENTS COMMITTEE ON PAYMENTS AND MARKET INFRASTRUCTURES & BOARD OF THE INTERNATIONAL ORGANIZATION OF SECURITIES COMMISSIONS, APPLICATION OF THE PRINCIPLES FOR FINANCIAL MARKET INFRASTRUCTURES TO STABLECOIN ARRANGEMENTS (Oct. 2021); FINANCIAL STABILITY BOARD, REGULATION, SUPERVISION AND OVERSIGHT OF "GLOBAL STABLECOIN" ARRANGEMENTS (Oct. 2020); G20 FINANCE MINISTERS & CENTRAL BANK GOVERNORS MEETING, G20 PRESS RELEASE ON GLOBAL STABLECOINS (Oct. 2019); FINANCIAL

I'll focus my comments today on "true" or "payment" stablecoins as described in the PWG Report.[117] As I've written previously,[118] true stablecoins are non-interest bearing financial instruments designed to maintain a stable value against a reference fiat currency—say one dollar. This reference value is also referred to as the stablecoin's par value. A well-designed stablecoin typically holds its value through a pair of promises. First, the stablecoin issuer agrees to sell and buy them back at par value (perhaps for a fee). Second, the issuer agrees to hold a pool of safe assets—the "reserve"—that has an aggregate market value at least equal to 100% of the aggregate par value of the stablecoins. Such a reserve is designed to back the issuer's obligation to repurchase stablecoins at par, and is replenished with the proceeds of stablecoin sales.

The reserve is meant to ensure that the issuer can always redeem outstanding stablecoins at their par value on demand. For this reason, reserve assets of a well-designed stablecoin would consist of cash and genuine cash equivalents, such as bank deposits and short-term U.S. government securities. This should enable the reserve to remain liquid even during stressed market conditions, minimizing the risk of loss if large numbers of stablecoin holders seek redemptions at once.[119]

The insight underlying a true stablecoin is not new. It's instead a form of "narrow bank"— a concept that has been in the public discourse since at least the Great Depression.[120] Narrow banks sometimes have not been considered

---

STABILITY BOARD, REGULATORY ISSUES OF STABLECOINS (Oct. 2019); G7 WORKING GROUP ON STABLECOINS, INVESTIGATING THE IMPACT OF GLOBAL STABLECOINS (Oct. 2019).

[117] PWG REPORT, *supra* note 2, at 2 (defining "payment stablecoins" as "those stablecoins that are designed to maintain a stable value relative to a fiat currency and, therefore, have the potential to be used as a widespread means of payment"). While there are many different types of stablecoins, including algorithmic stablecoins and stablecoins pegged to gold and other real assets, assessing the regulatory treatment of true stablecoins is an appropriate priority given their potential to play a wider role in consumer and business payment activities outside of cryptocurrency trading. *Id.* From here, any references to "stablecoins" throughout this written statement mean "true stablecoins" or "payment stablecoins."

[118] Christian Catalini & Jai Massari, Stablecoins and the Future of Money, HARV. BUS. REV. (Aug. 10, 2021), https://hbr.org/2021/08/stablecoins-and-the-future-of-money.

[119] Today, reserve assets vary among stablecoin issuers. For most U.S. dollar stablecoin issuers, their reserves are legally constrained by requirements under existing state money transmitter laws, with some making public commitments to maintain their reserves only in cash and genuine cash equivalents.

[120] *E.g.*, PAUL H. DOUGLAS ET AL., A PROGRAM FOR MONETARY REFORM (1939) (outlining the Chicago Plan), https://www.monetary.org/pdfs/a_program_for_monetary_reform.pdf; MILTON FRIEDMAN, A PROGRAM FOR MONETARY STABILITY (Fordham Univ. Press 1992); Ronnie J. Phillips, *The 'Chicago Plan' and New*

as economically useful as fractional reserve banks. This is because they do not engage in maturity and liquidity transformation—that is, using short-term deposits to make long-term loans and investments—which is the core function of modern banking and the lifeblood of the real economy.[121] But because narrow banks do not engage in maturity or liquidity transformation, they are generally considered safer than fractional reserve banks. We tolerate the risk traditional banking activities impose on the economy because of the benefits.

While stablecoin issuers have structural similarities to narrow banks, they provide potential new benefits that are worth recognizing. The basic business model for a stablecoin is to serve as a payment instrument. Today, stablecoins are used primarily in connection with cryptocurrency trading and decentralized finance (DeFi) applications.

For the moment, therefore, they are largely on the margins of the banking system and the real economy.

Some, however, view stablecoins as having a potentially broader use in retail payment services.[122] Payments using blockchain rails would complement existing payment systems grounded in the traditional banking sector such as cash, checks, credit and debit cards, and wire transfers. These incumbent technologies offer varying benefits and drawbacks. As stablecoins begin to play a role in retail payment transactions, they offer a way to decouple payment services from credit services, presenting us with the potential for increased competition from new entrants, expanded services, lower costs for consumers and greater opportunities for financial inclusion.

Particularly if they begin to realize this potential, and even more so if they approach systemic scale, stablecoins should be regulated in a manner that addresses the risks they present, which U.S. regulators have identified. As set

---

Deal Banking Reform, Working Paper No. 76 (June 1992), https://www.levyinstitute.org/pubs/wp/76.pdf; Jaromir Benes & Michael Kumhof, *The Chicago Plan Revisited*, IMF Working Paper (2012), https://www.imf.org/external/pubs/ft/wp/2012/wp12202.pdf. Some banking historians have argued that the concept of narrow banks has even deeper roots, tracing back to deposit banks in Medieval Europe and Rome, which were what we would call custody banks today.

[121] *E.g.*, Kenneth J. Arrow, *The Organization of Economic Activity: Issues Pertinent to the Choice of Market versus Non-market Allocation*, *in* JOINT ECONOMIC COMMITTEE OF THE CONGRESS OF THE UNITED STATES, THE ANALYSIS AND EVALUATION OF PUBLIC EXPENDITURES: THE PPB SYSTEM 48 (1969) ("The creation of money is in many respects an example of a public good").

[122] *See, e.g.*, PWG REPORT, *supra* note 2, at 8 ("Beyond digital asset trading, several existing stablecoin issuers and entities with stablecoin projects under development have the stated ambition for the stablecoins they create to be used widely by retail users to pay for goods and services, by corporations in the context of supply chain payments, and in the context of international remittances.").

out in the PWG Report, these include the risk of runs on poorly designed reserves, risks associated with the operation of payment systems generally, risks of scale, and risks arising from regulatory gaps.[123]

There already appears to be broad agreement among U.S. policymakers, regulators, and the industry on the general principles of stablecoin regulation. Regulation of stablecoin issuers should include restrictions on permissible types of reserve assets to ensure sufficient short-term, liquid backing; auditing and transparency standards so regulators and the public can evaluate reserve composition; restrictions that preclude maturity and liquidity transformation activities in order to shield reserve assets from the associated risks; obligations to address illicit financing and sanctions considerations; and requirements to address operational risks arising from settling transfers on blockchain networks. U.S. financial regulators have addressed these topics before and, with Congressional guidance, can do so again.

However, requiring stablecoin issuers to be insured depository institutions (that is, insured banks)—as suggested in the PWG Report—is not necessary and, unless certain adjustments are made, is not workable. I will explain why.

An insured-depository requirement is unnecessary because stablecoins can be structured and regulated to avoid the risks that require deposit insurance and the application of traditional banking oversight in the first place. Banks—by design—are in the business of maturity and liquidity transformation. Banks take in deposits that can be withdrawn on demand, against which they hold some short-term liquid assets, like cash in a Federal Reserve Bank account, but more importantly they hold long-term, relatively illiquid assets, like 30-year mortgages and long-term corporate loans. This activity creates economic value in the form of increased money supply and credit.

But it also creates run risk and the need for deposit insurance.[124] Limiting stablecoin reserves to short-term, liquid assets, and requiring the market value of those reserves to be no less than the par value of stablecoins outstanding, is an alternative way to avoid run risk—as U.S. policymakers have recognized since at least the 1930s.[125]

---

[123] PWG REPORT, *supra* note 2, at 12–14.

[124] *E.g.*, Douglas W. Diamond & Philip H. Dybvig, *Bank Runs, Deposit Insurance, and Liquidity*, 91 J. POL. ECON. 401 (1983) ("It is precisely the "transformation" of illiquid assets into liquid assets that is responsible both for the liquidity service provided by banks and for their susceptibility to runs.").

[125] DOUGLAS; FRIEDMAN; Phillips; Benes & Kumhof, *supra* note 7; *see also* DAVIS POLK & WARDWELL LLP, U.S. REGULATORS SPEAK ON STABLECOIN AND CRYPTO REGULATION (Nov. 12, 2021), at n.12–13 and accompanying text,

An insured-depository requirement is unworkable, without adjustments to the existing bank regulatory framework, because banks are subject to leverage and risk-based capital ratios that are calibrated based on the assumption that a majority of their assets are relatively illiquid and riskier than cash and genuine cash equivalents. Leverage ratios, in particular, are designed to backstop risk-weighted capital requirements. They treat cash and cash equivalents as if they had the same risk-and-return profile as long-term consumer and business debt, which they do not.

To take an example, a stablecoin issuer subject to a 4% leverage ratio would need to hold $104 billion of cash and genuine cash equivalents against $100 billion of circulating stablecoins—$100 billion backing the stablecoins on a dollar-for-dollar basis and a cushion of $4 billion of required capital in the form of shareholders' equity. A bank that engages in customary lending activities, such as credit card, real estate and business lending, is able to price its loan products to cover the cost of the required capital and still make a reasonable return. A stablecoin issuer, whose assets may be limited to zero-to-low interest paying cash and genuine cash equivalents such as bank deposits and short-term U.S. government securities, has no such ability. Therefore, unless Congress recalibrates the ratios to reflect the lower risk-and-return profile of stablecoin issuers who limit their reserve assets to cash and genuine cash equivalents, the stablecoin business model would be uneconomic for an insured depository institution—except perhaps as a sideline for a large, diversified financial services provider.

How, then, should stablecoins be regulated? Today, U.S. stablecoin issuers and digital wallet service providers are largely regulated by the states under money-transmitter regimes and trust-company authorities. New York regulates stablecoin activities under its special-purpose virtual currency licensing program, known as the BitLicense.[126] Wyoming has developed its own special-purpose bank license to accommodate cryptocurrency custody and payments activities.[127] The innovative work of state regulators has already played a key role in the expansion of stablecoin activities.

There is at present some federal regulation of stablecoin activities. U.S. stablecoin issuers and digital wallet providers are, for example, subject to the Bank Secrecy Act's anti-money laundering requirements as money services

https://www.davispolk.com/insights/client-update/us-regulators-speak-stablecoin-and-crypto-regulation.

[126] 23 NYCRR Part 200.

[127] HB0074, Special Purpose Depository Institutions, 2019 Wyo. Sess. Laws 328.

businesses registered with FinCEN, the U.S. Treasury's Financial Crimes Enforcement Network.

But an expanded federal role may well be appropriate and useful. This could include an optional federal charter for stablecoin issuers that would preempt the need for state-by-state licensing in return for supervision by federal regulators. A new and well-designed federal charter could accommodate a business model premised on the issuance of stablecoins fully backed by short-term, liquid assets and the provision of related payments services. This charter could impose requirements for reserve asset composition while tailoring leverage ratios or risk-based capital requirements and other requirements to the nature of the business model. And it could restrict the stablecoin issuer from engaging in riskier activities, to minimize other claims on reserve assets. This option would likely be welcomed by many stablecoin issuers even though it would entail comprehensive federal oversight.

I would like to close by thanking the Committee for its focus on these important issues. The Committee's work today in understanding how stablecoins work, how they can be used, and the risks they present is indispensable to developing a resilient regulatory framework. While I do not believe that stablecoin issuers should be limited to insured depository institutions, I strongly support common-sense regulation of stablecoins and their issuers in a way that takes account of their benefits and risks. And I am optimistic that there is much common ground among innovators, policymakers, regulators, and the public on these questions. This common ground can pave the way for a regulatory approach that safeguards consumers, the financial system and the broader economy, while continuing to promote innovation in this exciting and promising new financial technology.

I am happy to answer questions.

Written Statement of Dante Alighieri Disparte, before the United States Senate, Committee on Banking, Housing and Urban Affairs, Stablecoins: How Do They Work, How Are They Used, and What Are Their Risks?, Held on December 14, 2021 at 10:15 AM EST

Chairman Brown, Ranking Member Toomey, Members of the Senate Committee on Banking, Housing and Urban Affairs, thank you for the opportunity to share my testimony with you today.

My name is Dante Disparte and I am the Chief Strategy Officer and Head of Global Policy for Circle, a leading digital financial services firm and the sole issuer of USD Coin, or USDC - a dollar digital currency supporting the extensibility of the U.S. Dollar in a competitive, always-on global economy.

Having recently completed my 3-year term on the Federal Emergency Management Agency's National Advisory Council, and being no stranger to disaster displacement and hardship, I want to acknowledge the communities affected by last week's devastating storms. Indeed, as this disaster and others have shown, with the movement of financial aid and disaster relief, when speed matters most, friction stands in the way.

As a country, we have faced a Great Depression, a Great Deleveraging and in 2020 with the onset of the COVID-19 pandemic, we faced nothing short of a Great Correction. In this correction, the centrality of technology for any semblance of political, business, economic and household continuity was laid bare. What was also clear is that access to the internet and other digital public goods was unequal. How we engage with money and payments in digital form was clearly an area of pre-pandemic vulnerability in the U.S. and around the world.

The advent of stablecoins or what we like to refer to as dollar digital currencies like USDC, are an important innovation enabling greater control over how we send, spend, save and secure our money. To define a stablecoin - noting that, like money itself, not all of these innovations are created equal - is tantamount to the moment we converted our compact discs (CDs) into MP3s. The CD and music is still yours, but now enjoys the powers of programmability, user control and a digitally native form factor that works anywhere, on any device, across the planet.

Stablecoins, in effect, are designed to reference and import the economic properties of an underlying asset. By circulation the most successful of which all reference the dollar, with the economic aim of combating the "buyer's and spender's remorse" that plagued early cryptocurrencies. USDC is a now 3-year old dollar digital currency standing at more than $40 billion in circulation and cumulatively supporting more than $1.4 trillion in on-chain transactions, in a manner that enhances financial inclusion, responsible innovation and integrity. Critically, the dollar-denominated assets backing USDC, which are strictly cash and short-duration U.S. Treasuries of 90 days or less, are all held in the care, custody and control of U.S. regulated financial institutions.

Indeed, as this internet-native financial infrastructure continues to grow, we aim to do our part ensuring the future of payments and money is more inclusive than the past. Our recently announced Circle Impact initiative has four core components, each of which is close to home for me having grown up in poverty and being a first generation high school and college graduate.

These include:

- Allocating a share of USDC dollar reserves to Minority Depository Institutions (MDIs) and community banks across the country. We hope this will accrue to billions of dollars over time, strengthening the balance sheet of these banks and, thereby, strengthening their communities.
- Embarking on Digital Financial Literacy initiatives together with Historically Black Colleges and Universities (HBCUs) and other partners supporting the development of essential learning and hands-on approaches to entrepreneurialism.
- Leveraging our SeedInvest platform, which is one of the nation's leading equity crowdfunding businesses, to catalyze targeted campaigns for women and minority entrepreneurs across the country.
- Assisting humanitarian interventions and coordinating public-private partnerships to mobilize blockchain-based payments and USDC to deliver corruption-resistant, real-time aid and relief.

Because nothing worth doing is worth doing alone, our hope is to catalyze uncommon coalitions on these initiatives, which are deeply connected to our mission of raising global economic prosperity through the frictionless exchange of financial value.

While some argue the U.S. may lose the digital currency space race if it fails to issue a Central Bank Digital Currency (CBDC). I argue that we are winning this race because of the sum of free market activity taking place inside the U.S. regulatory perimeter with digital currencies and blockchain-based financial services. The sum of these activities are advancing broad U.S. economic competitiveness and national security interests.

Thank you again Chairman Brown and Ranking Member Toomey for the opportunity to speak with you today. I look forward to addressing the Committee's questions.

Reflections on the Policy Environment

With the emergence of digital currency innovations as important financial markets infrastructure, Circle has continued to prioritize engagement with

U.S. state, federal, and international regulators and policymakers. This culminated with the President's Working Group on Financial Markets report on stablecoins (PWG), which highlighted the recommendation that stablecoin arrangements be managed by insured depository institutions. The report goes on to raise a number of other potential risks to financial markets and consumers, which Circle has prioritized satisfying. It is important to note that the most enduring financial markets policies espouse a same risk, same rules technology-neutral approach to regulation. With the advent of digital assets, it is important to also look at the economic behavior of the digital asset or token.

Indeed, well before the PWG issued its recommendations, Circle announced its intention to become a federally chartered commercial bank. In the interim, USDC in circulation and the appropriate consumer protection, financial crime compliance and other standards are governed on a level footing to other major U.S. payments companies. One core difference, however, is that payments companies tend to build payment systems on proprietary technology, which creates a walled garden environment and often exacts the highest fees from those who can least afford it. Circle's approach, on the other hand, is to build on public blockchain infrastructure and in accordance with open source technology standards. This not only promotes innovation and competition, it promotes interoperability across payment systems, akin to how email networks work across platforms and service providers. Imagine how usable a Gmail account would be if Gmail could not send a message to a Hotmail user or a Yahoo account? Many of the world's payment networks labor under this walled garden challenge where the cost of interoperability, speed and distance travelled draw close parallels to pre-internet telecommunications networks.

Along these lines, Circle's services and USDC in particular, are increasingly being leveraged as a pro-competition open medium of exchange based on the U.S. dollar being the currency of the internet. Major credit card companies, small businesses, remittance companies, and many others, are making USDC a native settlement option for their businesses. This in turn is increasing market optionality with payments, while building a bridge between digitally-native financial services and real-world use cases. One recent example is the enablement of USDC as a settlement option on the MoneyGram network leveraging the Stellar blockchain as open financial infrastructure.

Some digital currency projects may resemble monetary airline miles, which are usable only if you wish to travel on a specific, closed network or if you were born in the "right" postal code. The structure of USDC and other Circle services based on public blockchain networks, promotes wide adoption, network effects and much needed price competition and interoperability, all without sacrificing requirements to protect the integrity of the financial system. Over time, important companion innovations in the digital identity domain will ensure privacy preserving approaches to financial access and novel internet-native financial markets based on digital currencies and blockchains can continue to grow.

In an always-on global economy, markets and people's financial needs do not take bank holidays. The advent of trusted digital currencies like USDC are enabling a wide range of use cases, including supporting cross-border remittances such as the MoneyGram example mentioned above. Remittances are the veritable flywheel of the global economy and are typically recession resistant money flows. However, with the onset of the COVID-19 pandemic, global remittance flows may have lost up to $200 billion in volume according to the World Bank (down from more than $700 billion pre-pandemic) due to the double-jeopardy of economic slowdowns, as well as the void of open payment networks. Digital currencies and the corresponding blockchain-based financial services ecosystem are beginning to fill this void as more than 200 million people worldwide (and more than 20 million) in the U.S. adopt these services.

Another use case in keeping with lower cost peer-to-peer payments and remittances, is the use of USDC and blockchain-based payments for disbursing aid and humanitarian relief. Moving physical cash into a humanitarian setting may often be a honey pot for corruption, bribery and fraud due to the limited traceability of physical money. The auditing fidelity of blockchains and the trust and price parity to the dollar of USDC can be used to support corruption-resistant, real-time relief payments. A successful program supporting doctors in Venezuela is emblematic of the opportunity for faster aid, development and humanitarian support using digital currencies.

Micropayments and programmable money, which are elusive but needed areas in our economy, are also made possible with dollar digital currencies and blockchain-based transaction ledgering. By prevailing payment standards, it often costs more to send a small amount of money than the sum of money sent. Micropayments for example for a freelance journalist who can accrue payments for each "like" of their article becomes a possibility with the increasingly widespread use of USDC for high-trust low-friction internet commerce and payments. Indeed, the bootstrap use case of USDC supporting the growth of digital asset market activity has satisfied exacting performance and operational standards.

In terms of market trust, transparency and accountability, Circle has consistently and voluntarily reported on the status of dollar-denominated reserves and their sufficiency to meet demands for USDC outstanding. This has been done with third party attestations from a leading global accounting firm. Circle has also prioritized building, designing and guarding the prudential standards for USDC inside of and conforming with prevailing U.S. regulatory standards that apply to leading fintech and payments firms such as PayPal, Square, Venmo and Stripe, among others.

Since its inception, USDC has always been easily redeemable and most redemptions happen speedily. Additionally, given the growing integration as a settlement option in leading merchant and credit card networks, the use of USDC in its digitally-native form for the procurement of goods and services remains a growing use case. The first USDC stablecoin was minted in September 2018. Since then, $95,976,829,528.16 have been issued and, as of December 1, 2021, $57,129,781,321.95 have been redeemed. This demonstrates a vibrant market is evolving around the use of USDC for payments, as well as a well functioning on and off ramp supporting redemption requests.

The extensibility of the U.S. Dollar as the reference currency of the internet is not a zero-sum proposition. As and when the potential for a CBDC becomes a possibility in the U.S. (notwithstanding some of the potential design risks and drawbacks), the experience, transaction throughput and openly competitive market powered by dollar digital currencies and blockchains, will be a useful pathway for future upgradability. In short, it is better to get it right, than to get it fast. The same also holds true with acknowledging that most "value added" money in circulation today, whether enshrined on a plastic card or stemming from the money creation of the fractional reserve banking system, is in fact privately issued. The advent of dollar digital currencies like USDC inherit, are answerable and additive to U.S. monetary, regulatory and compliance policy.

Emerging policy and regulation for the future growth of stablecoins and the digital assets market in the U.S. should aspire to do no harm, spur responsible financial services innovation and recognize the importance of U.S. states for being our fintech innovation labs. One challenge however, is that the states are not often represented in global macroprudential and regulatory bodies such as the Bank for International Settlements (BIS), the Financial Action Task Force (FATF), among others.

Harmonizing a broad U.S. approach to digital assets and competition in the digital currency space race, can improve U.S. competitiveness, security and lower fundamental costs for basic financial access.

Hearing on "Stablecoins: How Do They Work, How Are They Used, and What Are Their Risks?" before the U.S. Senate Committee on Banking, Housing, and Urban Affairs

Tuesday, December 14, 2021
Prepared Statement
Hilary J. Allen
Professor of Law
American University Washington College of Law

Chairman Brown, Ranking Member Toomey, and Members of the Committee:

Thank you for inviting me to testify at today's hearing. My name is Hilary Allen, and I am a Professor of Law at the American University Washington College of Law. I teach courses in corporate law and financial regulation, and my research focuses on financial stability regulation. I have authored several law review articles about fintech and financial stability, and I have also written a book, *Driverless Finance: Fintech's Impact on Financial Stability*, that explores the threats that crypto and other fintech innovations pose for our financial system. Much of my testimony is drawn from this book.

Prior to entering academia, I spent seven years working in the financial services groups of prominent law firms in London, Sydney and New York. In 2010, I worked with the Financial Crisis Inquiry Commission, which was appointed by Congress to study the causes of the financial crisis of 2007-2008.

I am not testifying on behalf of the Washington College of Law or any other institution; the views expressed here are entirely my own.

Executive Summary

The rise of crypto poses very real risks for financial stability, which I have explored at length in research that I would be happy to share with the

Committee.[128] In considering its response to crypto, I submit that Congress's most important goal should be to ensure that crypto does not cause a financial crisis. Proponents of crypto often cite the industry's potential to create jobs and improve financial inclusion, but financial crises destroy jobs and exacerbate inequality – including for people who never invested in crypto in the first place.

A "stablecoin" is a relatively new form of crypto asset. Stablecoins try to avoid the volatility associated with cryptocurrencies like Bitcoin by pegging their value to the US Dollar (or some other fiat currency). In November of this year, the President's Working Group on Financial Markets released a report on stablecoins (the "PWG Report") that identified a number of risks associated with stablecoins, and made three recommendations for addressing those risks. The PWG Report's first recommendation reads as follows:

> To address risks to stablecoin users and guard against stablecoin runs, legislation should require stablecoin issuers to be insured depository institutions, which are subject to appropriate supervision and regulation, at the depository institution and the holding company level.[129]

In this statement, I will set out why I share the PWG's general concerns about crypto and financial stability, but disagree with this specific recommendation. In short, stablecoins are not really being used to make payments for real-world goods and services. Instead, the primary use of stablecoins is to support the DeFi ecosystem. DeFi is a type of shadow banking system with fragilities that could – if DeFi reaches significant scale – disrupt our real economy. If lawmakers and regulators treat stablecoins as regulated banking products, that will lend legitimacy to and inspire confidence in stablecoins in a way that is likely to turbocharge the growth of DeFi. While stablecoins do have structural fragilities that may make them vulnerable to runs, the incidence and costs of stablecoin runs can be addressed by other policies that are less likely to encourage the growth of DeFi.

At the conclusion of this statement, I will summarize some of the policy options available to Congress in responding to stablecoins. These policy options range from an outright ban on stablecoins, through a licensing regime

---

[128] See, for example, *Driverless Finance,* 10 Harv. Bus. L. Rev. 157 (2020); *Payments Failure*, 62 B.C. L. Rev. 453 (2021); DRIVERLESS FINANCE: FINTECH'S IMPACT ON FINANCIAL STABILITY, Oxford University Press (2021).

[129] President's Working Group on Financial Markets, the Federal Deposit Insurance Corporation, and the Office of the Comptroller of the Currency, REPORT ON STABLECOINS, 2 (November 2021).

for stablecoins, to a multifaceted approach that uses aspects of securities law, antitrust, financial stability regulation, and banking law to respond to stablecoins' risks. While any regulation will inevitably create some barriers to innovation, this is a necessary trade-off when dealing with money and finance. Use cases for stablecoins and DeFi are often explained with analogies to other digital services – "send money as easily as sending a photograph," or "send money just like sending an email" – but these analogies underestimate the stakes involved. Because money and finance are the lifeblood of our economy, finance has always been highly regulated in a way that Kodak's provision of photographs, and FedEx's delivery of couriered letters, never were.

Introduction

Today's hearing is about stablecoins, how they work, how they are used, and their associated risks. A stablecoin is a new type of digital asset that is designed to have a value that is more stable than cryptocurrencies like Bitcoin, which are notoriously volatile (as a result, Bitcoin has never been useful as money or as a payments mechanism, even though it remains a popular investment). There are different ways that the creators of stablecoins seek to stabilize their value. The most widely-used stablecoins are backed by a reserve of real-world assets. This asset reserve is intended to inspire confidence in stablecoin holders that they will be able to redeem their stablecoin at any time at a rate that is pegged to the US Dollar (or some other fiat currency). There are also algorithmic stablecoins which rely on computer programs to adjust the supply of the stablecoins to keep the value stable in the face of demand.[130] Algorithmic stablecoins have not yet experienced significant uptake and so they are not the focus of my testimony (although they should still be on regulators' radar). The focus of my statement is on stablecoins backed by reserves, and how they are being used. Importantly, these stablecoins are not currently being used to pay for real-world goods and services in any meaningful way. Instead, their primary use is in the "decentralized finance" or "DeFi" ecosystem.[131] I will explain DeFi in more detail in Section 4; for now,

---

[130] On algorithmic stablecoins, *see* Ryan Clements, *Built to Fail: The Inherent Fragility of Algorithmic Stablecoins*. 11 WAKE FOREST L. REV. ONLINE 131 (2021) (available at http://www.wakeforestlawreview.com/2021/10/built-to-fail-the-inherent-fragility-of-algorithmic-stablecoins/).

[131] "At the time of publication of this report, stablecoins are predominantly used in the United States to facilitate trading, lending, and borrowing of other digital assets." PWG Report, *supra*

it suffices to say that DeFi creates digital versions of existing financial services like loans.

There are many different types of risks associated with stablecoins, and the DeFi ecosystem in which they are primarily deployed. There are risks for investors, whose investments may be vulnerable to fraud, hacks, and glitches; these risks are best addressed by the SEC and CFTC. Then there are risks that stablecoins could thwart public policy objectives, if they are used for money laundering or to avoid tax obligations or sanctions – FinCEN, the IRS, and OFAC are pursuing these issues. This statement, however, will focus on the risks that stablecoins and DeFi pose for financial stability. I will therefore start by elaborating on what "financial stability" is, and why financial stability regulation is important.

Financial stability regulation aims to prevent or mitigate financial crises, and so it must ensure that the financial system is robust enough to absorb future shocks. While some people have already forgotten the cost of the financial crisis of 2008, for others, the trauma of losing jobs and homes is still with them. Furthermore, the wealth disparities exacerbated by the 2008 crisis persist: for most middle-class families, their net worth in 2017 remained lower than it had been in 2007.[132] These disparities were even more pronounced for middle class African American and Hispanic families.[133] In short, the harm of the 2008 crisis fell disproportionately on the most vulnerable members of society. While supporters of crypto regularly cite its ability to create jobs and promote financial inclusion, a crypto-inspired financial crisis would destroy these, and more.[134]

To be clear, financial stability regulation does *not* aim to eliminate all risks from the financial system. Instead, the focus of financial stability regulation is on eliminating *systemic* risks that could compromise the ability of financial

Note 2 at 8. *See also* the Bank for International Settlements finding that "The growth of stablecoins has been exponential since mid-2020, when DeFi activities started to take off." Sirio Aramonte *et al.*, *DeFi Risks and the Decentralization Illusion*, BIS QUARTERLY REVIEW, 25 (Dec. 2021).

132 Nelson D. Schwartz, *The Recovery Threw the Middle Class Dream Under a Benz*, N.Y. TIMES, Sept. 12, 2018, https://www.nytimes.com/2018/09/12/business/middle-class-financial-crisis.html.

133 *Id.*

134 A recent research paper found that "inequality rises following recessions and that rapid credit growth in the run up to a downturn exacerbates that effect...These links between inequality, credit and downturns are particularly significant for recessions associated with financial crises." Jonathan Bridges *et al.*, *Credit, Crises and Inequality*, Bank of England Staff Working Paper No. 949 (Nov. 2021) (available at https://www.bankofengland.co.uk/-/media/boe/files/working-paper/2021/credit-crises-and-inequality.pdf?la=en&hash=9FC00E0CEA234D1E2C7C34A589A64183294F8FD6).

institutions and markets to perform the risk management, capital intermediation and payments processing functions necessary for broader economic growth.[135] In short, the endgame of financial stability regulation is sustainable economic growth, and ensuring the stability of financial markets and institutions is a means to that end. In the context of stablecoins and DeFi, this means that financial stability regulation should focus on protecting everyone who could be harmed by the impact of stablecoins and DeFi on our broader economy – especially those have chosen not to invest in stablecoins or DeFi, but could nonetheless be harmed by fallout from a crypto market failure.

There is significant uncertainty about how the markets for stablecoins, DeFi, and other crypto applications will develop. One possible response when faced with uncertainty is to wait and see what will happen. However, given the potential harm that crypto could cause for the broader economy, "wait and see" is not good policy. It is therefore commendable that the PWG has proactively engaged with the risks that stablecoins might pose for financial stability, and that Congress is proactively contemplating legislation on this issue. However, in my view, the PWG's recommendation that Congress enact legislation requiring "stablecoin issuers to be insured depository institutions" reflects an approach that is too microprudential in nature.

"Microprudential" regulation describes regulation that focuses on the stability of individual institutions, on the assumption that if an institution is stable, the financial system as a whole will benefit.[136] The PWG Report proceeds from the view that as long as there's no run on an individual stablecoin, then that will benefit financial stability. An important lesson from the financial crisis of 2008, though, is that financial stability regulation should be "macroprudential" in orientation, meaning that we should think through the systemic consequences of regulatory decisions[137] – for example, that microprudential regulation of stablecoins could fuel the growth of destabilizing DeFi. Macroprudential regulation also requires collaboration among regulators overseeing different parts of the financial system, with different perspectives on "how different developments fit together and where

[135] For further discussion of financial stability as a regulatory goal, *see* Hilary J. Allen, *Putting the "Financial Stability" In Financial Stability Oversight Council*, 76 OHIO ST. L. J. 1087, 1098 *et seq.* (2015).

[136] For a discussion of macroprudential and microprudential approaches to regulation, *see* Armour *et al*., PRINCIPLES OF FINANCIAL REGULATION (2016) 416-18.

[137] *Id.*

the unseen risks might be hidden."[138] In my statement today, I will highlight the dangers inherent in taking too microprudential an approach to regulating stablecoins, and suggest alternative policy responses that are informed by securities law, antitrust, and financial stability regulation, as well as banking regulation.

Stablecoins and Financial Stability

The PWG Report considers a number of risks associated with stablecoins, including the potential for runs on stablecoins. Put simply, a "run" is a self-fulfilling prophecy that arises when the holders of a seemingly safe asset start to lose confidence that they will be able to withdraw or redeem that asset at the expected value when they need to. Fearing the worst, they seek to withdraw or redeem the asset early – which means that the issuer of the purportedly safe asset has to sell off assets in order to raise enough cash to satisfy the withdrawal/redemption requests. Because the issuer has to sell quickly, assets are often sold at a discount, which depresses the price of the issuer's portfolio of assets and may ultimately drive the issuer into insolvency.

The paradigmatic example of this is a bank run, which occurs when panicking bank depositors seek to withdraw all of their funds from a bank, forcing that bank (which has invested the depositors' funds in long-term assets like loans) to start selling assets at a discount to raise the funds necessary to meet withdrawal requests. If the bank's assets shrink so much – as a result of these discounted fire sales – that the bank's liabilities outnumber its assets, the bank will fail, and then it will be unable to perform its usual functions of managing risk, intermediating capital, and facilitating payments for its customers. Furthermore, the discounted fire sales will not only affect the bank experiencing the run; they will also affect the market price of the assets that are sold, which (in a vicious cycle) can threaten the solvency of other institutions that have invested in similar assets.

In short, runs can cause financial stability problems in two ways: they can deprive the economy of capital intermediation services on which it relies, and they can ignite fire sales that drive down the prices of financial assets in a way that drags down other institutions and markets. As the PWG report and others have observed, asset-backed stablecoins may be vulnerable to runs because

[138] Martin Hellwig, *Financial Stability and Monetary Policy*, 20 (Aug. 2015) (available at https://www.coll.mpg.de/pdf_dat/2015_10online.pdf).

they purport to be redeemable against a fiat currency at a fixed value.[139] If something were to shake confidence in a stablecoin (as the PWG report identifies, this 'something' could range from a hack to a problem with the reserve assets),[140] then holders might come to doubt that the stablecoin could retain a stable value against their preferred fiat currency. We could then expect holders to redeem their stablecoins for fiat currency, forcing the issuer of the stablecoin to start liquidating the reserve of assets backing the stablecoin, depressing the market value of those assets, and incapacitating the stablecoin as a means of transacting.

Because of this potential for a run on stablecoins, the PWG Report has recommended that stablecoins should be treated more like bank deposits and brought within the sphere of banking regulation.[141] However, in my view, this recommendation misses some key context. Stablecoins differ from deposits in two important ways: (i) the expectations of the parties using them are different; and (ii) they play different roles in intermediating capital. Because of these differences, stablecoins should not be brought within the perimeter of banking regulation (at least, not now – the Financial Stability Oversight Council ("FSOC") and the Office of Financial Research ("OFR") should monitor stablecoins for changes in expectations and usage). Regulating stablecoins like bank deposits will lend them implicit government backing – and with it, confidence and legitimacy far beyond what stablecoin issuers could generate on their own.[142] Inspiring this type of confidence in the stability of stablecoins may counterproductively make runs more likely. Furthermore, legitimized stablecoins will turbocharge the growth of the DeFi (which relies upon stablecoins to facilitate "fund transfers across platforms and between users").[143]

Expectations Surrounding Stablecoins

Runs happen when people lose confidence that a particular asset (like a dollar in a deposit account) will continue to remain accessible at the expected value. This "confidence" aspect of runs means that runs are unlikely to occur if the

---

[139] PWG Report, *supra* Note 2 at 2.

[140] *Id.* at 12.

[141] The report recommends that "legislation should require stablecoin issuers to be insured depository institutions, which are subject to appropriate supervision and regulation, at the depository institution and the holding company level." *Id.* at 2.

[142] The PWG report recommends that "with respect to stablecoin issuers, legislation should provide for supervision on a consolidated basis; prudential standards; and, potentially, access to appropriate components of the federal safety net." *Id.* at 16.

[143] Aramonte, *supra* Note 4 at 24.

people holding an asset never expected it to have a stable value in the first place. Right now, stablecoins are not being used for payments for real world goods and services in any meaningful way, and so the people using them do not need them to maintain a stable value. The recent exponential growth in stablecoin usage has been driven by people who have purchased stablecoins to speculate in the DeFi markets,[144] suggesting that they do not care whether their stablecoins will maintain a consistent value.[145] Investor protection regulation can help tamp down on any limited expectations of stability that do exist, by preventing stablecoin issuers from advertising their stablecoins as being more stable than they really are, and by mandating disclosure of the assets in the reserve.

If stablecoins start to become widely used as payments mechanisms for real-world goods and services, then expectations will shift, and runs will be more likely. The FSOC and the OFR should monitor the stablecoin market for such a shift. However, (with some caveats I will discuss shortly) this seems unlikely to happen in the near term. Payments mechanisms benefit from network effects, meaning that they become more useful as more people and businesses use them. Stablecoins therefore have a "chicken and egg" problem when it comes to paying for real world goods and services: they need to develop a critical mass of merchants and users in order to become useful enough to attract more merchants and users. Before merchants and users are willing to start embracing stablecoins in this way, stablecoin issuers will have to address concerns about the ability of distributed ledger technology to process payments on a large scale. Changes in the size and usage of a payment system often create problems, and it will be particularly challenging for decentralized distributed ledger to respond to these changes.[146] If there is nobody "in charge" of the ledger on which the stablecoins are used, no fix can take effect unless and until it is adopted by the majority of the nodes that control that ledger. If majority approval cannot be achieved, the gridlock can be addressed by a "hard fork" that splits the distributed ledger in two, but given the network effects of payments systems, hard forks can be a very problematic response to governance problems.

---

[144] *See* Note 4.

[145] As one reporter observed about the stablecoin Tether, "It wasn't that they trusted Tether, I realized. It was that they needed Tether to trade and were making too much money using it to dig too deeply. "It could be way shakier, and I wouldn't care," said Dan Matuszewski, co-founder of CMS Holdings LLC, a cryptocurrency investment firm." Zeke Faux, *Has Anyone Seen Tether's Billions*, BLOOMBERG'S BUSINESSWEEK (Oct. 7, 2021).

[146] Hilary J. Allen, *Payments Failure*, 62 B.C. L. Rev. 453, 494 (2021).

While stablecoins face major hurdles to becoming a viable payments mechanism, there are two obvious scenarios in which these hurdles could be overcome more quickly. One is for lawmakers to follow the PWG's recommendation to regulate stablecoins like bank deposits, which would lend stablecoins greater credibility as a payments mechanism and attract merchants and users. It is perhaps telling that Jeffrey Allaire (the CEO of Circle, issuer of the USDC stablecoin) has welcomed this type of banking regulation for stablecoins.[147] In my view, this approach would be unwise – if the government wishes to promote better and faster payments frameworks for underserved consumers, there are simpler technological solutions to explore that don't require an inherently fragile asset like the stablecoin running on a distributed ledger with complex governance issues (complexity is itself a source of financial instability, and simpler solutions are less likely to cause problems).[148] Simpler technological solutions will also avoid the environmental costs of crypto mining.[149]

The second way in which a stablecoin could quickly become a widely-used payments system is if it is launched by a firm that already has a well-established network of users. Most pressingly, large tech firms already have large networks of users that they could encourage to adopt any stablecoin they issue. If a tech giant introduced a stablecoin, it could quickly become an important payments system that becomes critical to the real-world economy (particularly if the tech firm is willing to use a permissioned distributed ledger that will allow it to easily make changes to the underlying distributed ledger as its scale of usage changes). People *would* expect such a stablecoin to have a stable value, and in this sense, Meta/Facebook's Diem could pose a real threat to financial stability. That does not mean, though, that all stablecoins should be regulated like bank deposits. Instead, the problems related to Diem (and Meta/Facebook's other financial projects) should be dealt with directly –

---

[147] "But I would say at the highest level, the proposal that dollar stablecoin issuers in the US financial system should be regulated as banks at the federal level by the Federal Reserve is something that we think represents significant progress in the growth of this industry." *Circle CEO discusses stablecoin regulation and the bank charter process*, YAHOO NEWS (Nov. 9, 2021) (available at https://news.yahoo.com/circle-ceo-discusses-stablecoin-regulation-213747962.html).

[148] Allen, *supra* Note 19 at 464 *et seq.*

[149] "According to Marion Laboure, a Deutsche Bank analyst, mining one bitcoin consumes a larger carbon footprint than nearly two billion Visa transactions. Another incredible stat: an individual bitcoin transaction couldpower the average U.S. household for 61 days. Adding in the energy consumption of Ethereum, and the two major cryptocurrencies would rank 15th in the world, nearly equivalent to Mexico." Steve Goldstein, *Here's how many Visa transactions can be completed using the energy to mine one bitcoin*, MARKETWATCH (Dec. 10, 2021).

as should any other attempt by a tech giant to provide payments services. This may involve using antitrust law; a complementary approach would be to use the FSOC's designation power under Section 113 of Dodd-Frank to designate the tech giant in question as a systemically important financial institution and subject it to supervision by the Federal Reserve. Congress could also consider strengthening existing legislation that prevents commercial firms from accepting deposits so that commercial firms are prohibited from accepting deposits *and* from offering payments services.

The Role of Stablecoins in Intermediating Capital

When considering the problems associated with runs on stablecoins, it's important not to lose sight of why runs are a problem. Runs are not intrinsically bad, but they do become a problem when they interfere with the capital intermediation on which the broader economy depends (either by igniting fire sales that drag down the prices of assets held by other institutions and markets, or by disabling a capital-intermediating service for which there are no ready substitutes). For example, bank runs are a problem because they prevent banks from extending the credit that individuals and businesses rely upon for growth. In the worst case, runs can generalize into a broad-scale bank panic at multiple institutions, causing a widespread collapse in lending. Deposit insurance was adopted in 1934 to prevent this kind of panic and protect the flow of credit, notwithstanding valid objections from economists about moral hazard (in this context, "moral hazard" means that deposit insurance gives banks incentives to engage in riskier behavior in order to multiply their profits in good times, knowing that there is a government safety net that will absorb the losses in bad times).[150]

The moral hazard associated with deposit insurance was ultimately deemed a price worth paying to keep banks stable and funds flowing through them to the broader economy. But the value proposition for stablecoins is much less clear: what economic growth do they propel? And what moral hazard would government backing for stablecoins create? Right now,

---

[150] Moral hazard is the "tendency of an insured to relax his efforts to prevent the occurrence of the risk that he has insured against because he has shifted the risk to an insurance company." RICHARD A. POSNER, ECONOMIC ANALYSIS OF LAW 121 (5th ed. 1998). Lovett expressed the application of moral hazard in the banking context as follows: "If governments and modern nations do not allow most banks to [fail], how can the leaders and managements of banking institutions be disciplined and avoid unduly risky, negligent, or adventurous lending policies (or simply poor asset-liability management)?" William A. Lovett, *Moral Hazard, Bank Supervision and Risk-Based Capital Requirements*, 49 OHIO ST. L.J. 1365, 1365 (1989).

stablecoins are primarily being used to facilitate DeFi, and so the issue of whether we're worried about stablecoins' continuing ability to intermediate capital will depend on our conclusions about the utility of DeFi, and whether or not DeFi deserves implicit government support. These issues will be addressed in the next Section.

The remining concern about stablecoins, from a financial stability perspective, is whether run-inspired fire sales will have systemic consequences. This will depend on what assets are in stablecoins' reserves. The PWG Report observes that "[b]ased on information available, stablecoins differ in the riskiness of their reserve assets, with some stablecoin arrangements reportedly holding virtually all reserve assets in deposits at insured depository institutions or in U.S. Treasury bills, and others reportedly holding riskier reserve assets, including commercial paper, corporate and municipal bonds, and other digital assets."[151] It is possible that mass withdrawals by stablecoins from insured deposit accounts could trigger runs on the institutions that provide those deposit acccounts, but that doesn't mean that stablecoins need to be brought inside the perimeter of banking regulation. This possibility could be dealt with by prudential regulation of existing insured depository institutions: they could be prohibited from accepting deposits from stablecoin issuers on the grounds that it is an unsafe and unsound practice (there are already banking regulations that limit acceptance of other volatile deposits, like brokered deposits).[152]

To the extent that stablecoins invest in other assets types like U.S Treasuries, commercial paper, corporate and municipal bonds, and other digital assets, the impact of stablecoin runs will depend on the size of the stablecoin reserve. This is another argument for why Congress and regulators should not adopt policies that encourage the growth of stablecoins (and should take measures to keep tech giants out of the stablecoin business). If a stablecoin were to gain significant traction, then fire sales of its reserve assets would obviously be of significant concern, but if stablecoins remain modestly sized, then any fire sales will have limited impact on broader asset markets. Interestingly, the reserves of Tether, which currently has by far the largest market value of any stablecoin, may not actually be as big as expected. As one recent report put it: "[e]xactly how Tether is backed, or if it's truly backed at all, has always been a mystery. For years a persistent group of critics has

[151] PWG Report, *supra* Note 2 at 4.

[152] "The OCC does…discourage brokered deposits because of their high volatility and cost, and banks may bay a higher FDIC deposit insurance premium for such items" Richard Scott Carnell *et al.*, THE LAW OF FINANCIAL INSTITUTIONS, 118 (2021).

argued that, despite the company's assurances, Tether Holdings doesn't have enough assets to maintain the 1-to-1 exchange rate, meaning its coin is essentially a fraud."[153] If true, this would be highly problematic for investors in Tether, but it would also limit the systemic impact of any fire sale of Tether's reserve assets – because there wouldn't be so many of them. A run on Tether could, however, be disastrous for DeFi investors, as tens of billions of dollars of Tether are locked into DeFi protocols.[154]

DeFi and Financial Stability

DeFi, like any new and evolving business model or technology, is hard to pin down with a precise definition. Right now, the term is used to describe any simulacrum of traditional financial services performed using blockchain technology (relying in particular on smart contracts and stablecoins).[155] It can sometimes be hard to disentangle DeFi's aspirations from its realities. The term "decentralized finance" speaks to an aspiration – the hope that blockchain technology can be used to deliver financial services "without centralized intermediaries or institutions."[156] The expansion of DeFi is sometimes described as the foundation of "web3," an idealized vision for an internet that would run on a distributed ledger and therefore avoid the concentrated power of tech giants like Meta/Facebook and Google. In reality, though, distributed ledger technology is not as decentralized as claimed.[157]

Recent research from the Bank for International Settlements has observed that there is "a "decentralisation illusion" in DeFi due to the inescapable need for centralised governance and the tendency of blockchain consensus mechanisms to concentrate power."[158] There have been many illustrations of the lack of real decentralization in the cryptoverse.[159] One recent example involves BadgerDAO, which paused all of its smart contracts upon receiving

---

[153] Faux, *supra* Note 18.
[154] Aramonte, *suprat* Note 4 at 24.
[155] The Wharton Blockchain and Digital Asset Project, DEFI BEYOND THE HYPE: THE EMERGING WORLD OF DECENTRALIZED FINANCE, 2-3 (May 2021) (available at https://wifpr.wharton.upenn.edu/wp-content/uploads/2021/05/DeFi-Beyond-the-Hype.pdf).
[156] *Id.* at 2.
[157] *See* Angela Walch, *Deconstructing 'Decentralization': Exploring the Core Claim of Crypto Systems*, in CRYPTO ASSETS: LEGAL AND MONETARY PERSPECTIVES (ed. Chris Brummer) (2019).
[158] Aramonte, *supra* Note 4 at 22.
[159] For examples of actions within the Bitcoin and Ethereum blockchain systems that suggest centralized control, *see* Walch, *supra* Note 30.

reports of unauthorized withdrawals[160] – if decentralization lived up to the hype, there should be no person who could choose to pause the operation of these smart contracts. In addition to individuals who can control the governance of DeFi apps, many of the investors driving the growth of DeFi are institutional players, often engaging in transactions worth $10 million or more of cryptocurrency.[161] More generally, DeFi relies heavily on centralized crypto services (including stablecoins), which in turn rely on traditional financial services (like banks and fiat currencies).[162] DeFi is therefore not particularly decentralized, but using the term "decentralized" to describe these services serves a marketing purpose, and may also be intended to discourage regulation (if policymakers believe the decentralization hype, they may be misled into thinking that there are no intermediaries to regulate, notwithstanding that DeFi relies in part on the regulated financial system, wallets and exchanges are obvious candidates for regulation, and software developers and miners could also be regulated. Furthermore, just as some regulations and fiduciary duties are applied to significant shareholders of a corporation, concentrated owners of tokens could also be regulated).

In reality, DeFi's defining attribute is the technology it relies on, rather than decentralization. As already stated, DeFi relies on blockchain technology. Stablecoins are essential to DeFi's operation, as are smart contracts. A "smart contract" is simply a type of computer program that is designed to be self-executing and self-enforcing. These programs establish certain rights and obligations associated with tokens that are hosted on a distributed ledger, and execute on the distributed ledger (although they can be programmed to consult outside data sources, which are referred to as "oracles," before executing). The crypto industry's vision is that smart contracts, stablecoins, and distributed ledgers will be used in concert to provide new versions of "payments, lending, trading, investments, insurance, and asset management" services,[163] but it is still unclear who will use these services. A recent article in The Economist put it this way: "The problem is that all this fancy financial engineering has, as

---

[160] "Badger has received reports of unauthorized withdrawals of user funds. As Badger engineers investigate this, all smart contracts have been paused to prevent further withdrawals. Our investigation is ongoing and we will release further information as soon as possible," https://twitter.com/BadgerDAO/status/1466263899498377218 (Dec 1, 2021).

[161] Chainanalysis, *DeFi Whales Turned Central, Northern & Western Europe into the World's Biggest Cryptocurrency Economy* (Oct. 14, 2021) (available at https://blog.chainalysis.com/reports/central-northern-western-europe-cryptocurrency-geography-report-2021-preview/).

[162] "To the extent that DeFi relies on such stablecoins, it remains dependent on CeFi and traditional finance." Aramonte, *supra* Note 4 at 25.

[163] Wharton Blockchain and Digital Asset Project, *supra* Note 28 at 2.

yet, no "real" economy to service. Instead it underpins an incorporeal casino: most of those using DeFi do so to facilitate or leverage their bets on one of many speculative tokens."[164] If stablecoins are primarily used in DeFi, and DeFi is an "incorporeal casino," then treating stablecoins like regulated deposits will provide implicit government backing to that casino, encouraging its growth.

DeFi Growth

A recent report from the BIS described DeFi as largely self-referential, and concluded that "[g]iven this self-contained nature, the potential for DeFi-driven disruptions in the broader financial system and the real economy seems limited for now."[165] If Tether were to fail right now, for example, that would cause real problems for the DeFi ecosystem that relies upon it, but because DeFi still remains largely disconnected from both real-world economic applications and the established financial system, there would be limited pressure on the government to bail it out. However, as DeFi grows, the possibilities for something to go wrong, and for that something to impact the broader economy, increase.

Before the rise of crypto, the supply of new types of financial assets was always constrained—if only a little bit— because assets had to have some kind of connection to some kind of real-world economic good or service. Now, assets can be created out of thin air by anyone with computer programming knowledge, and an unconstrained supply of financial assets means more opportunities for asset bubbles to grow, and more assets to be dumped during fire sales. More assets also means more trading transactions which means more contractual relationships between counterparties that can transmit shocks through the system. Market practices requiring DeFi transactions to be overcollateralized with stablecoins could theoretically put some limits on the growth of DeFi, but when stablecoins are used as collateral for loans, the proceeds of those loans are often used as collateral for other loans, which can then be used as collateral for further loans, and so on.[166] This is multiplying the amount of leverage in the DeFi ecosystem, and the use of derivatives is also increasing the amount of leverage.[167] As the 2008 crisis amply demonstrated, increased use of leverage makes a system more fragile both by

---

[164] Alice Fulwood, *Decentralized Finance is Booming, But it Has Yet to Find Its Purpose*, THE ECONOMIST (Nov. 8, 2021).

[165] Aramonte, *supra* Note 4 at 21.

[166] *Id.* at 29.

[167] *Id.*

inflating asset bubbles on the upswing, and by causing fire sales on the downswing (if someone buys an asset with mostly borrowed money, then if the price of that asset falls, they will have to sell either that asset or some other asset in order to raise money to repay the loan).

DeFi could also grow as traditional financial institutions become increasingly interested in investing in, and offering, crypto.[168] The head of JPMorgan's blockchain team, for example, said earlier this year that "[w]e are keeping a very close eye on the DeFi evolution."[169] And the interest goes both ways, with some members of the crypto industry welcoming a relationship with traditional finance: the CEO of Circle recently said that "crypto needs to be integrated with the traditional financial system, creating "a hybrid model."[170] Regulated financial institutions could make huge profits by offering DeFi versions of their traditional products and services (in the past, financial institutions have had significant financial success in offering new versions of existing financial products that are exciting, but not much better at discharging their functions than previous versions).[171] Now that unlimited crypto assets can be created through computer programming, DeFi provides enormous opportunities for profit that may prove too seductive for the established financial industry to ignore. However, because the real economy relies upon the established financial industry for credit and other services, the government may feel compelled to bail out DeFi if it becomes integrated with the traditional financial system.

There are a number of avenues through which the financial industry's ventures into DeFi could cause problems for the traditional financial system, and ultimately the broader economy. First, financial institutions might make large, leveraged investments in DeFi and other crypto products. If the value of those products were to fall precipitously (for example, because of a hack), then the institutions invested in them would see their overall asset portfolios shrink, and could even experience a run. Either eventuality could have severe real-world consequences if it shuts down the availability of credit for individuals and small businesses, or ignites fire sales of unrelated asset classes.

---

[168] *Id.* at 31-32.

[169] Ian Allison, *Remember JPMCoin? Next Step is Programmable Money, Bank Exec Says*, COINDESK (Jun. 7, 2021) (available at https://www.coindesk.com/business/2021/06/07/remember-jpm-coin-next-step-is-programmable-money-bank-exec-says/).

[170] Ephrat Livni, *Congress Gets a Crash Course on Cryptocurrency*, N.Y. TIMES (Dec. 8, 2021) (available at https://www.nytimes.com/2021/12/08/business/house-financial-services-crypto.html).

[171] Dan Awrey, *Complexity, Innovation, and the Regulation of Modern Financial Markets*, 2 HARV. BUS. L. REV. 235, 263-4 (2012).

Furthermore, runs and other financial panics tend to be worse if there isn't much information available about the assets involved, or if that information exists but is impossible to understand. Most investors (including established financial institutions) are used to reviewing balance sheets and written disclosures to assess investments, not computer code. While it's possible for written disclosures to describe how smart contracts will operate, one study found that the written disclosure documents provided to crypto investors can be highly inconsistent with how the code of the relevant smart contracts actually functions.[172] This lack of clarity may exacerbate the problems associated with financial institutions investing in crypto.

Financial institutions might also be inclined to launch their own stablecoins (JPMorgan has already done so with its JPMCoin, although JPMCoin runs on JPMorgan's proprietary ledger rather than on a decentralized ledger).[173] If bank-issued stablecoins could be used in the DeFi ecosystem, than all the concerns raised in Section 3 about lending implicit government support to DeFi would be realized. There are also monetary policy and safety and soundness concerns associated with bank-issued stablecoins: a bank like JPMorgan has always been able to profit by making US dollar loans to borrowers, but regulations (most importantly reserve and capital requirements) ultimately limit the amount of loans that banks can make. In addition, banks have no right to create US dollars for their own spending—that right belongs solely to the central bank. JPMorgan could create JPMCoins for its own spending, though, and because JPMCoins are not subject to reserve and capital requirements, JPMorgan could also theoretically make unlimited loans in JPMCoins.

Disenchantment with the existing financial system has spurred interest in DeFi, and that disenchantment is understandable and often justified. However, we should be keenly aware that if there is money to be made in any substitute financial system, established financial intermediaries will seek to find a way in. Congress should therefore consider steps to keep regulated depository institutions and their affiliates separate from DeFi. One measure that would contribute to this goal would be to prevent these institutions from investing in DeFi or any other crypto; another would be to prevent these institutions from issuing any stablecoin that operates on a decentralized ledger. We should also be keenly aware, though, that even without the involvement of established financial intermediaries, DeFi will tend towards centralization and

---

172 Shaanan Cohney *et al.*, *Coin-Operated Capitalism*, 119 COLUM. L. REV. 591 (2019).
173 Allen, *supra* Note 19 at 495-6.

concentration, and that it suffers from many of the same problems as traditional finance – along with some new ones.

Speed and Rigidity

As previously noted, DeFi relies heavily on smart contracts as well as stablecoins. There have been a lot of news stories recently about hackers exploiting bugs in the code of these smart contracts, but even flawless code can cause financial stability problems.[174] In moments of crisis, "the elasticity of law has proved time and again critical for avoiding a complete financial meltdown."[175] Smart contracts, however, are designed to be as inflexible as possible, executing their preprogrammed instructions without waiting for any further input from a court or even the parties themselves.

When unexpected events occur, parties to regular financial contracts have the opportunity to amend them or agree not to enforce them. Legal systems have also developed the ability to relax and suspend contractual obligations in the face of a significant unanticipated event, whether through the use of bankruptcy courts, encouraging a contractual party not to enforce their rights, or even by enacting legislation that declares certain contractual terms illegal.[176] Because of their reliance on smart contracts, DeFi transactions will execute quickly, and will be harder to stop or undo (for example, DeFi loans are often structured so that they are automatically liquidated if there is insufficient collateral posted).[177] The execution of a smart contract can only be paused, changed, or undone with the consent of whoever controls the relevant distributed ledger, and where the ledger is decentralized and permissionless (like the Ethereum ledger) there is no single individual who can coordinate the process—even if the parties to the smart contract (as well as the public interest) all support it. Instead, any pause, change or reversal of a smart contract will require the consensus of all the nodes in the distributed ledger supporting the smart contract, which will take time (after the DAO hack in 2016, it took over a month for the nodes of the Ethereum distributed ledger to coordinate their response).[178] It seems highly unlikely that this kind of

---

174 Mark Hochstein, *The Downside of Programmable Money*, COINDESK (Nov. 30, 2021) (available at https://www.coindesk.com/business/2021/11/30/the-downside-of-programmable-money/).

175 Katharina Pistor, *A Legal Theory of Finance*, 41 J. COMPARATIVE ECON. 315, 321 (2013).

176 Anna Gelpern & Adam J. Levitin, *Rewriting Frankenstein Contracts: Workout Prohibitions in Residential Mortgage-Backed Securities*, 82 S. CAL. L. REV. 1075, 1128– 29 (2009).

177 Aramonte, *supra* Note 4 at 27.

178 Primavera De Filippi & Aaron Wright, BLOCKCHAIN AND THE LAW: THE RULE OF CODE, 188 (2018).

consensus could ever be achieved *before* the smart contract executes, and so any intervention is likely to come too late to prevent runs, fire sales, and other destabilizing harms.

While there are steps that can be taken to better equip a smart contract to adapt to unexpected events (for example, a smart contract can be programmed to consult an external oracle), taking these kinds of steps will increase transaction costs. The Ethereum ledger (which is "the predominant blockchain on which DeFi protocols and applications function")[179] charges a "gas cost" for any computing done, and consulting an oracle would increase the amount of computing power (and thus the gas charge) necessary to execute a smart contract. Participants in the DeFi markets will probably be willing to bear these charges up to a certain point, but eventually, these ongoing operational costs will discourage measures that cater for very unusual events. Unfortunately, when we're talking about financial stability, low-probability high-consequence tail events are the ones we're most concerned about.

An Illustration: AIG's Credit Default Swaps in the DeFi Era

It can be hard to conceptualize DeFi's implications for financial stability in the abstract. I therefore offer an illustration here, by explaining what would have happened in 2007-8 if credit default swaps issued by AIG had been issued as a form of DeFi.[180]

In the lead-up to the 2018 financial crisis, the insurance giant AIG had issued an estimated $1.8 trillion of credit default swaps ("CDS") that would require it to make payments if the mortgage-backed securities ("MBS") underlying those CDS suffered some type of credit event. AIG was not in a position to actually pay out on all of those CDS – at the time, AIG's parent company reported total capital of $95.8 billion – but AIG had assumed that the underlying MBS would never default and that payments would never be required. However, as time progressed, and the mortgages backing those MBS began to default in alarming numbers, people started to admit the possibility

---

[179] PWG Report, *supra* Note 2 at 9.

[180] This account of events relating to the credit default swaps that AIG issued to Goldman Sachs is drawn from Rena S. Miller & Kathleen Ann Ruane, Congressional Research Service, R41398, THE DODD-FRANK WALL STREET REFORM AND CONSUMER PROTECTION ACT: TITLE VII, DERIVATIVES (2012); and Financial Crisis Inquiry Commission, THE FINANCIAL CRISIS INQUIRY REPORT: FINAL REPORT OF THE NATIONAL COMMISSION ON THE CAUSES OF THE FINANCIAL AND ECONOMIC CRISIS IN THE UNITED STATES, 265-274 (2011).

that MBS themselves might default, which made AIG's position riskier. Worried that AIG might not be able to make payments on its CDS if the MBS failed, the banks and other investors that had bought CDS from AIG turned to provisions in their contracts that required AIG to provide them with collateral if the risks associated with MBS increased.

It was these calls for collateral that ultimately forced a government bailout – to the tune of tens of billions of dollars – to prevent AIG from failing. In particular, the investment bank Goldman Sachs demanded on several occasions that AIG post collateral in response to downgrades of the MBS referenced in the CDS that AIG had issued to Goldman. Pursuant to the agreements governing the arrangements between Goldman Sachs and AIG, these collateral calls were authorized if Goldman Sachs believed that the value of the underlying MBS had decreased. However, AIG had dismissed the possibility of such collateral calls – in fact, many senior people at AIG were unaware that the contracts authorized these collateral calls at all – and so no one at AIG had developed any way of assessing what the appropriate amount of collateral should be. As a result, Goldman Sachs was largely in a position to dictate how much collateral it was entitled to in a collateral call.

When Goldman Sachs did make its collateral call, AIG objected, the parties negotiated, and they ultimately agreed that AIG could post much less collateral than Goldman Sachs had initially demanded. However, if this had happened in an era of DeFi and the parties had used smart contracts to automate the collateral call process, Goldman Sachs would simply have had to inform a so-called "oracle" of the amount of desired collateral (remember that AIG didn't negotiate for any rights with respect to collateral calls). Upon consulting the oracle, the smart contract would immediately have withdrawn stablecoins from AIG's wallet on the distributed ledger and transferred them to Goldman Sachs. There would have been much less scope for flexibility or negotiation in Goldman Sachs' treatment of AIG, and AIG's solvency might have been in jeopardy as early as 2007.

When AIG ultimately did reach the brink of failure in September 2008, again as a result of collateral calls in connection with the many CDS it had issued, AIG's insolvency was averted by the government pledging to provide AIG with the funds necessary to cover those collateral calls. If the relevant CDS provisions had been automated as smart contracts, though, would there have been a way to suspend collateral calls until AIG received its infusion of government funds, or would collateral (in the form of stablecoins) already have been transferred away form AIG, rendering AIG insolvent before government aid could arrive? Parties to a paper contract can agree among themselves not to enforce a contract when it is not in their best interests to do so, but there is much less flexibility in a smart contract. Unless a smart contract were programed in advance to delay execution following the announcement of a government bailout of a counterparty (an unlikely event that would probably not have been contemplated at the time the smart contract was programmed), such news would not prevent default – even though, in reality, the announcement of government support succeeded in saving AIG in 2008.

A Note on Monetary Policy

This testimony is primarily focused on the impact of stablecoins and DeFi on financial stability. However, financial instability is not the only threat to broader economic growth. Central banks like the Federal Reserve carry out monetary policy functions in order to match the supply of money to the needs of the economy, and the rise of stablecoins has the potential to disrupt these functions. For example, central banks manage the money supply to respond to inflation. When there is a lot of money available in the economy, it is cheaper to borrow, and cheaper money increases purchasing power which can drive up inflation. The converse is also true: when there is less money available, inflation is reduced. If money increasingly takes the form of stablecoins issued by private entities, then that could displace the use of fiat currencies and limit the ability of central banks to match the money supply to the economic situation. Private sector institutions – who have no mandate to serve the public interest – will have usurped control over the money supply, undermining central banks' ability to rein in inflation or address deflation. This is yet another reason to avoid policies that encourage the growth of stablecoins.

Central banks are certainly concerned about the impact that widely-used stablecoins could have on their monetary policy. As a result, many central banks are contemplating adopting central bank digital currencies ("CBDCs") to compete with privately-issued stablecoins, notwithstanding that they have misgivings about the financial stability implications of CBDCs (particularly their potential to encourage runs from bank deposits to CBDCs).[181] Given these financial stability concerns (and also concerns about user privacy), if CBDCs are nothing more than a defensive response designed to outcompete the Diems of the world, that is another reason for Congress to consider whether

---

[181] Bank for International Settlements, CENTRAL BANK DIGITAL CURRENCIES: FOUNDATIONAL PRINCIPLES AND CORE FEATURES, 8-9 (2020).

Diem should be permitted in the first place. The need to protect monetary policy is also another justification for measures that prohibit regulated depository institutions from issuing stablecoins: if significant volumes of transactions are consummated in JPMCoins, for example, the Federal Reserve will also have lost some of its control of the money supply.

Possible Congressional Approaches to Stablecoins

Ban or Licensing Regime

Given stablecoins' inherent fragility, limited utility outside of the DeFi ecosystem, and potential to cannibalize monetary policy, Congress should consider whether banning stablecoins is appropriate. If Congress does not wish to enact a full ban, it could also consider a licensing regime for stablecoins whereby stablecoins will only be authorized if their issuers can demonstrate: (i) that the stablecoins have a purpose that is connected to real-world economic growth (i.e., growth outside of the DeFi ecosystem); (ii) that the issuers have the institutional capacity to manage the risks associated with the stablecoin's reserve and technology; (iii) that a run on the stablecoin would not impact financial stability; and (iv) that the stablecoin does not pose a threat to U.S. monetary policy. Although a ban or a licensing regime would need to be designed carefully to limit regulatory arbitrage, it would not be impossible to implement. As this statement has explored, stablecoins and DeFi are not as decentralized as advertised, and so there are intermediaries to whom regulation could be applied.

When considering measures like a ban or a licensing regime, Congress will no doubt wish to consider the impact of such measures on innovation. Innovation is important, but Congress should think critically about the type of innovation it wants to encourage. It would be wrong to assume that all crypto-related innovation is intended to make financial services more accessible to underserved populations. Stablecoins and DeFi services are used predominantly by people who already have access to the traditional banking system. If stablecoins and DeFi only provide marginal improvements over the financial services that are already available, but end up making our financial system more fragile, then chilling their development would be good public policy. It is worth noting that a World Economic Forum White Paper recently concluded that stablecoins currently offer limited benefits for financial inclusion:

> The principal finding of this white paper is that stablecoins are subject to many of the same barriers that constrain citizens from accessing other financial products and services, such as bank accounts, mobile money accounts or fully digital remittance providers. Where stablecoins are accessible, they generally address financial inclusion barriers to a similar degree as other digital financial services… stablecoins as currently deployed would not provide compelling new benefits for financial inclusion beyond those offered by pre-existing options.[182]

If Congress wants to encourage financial inclusion, it could consider focusing on supporting innovation in simpler mobile payments and remittance technologies, which might satisfy consumers' needs without the complications of runnable stablecoins, or distributed ledgers with convoluted governance structures. Simpler technologies would also avoid the environmental costs of crypto mining.

More Limited Interventions

A ban or licensing regime would respond to all of the financial stability risks identified in this statement (including the risk of runs on stablecoins), as well as responding to concerns about monetary policy. More limited interventions would inevitably entail tradeoffs. I have advocated against bringing stablecoins within the perimeter of banking regulation, which means that stablecoins will remain more fragile than they would be if regulated more like bank deposits. To limit the fallout of any run on a stablecoin, measures will therefore need to be considered to: (i) limit investors' expectations about the stability of stablecoins; (ii) monitor changes in the usage of stablecoins; (iii) prevent large tech firms and regulated depository institutions from issuing stablecoins; and (iv) prevent regulated depository institutions from accepting deposits from stablecoin issuers.

I will set out here some suggestions for measures that can be taken to address these objectives, and other objectives identified in my testimony.

- The SEC and CFTC should continue to oversee the stablecoins under their jurisdiction to ensure that investors are protected. More specifically:

---

[182] World Economic Forum, *What is the Value Proposition of Stablecoins for Financial Inclusion*, DIGITAL CURRENCY GOVERNANCE CONSORTIUM WHITE PAPER SERIES, 8 (Nov. 2021) (available at https://www3.weforum.org/docs/WEF_Value_Proposition_of_Stablecoins_for_Financial_Inclusion_2021.pdf).

    - The SEC and CFTC should prevent stablecoin issuers from misrepresenting that stablecoins are more stable than they are (for example, enforcement actions would be appropriate against stablecoins that claim they are covered by FDIC insurance).
    - The SEC and CFTC should compel disclosure of the contents of the reserves backing any stablecoin under their jurisdiction.
        - While various crypto industry members have asked that Congress create a dedicated crypto regulator, doing so would be problematic for many reasons, including that:
            - The US already has too many financial regulators, which leads both to duplicative regulatory efforts and issues falling through regulatory gaps. Adding another regulator would exacerbate this issue.
            - The more specialized the regulator, the more opportunities there are for the industry to "capture" the regulator. Concerns about captured regulators were an important impetus for the abolition of the Office of Thrift Supervision in 2010, and would be a real concern with a dedicated crypto regulator.
- The Office of Financial Research ("OFR") and the Financial Stability Oversight Council ("FSOC") should be charged with monitoring the growth of stablecoins. If a stablecoin becomes a widely-used and accepted payment service, the FSOC should consider:
    - Designating the stablecoin issuer as a systemically important financial institution, utilizing the designation power bestowed by Section 113 of Dodd-Frank. This would subject the issuer to supervision by the Federal Reserve.
    - If the stablecoin is decentralized, it may be more appropriate for the FSOC to use its authority under Section 804 of Dodd-Frank to designate the associated payment service as systemically important, and therefore subject to supervision by the Federal Reserve.
- Steps should be taken to prevent large tech firms like Meta/Facebook from issuing stablecoins:
    - The FSOC should explore how its designation power under Section 113 of Dodd-Frank could be applied to a large tech firm. The possibility of designation (and subsequent regulation by the

    Federal Reserve) may be enough to discourage Meta/Facebook from pursuing its Diem stablecoin.
        - A tech firm's size and the availability of substitutes for its stablecoins would obviously be relevant to determining its systemic importance, but the FSOC should also take into account the size of the firm's network, the breadth of the firm's non-financial services, and the firm's unique access to certain kinds of data.
    - Antitrust regulators should consider prohibiting a large tech firm from leveraging its network (as developed in a market where it has monopoly or near-monopoly power) into a payments platform.
    - Congress should consider amending existing legislation that prevents commercial firms from accepting deposits to prohibit such commercial firms from accepting deposits *and* offering payments services.
- Regulators of insured depository institutions and their holding companies should issue rules (or at the very least, guidance) designating the following practices as unsafe and unsound:
    - Holding stablecoin reserves in a deposit account.
    - Investing in any crypto asset.
- Insured depository institutions should be prohibited from issuing their own stablecoins. This could be achieved by legislation amending national banks' powers as specified in 12 USC Section 24 (seventh) (equivalent amendments would need to be made to the powers of state-chartered banks as well). Alternatively, banking regulators could effect this prohibition through a joint rulemaking.

Responses to Written Questions of Chairman Brown from Alexis Goldstein

Questions for Ms. Alexis Goldstein, Director of Financial Policy, Open Markets Institute, from Chairman Sherrod Brown:

1. Stablecoin companies frequently claim that their products are safe because reserves are invested in low-risk, highly liquid assets, such as bank deposits. Very low-risk assets, however, have low or even nominal returns. If stablecoin reserves are invested in these assets, do stablecoin providers face pressure to obtain revenue from stablecoin users in other ways, such as by cross-selling DeFi investments or charging transaction fees? Is there evidence in the market so far that firms face these incentives?

Stablecoin issuers that invest their reserves in very low-risk assets will likely face challenges generating positive returns. A recent example of this is Circle, the issuer of USDC, who disclosed in their amended S-4 (filed December 23, 2021) a net income loss of over $313 million, and an operating loss of over $42 million.[1]

Stablecoin issuers will likely branch out into other, more profitable (and higher risk) markets. Circle also indicates their plans to do just this in their original 8-K filing, which details plans to launch "Circle DeFi", a service they describe as allowing "companies to have connectivity to Compound, Aave, and other protocols through Circle Accounts and Circle APIs".[2] Ostensibly, DeFi product offerings would come with higher fees that could offset the USDC issuance business. But DeFi comes with its own set of risks, as nearly all DeFi platforms, including the platforms mentioned in the investor presentation – Compound, Aave, Maker – currently lack Know Your Customer, no Anti-Money Laundering, and no Countering Terrorist Financing checks. Maker is exploring adding KYC but is only in a research phase.[3]

2. Major stablecoin issuers, including Circle and Tether, do not allow retail stablecoin users to redeem their coins directly at the issuer. Yet most DeFi arrangements are used extensively or even predominantly by retail consumers, and, as discussed at the hearing, stablecoins are integral to these platforms. Are there risks that arise from the fact that DeFi is accessible to consumers, but important stablecoin redemption processes are not? Please explain.

U.S. retail investors can neither purchase nor redeem the top two stablecoins by market cap (Tether and USDC) directly from the issuer[4] – they are exclusively reliant on cryptocurrency exchanges to trade a stablecoin for a dollar. This embeds within the cryptocurrency ecosystem significant counterparty risk, not just to the stablecoin issuer but to the third-parties customers rely on to convert their stablecoins into fiat.

As the President's Working Group (joined by the FDIC and OCC) noted in its recent stablecoin report, stablecoins "play a central role in facilitating trading, lending, and borrowing activity in DeFi."[5] We see this reflected in a major DeFi exchange, Uniswap, where eight out of nine of the top Liquidity Pools on Uniswap have at least one leg in a Stablecoin, as of December 13, 2021.[6]

DeFi fees, especially on the Ethereum blockchain, can be prohibitively high for users with small amounts of assets.[7] The loss of a stablecoin peg would likely be particularly harmful to small investors on DeFi: they would not have access to redeem Tether or USDC, but would instead need to send their assets to a cryptocurrency exchange in order to be sold. But in times of volatility (as a loss of a stablecoin peg likely would be), Ethereum network fees tend to spike (As the Ethereum network can only process approximately 30 transactions a second,[8] fees often spike to extreme levels whenever there's increased congestion, as investors become increasingly willing to pay higher fees in order to get their transaction executed by an Ethereum miner). This may leave some users with small asset amounts stranded, as the fees may exceed the amounts they have locked into DeFi (stored in liquidity pools or locked into crypto lending or borrowing platforms like Aave or Compound).

[1] *Amended S-4*, CIRCLE (Dec. 23, 2021), https://www.sec.gov/Archives/edgar/data/0001876042/000110465921153174/tm2124445-4_s4a.htm at 112.

[2] *FORM 8-K, SUPPLEMENTAL PRESENTATION MATERIALS*, CIRCLE (Jul. 7, 2021) https://www.sec.gov/Archives/edgar/data/0001824301/000121390021036070/ea143875ex99-4_concordacq.htm at 15.

[3] *Grant Announcement: KYC/AML Compliance Research*, MAKERDAO (Feb. 2, 2022), https://forum.makerdao.com/t/grant-announcement-kyc-aml-compliance-research/12991.

[4] See: *FAQs*, TETHER, https://tether.to/faqs/. ("Unfortunately, Tether has decided to stop serving U.S. individual and corporate customers altogether. As of January 1, 2018, no issuance or redeeming services will be available to these users. Exceptions to these provisions may be made by Tether, in its sole discretion, for entities that are: Established or organized outside of the United States or its territorial or insular possessions; and, Eligible Contract Participants pursuant to U.S. law.") (last visited Dec. 12, 2021); and

[5] *Report on Stable Coins*, PRESIDENT'S WORKING GROUP ON FIN. MARKETS, THE FED. DEPOSIT INS. CORP. (FDIC), AND THE OFFICE OF THE COMPTROLLER OF THE CURRENCY (OCC) (2021), https://home.treasury.gov/system/files/136/StableCoinReport_Nov1_508.pdf.

[6] *Hearing on Stablecoins Before the U.S. Senate Banking Comm.* (2021) (written testimony of Alexis Goldstein), https://www.banking.senate.gov/download/goldstein-testimony-12-14-21 pp 11-12.

[7] *See* Liesl Eichholz, *Avalanche: The New DeFi Blockchain Explained*, GLASSNODE (Feb. 10, 2021), https://insights.glassnode.com/avalanche-the-new-defi-blockchain-explained/ ("With the price of ETH on the rise, even basic token swaps on Ethereum are becoming prohibitively expensive for entry-level players, while interactions with more complex DeFi contracts can come attached with fees exceeding 0.1 ETH (over $170 at the time of writing)."). *See also* Nivesh Rustgi, *Ethereum Miners Earn Record $110M Amid ETH Crash*, CRYPTO BRIEFING (May 21, 2021), https://cryptobriefing.com/ethereum-miners-earn-record-110-million-amid-eth-crash/.

[8] Luke Conway, *What Is Ethereum 2.0?*, STREET (Oct. 27, 2021), https://www.thestreet.com/crypto/ethereum/ethereum-2-upgrade-what-you-need-to-know.

3. When stablecoin issuers preclude retail users from redeeming directly, consumers can convert stablecoins into fiat currency by selling the tokens for dollars on exchanges. But as we saw on the day of the hearing—when major crypto exchanges experienced glitches in their price quote systems—exchanges have been prone to outages and malfunction. Please discuss how exchange outages or errors can affect stablecoin markets and stablecoin holders. Are there scenarios involving exchange failures that give rise to particular concern?

Without redemption rights, cryptocurrency exchanges are the only place where retail investors can exchange their stablecoins for U.S. dollars. This introduces additional counterparty risk on behalf of the customer to the exchange. It's an awkward second step not typically present in other kinds of digital payments – you don't need to *also* set up a stock brokerage account in order to send money electronically.

4. Please describe any risks and benefits that you believe are presented by smart contracts. In what contexts, if any, are smart contracts a valuable tool? Could smart contracts create systemic risks? As compared with traditional contracts, are smart contracts useful in consumer or small business contexts?

Smart contracts are immutable – unable to be modified once they are deployed onto a specific blockchain.[9] This makes DeFi platforms that rely on smart contracts particularly vulnerable to hacks and exploits, as platforms need to deploy new smart contracts to fix any bugs in old ones, leaving the platform and its assets at risk of catastrophic losses in the interim. This inherent vulnerability has led to massive losses in DeFi in 2021; a November 2021 report by Elliptic estimated that there were $12 billion total in losses in DeFi from January - November 2021.[10]

So-called "flash loans", which utilize smart contracts,[11] are often employed to hack DeFi protocols (that themselves rely on smart contracts). Flash loans are unsecured loans where capital is borrowed and repaid in a single transaction. As just one example, in October 2021, a flash loan was used to steal $130 million from the DeFi lending platform Cream Finance.[12]

---

[9] Erfan Andesta, Fathiyeh Faghih, and Mahdi Fooladgar, *Testing Smart Contracts Gets Smarter*, IEEE (Dec. 2020), https://ieeexplore.ieee.org/document/9303670. ("Smart contracts are immutable, verifiable, and autonomous pieces of code that can be deployed and ran on blockchain networks like Ethereum. Due to the immutability nature of blockchain, no change is possible on a deployed smart contract or a verified transaction").

[10] *DeFi: Risk, Regulation, and the Rise of DeCrime*, ELLIPTIC (Nov. 18, 2021), https://www.elliptic.co/resources/defi-risk-regulation-and-the-rise-of-decrime.

[11] https://www.coindesk.com/learn/2021/02/17/what-is-a-flash-loan/.

[12] Sam Reynolds, *Flash Loan Exploit Whips Cream Finance For $130 Million*, BLOCKWORKS (Oct. 28, 2021), https://blockworks.co/flash-loan-exploit-whips-cream-finance-for-130-million/.

3. When stablecoin issuers preclude retail users from redeeming directly, consumers can convert stablecoins into fiat currency by selling the tokens for dollars on exchanges. But as we saw on the day of the hearing—when major crypto exchanges experienced glitches in their price quote systems—exchanges have been prone to outages and malfunction. Please discuss how exchange outages or errors can affect stablecoin markets and stablecoin holders. Are there scenarios involving exchange failures that give rise to particular concern?

Without redemption rights, cryptocurrency exchanges are the only place where retail investors can exchange their stablecoins for U.S. dollars. This introduces additional counterparty risk on behalf of the customer to the exchange. It's an awkward second step not typically present in other kinds of digital payments – you don't need to *also* set up a stock brokerage account in order to send money electronically.

4. Please describe any risks and benefits that you believe are presented by smart contracts. In what contexts, if any, are smart contracts a valuable tool? Could smart contracts create systemic risks? As compared with traditional contracts, are smart contracts useful in consumer or small business contexts?

Smart contracts are immutable – unable to be modified once they are deployed onto a specific blockchain.[9] This makes DeFi platforms that rely on smart contracts particularly vulnerable to hacks and exploits, as platforms need to deploy new smart contracts to fix any bugs in old ones, leaving the platform and its assets at risk of catastrophic losses in the interim. This inherent vulnerability has led to massive losses in DeFi in 2021; a November 2021 report by Elliptic estimated that there were $12 billion total in losses in DeFi from January - November 2021.[10]

So-called "flash loans", which utilize smart contracts,[11] are often employed to hack DeFi protocols (that themselves rely on smart contracts). Flash loans are unsecured loans where capital is borrowed and repaid in a single transaction. As just one example, in October 2021, a flash loan was used to steal $130 million from the DeFi lending platform Cream Finance.[12]

---

[9] Erfan Andesta, Fathiyeh Faghih, and Mahdi Fooladgar, *Testing Smart Contracts Gets Smarter*, IEEE (Dec. 2020), https://ieeexplore.ieee.org/document/9303670. ("Smart contracts are immutable, verifiable, and autonomous pieces of code that can be deployed and ran on blockchain networks like Ethereum. Due to the immutability nature of blockchain, no change is possible on a deployed smart contract or a verified transaction").

[10] *DeFi: Risk, Regulation, and the Rise of DeCrime*, ELLIPTIC (Nov. 18, 2021), https://www.elliptic.co/resources/defi-risk-regulation-and-the-rise-of-decrime.

[11] https://www.coindesk.com/learn/2021/02/17/what-is-a-flash-loan/.

[12] Sam Reynolds, *Flash Loan Exploit Whips Cream Finance For $130 Million*, BLOCKWORKS (Oct. 28, 2021), https://blockworks.co/flash-loan-exploit-whips-cream-finance-for-130-million/.

Smart contracts may have some narrow use cases in finance. However, as in any system designed and run by human beings, the ability to rescind or amend certain transactions has proven useful over time. Whether it means canceling a fraudulent charge on your credit card or staying certain payments in a large firm bankruptcy proceeding, human judgment and discretion is often needed to maintain consumer and investor protection as well as financial stability.

5. Some stablecoin providers and commentators believe that Congress should create a new form of financial institution charter, specifically for stablecoin issuers. In a recently released framework for stablecoin legislation, Senator Toomey has also adopted this view.[1] From your perspective, would a novel stablecoin charter be preferable to requiring firms to follow existing law and conform to the regulatory categories it creates? Could new regulatory carve-outs incentivize regulatory arbitrages or otherwise undermine key existing rules?

It is preferable to mitigate the risks presented by stablecoins with the existing authorities of market and prudential regulators, rather than creating a novel stablecoin charter. The main use for stablecoins is as a waystation in between trades on more volatile crypto assets, and a custom stablecoin charter risks extending the federal safety net to a volatile and speculative asset class while ignoring the many secondary market risks already present.

6. In Senator Toomey's framework, he also suggested that some stablecoin issuers could, "based on their business models," choose to be regulated by "[r]egister[ing] as a money transmitter under the existing state regime and as a money services business under FinCEN's federal regime." Are state money transmitter and federal MSB rules adequate for managing the risks to consumers and the economy created by stablecoins? Please describe the strengths and limitations of these regimes, as applied to stablecoins.

Limiting the oversight of stablecoin issuers to federal MSB rules would present serious challenges, in large part due to the ongoing lack of sufficient funding for IRS enforcement. FinCEN delegates Bank Secrecy Act compliance examinations of virtual currency MSBs to the IRS. This raises challenges as IRS enforcement funding has been cut by 24 percent in inflation-adjusted terms since 2010.[13] This enforcement funding challenge appears to impact the IRS's MSB examinations, as it has only conducted 66 exams of virtual currency MSBs in five years (from 2015-2020), while there are 524 virtual currency entities in the IRS's examination database as of the end of FY 2020.[14] Thus, only some 12.5% of the virtual currency entities under the IRS's examination remit have been examined in the last five years.

---

[13] Chye-Ching Huang, *Depletion of IRS Enforcement Is Undermining the Tax Code*, CENTER ON BUDGET AND POLICY PRIORITIES (Feb. 11, 2020), https://www.cbpp.org/research/federal-tax/depletion-of-irs-enforcement-is-undermining-the-tax-code.

[14] *VIRTUAL CURRENCIES: Additional Information Could Improve Federal Agency Efforts to Counter Human and DrugTrafficking*, GOVERNMENT ACCOUNTABILITY OFFICE (Dec. 2021), https://www.gao.gov/assets/gao-22-105462.pdf at 45.

MSBs also face potentially lighter-touch regulation at the state level for operational and safety and soundness requirements. For example, exam cycles are not uniform and may be less frequent than bank or broker-dealer exams. State regulatory staff tended to be less well-resourced. Finally, state-licensed MSBs are subject to more permissive capital requirements than banks or broker-dealers. For example, in Pennsylvania and Ohio, my cursory review of money transmitter state law shows that each state requires only $500,000 in net worth to obtain the relevant license, in addition to coverage by a surety bond. Even with licenses and bonding in all 50 states, that amount of capital seems insufficient to cover potential losses associated with various risks inherent in stablecoins (ex: speculative use case, funding mismatch inherent in stablecoins' promise of redemption on demand versus investment in illiquid assets, etc).

7. Senator Toomey's framework further proposes that "[c]ommercial entities should be eligible to issue stablecoins, provided they choose one of these regimes [i.e., a bank charter, a special purpose stablecoin charter, or money transmitter and MSB rules]." Please discuss whether, in your view, it would be prudent to allow large, non-financial companies like Amazon or Alphabet to issue stablecoins.

There are a number of risks of large, non-financial firms issuing stablecoins, and there are also risks of such a firm creating cryptocurrency wallets that support other issuers stablecoins, as detailed in Open Markets Institute's November 2021 letter to the financial regulators about the risks of Facebook's Novi pilot.[15] These risks include the potential for predatory pricing, monetization of consumers' private financial data, conflicts of interest, and unchecked concentrations of corporate power. As Open Markets Institute noted in the letter, there are also questions as to the legality of such an offering by a large non-financial company:

> **"There are several legal and regulatory implications for Facebook's pilot that warrant particular attention by the agencies. The stablecoins sold by Facebook to Novi customers may be debt instruments and investment contracts that are 'securities' for purposes of the federal securities laws and thus may be subject to regulation by the Securities and Exchange Commission. In addition, Facebook may be engaged in the business of receiving deposits through Novi because Facebook agrees to hold stablecoins purchased by its customers and to allow those customers to transfer their stablecoins to others. Facebook represents that the stablecoins it sells to customers will maintain a one-for-one parity with the U.S. dollar. Court decisions since Marine Bank v. Weaver, 455 U.S. 551 (1982), establishes that financial offerings like Novi are both "securities" and "deposits" unless they are**

---

[15] *Open Markets Documents Grave Concerns with Facebook's Digital Wallet Pilot Program*, OPEN MARKETS INST. (Nov. 23, 2021), https://www.openmarketsinstitute.org/publications/letter-to-regulators-grave-risks-of-facebook-digital-wallet-pilot.

issued by FDIC-insured depository institutions or foreign banks that are subject to equivalent regulatory regimes.

The Biden administration's recent report on stablecoins noted that 'Relevant authorities, including the Department of Justice, may consider whether or how section 21(a)(2) of the Glass-Steagall Act may apply to certain stablecoin arrangements.' Facebook's Novi is a stablecoin arrangement that appears to provide deposit services (including safekeeping and payments) to its customers. Thus, through Novi, Facebook may be unlawfully engaged in the offering of unregistered securities, and they may also be in the illegal business of receiving deposits without a bank charter."[16]

8. Finally, Senator Toomey's proposal states that "[r]egulation should protect the privacy . . . and confidentiality of individuals using stablecoins." Could creating carve-outs for stablecoins from existing know-your-customer or BSA/AML rules raise national security concerns? If so, how?

There are already national security concerns with the usage of stablecoins on DeFi, as noted in my written testimony:

"Smart contracts on DeFi exchanges typically do not compare the cryptocurrency addresses executing their code against the Specially Designated Nationals and Blocked Persons list ("SDN list"). Stablecoins locked into Ethereum smart contracts could be helping to facilitate various forms of illicit finance, including the swapping of ransomware payments for other crypto assets."[17]

To explicitly carve-out stablecoins from KYC/AML or BSA rules would make existing problems worse, as stablecoin issuers would not be obligated to prevent entities on the sanctions list from redeeming stablecoins. This is concerning, given a February 2022 report by the United Nations which found that North Korean cyber-attacks have stolen millions of dollars worth of cryptocurrency to fund the country's missile programs.[18]

<u>Questions for Ms. Alexis Goldstein, Director of Financial Policy, Open Markets Institute, from Ranking Member Patrick J. Toomey:</u>

---

[16] *Open Markets Documents Letter Re: Facebook's Digital Wallet Pilot Program*, OPEN MARKETS INST. (Nov. 23, 2021), (Nov. 23, 2021), https://static1.squarespace.com/static/5e449c8c3ef68d752f3e70dc/t/619c15925a26166be151cf37/1637619090580/Concerns+with+Facebook's+digital+asset+pilot+project+.pdf.

[17] *Hearing on Stablecoins Before the U.S. Senate Banking Comm.* (2021) (written testimony of Alexis Goldstein), https://www.banking.senate.gov/download/goldstein-testimony-12-14-21.

[18] *North Korea: Missile programme funded through stolen crypto, UN report says*, BBC (Feb. 6, 2022), https://www.bbc.com/news/world-asia-60281129.

1. Ms. Goldstein, your hearing testimony lays out a series of discrete and very narrow hypothetical circumstances under which a stablecoin transfer from the United States to a European country would cost more than a money transfer using Western Union, which is a traditional money transfer service. Your hypothetical makes a number of assumptions that minimize the cost of traditional money transfers. In addition, you do not account for the significant speed advantage offered by stablecoins or the fact that many networks enable such transfers at low or no costs. For example, individuals have the capability to transfer stablecoins on networks like Solana, Stellar, Algorand, or Hedera in less than five seconds, far outpacing traditional means of money transfer. Stablecoins also provide the ability to transfer value to locations outside of Europe, including locations that are more expensive to reach using traditional payment transfer intermediaries. In these cases, stablecoins stand to be tremendously beneficial tools for remittances to family members across the globe.

   a. Do you agree that, under many circumstances, stablecoins could be a faster and less expensive mechanism to transfer value than traditional money transfer services?

For financial services to be effective and efficient for the average consumer, simplicity is essential. Currently, stablecoins are not accepted as legal tender in any nation. Therefore, using stablecoins as a mechanism for payments or remittances requires relying both on the existing rails of the banking system (as is the case with traditional money transfer services) and cryptocurrency exchanges (as is *not* the case with traditional money transfer services). — In other words, individuals seeking to pay for goods or services with stablecoins or individuals seeking to convert a stablecoin remittance into money they can use in the real economy requires relying on multiple intermediaries and taking multiple steps. These extra steps and extra players present added costs and speed disadvantages. I would agree with your premise that stablecoins could be faster and less expensive, but only in the narrow case where a user wanted to remain in the cryptocurrency ecosystem and not convert back to fiat.

As noted by the President's Working Group's (joined by the FDIC and OCC, shorthanded here as "PWG") report on stablecoins, stablecoins "play a central role in facilitating trading, lending, and borrowing activity in DeFi."[19] In contrast, PWG report discussed stablecoins' use of payments in a hypothetical, future use case. Even the network monopoly Facebook couldn't make stablecoins work as payments, as evidenced by the Diem consortium recently selling off its assets.[20]

---

[19] *Report on Stable Coins*, PRESIDENT'S WORKING GROUP ON FIN. MARKETS, THE FED. DEPOSIT INS. CORP. (FDIC), AND THE OFFICE OF THE COMPTROLLER OF THE CURRENCY (OCC) (2021), https://home.treasury.gov/system/files/136/StableCoinReport_Nov1_508.pdf.

[20] Olga Kharif, *Meta-Backed Diem Association Confirms Asset Sale to Silvergate*, BLOOMBERG (Jan. 31, 2022), https://www.bloomberg.com/news/articles/2022-01-31/meta-backed-diem-association-confirms-asset-sale-to-silvergate.

Some confusion over the costs and speeds identified in my testimony also stem from a distorted reality of how stablecoin transfers work in practice.

Ethereum is the dominant blockchain for stablecoin adoption. Ethereum's ERC-20 token standard is the only standard that is supported natively by *all* the top 5 stablecoins[21] by market cap;[22] hence it enables an apples to apples comparison, and was the reason why I used this example in my testimony. In addition, Ethereum's ERC-20 token standard is the only blockchain that *all* major exchanges support for stablecoins, again, which is why I used this example in my testimony.

For example, while FTX supports Solana's SPL token standard for stablecoins, Coinbase and Kraken do *not* support the SPL standard.[23] While Binance supports both the Binance Chain or the Binance Smart Chain BEP-20 and BEP-2 token standards, Coinbase, Kraken, and FTX do *not* support BEP-20 or BEP-2.[24] Neither the Coinbase, Kraken, FTX.us nor Binance.us (nor the non-U.S. Binance.com[25]) exchanges appear to support trading

---

[21] *How It Works,* TETHER, https://tether.to/en/how-it-works. ("Tether tokens exist as digital tokens built on various blockchains including Algorand, Ethereum, EOS, Liquid Network, Omni, Tron, Bitcoin Cash's Standard Ledger Protocol, and Solana."); *USDC: the world's leading digital dollar stablecoin,* CIRCLE, https://www.circle.com/en/usdc#:~:text=What%20blockchains%20support%20USDC%3F,Stellar%20as%20a%20native%20asset. ("USDC is available natively as Ethereum ERC-20, Algorand ASA, Solana SPL token, Stellar asset, TRON TRC-20, Hedera token, and Avalanche ERC-20."); *Why does Paxos use Ethereum?,* PAXOS, https://paxos.com/2019/03/03/why-does-paxos-standard-use-ethereum/, accessed February 6, 2022. ("Paxos stablecoins follow the ERC-20 protocol, which is a standard for smart contracts on the Ethereum blockchain. The ERC-20 standard specifies a set of standard functions to manage transactions and track account balances...Please note: In order to send and receive USDP, or BUSD, customers must have an Ethereum wallet that accepts ERC-20 tokens."); *Dai 1.0,* MAKERDAO, https://developer.makerdao.com/dai/1/. ("Dai 1.0 (beta) is a stable coin implemented as an ERC20 token on the Ethereum blockchain."); *TerraUSD (UST),* COINBASE, https://help.coinbase.com/en/coinbase/getting-started/crypto-education/ust. ("UST is hosted on the Ethereum blockchain."); Do Kwon, *Announcing TerraUSD (UST)— the Interchain Stablecoin,* MEDIUM (Sep. 21, 2020) https://medium.com/terra-money/announcing-terrausd-ust-the-interchain-stablecoin-53eab0f8f0ac. ("A few weeks ago, we launched TerraUSD (UST) with Bittrex Global, and announced plans to take it interchain to every major blockchain, starting with Ethereum and Solana.").

[22] https://coinmarketcap.com/view/stablecoin/, accessed February 6, 2022. Top five stablecoins by market cap were: Tether, USDC, BUSD, TerraUSD, and DAI

[23] https://support.kraken.com/hc/en-us/articles/360000678446-Cryptocurrencies-available-on-Kraken

[24] Coinbase, Does Coinbase support Binance Chain (BEP-2)?, https://help.coinbase.com/en/coinbase/trading-and-funding/sending-or-receiving-cryptocurrency/does-coinbase-support-binance-chain--bep-2–. ("Coinbase does not currently support Binance Chain (BEP-2) because it is a separate blockchain that is not integrated with our platform."); Kraken, Does Kraken support Binance Chain (BEP20/BEP2 tokens)?, https://support.kraken.com/hc/en-us/articles/360049417272-Does-Kraken-support-Binance-Chain-BEP20-BEP2-tokens- ("At this time Kraken does not support Binance Chain (BNB) or the Binance Smart Chain (BSC) (BEP20/BEP2 Tokens). BEP20/BEP2 tokens deposited to any Kraken address will not be credited and will result in the loss of your deposit."); FTX.us https://help.ftx.us/hc/en-us/articles/360043065054-Crypto-Deposits-and-Withdrawals ("USDT can be deposited or withdrawn as either OMNI, ERC20, TRC20, SPL."). All accessed February 6, 2022.

[25] *How to choose a network?,* BINANCE.COM, https://www.binance.com/en/support/faq/85a1c394ac1d489fb0bfac0ef2fceafd. ("BEP2 refers to the Binance Chain. Its native cryptocurrency is BNB. BEP20 refers to the Binance Smart Chain (BSC). Binance Smart Chain is a decentralized blockchain, its native cryptocurrency is BNB. ERC20 refers to the

stablecoins running on the Algorand, Hedera, or Stellar networks. Coinbase's separate Coinbase Wallet does support Stellar, but it appears to do so only via Steallar's native token XLM.[26] The counterexamples to my testimony cited in the hearing failed to account for these differences and elided over key nuances.

Some of the non-dominant blockchains mentioned above have additional challenges of stability, cybersecurity, and difficulty of access for those whose internet access is limited to smartphones. Solana has experienced 6 outages in January 2022 alone,[27] and recently, the most significant bridge between the Solana and Ethereum blockchain, Wormhole, was exploited and over $320 million was stolen.[28] Until recently, many Solana wallets were not available as native devices on mobile phones, a predominant means of accessing the internet for many households in need of remittances. For example, the Solana wallet. Phantom, launched an iPhone app on January 31, 2022.[29] Android is promised soon but not currently available; fake Android versions of Phantom aimed at stealing users' funds do exist, leading Phantom to dedicate a warning to these fake Android apps in their help pages.[30]

There are also additional risks with sending stablecoins through crypto exchanges, such as sending stablecoins to the incorrect wallet address, which renders funds unrecoverable.[31] Traditional money transfer services, in contrast, are subject to Regulation E rights around cancellation and refunds in the event of erroneous transfers.

Traditional money services can certainly use improving; the expense of remittances is something that Dodd-Frank attempted to address and which policymakers should continue to pursue. Research by the World Economic Forum on stablecoins, however, has shown it

---

Ethereum network. Its native cryptocurrency is ETH. TRC20 refers to the TRON network. EOS refers to the Enterprise Operation System network. BTC refers to the Bitcoin network....Please make sure that the selected network is the same as the network of the platform you are withdrawing funds from or depositing funds to. If you select the wrong network, you will lose your funds.").

[26] *Supported Assets and Networks*, COINBASE, https://help.coinbase.com/en/wallet/getting-started/what-types-of-crypto-does-wallet-support ("Coinbase Wallet supports the Ethereum, Polygon, Bitcoin, Dogecoin, Litecoin, Stellar Lumens, and Ripple network.").

[27] Mily Nicolle and Bloomberg, *Once billed as a rising star in crypto, Solana's sixth outage this month—and founder's 'lol' tweet—frustrates traders*, FORTUNE (Jan. 25, 2022), https://fortune.com/2022/01/25/solana-founder-anatoly-yakovenko-crypto-crash-blockchain-instability/.

[28] Olga Kharif and Yueqi Yan, *DeFi Project Known as Wormhole Hit With a Potential $320 Million Hack*, BLOOMBERG (Feb. 2, 2022), https://www.bloomberg.com/news/articles/2022-02-02/blockchain-bridge-wormhole-hit-with-potential-315-million-hack.

[29] Phantom (@phantom) TWITTER (Jan. 31, 2022, 9:34 AM), https://twitter.com/phantom/status/1488158676363845632 ("Phantom for iPhone is finally here! Everything you can do on desktop, now in your pocket.")

[30] https://help.phantom.app/hc/en-us/articles/4406705592339-Is-Phantom-available-on-mobile-iOS-or-Android- ("Phantom is NOT available on Android! Using a fake Phantom mobile app will result in your funds being stolen. Please help us by reporting these apps when you see them.")

[31] "FTX.US is not responsible if you send deposits or withdrawals to an incorrect address. If you are withdrawing from FTX.US to an incorrect address, there is likely nothing FTX.US can do to recover the tokens. If you deposit to an incorrect FTX.US address, we can attempt to recover it, but will charge at least $500 or 5% to do so." https://help.ftx.us/hc/en-us/articles/360043065054-Crypto-Deposits-and-Withdrawals.

to lack financial inclusion benefits due to barriers that include the need for internet connectivity, the need to open an account with a cryptocurrency exchange to obtain stablecoins, and the lack of acceptance with merchants (the WEF also cited a lack of options for small business loans, due to high fees and the requirements that loans be over-collateralized).[32]

The proliferation of blockchains, bridges, cryptocurrency exchanges, and stablecoins makes it very difficult to comparison shop across crypto payments systems or against traditional money transfers. The example in my testimony was a good faith effort to provide the Committee with a real world apples-to-apples comparison. I would welcome the opportunity to discuss this more with you or your staff.

Questions for Ms. Alexis Goldstein, Director of Financial Policy, Open Markets Institute, from Senator Robert Menendez:

1. White supremacy is an existential threat for our country. According to the Department of Homeland Security, domestic violent extremism is now the greatest terrorism threat to the U.S., and cryptocurrency is being used to fund these domestic terrorists.

    a. Is there any way to know how much funding white supremacists groups receive in cryptocurrency?

Following the transfers of assets is challenging in the cryptocurrency environment, given the prevalence of self-hosted cryptocurrency wallets identified only through pseudonymous cryptocurrency addresses (in Ethereum, for example, these are a 42-character hexadecimal string beginning with "0x"[33]). The lack of Know Your Customer (KYC) checks at most self-hosted wallet providers, and the lack of KYC throughout the decentralized finance ("DeFi") ecosystem makes any sort of analysis of cryptocurrency asset movements extremely challenging.

According to the Southern Poverty Law Center, it is more difficult now to track these hate groups and domestic terrorists because of their use of digital currencies.

    b. Is it in regulators and Congress' best interest to act and curb terrorist use of cryptocurrency?

---

[32] *What is the Value Proposition of Stablecoins for Financial Inclusion?*, WORLD ECONOMIC FORUMS (NOV. 2021), https://www3.weforum.org/docs/WEF_Value_Proposition_of_Stablecoins_for_Financial_Inclusion_2021.pdf.

[33] *What is an Ethereum Address?*, ETHERSCAN, https://info.etherscan.com/what-is-an-ethereum-address/#:~:text=An%20Ethereum%20address%20is%20a,with%200x%20appended%20in%20front.

Yes. For example, a February 2022 report by the United Nations found that North Korean cyber-attacks have stolen millions of dollars worth of cryptocurrency to fund the country's missile programs.[34] Chainalysis found that North Korean-linked hacks extracted nearly $400 million worth of digital assets in 2021, and that the value of North Korea-linked hacks grew by 40% from 2020 to 2021.[35] In addition, FinCEN recently identified in an October report that there were $590 million of ransomware reports in the first 6 months of 2021, more than all of 2020 combined. They also identified approximately $5.2 billion in outgoing BTC transactions potentially tied to ransomware payments.[36]

2. Despite key differences on a financial level, stablecoins are still cryptocurrencies just like any other when it comes to their increasingly widespread use in criminal activities thanks to the anonymity they offer. As stablecoins become more broadly used both as a payment method and as an investment vehicle, Congress and the financial regulators need to address the elements of the cryptocurrencies that make them attractive for illicit uses, including money laundering, fraud, cyberterrorism, and sanctions evasion.

   a. Does the anonymity offered by stablecoins and other cryptocurrencies make them more appealing for criminal use?

Yes. Please refer to the answer to question 2(c) below.

As Chairman of the Foreign Relations Committee, I'm particularly concerned about Venezuela, Russia, Iran, and other countries that develop, mine, or use digital currencies to evade sanctions, weakening one of our most effective foreign policy tools.

   b. How can Congress and financial regulators minimize the ability of bad actors to use stablecoins or other cryptocurrencies to evade sanctions?

In October guidance, Treasury's Office of Foreign Assets Control made it clear that all cryptocurrency market actors, including "exchangers, administrators, miners, wallet providers, and users" all play "an increasingly critical role in preventing sanctioned persons from exploiting virtual currencies to evade sanctions and undermine U.S. foreign

---

[34] *North Korea: Missile programme funded through stolen crypto, UN report says*, BBC (Feb. 6, 2022), https://www.bbc.com/news/world-asia-60281129.

[35] *North Korean Hackers Have Prolific Year as Their Unlaundered Cryptocurrency Holdings Reach All-time High*, CHAINALYSIS (Jan. 13, 2022), https://blog.chainalysis.com/reports/north-korean-hackers-have-prolific-year-as-their-total-unlaundered-cryptocurrency-holdings-reach-all-time-high/.

[36] *FinCEN Issues Report on Ransomware Trends in Bank Secrecy Act Data*, FINCEN (Oct. 15, 2021), https://www.fincen.gov/news/news-releases/fincen-issues-report-ransomware-trends-bank-secrecy-act-data.

policy and national security interests."[37] Compliance with this October guidance may face challenges, given past resistance from the cryptocurrency industry to Marathon Digital creating a sanctions-compliant mining pool.[38] The Treasury Department should work to ensure they take enforcement actions against those out of compliance with the October virtual currency guidance.

c. In general, what challenges do we face in trying to crack down on the use of cryptocurrency for illicit purposes?

As identified by the compliance firm Elliptic in a November 2021 report,[39] and by FinCEN in an October report,[40] those using cryptocurrencies for illicit finance have a range of tools available in order to hide their assets. These include "tumblers" and "mixers" (like Tornado Cash,[41] which is being used to launder the $15 million in Ether stolen from Crypto.com[42]) meant to obscure and hide cryptocurrency transfers from law enforcement, the use of DeFi to convert ransomware payments to other cryptocurrencies, and so-called "Layer 2" solutions which lack the transaction transparency of Layer 1 blockchains.[43] The lack of Know your Customer, Anti-Money Laundering and Countering the Financing of Terrorism compliance across DeFi, which has some $230 billion in assets,[44] is a particular challenge for countering illicit finance. In addition, cryptocurrency exchanges with insufficient KYC/AML controls are another challenge. In November, the Justice Department arrested two foreign nationals charged with deploying Sodinokibi/REvil ransomware to attack businesses and government entities in the United States.[45] The DOJ

---

[37] *Sanctions Compliance Guidance for the Virtual Currency Industry (Brochure)*, OFFICE OF FOREIGN ASSETS CONTROL (Oct. 2021), https://home.treasury.gov/system/files/126/virtual_currency_guidance_brochure.pdf.

[38] Kollen Post, *FinCEN Issues Report on Ransomware Trends in Bank Secrecy Act Data*, THE BLOCK (Jun. 2, 2021) https://www.theblockcrypto.com/linked/106865/marathon-ofac-bitcoin-mining-pool-taproot.

[39] *DeFi: Risk, Regulation, and the Rise of DeCrime*, ELLIPTIC (Nov. 18, 2021), https://www.elliptic.co/resources/defi-risk-regulation-and-the-rise-of-decrime.

[40] *FinCEN Issues Report on Ransomware Trends in Bank Secrecy Act Data*, FINCEN (Oct. 15, 2021), https://www.fincen.gov/news/news-releases/fincen-issues-report-ransomware-trends-bank-secrecy-act-data.

[41] https://tornado.cash.

[42] Sam Reynolds, *Crypto.com's Stolen Ether Being Mixed Through Tornado Cash*, COIN DESK (Jan. 18, 2022), https://www.coindesk.com/business/2022/01/18/cryptocoms-stolen-ether-being-laundered-via-tornado-cash/.

[43] Harry Halpin and Ania Piotrowska, *Achieving Network Privacy in Bitcoin: VPNs and Tor Help, But Mixnets Are Needed*, BITCOIN MAGAZINE (Jan. 20, 2022), https://bitcoinmagazine.com/technical/why-mixnets-are-needed-to-make-bitcoin-private.

[44] *DeFi Total Value Locked Hits All-Time High of $236 Billion*, BLOOMBERG/PR NEWSWIRE (Nov. 1, 2021), https://www.bloomberg.com/press-releases/2021-11-01/defi-total-value-locked-hits-all-time-high-of-236-billion.

[45] *Ukrainian Arrested and Charged with Ransomware Attack on Kaseya*, DEPARTMENT OF JUSTICE (Nov. 8, 2021), https://www.justice.gov/opa/pr/ukrainian-arrested-and-charged-ransomware-attack-kaseya.

issued a warrant to seize up to $13 million in funds stored on the cryptocurrency exchange FTX by one of the alleged ransomware attackers.[46]

3. Cryptocurrency certainly has the potential to broaden access to investments and financial services, but I'm worried that some crypto exchanges seem to be adopting some of the same measures seen in traditional banks that raise the barrier of entry.

    a. Isn't it true that newer users with the least assets often pay disproportionately high fees to access crypto services?

Yes. For example, Coinbase has two cryptocurrency exchange platforms: Coinbase, and Coinbase Pro. Coinbase is aimed at newer users — but charges astronomically higher fees than its Coinbase Pro offering: it costs $0.99 to purchase $5 worth of Bitcoin or the stablecoin Tether (USDT) on Coinbase, but only approximately $0.02 to do so on Coinbase Pro.[47] Another example is that users with smaller amounts to invest may face higher fees than they could overcome with trading returns or interest income. The crypto borrowing and lending platform Aave, which allows users to deposit crypto assets and earn rewards, and use their crypto as collateral for borrowing, is explicit about this in its FAQ, writing "You can deposit any amount you want, there is no minimum or maximum limit. Still, it's important to take into account that for really low amounts it is possible that the transaction cost of the process is higher than the expected earnings. It is recommended that you consider this when depositing very low amounts".[48]

---

[46] *Warrant to Seize Property Subject to Forfeiture*, DEPARTMENT OF JUSTICE (Sep. 10, 2021) https://www.justice.gov/opa/press-release/file/1447131/download ("In the matter of seizure...all funds up to $13 million in the FTX Trading Limited account")

[47] The precise fee schedule for Coinbase is vague and undisclosed. The Coinbase website states "Fees are calculated at the time you place your order and may be determined by a combination of factors including the selected payment method, the size of the order, and market conditions such as volatility and liquidity." https://help.coinbase.com/en/coinbase/trading-and-funding/pricing-and-fees/fees. By contrast, the precise fee schedule for Coinbase Pro is documented, but the fee depends on if the user is a Maker or a Taker of liquidity, and what the users' "fee tier" is; users that do larger volumes receive lower fees. The maximum fee on Coinbase Pro appears to be 0.50%. The maximum fee on Coinbase is far higher. https://help.coinbase.com/en/pro/trading-and-funding/trading-rules-and-fees/fees.

[48] Aave FAQ, *Is there a minimum or maximum amount to deposit?*, AAVE, https://docs.aave.com/faq/depositing-and-earning.

Screenshot from Coinbase app

b. Won't high fees for new users and traders with fewer assets keep many Americans from making use of these cryptocurrencies?

Yes. To elaborate, the Ethereum blockchain remains the dominant blockchain for DeFi, with an estimated 70% of all DeFi activity, according to an analysis by JPMorgan.[49] As many reports[50] have made clear, the Ethereum blockchain faces challenges of scalability, congestion, and extremely high fees.[51] The mean Ethereum transaction fee was $33.23 on February 5, 2022, and $56.45 on November 11, 2021.[52] Fees to merely transfer a crypto asset from one wallet to another were an estimated $22 on February 6, 2022, and were as high as $54 on November 11, 2021.[53]

---

[49] Joanna Ossinger, *JPMorgan Team Suggests Crypto's DeFi Boom Slower Than It Seems*, BLOOMBERG (Nov. 12, 2021), https://www.bloomberg.com/news/articles/2021-11-12/jpmorgan-team-suggests-crypto-s-defi-boom-slower-than-it-seems. ("The Ethereum network now has about a 70% share of DeFi activity, versus a near-total lock at the start of the year, the team added.")

[50] Jeff Benson, *War Over Ethereum Gas Fees and Usability Continues*, DECRYPT (Nov. 22, 2021), https://decrypt.co/86640/war-ethereum-gas-fees-usability-continues.

[51] Will Gottsegen, Ethereum's Fees Are Too Damn High, Coin Desk (Nov. 22, 2021), https://www.coindesk.com/tech/2021/11/22/ethereums-fees-are-too-damn-high/.

[52] Glassnode, Ethereum: Mean Transaction Fees [USD], https://studio.glassnode.com/metrics?a=ETH&c=usd&category=&m=fees.VolumeMean&s=1616752632&u=1644105600&zoom=, last accessed February 6, 2022 at 7:00 PM.

[53] Ethereum Gas Tracker, ETHERSCAN, https://etherscan.io/gastracker (visited Nov. 11, 2021, 6:00 PM and February 6, 2022 7:00 PM).

The problem is bad enough that some DeFi platforms acknowledge the high fees in their FAQs, as Aave does (discussed in the answer to 3(a) above).

This is the same paradigm we see in traditional banks. A recent report from the CFPB showed that in 2019 banks collected $15.47 billion in overdraft fees, which overwhelmingly affect the lowest-income Americans. If stablecoins are going to fulfill the promise of democratizing finance, they need to be accessible to everyone.

a. What changes should be made to ensure cryptocurrency is more accessible to smaller investors?

Exchanges like Coinbase could consider extending the lower fees it charges to its Coinbase Pro customers (noted in the answer to question 3b) to the users of the Coinbase platform.

However, a better policy option would be for Congress and the relevant regulatory agencies to examine methods to extend banking services to unbanked and underbanked households, continue work on reducing the cost of remittances and otherwise enable broadband access to allow users to connect to banking services cheaply and efficiently.

Responses to Written Questions of Senator Toomey from Jai Massari

Q.1. Ms. Massari, during your testimony you encouraged Congress to consider an optional Federal charter specific to stablecoin issuers. Specifically, you said that a "new and well-designed Federal charter could accommodate a business model premised on the issuance of stablecoins fully backed by short-term, liquid assets and the provision of related payments services. This charter could impose requirements for reserve asset composition while tailoring leverage ratios or risk-based capital requirements and other requirements to the nature of the business model. And it could restrict the stablecoin issuer from engaging in riskier activities, to minimize other claims on reserve assets. This option would likely be welcomed by many stablecoin issuers even though it would entail comprehensive Federal oversight."

How should a new charter designed for stablecoin issuers differ from existing bank charters at the State or Federal level?

A.1. The purpose of a new type of charter would be to accommodate the different business model of true stablecoin issuers from the business model of banks. As discussed in my testimony, banks engage in maturity transformation and liquidity transformation because they have short-term demand liabilities—that is, demand deposits—and are able to hold long-term loans and other illiquid and risky assets—for example, 30-year nonconforming mortgages, credit card loans, and real estate used as business premises. These activities are important to U.S. consumers, businesses, and the U.S. economy.

Accordingly, U.S. banking regulations have been developed to ensure that banks can execute their business model in a safe and sound manner. For example, banks are subject to leverage and risk-based capital ratios that are calibrated based on the assumption that a majority of their assets are relatively illiquid and riskier than cash and genuine cash equivalents. Deposit insurance requirements and lender-of-last resort facilities are designed to address the risk of bank runs that can occur when depositors lose confidence that their banks are able to convert their illiquid assets to cash fast enough to satisfy withdrawal requests.

True stablecoin issuers,[183] on the other hand, should not meaningfully engage in maturity or liquidity transformation in connection with their stablecoin activities. Their obligation to redeem the stablecoins they issue should be at least 100 percent backed by cash and cash equivalents. The stablecoin business, rather than generating returns from long-term lending and investments, is instead focused on payment services. Indeed, it is the potential for stablecoin systems to operate as retail payments systems at scale that has raised concerns among U.S. financial regulators, as reflected in the PWG report.[184]

A Federal charter for stablecoin issuers should be designed to address the business model of true stablecoin issuers and the characteristics of true stablecoins and the risks arising from the issuer's activities—which, in the case of credit, liquidity, and price risks, are substantially less than the same risks arising from maturity and liquidity transformation. Regulation of true stablecoin issuers should include restrictions on permissible types of stablecoin reserve assets to cash and genuine cash equivalents, auditing and transparency standards, obligations to address illicit financing and sanctions considerations, and requirements to address traditional and novel operational risks. In addition, permitting stablecoin issuers to be members of the Federal Reserve System with Federal Reserve master accounts would provide the

---

[183] I describe the characteristics of "true stablecoins" in more detail in my written testimony.

[184] President's Working Group on Financial Markets, the Federal Deposit Insurance Corporation, and the Office of the Comptroller of the Currency, Report on Stablecoins (Nov. 2021) 15, *https://home.treasury.gov/system/files/136/StableCoinReport-Nov1-508.pdf* (noting that "prudential concerns relate to the potential for stablecoin runs, payment system risks, and the possibility that some stablecoins may rapidly scale").

Federal Reserve with regulatory authority over those issuers. A new Federal charter should tailor existing leverage ratios to the business model of true stablecoin issuers. The current leverage ratios applicable to banks engaged in maturity or liquidity transformation are excessive, unnecessary, and unworkable when applied to true stablecoin issuers whose obligations to redeem their stablecoins are at least 100 percent backed by cash and cash equivalents. Likewise, a requirement that federally chartered stablecoin issuers obtain deposit insurance is not needed because a properly designed reserve requirement is an alternative to Federal deposit insurance, as recognized by leading economists since at least the 1930s.[185]

Responses to Written Questions of Senator Sinema from Jai Massari

Q.1. In recent years, digital assets have become increasingly popular holdings for publicly traded standards. Currently, the generally accepted accounting principles (GAAP) set by the Financial Accounting Standards Board use an intangible assets model for accounting digital assets. What potential issues, if any, may arise from using an intangible assets model to assess stablecoin holdings?

A.1. As you note, how digital assets, including stablecoins, are treated from an accounting perspective is an important issue. I am not an accounting expert and, therefore, I cannot provide input on the specifics of GAAP or the precise issues associated with any particular accounting method. Based on my experience as a legal practitioner, however, I believe it would be helpful for GAAP standard setters to evaluate whether differences in treatment between digital assets and other types of financial assets make sense, particularly in light of increasing corporate holdings of digital assets.

---

[185] See, e.g., Paul H. Douglas et al., "A Program for Monetary Reform", (1939) (outlining the Chicago Plan), *https://www.monetary.org/pdfs/a-program-for-monetary-reform.pdf*; Milton Friedman, "A Program for Monetary Stability", (*Fordham Univ. Press* 1992); Ronnie J. Phillips, "The 'Chicago Plan' and New Deal Banking Reform", Working Paper No. 76 (June 1992), *https://www.levyinstitute.org/pubs/wp/76.pdf*; Jaromir Benes and Michael Kumhof, "The Chicago Plan Revisited", IMF Working Paper (2012), *https://www.imf.org/external/pubs/ft/wp/2012/wp12202.pdf*; see also Davis Polk & Wardwell LLP, "U.S. Regulators Speak on Stablecoin and Crypto Regulation", (Nov. 12, 2021), at n. 12–13 and accompanying text, *https:// www.davispolk.com/insights/client-update/us-regulators-speak-stablecoin-and-crypto-regulation.*

Q.2. If a new model of accounting is designed for digital assets, should stablecoins be treated similarly to other cryptocurrencies?

A.2. I am not an accounting expert and therefore cannot speak to the appropriate accounting treatment of digital assets generally or stablecoins specifically. Based on my experience as a legal practitioner focused on U.S. financial regulation, however, I observe that different types of digital assets have different economic and legal characteristics. Viewing all digital assets as the same—either for legal or accounting purposes—merely because they are recorded and transferred on a blockchain seems inconsistent with the approach we take for other types of assets. Therefore, as should be the case with the legal classification of these assets, the accounting treatment of digital assets should be based upon the economic characteristics of the digital asset.

Q.3. How can the GAAP accurately account for stablecoin issuers' holdings with awareness of holdings for the purpose of stablecoin backing?

A.3. I am not an accounting expert and therefore cannot comment on the GAAP treatment of stablecoins. However, as a matter of consumer protection more broadly, I think it is critically important that stablecoin holders have clear and accurate information about stablecoin reserve composition.

Responses to Written Questions of Chairman Brown from Dante Disparte

Q.1. At the hearing, I asked whether Circle would continue to allow USDC to be used to facilitate cryptocurrency speculation if Circle received a bank charter. To be clear, if Circle received a bank charter, would it place any limitations on how USDC could be used in DeFi markets? If so, please describe such limitations.

A.1. As the sole issuer of USDC, Circle supports its broad adoption to enable U.S. dollars to exist in digital form on the internet. We will continue to support digital dollars on the internet as a medium of exchange, a store of value, and a unit of account, whether we receive a national bank charter or not.

Respectfully, Circle does not "allow USDC to be used to facilitate cryptocurrency speculation," any more than the United States Mint or a United States bank "allows" U.S. currency to be used to speculate on gold or individual stocks. The use of USDC for investments and digital asset capital markets activities still only confers the USDC holder with something denominated and pegged to a dollar. Put another way, USDC has the same use cases as a U.S. dollar, and because Circle is regulated by the appropriate authorities, we have the same relationship with USDC users as banks have with people and institutions that use U.S. dollars.

Circle does restrict its customers to institutions that comply with and satisfy the company's Know Your Customer (KYC) requirements and are not on sanctions lists, such as the U.S. Department of the Treasury Office of Foreign Assets Control (OFAC) list. Broadly speaking, if a USDC user breaks the law or violates applicable regulations, Circle will follow appropriate measures, including applicable financial crime compliance steps in collaboration with law enforcement.

We believe becoming a full-reserve national digital currency bank will enable frictionless, instant, and nearly free payments of U.S. digital dollars on open, permissionless blockchains. We believe a digital bank will create a safer and more resilient financial system. It will also build on open networks to support new forms of capital formation and intermediation. Traditional capital formation through today's banking system, including the borrowing and lending of money, is expensive, inefficient, and exclusive. Lending money to banks for most individuals yields near-zero interest returns. At today's inflation rate, individual depositors are losing approximately 7 percent of their wealth every year. We can do better. Digital dollars can increase global prosperity and economic freedom. New forms of digital asset capital market activities offer a less expensive, more prosperous, faster, and more inclusive alternative.

Q.2. In response to my question about limiting the use of USDC in DeFi, you noted that "Circle's counterparties, as a company, are other institutions and companies," and that "[w]e don't face the retail market as a retail payment system." You also said that the "advent of a whole host of internet-native capital markets, payments, and an always-on economy that is built around these innovations in public blockchains is important."

You emphasized in your testimony as well that USDC has important applications in strengthening financial inclusion, and could even be used in humanitarian contexts.

How can Circle ensure that USDC benefits consumers if its counterparties are institutions and companies, whose practices with respect to the retail market may undermine financial inclusion, and consumer and investor protection? Can Circle advance its goals if the policies and practices that govern how consumers use USDC are determined by other institutions?

A.2. Circle promotes responsible financial service innovation in the growing digital asset market. USDC provides an important component of a robust and interoperable payment system, fostering financial inclusion and competition, which in turn helps reduce costs for financial success. Circle strongly believes that institutions and companies, including Circle, must be committed to financial inclusion. That is why we have announced our Circle Impact initiative, and why we are deliberately focusing on where we can apply USDC to humanitarian use cases, such as our collaborative efforts to support doctors in Venezuela, among other efforts.

Moreover, for the reasons provided in response to Senator Brown's first question, Circle believes we are able to advance our goals notwithstanding counterparties who might not share Circle's commitment to financial inclusion and investor protection. There are two reasons for this: first, the very nature of USDC fosters increased financial inclusion and investor protection, for all the reasons previously identified. Second, the fact that other intermediaries might have policies or practices that are inconsistent with inclusion and consumer protection is not the fault of USDC itself. Once again, the proper analogy is to U.S. dollars: a company that transacts exclusively in U.S. dollars, but does bad things, does not implicate the dollar itself—it is that company and its policies that are to blame, not the currency in which it transacts business. The existence and increasing prevalence of companies with similar goals and compliance protocols as Circle will help strengthen financial inclusion, and reduce the risk to consumers and investors.

Q.3. Further, once USDC has been issued to a Circle institutional customer, is Circle deprived of control of the token? Could it regulate how that entity uses USDC, or regulate services the entity offers retail customers that employ USDC? If so, how?

A.3. Congress has the authority to prohibit certain activities, and regulators have the obligation to enforce the law. Users and issuers of stablecoins like USDC have the obligation to comply with the law. The issuer of a stablecoin should not use its position to either make law or regulate otherwise lawful conduct of a stablecoin user. Circle does not intend to use its position as issuer of USDC to control lawful use cases of USDC.

Circle's institutional customers make USDC available to their respective markets. Circle partners only with those institutions that comply with and satisfy Circle's KYC requirements and are not on sanctions lists, such as the OFAC list. Circle also verifies the identity all of its customers pursuant to the company's Anti-Money Laundering (AML)/Counter Terrorist Financing (CTF) and Sanctions Program in compliance with regulatory requirements and expectations, including but not limited to the Bank Secrecy Act (BSA). Circle has the ability to take action to freeze or seize USDC on its platform. That represents the first line of defense and the first line of control. Circle also works in accordance with its licensing and other regulatory requirements to support the safe and sound use of USDC on the blockchains that it supports. Similarly, once a USDC token is redeemed, Circle and law enforcement have a line of sight into whether illegal activity has taken place.

Additionally, the Centre Consortium has the ability to block individual blockchain addresses from sending and receiving USDC. Examples of such a scenario in which Centre would take action include to comply with applicable law, regulation, or court order, or a threat to the USDC network. Circle does not exercise control over USDC blocking.

Finally, a virtual asset service provider (VASP), digital wallet, bank or another intermediary, whether or not they are a Circle customer, also has the ability, and at times the duty, to freeze transactions or tokens, subject to their respective regulatory, legal, and compliance requirements.

Responses to Written Questions of Senator Toomey from Dante Disparte

Q.1. Mr. Disparte, as you and I discussed at the hearing, I am concerned about the misleading assertion that stablecoins are only used to facilitate lending, borrowing, and trading of other digital assets, and that stablecoins are not used to make payments for real-world goods and services. Contrary to this claim, your testimony noted that the stablecoin USDC is increasingly being leveraged by major credit card companies, small businesses, remittance companies, and others as a settlement option for their businesses. Could you provide data and/or examples regarding the extent to which USDC is being used for payments (including cross-border payments) and remittances?

A.1. Trusted digital currencies like USDC and blockchain-based financial services are building bridges between internet-native applications and real-world financial use cases and transactions. None is more important for financial inclusion than peer-to-peer remittances, which cumulatively in prepandemic times amounted to more than $700 billion a year. Circle is working to address inefficiencies that have plagued traditional remittance transfers, such as slow delivery and high fees for sending money across borders. Examples of Circle's work in this area include:

- Partnering with MoneyGram International, one of the world's largest money transfer companies, to enable USDC-denominated remittances on the Stellar blockchain and facilitate cross-border payments for millions of customers worldwide. With the global reach of MoneyGram's services and the speed and low cost of transactions on Stellar, people can convert their cash into and out of USDC, giving them access to fast and affordable digital asset services that may have previously been out of reach.
- Leveraging Circle's payments infrastructure and USDC, Bitso, the largest cryptocurrency exchange platform in Latin America with more than 3 million users, launched an initiative to make it easier, faster and more secure for Mexican residents to send and receive cross-border payments to or from the U.S. In 2020, remittances increased nearly 10 percent to over $40 billion. Remittances continued to increase in 2021, largely attributed to the growth of migrant labor in the United States.
- Helping the legitimate, elected Government of Venezuela distribute millions of dollars of desperately needed aid to the Nation's frontline medical workers as they battled coronavirus under horrendous conditions. Circle partnered with the Bolivarian Republic of Venezuela (led by President-elect Juan Guaido), U.S.-based fintech Airtm, and the U.S. Government to send the relief funds. The joint initiative established a disbursement pipeline that leveraged USDC to bypass the controls that Nicolas Maduro's authoritarian Government placed on Venezuela's financial system.

Additional examples of how Circle is powering USDC to facilitate payments include:

- Working in concert with Clothia, Visa, and Crypto.com, Circle is making it easier for a clothing marketplace to pay designers globally. Traditional cross-border payments are complex, costly and can take a long time to process. Clothia, a U.S.-based, curated marketplace that showcases the best up-and-coming fashion designers from around the world-managing operations and distribution so their designers can focus on design, artistic expression, and manufacturing. The company currently represents 140+ designers in 24 countries. Given their global business model, Clothia must make timely payments to designers around the world. Clothia chose Circle, USDC, Visa, and Crypto.com as their payout partner to improve the designers' payment experience.

- Partnering with Aid:Tech, a financial services company that brings transparency and accountability to Federal relief distribution, to leverage Circle's APIs and USDC to speed up the delivery of aid.
- Partnering with Wintermute, which selected USDC to convert digital assets into fiat in support of the Covid Relief Fund in India, an initiative to provide food, medical equipment and even vaccines to those affected by the virus. Wintermute selected Circle because of the company's swift minting and redeeming procedure, reliable transfer capabilities on multiple blockchains, and its worldwide presence which allows for efficient conversions to fiat.
- Coordinating with Visa, the Stellar blockchain and the fintech startup Tala to drive crypto adoption for underbanked customers in emerging markets. More than 3 billion people have limited or no access to services to borrow, save, or grow their money; Tala's partnership with Visa and Circle will help bring equitable financial tools to a massive underserved population.
- Partnering with the philanthropy Endaoment to create a disaster relief fund to help communities in the Midwest and South regions of the United States that were devastated by tornadoes in December 2021.

Additional data points on how USDC is helping to create and enable an internet-native ecosystem built on digital dollars, with U.S. Dollar assets held within the care and custody of U.S. regulated financial institutions:

- Over 100 billion USDC issued, with over 50 billion in circulation as of February 6, 2022, and 10,000 percent growth over 2 years.
- Nearly $2.5 trillion in on-blockchain payments and settlements in 2021, and 4.6 million active wallet addresses with USDC transactions in 2021 (Source: Internal Data Aggregations).
- 223 digital wallets support USDC transactions in over 175 countries (Source: Apple App Store and Google Play Store combined).
- 34 leading exchanges support trading and USDC conversion in 180+ countries, providing liquidity and convertibility to key currency markets around the world.
- More than 200 blockchain protocols supporting USDC.

- Hundreds of regulated financial institutions (VASPs) in financial centers around the world are supporting USDC.

Responses to Written Questions of Senator Sinema from Dante Disparte

Q.1. In recent years, digital assets have become increasingly popular holdings for publicly traded standards. Currently, the generally accepted accounting principles (GAAP) set by the Financial Accounting Standards Board use an intangible assets model for accounting digital assets. What potential issues, if any, may arise from using an intangible assets model to assess stablecoin holdings?

A.1. There are many different types of digital assets that exist today, and while these assets all rely on blockchain technology, there are significant differences among them in terms of economics, rights, obligations and risks, which need to be considered in determining the appropriate accounting framework. U.S. GAAP does not specifically address a holder's accounting for digital assets. The accounting therefore has to be evaluated based on the nature of the asset, the type of entity that holds the asset, and how the asset is held. In applying existing accounting standards, companies typically consider the definitions of intangible assets, financial instruments, inventory as well as cash and cash equivalents. In this response, we will differentiate between cryptocurrencies, such as Bitcoin, and reserve-backed stablecoins, such as USDC.

Cryptocurrencies

Current U.S. GAAP does not provide specific authoritative guidance related to the accounting for digital assets, and as such, cryptocurrencies like Bitcoin are typically classified as indefinite-lived intangible assets. As a result, holders record impairment losses as the cryptocurrencies' fair value falls below their carrying value, however such impairment losses are not reversed when the market values of these assets subsequently increase. Given the inherent volatility in many cryptocurrencies' market values, this accounting framework does not reflect the true economic value of the digital assets held by companies on their balance sheet at each reporting period. Therefore, companies that hold these digital assets generally use non-GAAP earnings measures in order to provide more relevant information to financial statement users, which reflect the true economics, rights, obligations, and risks of the digital assets held and more accurately explain their financial performance.

In the recent Financial Accounting Standards Board (FASB) Invitation to Comment (ITC) Agenda Consultation, many cryptocurrency industry members, public companies, and public accounting firms raised similar concerns about the application of the intangible asset accounting framework to cryptocurrencies, stating it does not provide relevant information to financial statement users because it does not appropriately reflect the underlying economics associated with digital assets and places unnecessary operational burdens on the financial reporting process for the companies that hold them. Our view is that a fair value accounting model for cryptocurrencies would give a more comprehensive view of the underlying economics and provide more relevant information to financial statement users.

Clear and authoritative U.S. GAAP guidance providing a fair value accounting model for cryptocurrencies would allow companies to more accurately present the economics, risks, and rewards of holding these assets, making financial statements more relevant and useful to financial statement users. Clear guidance would also minimize the operational burden on companies and align U.S. GAAP with International Financial Reporting Standards (which does provide an option to record upward movements after an indefinite-lived intangible asset has been impaired).

Stablecoins

A stablecoin is a blockchain-powered digital currency that combines the benefits of traditional digital assets (cryptographic security, digital transfer and settlement finality, fast transaction speeds, potentially lower transaction costs, and clear auditability) with the price stability of traditional fiat currencies. This is achieved by pegging the value of the stablecoin to a national currency or other reference assets. Because of the variety of facts and circumstances that may exist, there is no authoritative guidance around the accounting for stablecoins.

At Circle, we believe the accounting treatment of reserve-backed stablecoins should reflect the underlying economics of the reserves and the regulatory framework in which the stablecoin operates, which supports the value, intended use, functionality, and features of the stablecoin. Given the lack of authoritative guidance under U.S. GAAP, there is diversity in practice.

Holders may elect to apply the intangible assets model while others have regarded them as financial instruments, as they are entitled to redeem the coins for cash from the issuer. As previously outlined, the intangible assets model does not reflect the stability and rights related to a stablecoin, resulting in substantial operating burdens to accounting and financial reporting processes, and having little relevance to financial statements users.

The accounting treatment of stablecoins like USDC is a policy opportunity for the United States. In September 2021, the Conference of State Bank Supervisors released the Money Transmission Modernization Act for State adoption as part of States' broader effort to modernize their financial regulatory systems. This model law aims to replace 50 sets of State-specific money transmitter laws and rules with one single set of nationwide standards and requirements created by State and industry experts. The measure proposes a legal classification that applies to stablecoins, which reads as follows:

> (aa) "Stored value" means monetary value representing a claim against the issuer evidenced by an electronic or digital record, and that is intended and accepted for use as a means of redemption for money or monetary value, or payment for goods or services.

Notwithstanding the fact that there will likely be further accounting standard developments around digital assets and stablecoins, we believe reference to the underlying reserves, the rights conferred to holders of a stablecoin, and the applicable regulatory framework under which the stablecoin operates can inform the relevant U.S. GAAP framework to apply in the absence of authoritative guidance. In the case of Circle, the U.S. dollar-denominated reserves backing USDC are held in the care, custody and control of the U.S. regulated banking system and issued in compliance with money transmitter requirements under the electronic stored value definition above. The reserves are strictly comprised of cash and short-duration U.S. obligations, and we have consistently made publicly available reports on the reserves and their sufficiency to meet demands for USDC outstanding with third party attestations from a leading global accounting firm on a monthly basis.

Under the current U.S. GAAP framework, our view would be that U.S. dollar-denominated asset-backed stablecoins like USDC should be accounted for by holders as financial instruments (as USDC represents a right to receive cash from the issuer). Holders of a stablecoin from an issuer who meets the definition of a financial institution which functions similar to a demand deposit with rights to that deposit transferable over a public blockchain, could potentially meet the definition of and could be considered cash and cash equivalents under current U.S. GAAP.

We believe that a comprehensive framework under U.S. GAAP should be developed and given the prudential standards underlying USDC issuance, USDC should be accounted for in contemplation of a holders' right to redeem the tokens for U.S. dollars with consideration to the high-quality liquid assets the reserves supporting its value and the regulatory framework we operate in. The financial reporting of the reserves that support the stablecoin should focus on providing transparency about the nature and risks of these holdings to financial statements users.

We look forward to working with standard-setting bodies, public accounting firms, and others to advance those principles.

Q.2. If a new model of accounting is designed for digital assets, should stablecoins be treated similarly to other cryptocurrencies?

A.2. We believe that a comprehensive accounting framework designed for digital assets should reflect the different types of digital assets and the different underlying economics, rights, obligations, risks, and uses of those assets.

The purpose of USDC and other similar stablecoins, is to function as a stable store of value and convenient medium of exchange, with the same range of potential downstream applications as a U.S. dollar (or other equivalent fiat currency). USDC is not designed as an investment product as there is no reasonable expectation of profits by USDC holders, and accordingly is not a security. As the reserves backing USDC are solely invested in U.S. dollars and short-duration U.S. obligations, the instrument imports the monetary policy of the U.S. Federal Reserve Board. The regulatory framework under which we operate requires us to redeem USDC for one U.S. dollar; however, most digital assets, such as Bitcoin and Ether, do not hold value related to specific reference assets and are therefore subject to volatility and differing risks and rewards. Given the differing underlying economics and risks and rewards associated with different digital assets, we believe USDC and other stablecoins should be accounted for as a distinct class of digital assets within a future authoritative framework for accounting for digital assets.

When considering how stablecoins, as a distinct class of digital assets should be accounted for within a future authoritative accounting framework, we believe USDC and other similar stablecoins should be accounted for in contemplation of a holders' right to redeem the tokens for U.S. dollars and in relation to the high-quality liquid assets the reserves supporting the value are invested in. In our view this would mean that stablecoins like USDC should be accounted for as a financial instrument or as cash and cash equivalents by holders.

Q.3. How can the GAAP accurately account for stablecoin issuers' holdings with awareness of holdings for the purpose of stablecoin backing?

A.3. We value trust, transparency and compliance and would be supportive of U.S. GAAP disclosure requirements which provide financial statements users with relevant information to assist in their determination as to the stability, composition, and values of reserves supporting the stablecoins issued by the respective issuer.

In terms of market trust, transparency, and accountability, Circle has consistently and voluntarily reported our U.S. dollar-denominated reserves and the sufficiency of these reserves to meet the demands of all USDC outstanding as evidenced by third-party attestations published monthly. Circle has also prioritized building, designing, and guarding the prudential standards for USDC inside of and conforming with the prevailing U.S. regulatory standards that apply to leading fintech and payments firms such as PayPal, Block (formerly, Square), Venmo, and Stripe, among others.

Circle would welcome Federal regulations requiring rigorous standards for the assets backing U.S. dollar-denominated stablecoins as well as requirements for public disclosure and accountability. In Circle's view, the assets backing dollar-referenced stablecoins should be fully reserved and backed by U.S. dollars or short-duration U.S. obligations. In addition, financial statement disclosure requirements need to focus on providing transparency about the nature and risks of these assets and should be applied consistently by stablecoin issuers, who should be required to regularly report on the reserves and be subject to rigorous and consistent capital requirements.

From an economic competitiveness standpoint, this is an opportunity for the United States financial accounting standards setters, such as the FASB, to lay the foundation for how stablecoins are accounted for and disclosed on companies' balance sheets. The FASB should lead the way in developing a robust and clear accounting framework to provide financial statement users with high quality and comparable information, while balancing financial statement preparers' financial reporting and operational challenges, especially given consideration that the U.S. dollar is the reference asset of choice for the most widely used and popular stablecoins in circulation.

Responses to Written Questions of Chairman Brown from Hilary J. Allen

Q.1. Stablecoin companies frequently claim that their products are safe because reserves are invested in low-risk, highly liquid assets, such as bank deposits. Very low-risk assets, however, have low or even nominal returns. If stablecoin reserves are invested in these assets, do stablecoin providers face pressure to obtain revenue from stablecoin users in other ways, such as by cross-selling DeFi investments or charging transaction fees? Is there evidence in the market so far that firms face these incentives?

A.1. It goes without saying that firms need to generate revenue; if reserve assets generate insufficient returns, then stablecoin issuers will have to generate revenue elsewhere. If transaction fees are disclosed upfront and not structured to exploit consumers' cognitive biases, there is nothing wrong with charging fees for services that people are willing to pay for. A lack of transparency about revenue sources may be cause for concern, though; it may be that the stablecoin is being financially supported by hidden fees or by arrangements that conceal a hidden conflict of interest (as an analogy, in 2020, the SEC brought an enforcement action against Robinhood Financial LLC for failing to disclose to its customers that its commission free brokerage model was supported by "payments from trading firms for routing customer orders to them").[186]

Circle's Amended S-4 disclosure (filed with the SEC on December 23, 2021) states that for the 9 months ended September 30, 2021, it generated more revenue from what it terms "Transaction and Treasury Services" ($29,108,000) than "USDC interest income" ($21,214,000).[187] Circle projects that by 2023, $622,000,000 of revenue will come from Transaction and Treasury Services while $196,000,000 of revenue will come from USDC interest income.[188] Circle describes Transaction and Treasury Services as including "(1) Transaction Services, (2) Integration Services, and (3) Circle Yield. All three of the services are components of a unified suite of services that are accessed by, and integrated with, the Circle Account by providing

[186] SEC, "SEC Charges Robinhood Financial With Misleading Customers About Revenue Sources and Failing To Satisfy Duty of Best Execution", (Dec. 17, 2020) (available at *https://www.sec.gov/news/press-release/2020-321*).

[187] Circle Internet Finance Public Limited Company, Amendment No. 2 to S-4 Filing, p. 112 (Dec. 23, 2010) (available at *https://www.sec.gov/Archives/edgar/data/0001876042/000110465921153174/tm2124445-4-s4a.htm*).

[188] Id. at 132.

customers with the infrastructure required to process a wide variety of transactions and support their financial infrastructure."[189] One industry journalist described these transaction and treasury services as "probably the least understood and least detailed part of [Circle's] offerings"[190]—Circle may ultimately face conflicts between the interests of the businesses and financial institutions that utilize these transaction and treasury services on the one hand, and the consumers who use the USDC on the other hand.

Q.2. Major stablecoin issuers, including Circle and Tether, do not allow retail stablecoin users to redeem their coins directly at the issuer. Yet most DeFi arrangements are used extensively or even predominantly by retail consumers, and, as discussed at the hearing, stablecoins are integral to these platforms. Are there risks that arise from the fact that DeFi is accessible to consumers, but important stablecoin redemption processes are not? Please explain.

A.2. Consumers are vulnerable to many new types of scams proliferating in the DeFi ecosystem, including rug pulls.[191] Consumers may also find that the stablecoins themselves become worthless (at least outside of the DeFi ecosystem) if exchanges like Coinbase become compromised and so the stablecoins cannot be converted into cash. If this were to happen, any profits made in the DeFi ecosystem would be unavailable for the purchase of real-world goods and services. I discuss problems associated with exchange outages in more detail in response to the next question.

I would also observe that where stablecoin issuers do not allow retail stablecoin users to redeem their coins directly at the issuer, that calls into question the value of the reserve for consumers. If a stablecoin is backed by a reserve of assets held by the stablecoin issuer AND a stablecoin holder can redeem their stablecoin directly from the issuer, then the reserve inspires confidence that when the time comes for redemption, the stablecoin issuer will be able to honor the request by liquidating reserve assets (if necessary). In this situation, the stablecoin holder is in a similar position to the holder of a share in a money market mutual fund. If, however, there is no direct redemption right, it is unclear what claim stablecoin holders have on reserve assets. Do

---

[189] Id. at 107; see also id. at 182.

[190] Brady Dale, "USDC Is Only Circle's Second-Biggest Business", SPAC Filing Shows, *Coindesk* (Jul. 8, 2021) *https://www.coindesk.com/business/2021/07/08/usdc-is-only-circles-second-biggest-business-spac-filing-shows/.*

[191] Marco Castrovilli, "How To Spot a Rug Pull in DeFi", *Cointelegraph* (Nov. 11, 2021) (available at *https://cointelegraph.com/news/how-to-spot-a-rug-pull-in-defi-6-tips-by-cointelegraph*).

holders have contractual rights against an exchange that would force the exchange to convert their stablecoins at the expected value? If so, does the exchange have any direct contractual right of redemption against the stablecoin issuer at the expected value? Can these contractual rights be suspended in an emergency? I would humbly submit that the Senator might wish to seek answers to these questions to determine both the value of the reserve for stablecoin holders, and whether there is real run risk associated with stablecoins.

Q.3. When stablecoin issuers preclude retail users from redeeming directly, consumers can convert stablecoins into fiat currency by selling the tokens for dollars on exchanges. But as we saw on the day of the hearing—when major crypto exchanges experienced glitches in their price quote systems—exchanges have been prone to outages and malfunction. Please discuss how exchange outages or errors can affect stablecoin markets and stablecoin holders. Are there scenarios involving exchange failures that give rise to particular concern?

A.3. When a stablecoin is designed so that a holder has no direct right of redemption, holders are entirely reliant upon exchanges like Coinbase to "cash out" of their stablecoin. Because stablecoins aren't readily accepted by sellers of goods and services outside of the DeFi ecosystem, exchange outages can obviously cause real harm for a holder who needs to convert their stablecoins to cash to make time-sensitive purchases of real-world goods and services. At a systemic level, this kind of outage can damage confidence in the convertibility of stablecoins more generally, which could even cause runs on stablecoins through unaffected exchanges (assuming that stablecoin holders have a contractual right to compel those exchanges to convert their stablecoins, which they might not). During a panic, unexpected volumes of conversions could stress the infrastructure of exchanges, causing more operational problems and potential shutdowns, which would further damage confidence in a vicious cycle.

Q.4. Please describe any risks and benefits that you believe are presented by smart contracts. In what contexts, if any, are smart contracts a valuable tool? Could smart contracts create systemic risks? As compared with traditional contracts, are smart contracts useful in consumer or small business contexts?

A.4. I believe there are significant systemic risks associated with smart contracts, because of their automated execution. Rigid execution often seems appealing to parties in good times because it creates more certainty and the increased efficiency reduces transaction costs. However, in bad times, this can create systemic problems, as I explain in the following excerpt from my forthcoming book *Driverless Finance: Fintech's Impact on Financial Stability* (OUP 2022):

> because the future is inherently uncertain, no contract (paper or smart) will ever be able to cater for every possible eventuality that a financial asset might be confronted with. With paper contracts, though, the parties have opportunities to amend their contracts or agree not to enforce them. Courts can also intervene to fill in the blanks in paper contracts: law professor Katharina Pistor has observed that "the elasticity of law has proved time and again critical for avoiding a complete financial meltdown." In a financial system dominated by smart contracts, though, these kinds of interventions may come too late to prevent runs, fire sales, and other destabilizing harm. These problems arise because, even if the parties agree among themselves not to enforce a smart contract or a court issues an injunction preventing them from carrying out a smart contract, the parties can't effect this on their own. The execution of a smart contract can only be paused, changed, or undone with the consent of whoever controls the relevant distributed ledger, and where the ledger is decentralized and permissionless (like the Ethereum ledger) there is no single individual who can coordinate the process-even if the parties to the smart contract (as well as the public interest) all support it.
>
> Instead, any pause, change or reversal of a smart contract will require the consensus of all the nodes in the distributed ledger supporting the smart contract, which will take time. To give some context, after the DAO was hacked, it took over a month for the nodes of the Ethereum distributed ledger to coordinate their response. It seems highly unlikely that this kind of consensus could ever be achieved before the smart contract executes; undoing the transaction will probably be the only alternative. Undoing a transaction requires either a change in the ledger's underlying software, or what is known as a "hard fork," where the ledger is split in two with one version of the ledger not recognizing the problematic transaction. Identifying, contacting, and convincing a majority of the nodes of a decentralized ledger to accept either of these approaches would not be a quick process, and the run or fire sale we are trying to prevent could be over—and the damage done—long before the transaction were reversed.

Turning from systemic risk to the consumer/small business context, Professor Katharina Pistor has emphasized the hardships consumers faced because of the limited contractual relief available to them during the 2008 crisis. Pistor pointed out that the more rigid the contract, the more difficult the consumer's position:

> Consider the different fates of homeowners in the context of plummeting real estate markets in countries around the world. Homeowners in the U.S. may be on the periphery of the U.S. financial system.: While major financial intermediaries received emergency liquidity support from the Fed or Government bailouts, homeowners faced personal bankruptcy and foreclosure in accordance with the law. However, they are still better off than their counterparts in Hungary or Spain. The debt of Hungarian homeowners, for example, was compounded by the fact that two-thirds of mortgages were made in foreign currency—the euro or Swiss franc—and these currencies appreciated in the midst of the crisis (by 40 percent) relative to the domestic currency. Moreover, in Spain (and most other countries), mortgage-backed loans are full recourse loans (whereas in many States in the U.S. they are not. If property value is under water, homeowners still carry the burden of the entire amount they had contracted for.[192]

Self-executing smart contracts are more rigid than any contractual structures adopted before the 2008 crisis. For this reason, I would be very concerned by the mass adoption of smart contracts in consumer or small business contexts.

Q.5. Some stablecoin providers and commentators believe that Congress should create a new form of financial institution charter, specifically for stablecoin issuers. In a recently released framework for stablecoin legislation, Senator Toomey has also adopted this view.[193] From your perspective, would a novel stablecoin charter be preferable to requiring firms to follow existing law and conform to the regulatory categories it creates? Could new regulatory carve-outs incentivize regulatory arbitrages or otherwise undermine key existing rules?

A.5. From my perspective, it is preferable to require stablecoin issuers to follow existing law; a specialized charter for stablecoins is undesirable for a number of reasons. Creating specialized regulatory regimes often leads to duplicative regulatory efforts and turf wars on the one hand, and on the other hand, issues falling through regulatory gaps as private sector entities arbitrage the definitional boundaries of the specialized regime. Also, as I noted in my written testimony, "the more specialized the regulator, the more opportunities there are for the industry to 'capture' the regulator." Capture could become a

---

[192] Katharina Pistor, "A Legal Theory of Finance", 41 *J. Comparative Econ.* 315, 320 (2013).
[193] See "Toomey Outlines Stablecoin Principles To Guide Future Legislation", (Dec. 14, 2021), *https://www.banking.senate.gov/newsroom/minority/toomey-outlines-stablecoin-principles-to-guide-future-legislation.*

serious problem if a cadre of regulators were dedicated solely to a specialized stablecoin charter.

Speaking more specifically about regulatory arbitrage, any regulatory regime that is devised to apply to a particular technology at a particular moment in time is going to be particularly vulnerable to arbitrage by private sector entities (who can refine their technology to fall outside the regulatory definition). Legal tests that are more functional and technology-neutral (like the Howey test for what constitutes an "investment contract", and therefore a "security") are harder to arbitrage, and more like to withstand the test of time as technology evolves. As I concluded in my written testimony, the SEC (and the CFTC) should continue to oversee the stablecoins under their jurisdiction.

Q.6. In Senator Toomey's framework, he also suggested that some stablecoin issuers could, "based on their business models," choose to be regulated by "[r]egister[ing] as a money transmitter under the existing State regime and as a money services business under FinCEN's Federal regime." Are State money transmitter and Federal MSB rules adequate for managing the risks to consumers and the economy created by stablecoins? Please describe the strengths and limitations of these regimes, as applied to stablecoins.

A.6. As discussed during the hearing, stablecoins pose issues for consumers/investors, and for the stability of the financial system, and so any proposal that limits stablecoin regulation to State money transmitter rules and FinCEN will be inadequate. FinCEN is a financial intelligence unit, and has no consumer/investor protection or financial stability mandate. Instead, FinCEN's mission "is to safeguard the financial system from illicit use and combat money laundering and promote national security through the collection, analysis, and dissemination of financial intelligence and strategic use of financial authorities."[194] State money transmitter laws may involve consumer/investor protections, but they vary significantly by jurisdiction, which will provide consumers/investors with uneven protections. In addition, State regulators generally do not pay much attention to financial stability issues, because financial stability is a borderless public good that will accrue largely to persons residing outside of their State.[195]

Q.7. Senator Toomey's framework further proposes that "[c]ommercial entities should be eligible to issue stablecoins, provided they choose one of

---

[194] FinCEN, "What We Do", (available at *https://www.fincen.gov/what-we-do*).

[195] Daniel Schwarcz and Steven L. Schwarcz, "Regulating Systemic Risk in Insurance", 81 *U. Chi. L. Rev.* 1569, 1628 (2014).

these regimes [i.e., a bank charter, a special purpose stablecoin charter, or money transmitter and MSB rules]." Please discuss whether, in your view, it would be prudent to allow large, nonfinancial companies like Amazon or Alphabet to issue stablecoins.

A.7. In my view, allowing Amazon, Alphabet, or Meta/Facebook to issue stablecoins would be a worst-case outcome. To explain why, I excerpt here a few paragraphs from my forthcoming book *Driverless Finance* (in which I use the term "techfin" to refer to these tech firms):

> A payments service is . . . likely to be many tech firms' first foray into finance, but they won't necessarily stop there. As more users adopt the payment service, more user data is generated (about the customers and their transactions), which the tech firm can use not only to target advertising or identify potential customers for its non-financial services (which will yield yet more data) but also to expand into financial services that involve some data-dependent risk assessment (such as making loans or offering insurance). Offering more types of financial services will create new networks and generate yet more user data in a cycle that is virtuous for the tech firm, but not necessarily for a competitive marketplace or stable financial system.
>
> The techfins have a potential advantage over even the largest banks here, because they can exploit large troves of customer data (like social media posts or search histories or shopping patterns) that they have collected through their nonfinancial activities. In the United States, banks are prevented from engaging in nonfinancial activities, so the types of data that banks can collect are more limited (Goldman Sachs can't purchase a search engine, and Citibank can't start up an e-commerce platform). Because of the competitive advantages that come from their data supremacy (and because they are already huge), Google, Amazon, Facebook, and Apple could quickly become "too big to fail" providers of financial services. "Too big to fail" is used to describe a firm that is so critical to the provision of financial services (because of factors like its size, a lack of substitute providers, or interconnections with other parts of the financial system) that a Government simply will not allow it to fail. Unfortunately, firms that recognize that they are "too big to fail" are perversely encouraged to take extra risks: they will profit if those risks turn out well, but they know that any disastrous failures will probably be covered by a Government bailout. Profit therefore comes at the expense of the public, which is left holding the bag if the firm's risks don't pan out. And in some ways, that's a best-case scenario. What if a Government bailout isn't actually feasible?
>
> Google, Amazon, Facebook, and Apple are so big that in many ways, they make our existing notions of "too big to fail" seem quaint. A recent Government report concluded that Facebook and Google have monopoly

power in their defined markets, and that Amazon and Apple have "significant and durable market power." If any of these behemoths were to add payments or lending services to their existing markets, they could outcompete many of the alternatives, leaving few substitutes if they were to fail. In the absence of substitutes, a bailout seems inevitable—but what would a bailout on this scale look like? For example, might the Government have to bailout Amazon's e-commerce business as well as any lending arm? And which country's Government would be responsible? Some smaller countries (like Iceland and Switzerland) have already had to grapple with the issue that their banks might be too big for them to bail out, but when it comes to the techfins, even large countries like the United States might find them "too big to save."

Q.8. Finally, Senator Toomey's proposal states that "[r]egulation should protect the privacy—and confidentiality of individuals using stablecoins." Could creating carve-outs for stablecoins from existing know-your-customer or BSA/AML rules raise national security concerns? If so, how?

A.8. National security issues are largely beyond my expertise, but I see no reason why stablecoins should be treated differently from any other payment method when it comes to BSA/AML rules.

Responses to Written Questions of Senator Menendez from Hilary J. Allen

Q.1. The defining feature of stablecoins versus other types of crypto is that they are backed by assets such as fiat currencies or commodities. However, without proper transparency this feature only provides the illusion of stability.

Are market participants able to easily verify the portfolio holdings backing the stablecoins they invest in?

A.1. Generally speaking, there are no disclosure requirements pertaining to stablecoin reserves (although Tether is required to provide reports on the composition of its reserves pursuant to its settlement with the New York Attorney General).[196] However, an industry standard is starting to evolve where some stablecoin issuers make voluntary disclosures known as "attestation reports," where "the stablecoin issuer attests to its auditor how

---

[196] Letitia James, New York Attorney-General, "Attorney General James Ends Virtual Currency Trading Platform Bitfinex's Illegal Activities in New York" (Feb. 23, 2021) (available at *https://ag.ny.gov/press-release/2021/attorney-general-james-ends-virtual-currency-trading-platform-bitfinexs-illegal*).

many reserves it has, and the auditor examines this claim for validity. The auditor's findings then get posted for the public to see."[197] While better than no disclosure, such periodic voluntary disclosures are suboptimal because they only describe the reserve at a particular moment in time, and investors are forced to rely only on the information the stablecoin issuer chooses to disclose. Bad information may be omitted, insufficient detail may be provided, and disclosures will potentially be inconsistent as between stablecoin issuers, making comparisons difficult for investors.

Also, I would add that (as I noted in a response to Question 2 from Senator Brown (see above)), even with full disclosure, the value of the reserve assets to consumers is questionable if stablecoin issuers do not allow retail stablecoin users to redeem their coins directly from them.

Q.2. Transparency is a cornerstone of the economy. Consumers make the best decisions when they have the all of the necessary information, which is why I have always advocated for robust disclosure rules in across the financial system.

How can we increase transparency to ensure market participants properly disclose the value of stablecoins and other cryptocurrency so that the average investor is able to understand the true risks associated with such assets?

A.2. Unfortunately, it is hard to convey the true risks associated with investing in cryptocurrencies because we lack methodologies for valuing them. Nobel Prize-winning economist Robert Shiller has said that Bitcoin "has no value at all unless there is some common consensus that it has value. Other things like gold would at least have some value if people didn't see it as an investment,"[198] and that "no one can attach objective probabilities to the various possible outcomes of the current Bitcoin enthusiasm. How can we even start estimating the fundamental value of Bitcoin . . . ? Any attempt will soon sound silly."[199] In the absence of appropriate valuation methodologies, there is no metric that can convey to investors the true risks associated with most crypto assets.

Valuation of stablecoins is potentially more effective, to the extent that their value depends on the composition of their reserve assets. The danger here

---

[197] For more on stablecoin attestation reports, see J.P. Koning, "The Race for Stablecoin Transparency" (Aug. 16, 2021) (available at *https://www.coindesk.com/markets/2021/08/16/the-race-for-stablecoin-transparency/*).

[198] William Suburg, "Yale Prof. Shiller Thinks Bitcoin's 'Bubble' Could Actually Linger 100 Years", *Cointelegraph* (Jan. 19, 2018) (available at *https://cointelegraph.com/news/yale-prof-shiller-thinks-bitcoins-bubble-could-actually-linger-100-years*).

[199] Robert J. Shiller, "What Is Bitcoin Really Worth? Don't Even Ask", *N.Y. Times* (Dec. 15, 2017).

is that people will believe that the assets backing a single stablecoin will always be worth exactly $1, even though their value may fluctuate in reality. Investors in money market mutual funds face similar issues, and so some people have argued that all money market mutual funds should be required to have a floating value (to prevent investors from being misled about the stability of money market mutual fund share prices).

Additional Material Supplied for the Record

Blockchain Transaction Fees ("Gas") on FTX

This post describes and explains how FTX handles transaction fees charged by blockchains. To summarize, FTX absorbs and subsidizes fees charged by efficient, environmentally friendly blockchains. FTX absorbs almost all fees charged by other blockchains. However, FTX reserves the right to pass-through some or all of high per-transaction fees charged on some transfers on less efficient blockchains.

—

Exchanges like FTX must integrate with a variety of different blockchains so that customers can transfer cryptocurrencies in and out of the platform. Although each of these blockchains (Bitcoin, Ethereum, and Solana, just to name a few) have unique characteristics, they all share one common feature: all users of a given network must pay transaction fees to incentivize network participants to do the "work" (i.e., mining) required to add that transaction to the blockchain's distributed ledger. These fees are known as "gas" on the Ethereum blockchain, and are colloquially referred to as such in other contexts.

So how does FTX deal with blockchain transaction fees (which, as a fact, must be paid by someone)? When are such fees necessary to interact with FTX? What does FTX ultimately charge the customer, and why?

First, some background:

The "Deposit, Trade, Withdraw" Life Cycle

Cryptocurrency exchanges perform three primary functions necessary to facilitate customer transactions:

1. Accepting deposits of crypto and fiat currencies
2. Matching buy and sell orders (exchanging one currency for another)
3. Processing withdrawals of crypto and fiat currencies

Here's an example of what this life cycle might look like for a user: Alice sends 1 Bitcoin to her FTX wallet. FTX, which listens to all transactions happening on the Bitcoin blockchain, recognizes her deposit and credits her 1 Bitcoin in her FTX account (1). Later on, Alice decides to exchange her Bitcoin for Ether. She sends an order to buy 12 Ether for a price of 1 Bitcoin, and FTX matches her buy order with a seller and a trade occurs (2). Finally, Alice wants to withdraw her Ether from the exchange, and instructs FTX to withdraw her 12 Ether to her private wallet on the Ethereum blockchain (3).

For step 1, Alice had to pay a fee to the Bitcoin blockchain so that her deposit to FTX could be processed (she sent 1 Bitcoin from her BTC wallet to her wallet at FTX, and a small portion of that was deducted from the total transfer amount to pay the fee; the BTC network of miners only "confirm" or "do" this transfer if paid a transaction fee). Step 2 requires no blockchain fees, because trades on FTX occur entirely off-chain (one of the benefits of a "centralized" exchange such as FTX). Step 3 however, will require FTX to send a transfer request to the Ethereum blockchain, and therefore FTX will be required to pay gas fees on Alice's behalf.

The Size of Blockchain Fees

The actual amount that a blockchain requires to send a transaction differs widely based on the underlying structure of that blockchain. Platforms like Bitcoin and Ethereum are known as "Proof of Work" blockchains, where the "work" required to add that transaction to the blockchain uses a large amount of computing time and energy. On such platforms, average transaction fees are quite high: around $2 per transaction for Bitcoin, and around $40 per transaction on Ethereum! (again, even these figures can vary widely based on network demand, etc.)

There are other blockchains that use much more efficient means of validating transactions. Solana, Cardano, and Polkadot use variations of an algorithm known as "Proof of Stake." On Solana, for example, the average transaction fee is $0.00025.

FTX Withdrawal Fees

In practice, FTX does not charge fees for withdrawals on Proof-of-Stake blockchains, and it subsidizes about half of the blockchain fees for Proof-of-work blockchains (requiring the user to pay the other half). However, FTX reserves the ability to charge withdrawal fees, on small transactions especially (and particularly where there is a perception that a series of small withdrawals or other transactions are done in an abusive or otherwise unnecessary manner).

There are a few important considerations behind this approach:

Environmental Impact

Proof-of-work networks require substantially larger energy consumption than proof-of-stake networks. We aim to incentivize our customers to utilize blockchain technology with the lowest energy usage and therefore the smallest impact on the environment. A single Solana transaction requires about the same amount of energy as two Google searches. Empirically (based on our analysis of our customers' actual activity), more than 80% of the blockchain transactions originating from FTX occur on proof-of-stake blockchains.

Public Blockchain Usage

Blockchains are open-access public goods. It is therefore up to the users of these networks, especially large users such as exchanges, to encourage fair usage.

Imagine someone has $100 worth of Bitcoin they want to withdraw from FTX to their private Bitcoin wallet. They could instruct a single transaction for the full amount. They could also try and send 10,000 transactions for $0.01 worth of Bitcoin. FTX reserves the right to charge for small transactions to incentivize the former and disincentivize the latter, so that we are putting as little pressure on network bandwidth as possible, mitigating unnecessary and redundant costs, and ultimately mitigating unnecessary and redundant energy usage.

Business Costs

FTX wants to encourage users to bring their assets to our exchange for trading, because we believe we have the best approach to customer safety, technological robustness, and regulatory compliance. This is part of why we wish to subsidize blockchain transaction fees. However, with high-fee networks such as Ethereum, if we didn't pass some cost onto the user, then a customer could abuse the system by requesting lots of small transactions, which could become a prohibitive cost for FTX to do business (though a lesser concern than the environmental impact and network congestion effects of such behavior). Similarly, FTX does not charge fees to users for costs related to wire-transfer activity for transferring fiat onto or off of our platforms, which also can be quite costly. But FTX reserves the right to assess fees for wire-transfer activity if the amount of such activity becomes abusive, or to otherwise encourage users to employ more efficient methods for transferring their fiat. In practice, FTX only rarely passes along wire-transfer fees to our users.

Blockchain Choice

Finally, with advances in blockchain technology and interoperability, many cryptocurrency tokens can be transferred on multiple different blockchains. For example, on FTX you can withdraw Tether to an Ethereum wallet (where Tether originated), but you can also withdraw Tether to a Solana wallet. The latter is free on FTX, which we want to strongly incentivize our users to take advantage of given all the above considerations.

Chapter 2

Understanding Stablecoins' Role in Payments and the Need for Legislation*

Committee on Financial Services

Wednesday, April 19, 2023
U.S. House of Representatives,
Subcommittee on Digital Assets,
Financial Technology,
and Inclusion, Committee on Financial Services,
Washington, D.C.

The subcommittee met, pursuant to notice, at 10:02 a.m., in room 2128, Rayburn House Office Building, Hon. French Hill [chairman of the subcommittee] presiding.

Members present: Representatives Hill, Lucas, Davidson, Rose, Steil, Timmons, Donalds, Flood, Houchin; Lynch, Foster, Gottheimer, Torres, Sherman, Casten, and Nickel.

Ex officio present: Representatives McHenry and Waters. Also present: Representative Himes.

Chairman HILL. Good morning. Welcome to our first hearing on stablecoins, entitled, "Understanding Stablecoins' Role in Payments and the Need for Legislation."

* This is an edited, reformatted and augmented version of Hearing before the Subcommittee on Digital Assets, Financial Technology, and Inclusion, of the Committee on Financial Services, U.S. House of Representatives, One Hundred Eighteenth Congress, First Session, Serial No. 118–15, dated April 19, 2023.

In: Stablecoins
Editor: Olivier Bullock
ISBN: 979-8-89113-502-4

Without objection, the Chair is authorized to declare a recess of the subcommittee at any time.

I want to thank all of our witnesses for being here today, and I now recognize myself for 4 minutes for an opening statement.

Today's hearing marks the official resumption of the House Financial Services Committee's efforts to enact payment stablecoin legislation. Last Congress, Democrats and Republicans worked together on a proposal to bring payment stablecoin issuers under a regulatory framework in the United States, and to allow stablecoins to unlock their potential as a contributor to a modern payment system. That proposal from September was noticed for today's hearing.

Last year, Members from both sides of the aisle reviewed the proposal, provided feedback, and worked to reach a compromise, but the clock ran out on those efforts due to the fall elections. That bill is an infant. It is a baby. It is not necessarily a beautiful baby, but it is our baby, and it is named, "Maxine McHenry." And it is here today for both sides of the aisle to review and consider and to hear from our panelists, so today, we are going to discuss it, and think about revisions.

How do we address the benefits and risks described in the Biden Administration's 2021 report on stablecoins? The Financial Stability Oversight Council (FSOC) recommended that Congress pass a legal framework, and Chairman McHenry and I are committed to working across the aisle to pass payment stablecoin legislation. And we are hopeful that Members in this room on both sides of the aisle will build on the foundation of that work.

Luckily, we have made significant headway with the proposal that we noticed for today's hearing. By requiring payment stablecoins to be backed one-for-one by high-quality liquid assets held in reserve, the proposal mitigates run risk. The legislation also requires stablecoin issuers to comply with redemption requirements monthly at the station, and disclosures and risk management standards. These are just a few ways that this legislation established strong, much-needed consumer protections in this area, just as Ms. Hand outlines in her testimony today.

However, there is more work to be done. It is my goal that our payment stablecoin legislation will provide different ways for issuers to maintain and come into compliance. I believe innovation is fostered through choice and competition. And one way to do that is through multiple pathways to become a stablecoin issuer, with appropriate protections so that we prevent regulatory arbitrage or a race to the bottom. I am glad to have Superintendent Harris here from the New York State Department of Financial Services to explain the framework that is currently in place in New York and to discuss their requirements for payment stablecoin issuers.

Finally, I want to reiterate the urgency for those of us in this room to work together and pass this needed legislation. Recent reports indicate that digital asset developers are leaving the United States to go to countries that have more-established regulatory frameworks for digital assets. That is not good for innovation, jobs, or consumer investor protection here.

The ongoing turf war between the SEC and the CFTC over digital assets is not only unhelpful, but it is also unsustainable. When you have two agencies contradicting each other about whether one of the most-utilized stablecoins in the market is either a security or a commodity, you end up with uncertainty.

Federal regulators have made it abundantly clear that without an Act of Congress, they will continue to interpret their authorities broadly, even when in direct contradiction with each other. That is why it is time for Congress to act and pass legislation to establish a regulatory framework for payment stablecoins. We look forward to hearing from our witnesses, and I look forward to picking up where we left off last fall.

I now recognize the ranking member of the subcommittee, Mr. Lynch, for 4 minutes for an opening statement.

Mr. LYNCH. Thank you, Mr. Chairman, for holding this hearing to further examine the role of stablecoins in our financial system. I would like to also thank the witnesses for their appearance here to help the committee with its work. Thank you.

The last several months have marked the effective collapse of much of the crypto industry following the abrupt demise of Tether, FTX, and Silvergate Bank, and countless other cryptocurrency companies have also witnessed the massive failure of Silicon Valley Bank and Signature Bank, which is also a crypto-centric bank. In the wake of these destabilizing events and their devastating impact on the crypto sector, which lost two-thirds of its market cap and went from $3-trillion market capitalization to $1 trillion—$1.06 trillion as of this morning—stablecoins remain a relevant oversight topic, particularly considering that they fall within a subset of cryptocurrency, and are intended to be non-volatile digital assets by intent and design.

As reported by the President's Working Group on Financial Markets in its report on stablecoins, well-designed and appropriately-regulated stablecoins could support faster, more-efficient, and more-inclusive payment options. However, the panel also underscored that the stablecoins present a variety of risk factors that are not currently subject to robust regulatory standards and cohesive oversight.

To this extent, then-Chairwoman Waters led our committee's bipartisan investigation last Congress to examine the risks to investors, market integrity, and financial stability associated with stablecoins. We reviewed the technology behind stablecoins, their current use cases, State regulatory structures, and Federal oversight gaps. And we also examined the role of stablecoins in potentially promoting financial inclusion.

As we learned last year, stablecoins are a type of cryptocurrency that issuers assert is pegged to stable reserve assets such as the U.S. dollar. Issuers claimed that stablecoins serve the purpose of payments with the potential to improve payment infrastructure and increase access to financial services. In reality, however, we know that stablecoins are rarely used for payments, and are instead used to facilitate speculative cryptocurrency trading and investments.

Stablecoins also contain structural fragilities that make them vulnerable to runs and pose risks to monetary policy, national security, financial stability, and fair competition. It is worth revisiting questions of whether stablecoins are even needed, if they are hardly used for the purposes intended. If our goal is to improve our payment system and financial inclusion, we should instead consider advancing public sector options such as the FedNow payment system and a publicly-issued digital dollar.

Considering these insights, I have trouble understanding why this outdated legislation, which is not cognizant of the recent disasters in the crypto space that has structural flaws, is attached to this hearing. I share concerns about key parts of this with the 14 consumer advocacy groups that sent a letter yesterday expressing concerns about the numerous, grave risks that stablecoins pose to households and our financial system, and I will share a few.

For starters, giving States the authority to regulate stablecoins allows issuers to easily avoid Federal oversight and seek out more permissive States. Additionally, the bill identifies the Federal Reserve as the primary regulator for oversight and provides issuers with the access to Federal Reserve programs such as the discount window, master accounts, and payment services. These programs are typically limited to banks which are heavily regulated, and that is for good reason.

Most importantly, the bill does not address the biggest lessons we have learned in recent months. We have witnessed the risks that can occur when players commingle customer funds. This bill does not mention how conflicts of interest will be managed, particularly between issuers and exchanges. I also continue to have concerns about allowing non-bank entities with no regulation to issue bank-like products. If the recent bank runs have taught us anything, it is the danger of allowing shadow banking products, particularly stablecoins, to issue deposits-like products without FDIC insurance. So, I strongly believe we need to separate crypto assets from our banking system, and this bill does just the opposite.

With that, I ask that we take the time that we need to get this right rather than try to get there first. I yield back.

Chairman HILL. I thank the gentleman. The Chair now recognizes the Chair of the full Financial Services Committee, Chairman McHenry, for one minute.

Chairman MCHENRY. Payment stablecoins are an important part of the digital asset ecosystem and have the potential to be a cornerstone of modern payment systems. I want to thank the Subcommittee Chair and the Subcommittee Ranking Member for their engagement on this. I also want to thank the Ranking Member of the Full Committee, the former Chair of the committee, for her engagement. The Ranking Member and I spent a significant amount of time along with our staffs, working together with Treasury, with the Fed, and with members of our committee last Congress, and I thought it was important to acknowledge that good work as the foundation of our discussions and the frame laid out that between these negotiations between Ranking Member Waters and I last Congress when she was the Chair.

I think it is important that we lay that down for a public hearing and understanding of what we negotiated, and this is the continuation of that good work, but it is the first piece of committee work that we have done in a setting like this. A lot of things have happened since this draft, and we want members to engage in this, especially new members of this committee, and have ownership of the legislative product that we will be moving.

But I want to thank Ranking Member Waters for her engagement on this. And I think she and I both will confess that this bill is imperfect to us in many, many ways, to each of us in different ways. But I thought it was important to ensure that a Democratled committee, now a Republican-led committee, that we acknowledge the intellectual framework around us having a modern financial regulatory regime at the Federal level, like consumer interest is not served by us not acting. We need to have a Federal regulatory regime for stablecoins. It is important for us internationally and domestically. And it is very important that we have the understanding, on a bipartisan basis, of the utility and the importance of this legislation. And with that, I yield back.

Chairman HILL. I thank the chairman. The Chair now recognizes the ranking member of the Full Committee, Ms. Waters, for one minute.

Ms. WATERS. Thank you very much, Chairman Hill and Ranking Member Lynch, and I want to thank all of the witnesses for testifying today. Let me start by saying that last Congress, my staff and I worked extensively with then-Ranking Member McHenry on legislation to provide a regulatory framework for payment. He is absolutely correct about that. However, what did not happen was we did not complete the negotiation so that we can move forward, and, unfortunately, a lot of things have happened in between.

And, of course, in addition to FTX and a lot of other things going on, this bill that we have posted in no way represents any final work, and because so much has happened in between, we needed to get back together in negotiations. But Mr. McHenry alarmed me somewhat when he said that the Members on his side of the aisle had come up with a whole new bill, and I said to him, "Well, then, they come to any negotiations having made up their minds already." And I suggested that if he was going to have a Republican bill, that we would go back to work on a Democrat bill, and then we will get together and decide who is going to give, and what we are going to do to work out the differences, et cetera, et cetera. That has not happened.

So let me just say, the posted bill in no way represents the final work on stablecoins by negotiations between the two of us. The bill has been posted. The Chair wanted to post the bill. It does not represent a final product of any kind, so I think we are starting from scratch to deal with stablecoins. We must deal with it. We must get a stablecoin bill. I think we can do that, but we must disregard the bill that has been posted altogether. I yield back.

Chairman HILL. The gentlewoman yields back. My response to that would be that we welcome any legislative effort from the Minority in this regard, in a constructive way, and on behalf of Republicans. We have just been looking at the September draft led by Ms. Waters and Mr. McHenry and making our own changes, doing our own due diligence, and that is what this hearing is all about. So, we agree that in no way is the bill posted to this hearing the be-all or end-all. I made that clear in my opening statement. This really is an opportunity for both sides of the aisle to fully engage with this superb panel and think through the right way to revise the good work of Ms. Waters and Mr. McHenry last fall.

Before I call on our panel, I want to wish my colleague, Jae Jang, a Happy Birthday today. Nothing says, "Happy Birthday," like a stablecoins hearing.

We will now turn to our witnesses. First, the Honorable Adrienne Harris. Ms. Harris is the Superintendent of the New York Department of Financial

Services. Prior to her service there, she was in senior roles at the Treasury Department and the White House.

Second, Professor Jesse Austin Campbell joins us. He is an adjunct professor at Columbia Business School, where he teaches a class on blockchain markets and infrastructure, as well as serving as a managing partner at Zero Knowledge Consulting.

Third, Mr. Jake Chervinsky. Mr. Chervinsky is the chief policy officer of the Blockchain Association, a digital asset association based here in Washington, D.C.

Fourth, Mr. Dante Disparte. Mr. Disparte is the chief strategy officer and head of global policy at Circle, the issuer of USDC, as well as a member of the World Economic Forum's Digital Currency Governance Consortium.

And our final witness is Ms. Delicia Reynolds Hand. Ms. Hand is the director of financial fairness at Consumer Reports.

We thank each of you for taking the time to be here today. Each of you will be recognized for 5 minutes to give an oral presentation of your testimony. And without objection, each of your written statements will be made a part of the record.

Ms. Harris, you are now recognized for 5 minutes to give your oral presentation.

Statement of the Honorable Adrienne A. Harris, Superintendent, New York State Department of Financial Services

Ms. HARRIS. Thank you, Mr. Chairman. Good morning, Chairman McHenry, Ranking Member Waters, Subcommittee Chair Hill, Subcommittee Ranking Member Lynch, and members of the Subcommittee on Digital Assets, Financial Technology, and Inclusion, and to the hardworking staff. I am Adrienne Harris, Superintendent of New York's Department of Financial Services (DFS). Thank you for inviting me today.

Strengthening the nation's regulatory oversight of virtual currency is critical to protecting consumers and ensuring the safety and soundness of institutions. I look forward to sharing with you some key features of the DFS framework and to offering continued assistance as you work to develop a comprehensive national regulatory framework.

DFS has been a prudential regulator of virtual currency since 2015. Our virtual currency regulatory framework is the most comprehensive in the country, built on the model of full-scope banking supervision, but tailored for the unique considerations of the industry. It has served well to protect New York consumers, keep virtual currency entities safe and sound, and hold the bad actors to account.

The Department has a wide range of tools to regulate the virtual currency industry, including licensing, supervision, examination, and enforcement. The core provisions of the DFS regulatory and supervisory framework are robust capital and financial standards, strong consumer protections, sophisticated cybersecurity requirements and strong anti-money laundering provisions. For example, virtual currency entities are subject to custody and capital requirements designed for industry-specific risks. Entities must hold virtual currency in the same type and amount on a one-to-one basis that is owed or obligated to a customer that is distinct from the traditional banking fractional reserve system.

Once an entity meets rigorous standards to be licensed or chartered, DFS creates a detailed supervisory agreement that is tailored to each company's risks. Companies must get approval from the Department for material changes in business, including for new product offerings, and stablecoin issuance. Entities also are subject to ongoing supervision and are regularly examined for compliance with regulations and those supervisory agreements. If, through our supervision, we find that a regulated entity is not in compliance with our rules, DFS' enforcement division can investigate and take appropriate actions to ensure that companies pay penalties for violations, remediate issues, and return lost funds to customers.

Specific to stablecoins, DFS was the first agency to provide regulatory clarity for these products. In June 2022, DFS provided guidance related to the issuance of U.S. dollar-backed stablecoins. The DFS stablecoin guidance requires one-to-one reserving with cash or cash equivalents, redemption fulfillment within 2 business days, and independent public audits to confirm reserves.

As members of this committee contemplate Federal legislation for stablecoins, I believe the best path forward is to build on the well-established dual-banking regulatory system. Any legislation that preempts the State's ability to regulate innovative financial services would be harmful to valuable regimes that already exist, and hamper State regulators' ability to respond nimbly to a changing financial ecosystem.

I am proud of the work DFS has done to develop a comprehensive supervisory framework and to foster a well-regulated virtual currency industry in the State. We welcome further collaboration with you to take advantage of our lessons learned and develop a comprehensive national regulatory framework to protect markets, entities, and consumers. Thank you.

[The prepared statement of Ms. Harris can be found on page 80 of the appendix.]

Chairman HILL. Thank you.

Mr. Campbell, you are now recognized for 5 minutes for your presentation.

Statement of J. Austin Campbell, Managing Partner, Zero Knowledge Consulting, and Adjunct Professor, Columbia Business School

Mr. CAMPBELL. Thank you very much. I would like to start by thanking Chairman McHenry, Ranking Member Waters, Subcommittee Chair Hill, and Subcommittee Ranking Member Lynch, and all of the members of the subcommittee and the hardworking staff for the opportunity today.

I want to start with something of an apology, which is to say the debate around stablecoins has been incredibly confusing. It has probably been harmful to consumers. It has probably been harmful to the nation. One of the problems is that with the lack of clarity from Congress, many things are called stablecoins which should not be. What we need is clarity to define stablecoins so that we understand that stablecoins built right are actually not new and are relatively mundane financial instruments.

If you look at frameworks that have worked, like the framework from the NYDFS, these things look like conservative banks, maybe government money market funds. These are the sorts of things we know how to address as a financial system. We can regulate them, and I think there are also answers to some of the issues that already exist in our current system, such as State versus Federal. I suggest in my testimony for small to medium-sized stablecoins, they are fine at the State level. When they become very large and systemic, they should probably exist at the Federal level. We don't need a $2-million stablecoin being regulated by the OCC or the Federal Reserve. It is not an effective use of time, but nobody is suggesting that JPMorgan be only State-regulated.

I think there is a way to make these things work. They serve the purpose of money on a blockchain, and that is what is ultimately the real innovation here is the blockchain itself and the opportunities for transactions that creates. In the current environment, we are failing at making this happen as a country. Our regulation is currently chaos for stablecoins. If I am an issuer and I want to create a stablecoin, I technically don't know if I am going to be answering to a State regulator, a Federal banking regulator, the SEC, or the CFTC.

And it puts you in the same position as if you are out with friends and you are going to play some sports game, and somebody tells you, well, we may enforce the rules of baseball, or football, or basketball, and we are not going to tell you which in advance. And maybe some of them will all apply at the same time. It is unworkable.

And what this means, and it pains me to say this as an American, is that things are moving offshore. I can say this with certainty because I advise my clients right now to do exactly that. There are other regimes with significantly more regulatory clarity than what we have provided here, where if you are a good actor who wants to comply with the law, who wants to do the right thing, you want to go there because you know you can do it with certainty.

And this is bad for jobs. It is bad for the strength of the dollar. It is bad for our status as a reserve currency. And it is particularly bad for national security, as blockchains have a significant degree of transparency that is not present in markets like actual cash markets, right? When somebody transacts on a blockchain, it is public. We may not always know right now who transacted, but you know the amount, the time, the wallets they traded with, and what they sent back and forth. And with the richness of data, it is just a matter of time until you can identify the wallets. This is a huge data analysis tool to enforce our rules on the financial system that we are potentially giving away.

Right now, over the past year, the biggest winner has been Tether. They are offshore. They don't work well with us. They facilitate some activity they probably shouldn't, but the chaos is leading that stablecoin to grow while others shrink. The other thing that is happening is other countries are moving into this space.

Just this morning, before the hearing, I saw news that Russia is exploring legislation to formalize their ability to transact in crypto. If we don't take the field, others will do so before us, and they may not be doing it in ways that we like, so in the end, this matters. I would call upon the subcommittee to think deeply about passing some sort of bill about stablecoins. We can't let perfect be the enemy of good when one of our enemies here is time.

Right now, doing this right will bring financial inclusion through the dollar to billions of people globally. This is not just a U.S. concern; it reinforces the strength of the dollar in the world. It will help us fund the deficit. Every dollar that goes into stablecoins ends up in traditional financial instruments that we can use to fund our government, like T-Bills. It will bolster our reserve currency status, and it will ensure that if the blockchain continues to grow at the pace it has from 2012 to present, the standard of transaction on there for a currency is the dollar. Thank you very much.

[The prepared statement of Mr. Campbell can be found on page 36 of the appendix.]

Chairman HILL. Thank you, Mr. Campbell.

Mr. Chervinsky, you are now recognized for 5 minutes for your oral presentation.

Statement of Jake Chervinsky, Chief Policy Officer, Blockchain Association

Mr. CHERVINSKY. Thank you, Subcommittee Chairman Hill, Subcommittee Ranking Member Lynch, Full Committee Chairman McHenry, Full Committee Ranking Member Waters, and members of the subcommittee for inviting me to testify today. My name is Jake Chervinsky, and I am chief policy officer for the Blockchain Association, a nonprofit trade association dedicated to advancing good policy so that all of the benefits of public blockchains can be realized here in the United States. The Blockchain Association includes over 100 leading U.S. companies who are committed to responsible innovation, to advancing and strengthening the United States strategic position in global finance and technology, and to making financial services more accessible to American consumers.

My message for you today is simple: Congress must pass stablecoin legislation. Given the right policy, stablecoins can revolutionize the payment system and reinforce the dominance of the U.S. dollar at a time when our foreign adversaries, like China, are seeking to undermine its status as the global reserve currency.

In my time this morning, I want to give you three reasons why stablecoin legislation is so necessary. First, our financial system has a problem. It is stuck in the analog era of the last century, constrained by intermediaries who act as gatekeepers and middlemen to outdated infrastructure that has failed to keep pace with the digital age.

Today, the global economy is on all the time. It is always connected, and yet, our payment system is still slow, inefficient, unreliable, and inaccessible to many Americans. Public blockchains are the solution to that problem, a revolutionary upgrade on the technology that powers the global financial system. And U.S. dollar stablecoins are one of their best applications, allowing anyone with an internet connection to send any number of dollars to anywhere in the world, nearly instantly, and at nearly zero cost. Stablecoins outperform legacy payment rails across-the-board. They are safer, they are faster, they are cheaper, they are more reliable, and they are accessible to everyone. Now, new legislation is necessary to maximize the benefits of stablecoins and also to protect consumers and to ensure that the financial system is safe and sound.

Second, the status of the U.S. dollar as the global reserve currency is under threat by foreign adversaries like China, which is pushing the digital yuan as a competitor to the dollar. The best way for us to maintain U.S. dollar-dominance worldwide is to spread stablecoins all over the world. Stablecoins are indeed best suited to perform that task.

Third, if Congress fails to act, we will not only forfeit a huge competitive advantage to our adversaries, we will also lose entrepreneurs and innovators to other, more-welcoming jurisdictions like Europe, the United Kingdom, Singapore, Japan, Australia, and many others that are far ahead of the United States in regulating digital assets. Make no mistake, regulatory uncertainty is already driving innovation overseas. Adopting stablecoin legislation now will send an important message to the job creators and the taxpayers in the U.S. blockchain industry that they are still welcome here at home.

Members of the subcommittee, stablecoin legislation has already received bipartisan, bicameral support, and the Financial Services Committee has already made great strides toward a balanced and effective bill. I urge you to continue that work on a bipartisan basis, and I, along with the Blockchain Association and all of our member companies, stand ready and willing to help. I appreciate the chance to testify today, and I look forward to your questions. Thank you.

[The prepared statement of Mr. Chervinsky can be found on page 51 of the appendix.]

Chairman HILL. Thank you very much.

Mr. Disparte, you are now recognized for 5 minutes for your oral statement.

Statement of Dante Alighieri Disparte, Chief Strategy Officer and Head of Global Policy, Circle

Mr. DISPARTE. Full Committee Chairman McHenry, Full Committee Ranking Member Waters, Subcommittee Chairman Hill, Subcommittee Ranking Member Lynch, and members of the Subcommittee on Digital Assets, Financial Technology, and Inclusion, it is my honor to submit my testimony to you today. My name is Dante Disparte, and I am the chief strategy officer and head of global policy for Circle, a leading global financial technology firm, and the issuer of the USD coin, or USDC.

USDC is a dollar digital currency supporting the extensibility of the U.S. dollar in a competitive, always-on, internet-based global economy. Indeed, as fears grow of de-dollarization, or the rise of alternative payment systems that are non-conversant with U.S. values or broader norms in the rules-based financial system, Circle, USDC, and dollar-denominated payment stablecoins can help to ensure the dollar remains the global currency of preference, including natively on the internet.

Over the course of our 10 years of activity in the U.S. and around the world, we have always aspired to a regulation-first approach based on trust, transparency, accountability, and financial integrity. It has been 5 years since the first USDC was issued, which, for the purposes of this hearing and proposed legislation, can be considered a dollar-denominated payment stablecoin.

Today, USDC has supported more than $10 trillion in cumulative transactions on the public internet. A USDC-enabled, wallet-supported global payment network is in more than 190 countries, which is akin to a mobile money network like M-PESA, but at world scale. More than 75 percent of all USDCs in circulation are held in digital wallets and smart contracts rather than on digital asset exchanges, suggesting a strong correlation as a dollar-denominated store of value. Indeed, there is a, "Cambrian explosion," of use cases and responsible innovation, courtesy of the programmable, composable, trusted, and open nature of USDC. Rather than disrupting traditional financial systems or markets, we are seeing growing acceptance of USDC as a dollar settlement option among major financial services firms including Visa, MoneyGram, and Worldpay, among many others.

By every measure, courtesy of this early adoption of dollars as the currency of reference in digital assets markets, more than $132 billion of stablecoins in circulation reference the dollar, albeit to varying degrees of prudential regulatory standards. While some of these dollar-referenced stablecoins are starting to embrace sunlight and transparency, USDC was born in it. From the first issuance through to today, we have adopted macroprudential risk standards and transparency that is a hallmark of trust, even when compared to traditional financial services firms. As a result, a proliferation of enterprise use cases and adoption has followed.

Enterprise use cases for USDC run the gamut from Treasury management to easing the exacting cost and slow speeds of crossborder payments, which remain stubbornly high, and inconveniently slow, with little meaningful competition. Indeed, one of the partnerships we are the proudest of shows the art of the possible with USDC and the advantages of open interoperable payment systems. Last year, Circle, together with the Stellar Development Foundation and MoneyGram, partnered with the United Nations High Commissioner for Refugees (UNHCR), to enable USDC as a form of digital dollar cash assistance supporting war-displaced Ukrainian refugees.

As the sole issuer of USDC, Circle has always operated under the highest-prevailing regulatory standards for electronic-stored value and money transmission in the United States. While other countries regulate payments and electronic money activity at a national level, the U.S. framework empowers State banking and money transmission supervisors to foster, develop, and regulate the payments industry at the State level.

Although this sum-of-the-parts approach may be subject to potential operating and regulatory gaps, it has nonetheless produced an economic development model that has enabled companies to start up and scale across the United States. Our States are not only the laboratories of U.S. democracy, and crucibles for economic development, they are also the laboratories of payment services innovation. Rather than framing financial innovation and regulation as competing forces, Circle's operating experience over the last decade has prioritized public-private regulatory partnership and personhood.

In short, financial innovation, inclusion, and protecting the integrity of the financial system are not competing objectives. Today, we are comprehensively licensed as a State-supervised money transmission and electronic stored-value company across 48 States. We were the first company to receive a BitLicense from the New York State Department of Financial Services in 2015. We have been and remain a registered money services business conforming with the Financial Crimes Enforcement Network's (FinCEN's) guidance on combating illicit financial activity. The net result is a company that went from a mere idea 10 years ago, to a business that has approximately 1,000 employees in 35 States and 12 countries, with both strong prospects and the desire to become a U.S.-listed company.

Thank you for the opportunity to testify today. I look forward to addressing the committee's questions.

[The prepared statement of Mr. Disparte can be found on page 63 of the appendix.]

Chairman HILL. Thank you, sir. Ms. Hand, you are now recognized for 5 minutes for your oral presentation.

Statement of Delicia Reynolds Hand, Director, Financial Fairness, Consumer Reports

Ms. HAND. Thank you. Good morning, Full Committee Chairman McHenry, Full Committee Ranking Member Waters, Subcommittee Chairman Hill, Subcommittee Ranking Member Lynch, and members of the subcommittee. I am honored to participate in this important conversation about stablecoins and the need for legislation today. My name is Delicia Reynolds Hand, and I am the director of financial fairness at Consumer Reports, where I lead the organization's work to evaluate and rate digital financial products and services.

Today, these products and services promise all kinds of things— financial security, well-being, and even the ability to leverage new forms of asset classes—without financial intermediaries, with a simple swipe or click. Whether these products and services live up to these promises is still an open question, but it's one that we aim to answer through our product testing and consumer research.

Cryptocurrencies can be appealing to everyday consumers, whom traditional finance has never appropriately served. Our own 2022 Consumer Reports survey showed that African Americans once owned cryptocurrencies at a higher rate than other ethnic groups. These consumers have never been a priority of the traditional finance and banking system. They continue to live, however, in credit and intergenerational wealth deserts, so there is a certain appeal to something outside the very financial system which has largely ignored them. They are the targets of Super Bowl ads, influencers, and cryptocurrency kiosks.

But consumers are caught in a vicious cycle of boom and bust of crypto experimentation. It is a public policy disaster that there yet no uniform and meaningful regulatory frameworks in the United States. These risks are significant and include an unlimited supply of tokens and coins serving as collateral for loans, rigid self-executing smart contracts, non-existent reserve requirements, lack of interoperability requirements, lack of meaningful disclosures, and the creation of debtor-creditor relationships.

We need to see common-sense, consumer-first, comprehensive regulation, and the bill as posted, while it has some positive things, does create some concern. First, the bill creates the potential for regulatory arbitrage. An important check on our banking system is that even State-chartered institutions have to obtain Federal approval. But this bill has no equivalent requirements for Federal regulatory review, as the Federal Reserve Board or other regulators would have no authority to reject State licensing.

Second, while the bill does outline an important role for Federal oversight, and require parent companies of bank subsidiaries authorized as stablecoin issuers to be insured depository institutions, it doesn't provide the same requirement for non-bank issuers, and allowing this will create confusion and less protection for consumers who choose to purchase stablecoins that do not offer such insurance. While the bill sets up a regime to approve issuers of payment stablecoins, it doesn't outline how payment activities conducted or facilitated by the issuers or their coins will have adequate consumer protections. Consumers need to be able to prevent, cancel, replace, or override a transaction. And this is a critical, critical function necessary to ensure that payment system operators are able to conduct chargebacks or facilitate disputes over payments.

Consumers have come to rely on interoperability, and they should have the same benefits in stablecoin payments. But this bill does not require interoperable technology protocol, although the bill calls for the development of standards. This may still impede consumer access and leave consumers walled off into each institution's specific system.

We would also like to see additional language associated with custodial wallets. While custodial wallets may help consumers keep track of their keys, this has created a legal gray area that should be clarified. The law should prevent a debtor-creditor relationship from being formed, and this should be clearly required in the disclosures.

There are additional consumer investor protections that we would like to see included or improved in the bill such as moving from outdated notice and disclosures, prohibiting the commingling of funds, requiring a 24-hour calendar day redemption requirement, and ensuring that a consumer's use of stablecoins does not create the debtor-creditor relationship. Notably, we want to see all Federal regulators have a clear and meaningful role in this space. I encourage committee members to continue to work together on a bipartisan basis, and I appreciate the ability to be here with you today. Thank you.

[The prepared statement of Ms. Hand can be found on page 73 of the appendix.]

Chairman HILL. Thank you very much for your testimony. We will now turn to Member questions, and the Chair recognizes himself for 5 minutes for questions.

Currently, the SEC and the CFTC are taking contradictory positions in court about whether one of the most-utilized stablecoins in the market is a security or a commodity. This creates an impossible situation for the private sector, for other regulators, and for stablecoin issuers, who can't possibly comply with both securities and commodities laws at the same time. One of the main goals of our legislation is to resolve this regulatory uncertainty once and for all.

Let me start with you, Mr. Disparte. Can you discuss the impact of that conflict?

Mr. DISPARTE. Thank you, Chairman Hill. Indeed, this is what I like to classify as sort of a regulatory Game of Thrones at the Federal level, and it isn't helpful. I think we saw that yesterday in the committee. Looking at securities issues alone, it isn't particularly helpful. There is a proliferation of digital assets in circulation. However, virtually every country of substance in the world treats payment stablecoins under an equivalent national regime that would conform with electronic money rules and as a payments and banking innovation, not as a securities or commodities innovation. They might be used in digital asset trading, but their core function, particularly when treated as a payment stablecoin, is to solve the buyers and spenders remorse that were one of the original sins, if you will, of the digital assets industry.

Chairman HILL. Thank you.

Mr. Campbell, in your view, should non-interest-bearing payment stablecoins be considered securities?

Mr. CAMPBELL. No, I would echo Mr. Disparte's comments. These fundamentally work like money. They operate like banking products. Unless you believe that something like JPMorgan's bank deposits or physical U.S. dollars should be securities, then they should not be either. They should note that well.

Chairman HILL. Okay. That is helpful. Let me switch gears. The current regulatory framework for stablecoins is mostly handled by State regulators and FinCEN. The State frameworks, New York being the most recognizable, provide critical consumer protections and regulatory oversight. As we seek to set up a Federal framework, it is critical that we also retain multiple pathways for payment stablecoin issuers. This is an aspect of the proposal that I particularly want to make sure we get right. We had a version of that in the draft.

So, Superintendent Harris, what role do you think State regulators currently play, and should play in regulating payment stablecoin issuers?

Ms. HARRIS. Thank you so much, Mr. Chairman. I think the State regulators can play an incredibly important role. As you have seen in New York, we work very closely with FinCEN, among other Federal regulators, but we have been able to nimbly respond to all of the changes in the marketplace, laying out a flexible licensing and charter regime both through our BitLicense and limited purpose trust, and engaging in supervisory agreements with each of our licensed entities, so that we can tailor our oversight to each of the risks that those entities present, examining on a regular basis, and bringing enforcement actions when necessary.

And as I noted in my testimony, everything that we do is based on the banking supervision model, and I think it would be very helpful to see the dual regulatory framework that we use in banking duplicated for cryptocurrency and stablecoins as well.

Chairman HILL. Good. Thank you. And consumer protection is at the forefront of what you do and investors, right?

Ms. HARRIS. Absolutely, we require—

Chairman HILL. I thought Ms. Hand made a good point about making sure that is at the forefront of what we are doing, and you would echo that as a State regulator?

Ms. HARRIS. Absolutely. We require robust disclosures about fees and risks. We require one-to-one reserving and attestations, we don't allow lending of consumer assets, and we require segregation, all of which are very important consumer protections.

Chairman HILL. Thank you. Representative Himes is visiting our subcommittee today. We are glad to have you, Mr. Himes. He and I have a bill called the 21st Century Dollar Act. The mission is to ask the Treasury to inform Congress about how to keep the pre-eminence of the dollar-based trading system in the world, which is integral to the economic success of the U.S., and has been a boon for countries all over the world in the past 8 decades. It is a positive thing, not a negative thing, and only people who think it is negative are people who are sanctioning. So, you have to think about that for a little bit. We are not here to emulate whatever the surveillance State policies are of Iran or China.

In my view, one of the benefits of creating regulatory certainty in America is preserving this innovation in our country and preserving the U.S. dollar's status as the global reserve currency.

Mr. Disparte, could you reflect on the role stablecoins can play in supporting U.S. dollar dominance?

Mr. DISPARTE. Thank you, Mr. Chairman. As I mentioned in my testimony, cumulatively, in 5 years alone, Circle's USDC has processed $10 trillion of internet-native payments. This is an activity that is not possible by any other means and any other transactions. Most of the world's payment systems labor under what is known as the, "walled garden," problem. That would be the equivalent of a Gmail account not being able to send an email to a Hotmail account because the two systems are not conversing.

Chairman HILL. Thank you very much. If there are any further thoughts from witnesses on the panel, please respond in writing.

I'd now like to turn to my friend, Mr. Lynch, the ranking member of the subcommittee, for 5 minutes.

Mr. LYNCH. Thank you, Mr. Chairman. Ms. Hand, the landscape of stablecoins has changed considerably in recent months. In particular, it has shrunk due to failure of some stablecoin issuers following the collapse of FTX, the crypto exchange. About a million customers lost all of their money, totaling about $8.9 billion. All of this has revealed some complex risks associated with stablecoins, including their lack of stable values. Obviously, stablecoins are not stable. I know that there have been warnings to the banking system about the custody of stablecoins and dealing with other cryptocurrencies and also the vulnerability to runs that we have seen recently. Can you talk about some of the other risks that have been exposed in recent months? And could you also discuss the ways in which the current legislation that is tied to this hearing does not reflect those vulnerabilities and does not offer ways to address those new risks?

Ms. HAND. Certainly. Thank you for the question. I think one of the primary risks has actually been brought up in testimony here today with reference to the growing acceptance of USDC by financial institutions. So, despite the recent instability and volatility that has impacted the fiat currency banking system, we continue to see the traditional financial industry invest, and this is at the risk of consumers. We need to see in a bill clear activity limitations that reflects some of the issues that came up in recent months.

We need to see limitations on commingling. That was an issue with FTX. We also need to see restrictions on self-dealing, and undisclosed conflicts of interest. And very explicitly for the consumers in Celsius, who were not able to recover, we need to prevent a debt-or-creditor relationship so that my coins are my coins, and not those of the company. Those are some of the key risks that we see are not addressed, among other things.

Mr. LYNCH. I do want to make one correction in what I said before. I think I talked about Tether's collapse, but it was actually Terra, not Tether, that collapsed. Tether just dropped in value. One of the things I worry about in this current legislation being proposed is that it would allow stablecoin issuers access to the Federal Reserve services, the discount window.

One of the saving graces of the FTX collapse, and other subsequent collapses, is that it wasn't tied to the traditional banking system. We had ring-fenced the crypto industry so well that most of those losses were occurring in the crypto industry itself, and did not infect the traditional banking system, which is the envy of the world, and provides so much power to the U.S. dollar, and provides us a safe haven for much global investment. Can you discuss the risks that can come with allowing stablecoin issuers to act like banks without the regulatory framework that provides protection to depositors and provides integrity to our entire system?

Ms. HAND. Certainly. I will start with an historical point, which is the reason why we have the National Bank Acts. They stemmed from a series of bank failures, and systemic runs, and a complete lack of Federal oversight. So in the equivalent here, we need that clarity. We cannot treat non-bank entities like banks without the equivalent restrictions to their access to consumers and not having substantive consumer protections in place.

Mr. LYNCH. My time has expired, and I yield back.

Chairman HILL. The Chair now recognizes Mr. Lucas of Oklahoma for 5 minutes.

Mr. LUCAS. Thank you, Mr. Chairman. I appreciate that. I think it is helpful as we work through this process to do just a little bit of housekeeping on some of the definitions. "Stablecoin" attempts to provide a relatively stable value in pegging its value to realworld assets.

Mr. Campbell, could you elaborate on the different categories of underlying assets that can back a stablecoin, and then specifically on the payment stablecoins in the legislation we are discussing today?

Mr. CAMPBELL. Yes, thank you very much. If we look out in the wild, there are really three kinds of stablecoins that have existed. The first is what I would call fiat-backed stablecoins. They kind of work the way you have in your mind, which is there is a pile of some sort of financial instruments behind them. The second is crypto-backed. This is people attempting to over-collateralize with things like Bitcoin or Ethereum. And then, the last version is algorithmic, which are backed by some sort of mathematical relationship.

I can tell you that the first category has been largely successful. The second two are highly-experimental financial products that probably should not be called, "stable." And I would say specifically within this bill, defining stablecoins as the first category with good reserve guidelines and then consumer protections around what you are allowed to call a stablecoin would be greatly helpful. Thank you.

Mr. LUCAS. Ms. Harris, you discussed the general approval process for a BitLicense through the New York State Department of Financial Services (DFS) and how DFS enters into supervisory agreements with companies based on their individual risks and business models. Could you elaborate a bit more on examples of specific risks presented by a firm that could be addressed in a supervisory agreement?

Ms. HARRIS. Absolutely. Thank you, sir. First, I want to note that we have one licensing and one chartering regime in New York, so it gives companies the flexibility to choose a regime that matches their business model without sacrificing any regulatory rigor. Then, once a firm has a license or a charter, as you noted, we engage in the negotiation of a supervisory agreement that allows us to tailor our oversight to risks.

So, imagine a company that wants to offer a coin on two different protocols. We can require separate disclosures, enhance cybersecurity controls, and enhance Bank Secrecy Act/Anti-Money Laundering (BSA/AML) controls, based on the risk that those protocols might present. We also have preapproval for every new product or material change in business a licensee seeks to offer.

Mr. LUCAS. Mr. Disparte, Circle's USD Coin fell below its $1 peg during the banking turmoil that stemmed from Silicon Valley Bank (SVB). SVB was, of course, one of the banks that Circle used to manage cash reserves. And as we all know, the regulators stepped in to fully insure those deposits. Mr. Disparte, could you discuss the lessons learned from the collapse of SVB and what the potential impact of the SVB collapse was to USDC?

Mr. DISPARTE. Thank you for the question, Congressman. We learned a lot of lessons, the first of which is that while many of the policy conversations have been about what risks could crypto and digital assets introduce to the traditional banking system in the traditional sector, we learned with the failure of not one bank, but three successive bank failures consecutively over the course of several weeks, that we had to protect our business from risks in banking. And one of those risks obviously could have been an existential-level event for America's commercial banks, but for the Federal intervention. And over the course of the weekend, Circle, like any other U.S.-regulated money transmitter, had a fiduciary obligation to redeem all USDC demands at par. We were able to make that promise on the Saturday after the bank failures began, closing the temporary DPAC of USDC from $0.88 to $0.98.

And today, as we advocate for this legislation, one of the points that we could separate is payments activity from banking because Circle, like any other company that relies on banks for payments, had an exposure, and that exposure was what happens with uninsured deposits inside the banking system.

Mr. LUCAS. Absolutely. I thank the witnesses for their observations, and with that, Mr. Chairman, I yield back.

Chairman HILL. I thank the gentleman from Oklahoma. And I recognize the distinguished gentlewoman from California, the ranking member of the Full Committee, Ms. Waters, for 5 minutes.

Ms. WATERS. Thank you very much. First of all, I am a little bit surprised that Superintendent Harris is here today. I didn't know that you have a regulatory framework for stablecoins. Do you?

Ms. HARRIS. Yes, ma'am, we do, quite a robust one that exists both in regulation in our supervisory agreements and in our recent guidance that we issued.

Ms. WATERS. I agree with most of our panel that we should move very quickly to establish the stablecoin bill and get that legislation going. But since I have you here, Ms. Harris, I cannot help but ask you a few questions about the stablecoins that we are concerned about, which certainly are very important. But you just had a big bank failure in New York, and I want to take a moment or so to understand that. What happened with one of the biggest bank failures in the country as it relates to cryptocurrency, if I may?

Ms. HARRIS. Absolutely, ma'am. It is a misnomer that the failure of Signature Bank was related to crypto. What we saw with Signature Bank is that it had a new-fashioned bank run and the outflow of deposits were from a broad depositor base, including wholesale food vendors, fiduciaries' trust accounts, and law firms. And in fact, the outflow of crypto deposits was in exact proportion to the representation in the depositor base overall, and, in fact, some of those deposit outflows were actually pre-planned. It is, of course, unfortunate that there was a run on the bank at Signature prompted by what we saw with SVB, but it is not the case that the failure of Signature was related to crypto.

Ms. WATERS. Again, why is it understood or believed that it was related to cryptocurrency? How do you absolutely excuse cryptocurrency from being a part of the problem at Signature, that caused it to be in the situation where it had to be closed down?

Ms. HARRIS. Yes, ma'am. I think it is part of what has transpired with social media and other things. It is true that Signature banked a healthy proportion of crypto customers; about 20 percent of its depositor base was crypto companies. They were known and had announced previously that they were de-risking from the crypto space. But again, with the run we saw on the bank that Friday evening, about 20 percent of the deposits left the bank, but 20 percent of that 20 percent was crypto. The rest were normal commercial customers with uninsured deposits that were leaving the bank.

And so, we did not see the collapse as a result of crypto deposits and their instability. There was a broad base of depositors that left the bank. The crypto depositors that left the bank were in exact proportion to their depositor base, so it really was just a new-fashioned bank run prompted by what happened with SVB.

Ms. WATERS. As you know, there will be continued discussions and hearings and investigations on the issue. But since you do have a regulatory regime for the stablecoin, much of the concern that we have learned about has to do with assets and whether or not they are credible, and what can be called an asset, and how can we be sure that we are going to protect the investors with assets that may not be real. What have you learned about that?

Ms. HARRIS. We have learned a great deal, and let me start by saying in New York, we did not license FTX. They could not do business in New York. The same is true of Voyager, and the same is true of Celsius. They did not meet our standards, so they could not operate in New York, even though they could operate in the rest of the country. We require our stablecoin issuers to back their stablecoins one-to-one with cash and cash equivalents. They have to provide redemption to their customers within 2 business days. They have to provide public and independent attestations of their reserve mix on their websites. And we have robust capital requirements based on a very sophisticated formula that we require our companies to have, which is why no New York-licensed entity has gone bankrupt.

Ms. WATERS. What advice would you give us, since we are still at the point of putting together legislation and hopefully working in a bipartisan way to do that? What advice can you give us about determining what is and what is not a real asset?

Ms. HARRIS. I think, ma'am, the framework that we have put together in New York is a very good model that has served well to protect New Yorkers. And I would urge the committee to do what it can to duplicate that and to allow for a State pathway so that nimble regulators can continue to police the space appropriately.

Ms. WATERS. Thank you very much.

Ms. Hand, given the implications of our national payment system, should we allow States to regulate payment stablecoins on their own? Does a Federal agency, like the Fed, need a role to approve payment stablecoins before they are issued in addition to regulating their digital wallet providers?

Chairman HILL. Could you submit that answer in writing?

Ms. HAND. Yes, I am happy to do so.

Chairman HILL. The gentlewoman's time has expired.

Ms. WATERS. Thank you.

Chairman HILL. The Chair now recognizes Mr. Davidson, who is also the Vice Chair of this subcommittee, and the Chair of our Housing and Insurance Subcommittee, for 5 minutes.

Mr. DAVIDSON. Thank you, Mr. Chairman. And thanks to our witnesses for being here today. I also thank the staff on both sides of the aisle for all of the work that has gone into getting to this point on the stablecoin bill. The market has been pleading for this for a long time, except in New York.

The New York regulators have been way ahead of the curve. I am glad that more of my colleagues are learning that not only is there a regulatory framework in place, but that it is essentially impossible for a stablecoin to go to zero. And the reason is that it is backed by Level 1 high-quality liquid assets or, in at least one case, physical custody of a commodity, not a derivatives contract like a net asset value fund, but actual audited, physically-present custody of a commodity.

Superintendent Harris, you regulate those things, so what would you say are the key elements of the guidance that gives people confidence that a stablecoin really is stable and backed by the full value, whether that is $1, or in the case of a commodity, the value of the commodity?

Ms. HARRIS. Thank you so much for your questions, and they are precisely the elements that you mentioned. And I will also note that in New York, we have not approved any algorithmically-backed stablecoins for issuance or listing in New York, but it is that one-to-one backing. It is our prohibition on commingling rehypothecation lending. It is our T+2 redemption, and it is our audit and reporting requirements, I think, that gives consumers quite a bit of confidence in a New York-regulated entity.

Mr. DAVIDSON. Just as a follow-up, when you look at the implications of that—I am from Ohio, and we don't have an Ohio regulator that is doing what you are doing. But a Federal framework for payments stablecoins would say, we can trust that the New York financial services regulators have this. At some level, we would have some Federal supervision that would interact like we do in other financial services, and that would be highly compatible with your existing State-based regulatory framework?

Ms. HARRIS. Absolutely, sir.

Mr. DAVIDSON. Thank you very much for that clarification.

Mr. Campbell, Tether is the largest stablecoin in the ecosystem, and it is headquartered in Hong Kong. What does it mean for the stablecoin ecosystem that Tether is located offshore, and how has Tether become such a large player in the space?

Mr. CAMPBELL. Thank you for the question. I would say, one, Tether has become a large player because they had a first-mover advantage. They started in 2014 before other stablecoins, and that just speaks to the problem of inaction. When people can't move elsewhere, you end up with entrenched incumbents.

Two, Tether has not faced the same kind of regulatory uncertainty. They don't have the concerns that others do about having to conform with something relatively strict and relatively demanding like the NYDFS guidance, which, by the way, I greatly support, having worked in that space as well, that keeps consumers safe. They are not transparent. It is unclear if they have always had all the reserves, and it puts people at risk, but when they are the default option because others are being hamstrung, it is what people use, because there is demand for dollars on a blockchain. So, I think it is there just because it has been available.

Mr. DAVIDSON. Yes. I think that is a big part of it, and thanks for your clarification. Because they don't have the transparency and disclosure requirements, I have at times referred to it as a, "time bomb," because we have clarity in New York, but we don't have clarity into Hong Kong's market. And frankly, the move to Hong Kong is a step in the right direction, because for a while it wasn't even clear that they were accountable even in Hong Kong, so hopefully, Tether is as stable as it is purported to be. But I think the real opportunity for us is for this body to create legal clarity.

And look, we hit SEC Chairman Gensler pretty hard yesterday on his failure at the SEC to provide clarity, but ultimately, we should be clear: The job to provide legal clarity at the Federal level is right here in this body. And I just want to thank Chairman McHenry, and, when she was Chair, Maxine Waters, for paying attention to this space. The market really needs this legal clarity, and I think that is something that both of you have highlighted.

Let me close with Mr. Chervinsky. If stablecoins are to eventually be used as an actual medium of exchange to move that store of value that is stable, do you believe it is necessary that they retain the attributes of cash, which is permissionless, peer-to-peer transactions versus an intermediary third-party that facilitates the transactions?

Mr. CHERVINSKY. Thank you for your question, Congressman. I think that is absolutely critical. I think that we are currently moving toward a cashless society, and we can go in one of two directions. We can either follow China and have a currency that is totally controlled and surveilled by governments and also by corporations to sort of a business model of surveillance capitalism where we can reproduce the benefits of cash. I think we all agree that cash is a very important tool for people to use and we can do that in the digital space using stablecoins.

Chairman HILL. The gentleman's time has expired.

Mr. DAVIDSON. To be trusted, it has to have those characteristics. My time has expired, and I yield back.

Chairman HILL. Thank you. And I now recognize my friend from Illinois, the distinguished ranking member of our Subcommittee on Financial Institutions and Monetary Policy, Dr. Foster, for 5 minutes.

Mr. FOSTER. I guess I will start with a question that I asked a little more than a year ago when we had SBF and all of the crypto luminaries in front of our committee, and what I regard as the foundational question on identity, which is, if we wish to prevent crypto assets from being used for ransomware and a long list of illicit activities, is there any alternative to having every crypto transaction traceable to the secure digital identity issued by a country with which we have extradition treaties, or is there any technological solution to that of which anyone is aware, or do we have to just say, we cannot have self-custody? We can't have any of these? We can't have anonymous transactions? Is there anyone who believes there is a solution that prevents ransomware, and doesn't violate that?

Mr. CHERVINSKY. I will take that, Congressman. I think that there will be those solutions, and I can tell you—

Mr. FOSTER. No, that is not acceptable. I am talking about doing something right now. Right now, is there a technology that stops ransomware, if we allow self-custody on anonymous transactions?

Mr. CHERVINSKY. There are many companies working on very important—

Mr. FOSTER. That do not have solutions that work. I understand there are many companies that are anonymous Monaro-type collaborations that are trying to make the exact opposite happen. I think everyone watching this debate should understand that either you support continuation of ransomware and all of that illicit stuff or you don't, and it is a pretty much a binary choice that we have to face. Another example of this is, let's say that someone puts a gun to your head, drags you into an alley, and says, get out your phone and transfer all of your digital assets to me, are you screwed or not? In your ideal world, are you in your utopia? What is your reaction to that?

Mr. CAMPBELL. I will say that if you look at the models of existing stablecoins, including the Paxos stablecoins that I previously ran, we do have a solution to this problem, and I advocate for it in my testimony. Stablecoins that exist on public blockchain should have freeze and cease capabilities. If there is illicit action, we need the ability to take those coins back and prevent them from being spent. We also need blockchain surveillance tools, which Superintendent Harris talked about, and they exist: Chainalysis; Elliptic; Inca Digital.

Mr. FOSTER. But these are being defeated by more anonymous coins all the time.

Mr. CAMPBELL. Only when using crypto assets that are not the regulated stablecoins.

Mr. FOSTER. Okay. So, part of your vision is that there be mandatory transparency so that ultimately, regulators can see the true identities behind the participants in transactions?

Mr. CAMPBELL. That is one option. I would say the other is right now, given the lack of clarity and the inability of many of the most-regulated financial institutions to operate in this space, you have many bad actors. If you create a Federal pathway where they use specifically-regulated stablecoins that have these properties—

Mr. FOSTER. Yes, ultimately, what we need is the equivalent of a license plate on every digital wallet because if you think about how essential the development of license plates and driver's licenses were to the healthy development of the automobile industry, you know that this was crucial. It would be completely unacceptable to have unlicensed cars and unlicensed drivers driving through your neighborhood or across your international borders.

And it can be anonymous, like a license plate is anonymous, under most circumstances, but you have to have that guarantee that if someone drives through your neighborhood and runs over your dog, you can jot down the license plate, take it to a trusted court system, de-anonymize the owner of that car or that wallet, and haul them into court.

Mr. CAMPBELL. I would say, in fact, in the freeze-and-seize regimes for stablecoins, you don't even need anything other than their license plate. I don't need to know who owns a wallet address to take the assets out of it. If somebody was hacked, and all we know is the wallet address, you can take those assets back.

Mr. FOSTER. You have to know the private key associated with it.

Mr. CAMPBELL. No. No. With the freeze of stablecoins—

Mr. FOSTER. If you have or if you are willing to—

Mr. CAMPBELL. —if the token is standard, we can take it back.

Mr. FOSTER. With some kind of governance superseding and overpowering the blockchain, in which case the blockchain doesn't rule, you have a trusted third party that can reverse transactions.

Mr. CAMPBELL. That is essentially correct in how the centralized fiat stablecoin issuers—

Mr. FOSTER. Okay. For my last 30 seconds here, there is a whole bundle of things associated with rapid run risk, fraudulent minting implications on monetary policy, that all seemed like they would be perfectly addressed with a simple rule that any stablecoin that is issued has to be associated with an account at the Federal Reserve, and that no issuance is valid until it is accompanied by an attestation from the Fed that the total amount that has been issued is less than what is on reserve at the Fed. And a simple API that the Fed would provide, as well as the license, seems like an answer to that whole bundle of things.

Is there anyone, if you can answer for the record, who sees any problems with that simple rule? Among other things, it provides a business model for issuers, because they get to collect the interest from the Fed.

Chairman HILL. I would invite the panel to respond to that good question in writing.

Thank you, Mr. Foster. The Chair now recognizes the gentleman from South Carolina, Mr. Timmons, for 5 minutes.

Mr. TIMMONS. Thank you, Mr. Chairman. Mr. Disparte, in the last few weeks, $6 billion has been transferred from USDC to foreign stablecoins. That $6 billion left the U.S. economy. That $6 billion is no longer subject to the same U.S. AML/KYC standards. Could you opine on this? What do you believe are the reasons for this mass exodus of U.S. funds, and do you believe it is due to the lack of regulatory clarity? And what implications does that have for our national security?

Mr. DISPARTE. Thank you for the question, Congressman. I do think for a lot of users of these alternatives in the world, be it alternative payment systems, or in this case, Tether, opacity is the future they are looking for the most, and that should be neither conflated nor confused with the presumption of privacy in financial services, whether digital or analog. But I do think there is a race to the bottom taking place in corners of this market segment, and candidly, the void of regulatory clarity in the United States is partly filling that vacuum.

And there is also a geopolitical digital currency space race taking place around the world that I think, more importantly and perhaps more kinetically in the short run, also manifests itself as a digital assets 5G war. So, just as there are certain companies you wouldn't want building hardware and software in your telecommunications infrastructure, I think there are certain firms in this industry that you wouldn't want building the financial plumbing of the future. And many of those firms are operating with impunity outside of the perimeter of major jurisdictions including the United States.

Mr. TIMMONS. Thank you for that. It seems direct contradictions from regulators are just one of the many signs that show Congress needs to act. Many stablecoin projects are fleeing the United States for countries that have established clear frameworks for payment stablecoin issuance. The longer the U.S. goes without a clear regulatory framework for stablecoins, the more this will accelerate.

Mr. Chervinsky, would you describe what the impact will be if legislation is not enacted?

Mr. CHERVINSKY. Thank you for your question. I think if Congress doesn't act, then stablecoins will be issued in other countries. There is a clear desire for this type of technology and for its application to national currencies, and there are many other jurisdictions that are adopting workable frameworks. And I think what that means is that the United States will not be able to ensure that stablecoin issuers are observing American principles. It also may mean that stablecoins will not be based on the U.S. dollar to begin with. We will see euro stablecoins in Europe, and yen stablecoins in Japan, and that will be a hit to U.S. dollar dominance, and is something that we should avoid.

Mr. TIMMONS. Thank you. The draft legislation attached to this hearing would require stablecoin issuers to produce information such as financial inclusion reports annually.

Mr. Campbell, in your view, what is helpful to know about a stablecoin issuer? Would you consider financial inclusion reporting as materially-important enough to be statutorily-required?

Mr. CAMPBELL. Thank you for the question. I would start by saying I primarily think of these as banking products, which means the first thing I think about is safety and soundness when I think about stablecoins. Number one on the list when you think about transparency is transparency of reserve assets, composition of reserve assets, and giving everybody from a financial inclusion perspective, the faith that they can use this instrument, and it is backed by things like cash at U.S. banks that is insured, it is backed by T-Bills, it is backed by the correct forms of assets. Then, where you end up with from an inclusion standpoint is regardless of reporting at very low cost with very low friction, every American and others can use this product.

Mr. TIMMONS. Thank you for that. Mr. Chairman, I yield back.

Chairman HILL. The gentleman from South Carolina yields back. The gentleman from New York, Mr. Torres, is now recognized for 5 minutes.

Mr. TORRES. Thank you. Superintendent Harris, I said to you privately and will reiterate publicly that I will not support any stablecoin legislation that preempts the New York State Department of Financial Services or otherwise encroaches on the sovereignty of New York State. As a New Yorker, that is a red line for me.

When it comes to finance, there is a long tradition of dual regulation. Just like banking has both a Federal option and a State option, stablecoin issuance should have both a Federal option and a State option, and a State option should exist not only on paper but in practice. The Federal Government should certainly have a floor that prevents regulatory arbitrage to be sure, but there is no need for a ceiling that preempts either in theory or in practice does the proposed legislation before us create a genuine system of dual regulation.

Ms. HARRIS. Thank you so much, Congressman. It has been such a pleasure to get to know you and work with you since taking on this role, so I appreciate your partnership. I think there are certainly improvements that could be made to the present legislation, although it has language which states that nothing in the legislation will preempt States in practice. I think there are a number of provisions that give Federal regulators veto authority over State regulators and their judgments and oversights that would be counterproductive and provide a disincentive for companies to take a State path.

Mr. TORRES. So, we are not quite there yet.

Ms. HARRIS. Not quite yet.

Mr. TORRES. Do you agree that stablecoin issuers should be fully reserved and that those reserves should consist of 100 percent cash or cash equivalents?

Ms. HARRIS. Absolutely, and that is what we do in New York.

Mr. TORRES. And do you agree that those stablecoin reserves should be verified not only by self-attestation, but also by a third-party audit?

Ms. HARRIS. Yes, and that is what we do in New York.

Mr. TORRES. Common sense dictates that you cannot have an honor system in which a charlatan like Sam Bankman-Fried claims to be fully reserved and then the regulators take his word for it.

Ms. HARRIS. Exactly.

Mr. TORRES. The President's Working Group (PWG) report proposes banking regulation for stablecoin issuers, but since a stablecoin issuer has no fractionalization of reserves and no lending function like a bank, it would seem to me that a stablecoin issuer operates differently from a bank and therefore should be regulated differently.

Mr. Chervinsky, do you agree with that analysis?

Mr. CHERVINSKY. I completely agree, and I think that we can design reasonably-tailored regulations for non-bank entities to issue stablecoins in a way that is just as safe and sound as a bank doing the same.

Mr. TORRES. SEC Chair Gary Gensler asserts that an alternate regulatory framework for crypto would undermine 90 years of securities law. Since American federalism has 50 laboratories of democracy, we can actually test that thesis, that hypothesis against the regulatory experience of one of those laboratories, New York State. New York State crypto regulation is segregated from securities regulation. The New York State Department of Financial Services regulates crypto, whereas the New York State Attorney General regulates securities. So, has the Gensler hypothesis been proven right or wrong in New York? Has a separate regulatory framework for crypto undercut securities regulation?

Ms. HARRIS. What I would say is our authorities do not depend on definitions about what is a security, what is a commodity, or what is a currency. At DFS, we have blanket authority over virtual assets, and we exercise it accordingly. Some of our companies are also subject to registration requirements with the Attorney General, and I think what we have done in New York has proven to be quite successful for some of the reasons we have discussed today.

Mr. TORRES. So, has a separate licensing regime for crypto come at the expense of regulatory rigor?

Ms. HARRIS. No, not at all, to the contrary.

Mr. TORRES. In fact, New York State DFS is the most rigorous regulator of crypto in the country.

Ms. HARRIS. And I would say in the world.

Mr. TORRES. In fact, who was the first to raise red flags about the insufficient reserves of Tether? It was not the SEC. It was not the CFTC. It was the State of New York.

Ms. HARRIS. Correct.

Mr. TORRES. So, the notion that a separate regulatory framework for crypto would undermine 90 years of securities law has been definitively disproven in New York State. The legacy financial system has high fees and long delays that prey upon the lowest-income Americans. Poor people of color have to pay predatory fees in order to transfer their own money to loved ones abroad. Stablecoin has the ability to function as a currency, and blockchain has the ability to move money from peer to peer in real time.

Mr. Campbell, is it fair to say that the combination of those two technologies has the potential to create a better, cheaper, and faster payment system? Actually, that question is for both Mr. Campbell and Mr. Disparte.

Mr. CAMPBELL. I thank you for the question, and I would say yes, unequivocally. The beauty of a blockchain is it treats everybody the same. If you have low fees, high transparency, and a high ability to transact, everybody can use it regardless of the amount of money they have, and I think that is one of the best features of this new technological innovation.

Mr. DISPARTE. Unequivocally.

Mr. TORRES. Short and sweet. I yield back.

Chairman HILL. The gentleman from New York yields back. The gentlewoman from Indiana, Mrs. Houchin, is recognized for 5 minutes.

Mrs. HOUCHIN. Thank you, Chairman Hill and Ranking Member Lynch. And thank you to the witnesses for your testimony and for speaking with us today.

As I highlighted yesterday in our hearing with SEC Chair Gensler, I am concerned about the lack of regulatory clarity from agencies and the restrictive, overly-burdensome approach that many of our Federal regulators are taking with the digital assets ecosystem. The constant threat of regulation by enforcement has done nothing to help businesses and innovators here in the United States. Instead, an unclear approach by the Federal agencies has only served to push innovators elsewhere.

Mr. Disparte, Circle just announced it is opening its European headquarters in Paris. What does the regulatory environment for stablecoins look like in the European Union?

Mr. DISPARTE. Thank you for the question, Congresswoman. The European Union, since 2019, has embarked on a whole-of-region, whole-of-economy framework for digital assets known as the Markets in Crypto-Assets Regulation framework. Originally, this was in response to fears of Big Tech and, at some level, fears of China tech or geopolitical competition in technology. But today, that framework has evolved into perhaps the world's most comprehensive framework for digital assets that including the topic of stablecoins would acknowledge them as electronic money, tokens, and would passport those licenses across the European Union.

Circle has just announced the submission of two licenses in Europe and Paris, and France is the venue of choice. One is an electronic money license and the second is a digital assets service provider license. And the two of them would allow for all of the activity that we support here to be effectively exported to Europe. I should add, we have also filed for a similar license in Singapore as a major payments institution.

Mrs. HOUCHIN. How does it compare to the draft proposal from the 117th Congress that is attached to this hearing?

Mr. DISPARTE. On the one hand, it is a much broader framework. The European framework, Markets in Crypto-Assets (MiCA) framework, contemplates broader activities and payments stablecoins. It contemplates digital asset trading, which types of assets would be systemic, definitional issues around market conduct, and so on, but it does have many aspects that would be comparable. For example, the requirement of prudential treatment of stablecoin reserves, segregation of funds, a lot of the disclosure points that we have highlighted so far in this hearing.

Mrs. HOUCHIN. And to be clear, the EU is not the only foreign political entity that is moving on this issue. Mr. Campbell, Mr. Disparte, could you shed some light on what other countries' regulatory frameworks for stablecoins look like, and what the frameworks require of issuers? I am looking at what are the implications of the United States not being the first mover in this space, and how has that impacted the current dynamics of the overall ecosystem?

Mr. CAMPBELL. Thank you for that question. I would say, if you look around the world, you are starting to see legislation that deals specifically with fiat-backed stablecoins, so nobody is really embracing crypto-backed. Nobody is really embracing algorithmic. But places like Singapore, Dubai, Abu Dhabi, and the U.K., which is now working on a framework like the European Union, all have frameworks that I would say are substantially similar to what has been proposed in the 117th Congress bill. I think we can do better in America. Our financial regulation and systems are more robust than some of those places, but, in general, if we don't act, those are the best options, and people will take advantage of them. Thank you.

Mr. DISPARTE. And for my part, I don't subscribe to the view that it is a zero-sum proposition. I do think the stakes are increasingly higher and there are more choices in terms of jurisdictions and venues, but it should be made clear that Circle, or a company like Circle, probably wouldn't have been started successfully in any other country around the world. But the fact that we are now a net exporter of our operating model and business model does require, I think, that the U.S. pay attention to these alternative jurisdictions.

There are other places as well. Later in June, Japan will issue broad, comprehensive stablecoin guidance. Hong Kong has come back online in a broad way. But the innovation ultimately will conform, I think, with all of the rules that we could set forth in this committee. And I do think it is really critical that the path for digital assets is increasingly shaped by city states as opposed to nation states. And we see that, of course, with New York, Singapore, Hong Kong, and many other jurisdictions around the world.

Mrs. HOUCHIN. Thank you. Without proper action, I certainly fear the U.S. could lose its leading role in digital assets. Many stablecoin projects are fleeing the United States for countries that have established clear frameworks for payment stablecoin issuance. Without guidance, I think this problem will only worsen. As a member of the subcommittee, I am certainly excited to tackle these important issues to make sure that we get it right here in the United States. I yield back, Mr. Chairman.

Chairman HILL. The gentlewoman yields back. And I now recognize the gentleman from California, Mr. Sherman, who is also the ranking member of our Capital Markets Subcommittee, for 5 minutes.

Mr. SHERMAN. There is a lot of money in the crypto and the crypto-adjacent space. The crypto world makes money by literally making money. They had it up to $3 trillion. It has dropped down to $1.2 trillion, but $1.2 trillion out of thin air pays for a lot of lobbyists, and a lot of propaganda. In my City, Los Angeles, the Lakers play in a crypto arena. They do not play at a, "Know Your Customer," arena. They do not play at an, "Enforce Our Tax Laws," arena. They do not play at a, "Prevent Drug Dealers from Being Able to get Their Financial Transactions Handled," arena.

We have a very good payment system. We have an excellent currency. The entire world tends to like the dollar. It is a good store of value, a good measure of value, and a good means of transaction. If you use Apple Pay, it comes right out of your checking account. It is not as good as what the crypto world promises they will deliver in some future decade, but it is way better than what the crypto world delivers now, and I am sure that payment systems using the dollar will get better.

So, what is the problem? The problem is that it is so hard to cheat on your taxes, and it is hard to run a drug sales operation with the U.S. dollar because we have Know Your Customer (KYC) and we have Anti-Money Laundering (AML), and we need a payment system that meets the needs of the millions of Americans, or at least the hundreds of thousands of Americans who want to engage in major illegal activity.

Other countries are moving forward with this, and we have to catch up with them. Peru is ahead of us in cocaine manufacture and cocaine cultivation. China is ahead of us in organ harvesting, and it is time for America to catch up.

Ms. Hand, if we allow every State to have its own rules, and say, a State like Wyoming, which doesn't have that many people and cows don't always sell for as much as they would like, if they could make a billion dollars by just having a regulatory system that was perfect for tax evaders, what would stop them?

Ms. HAND. Thank you. Currently, nothing would stop them because there is no overarching equivalent Federal regulatory framework, and we would continue to see a race to the bottom, which is not good—

Mr. SHERMAN. Yes. What the payment system needs is regulation so that you can be sure that while you are hiding your money from the IRS, and that is the big market for this. Drugs are important, sanctions evasion is important, but the IRS has testified that there is nearly a trillion dollars of unpaid taxes every year, almost exclusively from the very wealthy. And in order to not pay a trillion in taxes, you need to hide a trillion of income, which means over a decade, you have to hide $30 trillion of assets. That is a huge market, and I think it could be more important to Wyoming than cows. And of course, it all goes away if your payment system has Know Your Customer and Anti-Money Laundering provisions.

And a stablecoin, talk about an oxymoron. The problem for those who want to use the system is that it is so completely unregulated that they might find that their money in the Bahamas isn't there anymore. So, they need regulation to protect those who put their money in while at the same time, who don't have Know Your Customer and Anti-Money Laundering. And that is something that I think the State of Wyoming or anyone else trying to provide this service will make sure that there is actually reserves behind the coin. But at the same time, the IRS can't find out who owns the coins. So, every day, drug dealers get cheated because they try to buy a kilo and the scale is deliberately cheated against them. They need regulation too, and a fair system to have a concealed currency is what cryptocurrency is all about. I yield back.

Chairman HILL. The gentleman yields back. Mr. Flood is now recognized for 5 minutes.

Mr. FLOOD. Thank you, Mr. Chairman. I appreciate all of the witnesses' time and testimony today. As someone who passed the Nebraska Financial Innovation Act to allow State-chartered banks to custody digital assets in my home State, I am really interested in the pathway for States, and I appreciate, Superintendent Harris, you being here today and your testimony. As we think about legislation, can you describe why maintaining a robust role for State regulators is important?

Ms. HARRIS. Absolutely, sir, and thank you for your question. I think we see the success of the dual regulatory framework on the banking side, and it is something that we should seek to duplicate when it comes to stablecoins. I think the main virtue is the nimbleness with which State regulators can act and you see that evidence in New York with our one-to-one reserving requirements. All of the things we have talked about here today are already in place in New York because we can move more quickly and stay abreast of developments in the space.

Mr. FLOOD. In your position, can you tell me other States that you think are at the forefront of stablecoins and understanding the space and State regulators that have maybe taken some steps to be more innovative?

Ms. HARRIS. Illinois has recently announced that they are going to take the New York framework and duplicate it, and I understand that a number of other States that are exploring that as well.

Mr. FLOOD. Okay. Thank you. It is important that the pathway to becoming a stablecoin issuer remains open for new entrants.

Mr. Disparte, do you view the current path for non-banks in the current draft legislation attached to this hearing as achieving this goal?

Mr. DISPARTE. Thank you for the question, Congressman. I do think it is really critical. The United States of America is an outlier among the advanced economies in the world and not having a Federal payment system charter. The best alternative we have is companies like PayPal, and Stripe, and Apple Pay, and all of these other services. And I do think it is really critical that a Circle enjoys competition in the future, where a comparably regulated and structured stablecoin might exist also, referencing the dollar. The next real breakthrough is fungibility and interoperability of those payment systems as well. So, preserving a bank and non-bank pathway for digital currency issuance in the country is going to be really critical.

Mr. FLOOD. One of the issues that I have dealt with in Nebraska is, I think consumers don't appreciate that the word, "bank," comes with a level of security that you can't get in a lot of countries around the world. Allowing non-bank entities access to the Federal payment system is a big step for Congress. It is a big step for this process. It comes with FDIC oversight, and the Federal Reserve. Can you respond to the concerns that someone might have about allowing an entrant into the Federal payments system? And how do we weigh whether or not we do it with a non-bank entity, which I really think is an open question. I am concerned about it. I would like to know your thoughts.

Mr. DISPARTE. Again, here, too, if you want to really understand the competitiveness gap the United States faces, the inability for the central bank of the United States, the Federal Reserve Board, to provision Federal services to non-bank actors is an enormous gap. Again, we are an outlier compared to the United Kingdom, Europe, Singapore, and many other countries around the world and indeed, the digital currency space race analogy is precisely that. There are 114 central banks around the world representing 95 percent of global GDP, developing solutions around this digital currency question, and that could include the provision of central bank custody for cash reserves. We have just run the cusp of launching FedNow in the United States. If FedNow is going to work, FedNow has to be provisioned to non-bank actors.

The banks, I hate to say, have no incentive in competing past fee interest incomes—to be banked is expensive in this country. To use basic payment services is expensive in this country, and we exact the highest fees from the people who can least afford it, for very basic services. Those services, I might add, also enjoy a public backstop. The last time we socialized losses to trillions of dollars was in bailing out the very banking system; we just saw three banks bailed out recently. So, payments competition is critical. Legitimizing it at the Federal level would merely level the playing field between the United States and other countries.

Mr. FLOOD. Do you think that non-bank entities would also welcome all of the steps that we require like, Federal FDIC insurance, and the exams? One of my concerns, and I think it is an honest concern, is if we let non-bank entities enjoy the benefits of banks, that could make it difficult. We can't have a collapse. We can't have a calamity. We can't miss for the American consumer. Thank you. I yield back.

Chairman HILL. I thank the gentleman from Nebraska, and I now recognize the gentleman from Illinois, Mr. Casten, for 5 minutes.

Mr. CASTEN. Thank you, Chairman Hill. And thanks to all of our witnesses. Mr. Disparte, I want to start with you. When Mr. Lucas asked you what lessons you learned from this period in March, when that essentially broke the buck, if you will, on stablecoin, and you had mentioned that—I think you said you were exposed to some risks in the banking sector. I want to challenge you a bit on that because there were no money market funds that broke the buck and they were just as exposed to the banking sector. First question, do I have it right that you had about $40 billion in cash deposits on March 9th, of which $3.3 billion was at SVB? Is that right?

Mr. DISPARTE. That is correct.

Mr. CASTEN. Okay. Have you since that point made any efforts to increase your dollar holdings, diversify your dollar? What have you done to protect against the fact that you did have exposure to a part of the banking sector, but not to the majority of your dollar holdings?

Mr. DISPARTE. Yes. Thank you for the question, Congressman. Circle, prior to the failure of Silicon Valley Bank, continues to operate what we think of as the safest dollar settlement infrastructure on the internet. USDC's entire composition—

Mr. CASTEN. I don't want to be rude, but I don't want to get into a whole pitch for Circle. I am just trying to understand, did you take measures to increase the diversity or the liquidity of your dollar holdings?

Mr. DISPARTE. Sure. Today, the cash component of USDC is held at a large cash custodian, New York bank, and the remainder, typically 80 percent of USDC, is short-dated U.S. Treasuries.

Mr. CASTEN. Okay.

Mr. DISPARTE. Of 90 days or less.

Mr. CASTEN. Okay. And was there significant volume of loss on the trading during that period before you got back to the dollar peg?

Mr. DISPARTE. Well, yes, USDC lost about $10 billion of circulation. But we think of it as fulfilling the right that the coin holder has of redemption at par for a U.S. dollar, even in a situation of extreme stress in the banking system. The three banks that failed had connectivity to the digital assets industry, although their failure wasn't caused by the industry.

Mr. CASTEN. I understand. So, I asked that question. Now, I just want to put a question to all of you, and I was going to ask you all to be New Yorkers in 1975, but then I realized some of you may be conflicted out from that question. So, let me ask instead that you all be Michiganders in 2013. The largest city in your State is about to go bankrupt. You were the treasurer of Michigan. Would you support legislation that would allow States to print paper money issued by the State of Michigan with a peg to the U.S. dollar without any approval from the Fed that would allow you to print your way out of the bankruptcy of Detroit? Would any of you support that legislation, or would that feel like a moral hazard to you?

Mr. CAMPBELL. I will answer that one and say, one, no, you shouldn't be having unbacked instruments, but two, their—

Mr. CASTEN. No, no, they are backed. They are backed by the Fed. We are going to mandate that the Fed has to fully back that Michigan dollar.

Mr. CAMPBELL. I would say I think the model you should think about in this context is things like prepaid cards or money market funds, which are different—

Mr. CASTEN. I am just asking, should you be able to print, as we did before the Civil War—just have States print currency, but then say that the Federal Government is going to backstop that currency? It feels like a big moral hazard to me. The reason I ask that is because Section 103 of the draft legislation says that a stablecoin issuer could ask for approval from a State, that State could then choose to accept that, and the Federal Reserve would have to approve that within 60 days, and the Fed would have no backstop.

Look, it is currency, right? You could have a situation under Section 103 of this rule, where if I am a State, if I am New York in 1975, and Michigan, if I am the next State that is facing a fiscal crisis, I can just say, can somebody please issue a stablecoin so that I can back my way through this and dump all the risk on the American taxpayer?

Mr. CAMPBELL. Yes, I would say that is the value of the reserve guidelines that are also within this bill, is that to create a stablecoin—

Mr. CASTEN. No, no, I am asking, should the Fed not have the right, if we are going to give the Fed the obligation to backstop that risk. And the reason I framed this by starting about the Circle question is, the money market funds did not blow up because for better or for worse, there is a Fed backstop.

Ms. Hand, with the time I have remaining, do you have any thoughts on how we might improve this legislation to remove the moral hazard?

Ms. HAND. Absolutely. We need that clear backstop and the Federal Reserve to minimally have the ability to reject applications that don't come up to par.

Mr. CASTEN. Okay. I would hope that at a minimum, we can improve this legislation by making sure that if we are going to put that obligation on our Federal Government, the Federal Government should have some authority to say whether or not they are willing to accept it. Thank you. I yield back.

Chairman HILL. I thank the gentleman. Mr. Nickel is now recognized for 5 minutes.

Mr. NICKEL. Thank you. And thank you all for being here today. I share the same concerns as Ranking Members Waters and Lynch and agree that we need to ensure robust consumer protections when it comes to digital assets. I also want to thank Chairman Hill for holding today's hearing and I look forward to working on bipartisan stablecoin legislation.

After our committee's hearing with SEC Chair Gensler yesterday, it is still evident that there is a lack of clarity in regulation impacting the digital assets industry. Without clear rules of the road, this innovative technology could head overseas where we can't protect investors. I am committed to working in a bipartisan way to make progress wherever we can on this issue.

Mr. Chervinsky, how would effective stablecoin legislation bring more clarity to the way digital assets are regulated?

Mr. CHERVINSKY. Thank you for the question, Congressman. I think stablecoin legislation would bring clarity in two ways. One, specifically, it would provide clear rules of the road for stablecoin issuers as to how they can set up their businesses and put these products into the market here in the United States subject to American principles and so that, as Congressman Foster asked earlier, they would be required to freeze assets, if it were required in order to keep illicit actors and other bad actors out of the crypto ecosystem. I think that is very important.

But secondly, it would also send a message that the United States is open for business to this technology. That is not the message that the industry has been receiving from many other regulators so far, who have been substituting their own judgments about the value of digital assets for Congress' judgment. But indeed, it is Congress' role to answer the major question of how digital assets should be regulated, and I think that Congress should begin with stablecoin legislation.

Mr. NICKEL. Thank you.

Mr. Disparte, I understand that the U.S. has an opportunity with stablecoins to reinforce the dominance of the U.S. dollar as the global reserve currency. This comes at a time when the status of the dollar is under threat by foreign adversaries like China and Russia. Mr. Disparte, can you provide some examples of how stablecoins have improved cross-border transactions and empowered those living in economically-disadvantaged countries? And can you please explain how stablecoins may enable individuals and businesses across the globe to transact in U.S. dollars?

Mr. DISPARTE. Thank you for the question, Congressman. One of the most powerful examples is a very recent one, which is our partnership with the United Nations High Commissioner for Refugees (UNHCR). Circle, together with Stellar and MoneyGram, as I shared in my written testimony, helped design a sort of digital cash assistance program for Ukrainian refugees. This program worked in a manner that no other alternative payment system could have supported, which is that if you think of the way we as a country move foreign aid today or disaster assistance, it is pallets of physical cash, which are literal honey pots for corruption, bribery, and fraud. The idea that you have device-centric money that is corruption-resistant, near-instant, and auditable is a very powerful feature, and the stablecoin, a dollar-denominated stablecoin, in this case USDC, is the payload that supports that innovation.

Mr. NICKEL. Thank you. Public blockchains offer a revolutionary solution to our current financial system. Public blockchains can be accessed by anyone in the world who has an internet connection and are faster, less expensive, more reliable, and more transparent than legacy payment rails. But as we have seen, the value of various cryptocurrencies is volatile when compared to many currencies, especially the U.S. dollar.

Mr. Chervinsky, how do stablecoins differ?

Mr. CHERVINSKY. Stablecoins combine the best of both worlds of the traditional financial system and public blockchains. They take the benefits of the public blockchain—efficiency, security, reliability, and accessibility—and combine that with stable value. Now, many other types of digital assets like cryptocurrencies are volatile against the U.S. dollar. And that is not to say there aren't great reasons why people should use those assets for any number of purposes in a decentralized environment. But for the purpose of payments, it is best to have an asset that is stable against a national currency so that it can be used to exchange for goods and services without worrying that tomorrow, the price of what you bought yesterday is going to be way higher or way lower. So with stablecoins, we get all the benefits of the technology without that issue of volatility.

Mr. NICKEL. Thank you so much. I yield back.

Chairman HILL. The gentleman yields back. I want to thank our witnesses for being an excellent panel today. I thought the conversation was very helpful in clarifying the direction to take on stablecoin legislation. I certainly have heard unanimity from the panel that a regulatory framework designed by

Congress is something that would benefit the U.S. economy and U.S. investors and consumers.

The Chair notes that some Members may have additional questions for this panel, which they may wish to submit in writing. Without objection, the hearing record will remain open for 5 legislative days for Members to submit written questions to these witnesses and to place their responses in the record. Also, without objection, Members will have 5 legislative days to submit extraneous materials to the Chair for inclusion in the record.

This hearing is now adjourned.

[Whereupon, at 11:49 a.m., the hearing was adjourned.]

Testimony of J. Austin Campbell Managing Partner, Zero Knowledge Consulting Adjunct Professor, Columbia Business School

Introduction

First of all, let me thank Chairman McHenry, Ranking Member Waters, subcommittee Chair French Hill, subcommittee Ranking Member Stephen Lynch, the members of the committee and the hardworking staffers behind all of them for giving me the opportunity to testify. It is an honor and a privilege to share my thoughts on how America has a historical opportunity to expand our leadership of the global financial system, bring sound money and property rights to billions of people globally in a responsible, risk-conservative manner, and modernize the now creaky and aged inner workings of the United States' own financial system.

As, if we fail at that, we risk giving away control of the financial rails of the future, the reserve status of the dollar, and financial inclusion for billions of people denied the opportunity we take for granted in the United States.

My CV is included with this testimony, so here is the summary version: I have been on the sell side and the buy side in finance at large banks, I've worked in crypto and managed the reserves of a large stablecoin, and now I run an independent consulting firm and teach.

Overview

There are many topics I wish to address in writing for the committee today, so I will start with an overview of the important points. I also want to note that I direct my comments to all of the members of this committee, as stablecoins are not and should not be purely a partisan issue. Representatives Hill, Torres (shout out to a fellow crypto-constructive New Yorker), Emmer, many other members of this subcommittee who are seeking common ground, or in the House proper, members like Ro Khanna demonstrate we can all work together here. I commend chairman McHenry and ranking member Waters for being early to advocating for clarity and developing legislation for stablecoins. I am here today to be part of that effort.

First, the overall discussion on stablecoins has been chaotic, confused, misinformed, uninformed, and likely value subtracted for those watching from the outside and trying to understand the space, such as the members of the committee. As a result, we have dueling narratives that stablecoins are the most important financial innovation of all time and should be special exempt magical instruments and that stablecoins are a dire threat to the financial system and essentially a criminal conspiracy to launder vast sums of money. Both are wrong.

Stablecoins are not new; they look a lot like pretty basic cash instruments. If a pile of t-bills and bank deposits are an existential threat to the financial system, Vanguard's government money market fund would have destroyed us a long time ago. Conversely, this also means stablecoins are not some innovation so futuristic that they deserve exemptions from many of the rules around basic financial risk management, disclosure, and controls that characterize banks, money market funds, and insurance products in our current system. In short, stablecoins are actually mundane.

Second, stablecoins are a key to expanding the reach of the dollar. The United States runs a significant deficit we must fund. Simultaneously, the dollar, thanks to the strength of the American economy, the solidity of our legal system, and the core rights that come with that, is demanded globally. In the world of blockchain and crypto, the preferred fiat currency is, unsurprisingly, also the dollar. The only thing that could stop that would be the interdiction of usage of the dollar on blockchains, meaning that if the United States embraces the innovation of stablecoins, then as the usage of blockchains and crypto grows, the reach of the dollar will also grow commensurately. US Dollar stablecoins expand the reach of the dollar into a new, rapidly growing market, cementing the usage of the dollar for global trade. Additionally, the reserves for stablecoins, if appropriately regulated, provide a pool of additional capital purchasing treasury debt or lending to the American financial system that did not previously exist, allowing stablecoins to draw in new foreign capital to fund the government.

Third, stablecoins are a key to financial inclusion. In my course at Columbia Business School, one of the exercises we do is to create a crypto wallet. It takes approximately thirty seconds. This is far faster than opening a bank account. A new option creates competition for banks, who have a long history of things like excessive overdraft charges, opening fake accounts, underpaying depositors while taking significant risks with their money, and generally treating their retail customers poorly, only to eventually require bailouts when they fail. For those who are traditionally most mistreated by banks or for those who live in parts of the world where the official system itself is untrustworthy (due to inflation, arbitrary confiscation, or worse), stablecoins can be an immediate outlet where each individual requires only access to the internet and a phone to become their own bank vault and store stablecoins in that vault. Taxi drivers in Ulaanbaatar, a recent immigrant with no credit history in the Bronx, Russian dissidents secretly supporting Ukrainian refugees, or just a random college professor at an American university demonstrating for a class can all use this technology. They can all send stablecoins to each other, choosing (if we allow and foster their growth) the US dollar over any particular local system. Stablecoins are a tool to allow billions of people globally to adopt the dollar and the benefits that come with it, especially those with poor access to traditional financial services.

Fourth, the current situation in America is rapidly evolving into a ban on stablecoins. There are going to be those who say that regulations are sufficient currently, and there will be others who believe that current institutions can engage in many of these activities. The reality is not that. Right now, we have a handful of state regulators who have attempted to blaze trails in the space, such as the NYDFS and superintendent Harris, or more recently, director Lammers in Nebraska. We also have federal banking regulators who have said the following: "The Board generally believes that issuing tokens on open, public, and/or decentralized networks, or similar systems is highly likely to be inconsistent with safe and sound banking practices."[1]. Note that this is directly contradictory to the efforts of the state regulators, who have permitted literally the opposite. This same note in the Federal Register has also caused banks to

---

[1] https://www.federalregister.gov/documents/2023/02/07/2023-02192/policy-statement-on-section-913-of-the-federal-reserve-act.

back away from banking the crypto sector, meaning that stablecoin projects now also face some difficulty establishing very basic banking relationships (operational accounts, reserve accounts, and securities custodians) that are taken for granted by virtually every corporate client in America. On top of that, we also have the SEC, who has sent a Wells Notice to Paxos, the issuer of BUSD, alleging that the stablecoin is a security. In short, someone attempting to launch or manage a stablecoin in the United States doesn't know if they can issue on a public blockchain, doesn't know if they can get banking relationships, and doesn't know if they have to answer to a state financial regulator, a federal banking regulator, or the SEC, who all often have mutually contradictory answers as to responsibilities.

Fifth, in the face of all of this, the market is moving outside of the United States. The Monetary Authority of Singapore, the European Union, Dubai, Abu Dhabi, Hong Kong, Bermuda, and others are all moving forward with legislation, have passed legislation, have opened sandboxes for experimentation, or in many cases, some of all three. This means that a good actor wanting to run a stablecoin with appropriate financial controls, risk management, transparency, consumer protection, and operations would be better served leaving the United States and the incredible chaos inside of our regulatory system and instead creating what is essentially an offshore eurodollar version of a stablecoin. I will transparently warn the committee that not only am I aware of multiple efforts going down this path outside of the United States, but also that the biggest winner of the US regulatory actions and legislative inaction over the past year has been Tether, an offshore stablecoin that provides very little in the way of transparency or consumer protection. When I am asked to consult or advise for projects attempting to build stablecoins or use stablecoins, my first advice has now become to avoid US operations and a US domicile. The jobs are going elsewhere. Soon, they may also be in a different currency instead of the dollar.

Sixth, this paradigm creates what is ultimately a national and financial security problem for the United States. Remember this: a stablecoin operating outside of the United States is far less likely to be responsive to US government efforts to protect the financial system. We lose the data. We lose direct access to the persons operating such an effort. We may even lose the ability to enforce our laws or sanctions regime, depending on the domicile of a stablecoin.

Similarly, we have no guarantee of strong financial protections for the users. While some jurisdictions provide financial protections on par with the United States, that is not universally true, and certainly, the United States has been a global leader with significant expertise in regulating financial instruments. Why would we want to offshore that? Why would we want to open the door for stablecoins to use other currencies as their primary backing by blocking efforts to create US dollar stablecoins? What will the future financial system look like if the euro or perhaps the e-yuan CBDC becomes the preferred currency for blockchains and crypto while the space continues to grow at the same pace it has from 2012 to present?

Seventh, I have implied or said several times above that stablecoins can be done in a safe, sane, risk-conservative way. Let me lay out the principles that I believe can ensure that, some of which are similar to the ones I discussed with the NYDFS[2] in the past, that I would propose be enshrined in the 117th Stablecoin proposal:

1. Stablecoins should have clear reserve guidelines that restrict the reserve assets to those which are appropriate for cash stability products. In particular, I would expand the assets permitted to cash and bank deposits, T-Bills, Agency Debt of less than 1 year maturity, Overnight Repo and Reverse Repo secured by treasuries or agency debt, and potentially small (<5%) holdings of certain highly rated types of municipal bonds[3]. The overall portfolio should be limited to a weighted average maturity of 90 days or less. Government money market funds that fit within these guidelines should also be permissible assets.
2. Stablecoins should have a bankruptcy remote form factor for the reserves or strict guidelines around capital and controls, and thus, stablecoin issuers should either be insured depository institutions, uninsured depository institutions, or trusts, and subject to appropriate regulatory oversight around their risk, capital, and controls. They should not be corporations without strict rules around these activities and they should not be able to operate using only money transmitter licenses, as those are insufficient for the protections needed for consumers and the financial system.

---

[2] Here, Matt Siegel deserves some significant credit for leading the development of reserve guidelines that have allowed the 3rd largest stablecoin to liquidate over 60% of its holdings in a short period of time with zero disruption to the peg or reserve stability. Well done to Matt and the rest of the NYDFS team showing this can and should be done safely.

[3] This expanded definition escapes the problem of stablecoins being too much like a narrow bank, as here they invest extensively in forms of funding beyond just risk-free deposits. Likewise, this addresses some of the monetary policy concerns of the Federal Reserve by allowing t-bills to be repo'd back out to the market to provide liquidity in times of stress.

3. Stablecoins should have a legal requirement to allow users to mint and burn[4] coins at a stable $1 peg, or if such a requirement cannot be fulfilled due to severe difficulties with the issuer, the ability to suspend redemptions and go into unwind or receivership under the supervision of an appropriate regulator (to avoid advantaging or disadvantage specific token holders if such an event occurs). While small fees for mint and burn may be permissible, they should be limited in size and scope.
4. Stablecoins should have appropriate controls around the mint/burn process to ensure their KYC/AML processes are on par with other regulated financial institutions, and stablecoins should only be allowed on blockchains that permit freeze and seize of stablecoins so that the tokens can be interdicted in the case of usage by criminals or other bad actors, either in response to legal orders or the stablecoin issuer's own risk policies and rules. Blockchain monitoring should also be required, as while blockchains operate pseudonymously, meaningful data analysis and tracking tools do exist and should be used to detect malicious activity and bad actors.
5. Transparency should be mandatory, with stablecoins required to publish their entire reserve holdings no less frequently than monthly, publicly disclose the reserve guidelines that they are bound by so holders of the token are aware of what future reserve composition may look like, and to have audits or attestations (as appropriate) which include a review of these reports.
6. Stablecoins with these features should be expressly permitted on public blockchains, as limiting them only to private blockchains or walled gardens ensures that they will not develop a network effect, will be captured by incumbent interests and will not benefit consumers, and likely have very significant privacy concerns that emerge about their usage.
7. There should be rules around commercial speech that ensure only stablecoins that fit the guidelines laid out above are able to be called stablecoins. I can't just rent an office, buy a computer, and then start taking deposits and calling myself a bank without appropriate regulatory approval; stablecoins should be no different. A regulatory regime that expressly defines stablecoins and requires compliance

[4] Mint/Burn is the process of creating and destroying stablecoins. Give $1, get a token. Give a token, get $1. This should require AML/KYC at the point of transaction, always.

with that regime would have prevented things like UST from catching on based on false promises of safety.

8. Stablecoins should be allowed to pay interest to their holders, if and only if those holders have KYC'ed with the stablecoin issuer and their wallets are known, just like a bank account.
9. It should be made clear that stablecoins within this framework are not securities. Restricting trading in stablecoins in the way securities are restricted, requiring registration with the SEC and the disclosures appropriate for instruments like stocks, or putting trading rules intended for assets with volatile prices in place around stablecoins would be a little bit like saying dollar bills themselves are securities. Stablecoins need to work like money, to make a very simple statement, and belong in the hands of the banking regulators.
10. There should be both a state and federal pathway for stablecoins. We are early in the space; there will be a lot of experimentation and many efforts. It does not make sense for the OCC or the Federal Reserve to be spending significant amounts of time on a $2mm market cap stablecoin run out of Alabama, but nor does it make sense for Alabama[5] to be the sole overseer for a $500b market cap stablecoin. Therefore, I would suggest that we take advantage of the relative strengths of the American system and allow each state to regulate stablecoins below a $100b threshold that conform with these rules, but that any stablecoin that expands above this threshold must transition to federal regulation. For all state regulated stablecoins, I would suggest also allowing one of the federal regulators to be provided with all the same data and access to information as the state regulators, so that even if they are not the prudential regulator at the time, they have visibility into efforts nationwide.

Stablecoins within this framework are highly unlikely to be dangerous to the US financial system, as they are limited to highly liquid, safe, relatively boring assets that are similar to conservative bank assets under the Basel 3 framework or money market funds. Put differently: if stablecoins in the structure I have described are actually a safety and soundness concern, our regulators should be positively panicking about the >$22T of riskier assets that compose our banking system.

---

[5] If you are wondering why I picked Alabama, it's because I let my 7 year old daughter Leandra pick a random state for this example.

Stablecoins within this framework will also be maximally protective of consumer interests, facilitate financial inclusion and the ability to use dollars safely for the disenfranchised or less well off both within our nation and globally, and provide a significant pool of funding for US debt securities that previously did not exist at exactly the time where we run a significant deficit at the federal level. There are no losers here, other than those countries that wished to take parts of the US economy and financial system away for themselves.

Therefore, I would like to conclude here with a call to action for the committee. You have been leaders in the American political system by moving forward with a bill that is badly needed. I would ask you to finish your work; if we don't manage to pass something, I will be forced to continue to advise clients to leave the country and take their jobs and capital with them to build things elsewhere. Others will continue to build the future financial rails in places other than America. We will open the door to the dollar not being the preferred currency on blockchains, and other nations eroding our status as the reserve currency.

I would like to see America be a global leader in this space, where consumer protection, financial inclusion, innovation, and strengthening the dollar are all benefits of the actions that we take today. I urge you to lead us down that path. Thank you.

Further Discussion of Key Points

What Is a Stablecoin?

This has been a topic of much confusion, so I think it is worth discussing here what a stablecoin actually is for the committee and the record.

Definition: "A stablecoin is the representation of a unit of fiat currency on a blockchain."

That's it. In the most simplistic form, one could take literal, physical dollar bills, put them in a vault, and issue tokens for each dollar in the vault. This would be a basic form of stablecoin, and ironically, somewhat similar to a CBDC as it would be the physical version of the central bank's currency, just tokenized[6].

While there are many implementations of stablecoins in the wild, the core definition is always simple. It's a dollar (or euro, or yen, etc.) on a blockchain.

---

[6] A CBPC (Central Bank Physical Currency)?

The innovation is no more complex than a dollar being an electronic bank deposit, or in PayPal or Venmo, or a prepaid gift card.

For those arguing either for or against stablecoins, this also creates a useful rule of thumb: substitute in the word Zelle or gift cards or prepaid debit cards for what they say. Anyone arguing that these things are either existential threats to the financial system or such unique and novel financial instruments that they should be completely exempt from our current rules sounds pretty silly when you do that, no?

How Have Stablecoins Been Constructed so Far?

There are essentially three major models of stablecoins that have existed in the world, as the definition is commonly used: fiat-backed stablecoins, like USDT, USDC, BUSD, and others, crypto-backed stablecoins like DAI, and algorithmic stablecoins, like the ill-fated IRON and exceptionally ill-fated UST. Each of these work a bit differently, but in general terms they are as follows:

Fiat-backed stablecoins are those which attempt to hold their peg to a unit of fiat currency by actually having that fiat currency. Be it in the form of bank deposits, t-bills, or gold, commercial paper, or private loans, they are essentially engaging in an activity somewhere between running a money market fund, an old school trust, or a bank. To me, as someone who worked for a decade in fixed income at JPM analyzing various forms of cash stability instruments, they fit best within a banking framework, though I would be very conservative about the types of assets they are allowed to hold and the capital and risk controls framework around them.

Crypto-backed stablecoins are, essentially, securitizations using crypto. Someone minting the stablecoin must provide excess collateral, say $2 worth of BTC for every $1 of stablecoin. This collateral is supposed to provide a buffer, and if it declines in value enough, it will be auctioned off and liquidated with the proceeds put into more stable assets such as, ironically, fiat-backed stablecoins. This model is both dependent on the demand for leverage and prone to the same sort of instability as things like senior tranches of AAA CLOs in traditional financial markets. While it might hold a stable peg to a unit of fiat currency, there is no particular guarantee here, and they are likely to be more volatile than conservatively reserved fiat-backed stablecoins.

Algorithmic stablecoins are an exciting and wildly destructive (so far) attempt at creating what is essentially a synthetic fiat currency. They exist by attempting to preserve an exchange-based relationship to another token that, in theory, has independent value. For example, in the case of UST, $1 of

LUNA (the main token for the Terra blockchain) could be exchanged for 1 UST, or 1 UST could be exchanged for $1 of LUNA. This worked so long as LUNA had independent value and continued to have demand. However, when the main value of LUNA was the UST token itself, it meant that when UST lost its peg, LUNA also collapsed into a death spiral that destroyed $40B of market cap in a very short period of time. While I do not foreclose upon the possibility of an algorithmic stablecoin working someday, for now, a better term for them would be algorithmic unstablecoins.

So what does this tell us? Fiat-backed stablecoins, properly constructed, look a lot like boring old financial instruments that we handle every day in the trillions. The only excitement here is putting them on a blockchain, and I would suggest that is a feature, not a bug. We can, and should, create a regulatory framework to allow these instruments to exist.

As to the other two types of stablecoin products, we would not consider CLOs or highly novel exotic instruments to be stable instruments, and so while they are interesting and perhaps have some utility, it's probably a stretch to call them stablecoins.

Therefore, my recommendation is a simple consumer protection addition to the 117th Stablecoin proposal: the only things where people should be allowed to call them stablecoins, market them as stablecoins, or make any promise of stable redemption should be fiat-backed stablecoins within an appropriate regulatory framework. This should be made explicit so that consumers are protected from unfair, deceptive, or abuse acts or practices in marketing, disclosures, or statements by issuers. A benefit here is that enforcement under this angle is likely easier than litigating complex financial issues.

This will be far more effective than attempting to ban non-payments stablecoins, the constitutionality of which is likely questionable in some cases. Rather, just ban misrepresentations about their status, risk, or characteristics. This will also make enforcement actions easier to bring where necessary.

Dollar Stablecoins Expand the Reach of the Dollar

Every economic system has a preferred form of money. In the United States, I use dollars. When I travel to Singapore, I am using Singaporean dollars. In France, I use the euro. In Japan, I use the yen. In Korea, I use the won. In Argentina, I use the US dollar.

Wait, what? Notice that last point. Another interesting aspect of an increasingly global economy is that in countries where the currency is not viewed as legitimate, usually due to some combination of inflation, poor governance, or arbitrary confiscation, people will substitute in another currency where possible.

Right now, the most frequent choice for this is the US dollar. The safety, security, property rights, stability, and reach of the dollar make it the primary choice globally, for many forms of transactions. There are other well regarded currencies, like the euro and the yen that I mentioned above, so the dollar does not stand alone, but it does have the pole position and majority share. In fact, the dollar is so well-regarded and widely accepted that it is considered the reserve currency of the world.

Against this backdrop, we have crypto and blockchain technology. For something that literally did not exist 20 years ago, it has made quite an impact. Billions of dollars of value transact on blockchains, and the ecosystem continues to grow in volatile fashion, prone to fits and starts, exactly as one would expect for a nascent technology. It's important to remember how early we are in the history of blockchains and crypto. After all, at a similar time in the history of the internet, we were still using modems that sounded like a cybernetic goat was being tortured to death when they connected. We are early.

At this early point, though, one thing is clear: the currency of choice on blockchains is the dollar. In fact, it's often the choice of those who did not have good dollar access before; by my best estimate, when I was at Paxos and running BUSD, roughly 95%+ of BUSD token holders were non-US citizens. This means people were opting into the dollar, globally, to the tune of billions upon billions of new funding for the US Treasury! Every dollar in a stablecoin is potentially a human being lifting themselves out of a corrupt regime and into the US financial system. Arguably, we have never created a more inclusive financial technology.

This is part of what makes the current US regulatory response to stablecoins a bit confounding for me. It's very rare that a country with the reserve currency, a large deficit, which cares deeply about inclusion and freedom, and has a need for funding encounters a rapidly growing new source of money and financial empowerment and says "Nah, we're good, go away."

But that is what we are doing when our federal banking regulators say that stablecoins on public blockchains are incompatible with safe and sound banking practices. Why is this? Are we threatened by having more funding for the treasury? By having people buy t-bills and hold them in a fashion similar to the $5T of money market funds in the world? Or is this a misunderstanding of these instruments, assuming they are primarily used for criminal activity[7], where the freeze and seize capabilities of stablecoins mean that even if people are using crypto for illicit purposes, they tend to prefer native crypto assets that cannot be confiscated and that such activity is still likely lower than the rate of crime via regular dollar rails[8]? My best guess is this stance comes from a combination of misunderstanding of what stablecoins are and preferring the short-term stasis of well-understood old legacy systems, even if that path ultimately leads to obsolescence and a slow death in the long-run.

In short, the United States has every incentive in the world to make sure the dollar is the base currency of the fastest growing financial market in the world, rather than impeding that development and allowing another country to step in and fill the void. After all, if we embrace technophobia and assume blockchains and crypto will fail, how will that look in 30 years if the majority of assets trade globally on blockchains, priced in Yuan? Oops.

Competition From Stablecoins & Financial Inclusion

If I were still working at a large global bank, I would have a significant financial incentive to oppose stablecoins. Why? They are competition for deposits. In the current system, banks still take in deposits, pay essentially zero interest on them, and loan them out for significantly higher sums. My old employer, JP Morgan, recently released their quarterly results and they were impressive[9]. The success was driven by an increase in interest income, so naturally, I went into the Chase app, looked up my checking account, and assumed they would be passing some of those gains to me, as a depositor of the bank.

Nope! Still 0%[10].

For the privilege of having a bank account, many people are also subject to mandatory minimums, monthly or annual fees, overdraft charges, and

---

[7] This is not legal advice, financial advice, or in fact advice of any sort, but if you're going to commit a crime, use cash. Blockchains leave a lot of evidence, and firms like Chainalysis and Inca Digital are getting better every single day at using that evidence to find bad actors. Do not underestimate the public part of public blockchains.

[8] https://blog.chainalysis.com/reports/2023-crypto-crime-report-introduction/.

[9] https://www.jpmorganchase.com/content/dam/jpmc/jpmorgan-chase-and-co/investor-relations/documents/quarterly-earnings/2023/1st-quarter/be0fc3a0-c499-4af9-933c-6e7f75025097.pdf.

[10] Technically 0.01%.

upcharges for many basic services, like wires. They also have the benefit of still likely earning 0% or near 0% on their balances.

Those who are most disadvantaged in this paradigm are, of course, those with less money to begin with. If you don't meet the monthly minimum? Fees. If you have less money to begin with, a $10 fee can matter. $10 out of $1000 is a big chunk, but $10 to a billionaire is just not going to move the needle. In fact, as you get wealthier, you get access to things like money market funds and other investments, so your opportunity to earn interest income goes up, not down!

Enter the stablecoin. More so, let us posit the existence of a stablecoin that conforms with the principles that have been laid out in my testimony. Now, as a worker earning minimum wage and struggling to make ends meet, you have an option where you will likely be paid a higher rate of interest, pay lower fees, and not be subject to some of the complicated financial risks that come along with using a bank. Instead, you get a very simple payments tool without added bells and whistles, and on the right blockchain, you can pay people with it for essentially zero.

This sort of simplified, open-source, cheap access financial system is life changing, especially when it is a global and peer-to-peer. I've talked so far about basic use cases to reduce some of the influence of the too-big-too-fail bank crowd or monopolistic payments providers, but imagine the benefits for things like remittances, international transfers, or simply a vendor paying a supplier in another country.

Stablecoins, properly designed and regulated, reduce rent-seeking by intermediaries and put financial control and profits back into the hands of the most vulnerable and underserved in our systems.

American Regulatory Landscape

Right now, it's growing close to impossible to be a stablecoin issuer in America. To do so, one needs to have the following things in place to construct a properly designed stablecoin: banking relationships, trading, securities, and custodial relationships, a regulatory framework, and distribution across the blockchain and crypto space.

Right now, thanks to the actions of federal regulators, the first is becoming increasingly difficult to find. While a small subset of crypto firms retain their banking access, new entrants are increasingly finding it difficult to even open operating accounts, much less do things like trade treasuries or overnight reverse repo. Similarly, given the statement that public blockchains are not compatible with safe and sound banking practices and the extreme emphasis on crypto risks by the FDIC, OCC, and Federal Reserve (up to and including requiring non-objection for all new crypto activities, daily and monthly activity reporting far in excess of that required for other business lines, and soft caps on the amount of exposure a firm can take), even those banks providing services are largely not expanding those services. Simultaneously, it's unclear what regulatory framework applies, as the three aforementioned regulators, the SEC, the CFTC, and various state regulators have all thrown their hat into the ring, many of which bring mutually incompatible requirements when it comes to issuing a stablecoin.

All of this sound and fury, by the way, about an industry that is a tiny fraction of overall cash instruments:

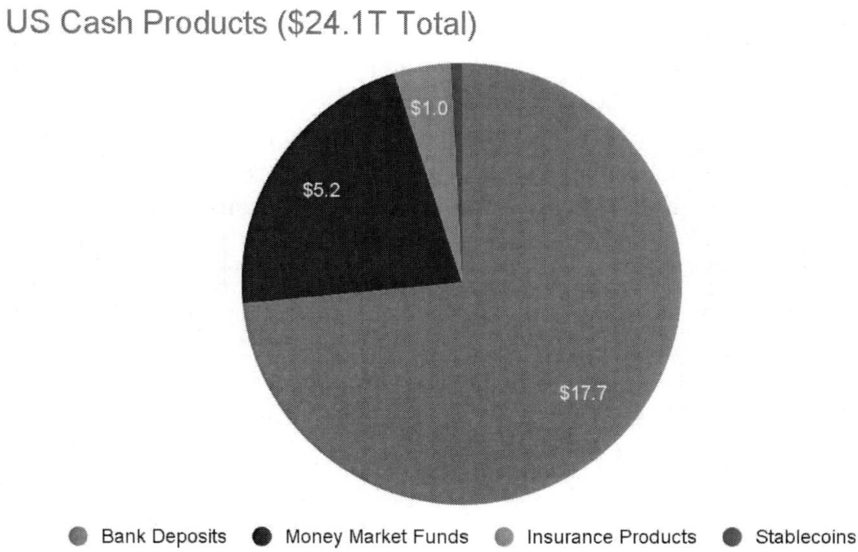

That tiny green slice that is so small I couldn't even fit a label on the chart in a way that is readable? That is the <$0.2T of stablecoins that exist in the world, or put differently, a less than 1% rounding error on the amount of cash products in the US financial system. Yet even now, we have a five-way (minimum) fist fight between regulators over that sliver.

At the same time this is the landscape in the United States, there are now foreign jurisdictions where one could do the following: face a single regulator with absolute clarity on legality, establish banking relationships which are stable, and have complete certainty about product taxonomy and rules around facing consumers. Many of these jurisdictions might also prefer those stablecoins not be in dollars, before we even get to the more complicated topic of CBDCs.

From the perspective of an entrepreneur, this makes for a very easy decision: leave the United States. Staying here to attempt to build currently means years of confusion and huge costs to respond to multiple contradictory requests while trying desperately to hold onto banking relationships, and going abroad means foreign jurisdictions that may well offer tax breaks or incentives to build there with a clear legal framework.

America, in this one particular space, has become the thing we often criticize other nations for: a system where the government is used as a weapon against non-incumbents in an anti-free-market anti-consumer fashion to entrench legacy interests. Nobody, after all, is happier about the complete blockage of stablecoins than legacy banks. If one bans consumers from having options other than the traditional zero-rate checking account with excessive fees, they don't have to compete. Meanwhile, talent and economic growth will happen, they will just happen somewhere else, eventually in another currency.

The final point here is that "do nothing" is not benign neglect to allow a fledgling industry to evolve, nor is it consumer protective, as the stablecoin that has grown the most in response to the actions of US regulators this year is Tether! Do nothing is an affirmative statement that the United States does not intend to provide onshore consumer protections, and instead other jurisdictions should lead the way on what will be used as money on a blockchain while the United States does everything it can to hold the space back from using dollars. This would be a huge tactical mistake, unless I am completely wrong about blockchain and crypto, and it turns out that despite hundreds of thousands of extremely talented young people, multiple billion dollar companies, and global adoption, this whole space is going to zero.

Set that against the "danger" of allowing properly regulated, very conservative, highly transparent stablecoins, and it becomes clear that the path of least damage is to allow the experiments, but in controlled fashion.

It would also be a mistake to attempt to do too much in this one bill. There are extremely important market structure, trading, and custodial concerns that apply to the crypto space. I know this has also been a focus of both chairman McHenry and ranking member Waters, but I would urge the committee to understand the plight of the space and how much confusion there is right now. Please do not let perfect be the enemy of good - those concerns can and should be addressed, but not at the expense of giving us clarity on how to use money at the base layer. Similarly, payments stablecoins themselves do not necessarily share many of the market structure concerns that exist for price volatile instruments (for example, Starbucks using a stablecoin in their app to allow a consumer to simply pay for coffee is not the same as trading a manipulated token through an unregulated exchange). Address them, certainly, but don't hold up a stablecoin bill for them.

National Security

It is a common refrain that blockchains and crypto are primarily used for criminal activity. While this is confused as a general statement (for instance, I am very confident that JP Morgan's Onyx is not a hotbed of terrorism financing), even when this statement is narrowed to tokens on public blockchains, this is not particularly true. Certainly, there are some bad actors in the crypto space: ransomware attackers prefer crypto[11] as a form of payment (though each day, law enforcement gets better at interdicting this activity), North Korea's state-sponsored hacking group has misappropriated funds from crypto projects, and money launderers have used crypto as a way to attempt to obfuscate their activities.

Even so, I have doubts about the long-term viability of public blockchains for criminal activity. With each passing day, we have more metadata available to us to attempt to identify wallets, both data from the blockchain itself and data from various other sources, such as social media, to triangulate wallet ownership. Each wallet that is owned forms part of a chain that can be used to trace transactions. Already, the Treasury has been able to place wallet addresses on the SDN list, and as our intelligence agencies, law enforcement divisions, and regulators improve their technological capabilities, our ability to use the rich data provided by blockchains to detect illicit activities will grow exponentially.

After all, consider the parallels between a stablecoin and cash. In the case of cash, once it leaves a bank through an ATM, we know only the person who took the cash out and then, much later, the person who put the cash back in. All of the transactions between those two endpoints are often completely invisible, or at least only partially visible after very significant efforts. On the other hand, imagine the same scenario with a stablecoin. We know who minted it, and we know who burned it, just like in the ATM example. Only here,

[11] However, typically they do not prefer stablecoins, as those can often be frozen and seized!

because of a public blockchain, we have a complete and total record of every single transaction in the chain between those two points: wallet addresses, time of transaction, amount of transaction, and who they transacted with. We may not always know who owns the wallets (yet), but we know the entire chain. One of those two fact patterns is a much better long-term paradigm for law enforcement, and we should embrace the one providing us with rich data.

At this point, I also want to take a moment to say one of the strategic imperatives of the committee should also be to greatly strengthen our regulators on this front. I am privileged to have many friends in the regulatory community, and I am sympathetic to the fact that they are underpaid, under-resourced, and often trying to do the best they can with the hand they are dealt while getting blamed whenever things go wrong. I know I have raised comments throughout this document critical of their performance, but I want to stress that this is an outcomes based analysis, not one motivated by any belief in personal malice or bad intentions on their part.

As a final point on national security, it would also be a crippling mistake to leave this technology in the hands of foreign nations who might be hostile to American interests. Imagine a semi-private blockchain, where validator nodes are run by a consortium of foreign governments that provide visibility to each other on transactions, but not to the United States. This sort of endgame, with stablecoins in other currencies being a staple of transacting on such a chain, would blight our efforts to use the financial system to combat bad actors. We are faced with a growing, data-rich, open-source system. We should not force it into the hands of others and out of our own.

Conclusion

I want to end by again thanking you all for the opportunity to testify. I truly believe we are at a pivotal moment in the history of American financial markets, and I hope I have played a small role in pushing us in the right direction (behind the much larger efforts of chairman McHenry, ranking member Waters, and the entire committee and their respective staffs). I salute the committee for the attention paid to this important issue, for bringing together a diverse set of voices to testify today, and for any and all future actions to provide clarity, financial safety, and opportunity for Americans as a whole.

I will re-iterate my points that stablecoins are not novel from a financial perspective and can and should be safely regulated. I would re-emphasize that

I have laid out principles of good governance above, and as someone who has traded cash instruments in the 100s of billions over a career in traditional financial services before running a stablecoin myself, I am confident I have covered the major points to protect consumers and encourage innovation. Similarly, I hope the committee will remember my comments on regulatory realities, how both a state and federal path should be created so we can appropriately allocate efforts and responsibility, and finally, that some of our hard-working regulators get some badly needed reinforcements in their policy, innovation, research, and tech groups so that they can lead from the front.

Written Testimony of Jake Chervinsky, Chief Policy Officer of the Blockchain Association, before the United States House of Representatives, Committee on Financial Services, Subcommittee on Digital Assets, Financial Technology and Inclusion, in a Hearing Entitled Understanding Stablecoins' Role in Payments and the Need for Legislation, April 19, 2023

Chairman Hill, Ranking Member Lynch, and Members of the Subcommittee:

My name is Jake Chervinsky and I serve as Chief Policy Officer for the Blockchain Association (the "Association"). I am an attorney by training: I started my career in private practice in 2013, where I focused on anti-money laundering and anti-corruption compliance and investigations, financial services litigation, and government enforcement defense. In 2019, I recognized the transformative power of blockchain technology and joined Compound Labs, Inc., a prominent software development company in the decentralized finance ("DeFi") space, as General Counsel. I joined the Association to focus full-time on public policy in November 2021.

The Association is the leading nonprofit membership organization focused on promoting a pro-innovation policy environment for the U.S. blockchain industry. We represent more than 100 member companies from every sector of this dynamic industry, including software developers, infrastructure providers, exchanges, custodians, investors, and more. Our members are strongly committed to regulatory compliance and have long requested clear rules of the road so that they can build safe, sound, and successful businesses here in the United States.

Thank you for the opportunity to testify about one of the most promising applications of public blockchains, and one for which tailored legislation is needed: U.S. dollar stablecoins.

Executive Summary

Our current financial system has a problem: it is dominated and constrained by intermediaries. Modern commerce relies on a small number of large financial institutions to operate proprietary infrastructure for which they serve as the exclusive gatekeepers and middlemen. Although these institutions historically formed the backbone of a strong, well-functioning financial system, they have failed to keep pace with the digital age. The global economy is always on and always connected, but traditional financial institutions continue to use slow, inefficient, and unreliable tools that were developed for the analog era of the last century before the rise of the internet.

Public blockchains offer a solution to that problem: a revolutionary upgrade on the technology that powers the global financial system. First and foremost, blockchains offer public payments infrastructure to go along with the public internet. Blockchains can be accessed by anyone with an internet connection to transfer any amount of value to anywhere in the world, nearly instantly and at nearly zero cost. Blockchains outperform legacy payment rails in practically every way, since they are faster, less expensive, more reliable, more transparent, and inclusive by default.

Stablecoins are a particularly powerful application of blockchain technology. For the time being, other blockchain-based cryptocurrencies remain highly volatile, and thus are poor performers as "units of account" — a term describing the important role of currency in setting consistent prices for goods and services. Stablecoins, on the other hand, take advantage of all the benefits of public blockchains while maintaining a stable value against a national currency like the U.S. dollar. As a result, stablecoins represent a categorical improvement for global payments.

U.S. dollar stablecoins also offer an extraordinary opportunity to advance U.S. interests at home and abroad. At present, foreign adversaries such as China and Russia are seeking to undermine the status of the U.S. dollar as the global reserve currency. To strengthen the dollar's dominance, our main priority should be to spread dollars far and wide, and blockchain-based stablecoins — which enable billions of people around the world who lack financial services to join the global economy for the first time — provide the best mechanism to achieve that priority.

To maximize the benefits of U.S. dollar stablecoins, Congress must move quickly to pass tailored legislation providing regulatory clarity to U.S.-based stablecoin issuers. As a matter of law, only Congress, not the federal agencies, can decide how digital assets like stablecoins should be regulated. The consequences of failing to act — losing ground to competing national currencies like China's digital yuan, losing out on the benefits of a revolutionary upgrade to legacy payment systems, and losing innovators to other jurisdictions — are dire. There is no time to waste.

Below, I outline five principles for effective stablecoin legislation that the Association believes would protect consumers while promoting innovation. We urge the Committee to resume its focus on drafting and introducing stablecoin legislation through a bipartisan process. We, along with all of our member companies in the blockchain industry, stand ready and willing to help.

Introduction to Stablecoins

"Stablecoin" is a term for a blockchain-based digital asset that seeks to maintain a stable value compared to a reference asset, typically a national currency. For example, a stablecoin that references the U.S. dollar seeks to maintain a stable value of $1.00 per unit. Stablecoins, like other digital assets, run on decentralized public blockchains, meaning anyone can use them without having to rely on a trusted third party.

There Are Three Main Types of Stablecoins

There are different types of stablecoins, which all use different models to achieve the goal of maintaining stable value, each with their own benefits and drawbacks. There are three main types of stablecoins, as described below.

Custodial stablecoins are issued by an operating company and backed by collateral held in a bank or other institution. Custodial stablecoins are *fully collateralized* — $1 of assets held in reserve for every unit of stablecoin in circulation — and seek to maintain their value based on the operator's promise to maintain the reserve and pay redemptions on demand. Custodial stablecoins represent approximately 95% of global U.S. dollar stablecoins in circulation.[12]

---

[12] *See Total Stablecoin Supply*, The Block, https://www.theblock.co/data/decentralized-finance/stablecoins (last visited Apr. 16, 2023).

The largest custodial stablecoins are Tether's USDT (~$81b) and Circle's USDC (~$30b).

Decentralized stablecoins consist of autonomous software protocols on public blockchains that seek to maintain stable value without relying on a trusted central issuer. Decentralized stablecoins are backed by digital assets held in transparent smart contracts rather than in a bank or other institution. They are typically *overcollateralized* — more than $1 of digital assets held in reserve for each unit of stablecoin in circulation — and maintain their value based on the holder's ability to audit and redeem collateral at any time without relying on a third party. The largest decentralized stablecoin is DAI (~$5b), which is part of the MakerDAO protocol.

Algorithmic stablecoins seek to maintain stable value without any backing at all. Algorithmic stablecoins are *uncollateralized* — Instead of collateral, they rely on financial incentives designed to influence market forces of supply and demand. The best-known algorithmic stablecoin was TerraUSD, which relied on a unique mechanism to adjust its total supply for stability.[13] For reasons both internal and external to TerraUSD's design, including the potential impact of alleged fraud on the part of TerraUSD's creator Do Kwon,[14] its stability mechanism failed and the stablecoin collapsed. It is unclear if an algorithmic stablecoin with different characteristics could succeed in the future, but after the collapse of TerraUSD, the blockchain industry has moved away from research and development on algorithmic stablecoins.

Different Types of Stablecoins Merit Different Kinds of Regulation

Different stablecoin models present substantially different risk profiles and therefore demand different regulatory treatment. Although the three main types of stablecoins identified above are all colloquially described by the term "stablecoin," they each operate so differently that the regulatory principle "same business, same risks, same rules" does not apply.

To illustrate this difference, compare the distinct risk profiles of custodial and decentralized stablecoins. Custodial stablecoins are issued by an intermediary that maintains custody of a reserve backing the stablecoins. Holders of custodial stablecoins are thus essentially holding a liability of the

---

[13] Matt Levine, *Terra Flops*, Bloomberg (May 11, 2022), https://www.bloomberg.com/opinion/articles/2022-05-11/terra-flops.

[14] David Yaffe-Bellany, *Crypto Fugitive Do Kwon Is Charged With Fraud by U.S. Prosecutors*, N.Y. Times (Mar. 23, 2023), https://www.nytimes.com/2023/03/23/business/do-kwon-arrested-crypto.html.

issuer, and are exposed to the risk of the issuer mismanaging the reserve, refusing to process a redemption request, or otherwise failing to honor their liability.

Decentralized stablecoins remove the main risk of custodial stablecoins by replacing their trusted central operator with autonomous code storing collateral on a transparent public blockchain. Users of decentralized stablecoins benefit from that transparency, since they (along with regulators and the rest of the public) can audit the reserve of the stablecoin in real-time. This differs from holders of custodial stablecoins, who must wait for the issuer to publish periodic audits or attestations, and then must trust in their accuracy.

On the other hand, decentralized stablecoins may expose users to risks that are not present for holders of custodial stablecoins. Because decentralized stablecoins consist of blockchain-based code, which is typically immutable, they are only as safe and sound as the quality of that code. As a result, decentralized stablecoin holders may be subject to technical risks — code flaws and other vulnerabilities — that do not arise in the context of a custodial stablecoin.

Given the distinct benefits and risks involved in custodial and decentralized stablecoins, as well as the distinct constitutional rights at issue — for example, the speech rights of software developers — it would be a grave policy error to apply the same rules to all types of stablecoins. The Association urges Congress to begin by developing tailored legislation for custodial stablecoins, since that category of stablecoin makes up the vast majority of total market share, and because the benefits and risks of custodial stablecoins are already well-understood.

The Current Regulatory Landscape for Custodial Stablecoin Issuers

Today, custodial stablecoin issuers are subject to a patchwork of regulatory requirements administered by a number of agencies at both the state and federal level. These regulations have proven effective in many ways, but fall short of a much-needed federal framework.

At the state level, issuers are generally required to obtain a money transmitter license ("MTL") in each state where they do business. The purpose of the state MTL regime is to protect consumers by ensuring that their funds aren't lost due to theft or mismanagement. Although the state MTL regime is somewhat burdensome, forcing custodial stablecoin issuers to comply with bespoke requirements in dozens of different states, it does offer some protection for consumers by requiring stablecoin issuers to post surety bonds, provide various statements and reports, undergo examinations, and submit to fingerprinting and other security measures.

In addition, custodial stablecoin issuers are subject to the states' various consumer protection laws, which generally outlaw deceptive and unfair trade practices. Some issuers have also obtained trust or similar charters, which subject them to more rigorous oversight by state banking and financial services regulators.

At the federal level, custodial stablecoin issuers generally qualify as money services businesses under the Bank Secrecy Act ("BSA") and therefore must register with the Financial Crimes Enforcement Network and implement BSA-compliant anti-money laundering programs. Some issuers have sought or received a national trust charter, which places them under the regulatory authority of the Office of the Comptroller of the Currency ("OCC").

Given stablecoins' economic and geopolitical importance, the Association believes Congress must adopt a comprehensive federal framework governing firms that issue, maintain, and redeem these assets. Our recommendation is aligned with those of current leaders in government. In November 2021, the President's Working Group on Financial Markets ("PWG") published a report recommending that "Congress act promptly to enact legislation to ensure that [stablecoins] are subject to a federal framework on a consistent and comprehensive basis."[15] In May 2022, Treasury Secretary Janet Yellen reiterated this recommendation during testimony before this Committee, stating that she was "eager to work with [Congress]" on legislation through "a bipartisan effort."[16]

Stablecoins Offer a Revolutionary Upgrade on Traditional Payment Systems

Stablecoins represent a categorical improvement on legacy payment infrastructure, allowing users to transfer any amount of value to any person anywhere in the world nearly instantly and at nearly zero cost. Unlike

---

[15] Press Release, U.S. Dep't of the Treasury, President's Working Group on Financial Markets Releases Report and Recommendations on Stablecoins (Nov. 1, 2021), https://home.treasury.gov/news/press-releases/jy0454.

[16] *The Annual Report of the Financial Stability Oversight Council: Hearing Before the H. Comm. on Fin. Servs.*, 117th Cong. 6-7 (2022) (statement of Janet Yellen, Sec'y, U.S. Dep't of the Treasury), https://www.congress.gov/117/chrg/CHRG-117hhrg47651/CHRG-117hhrg47651.pdf.

traditional payment methods, stablecoins are accessible to all, enabling billions of people around the world who lack financial services to join the global economy for the first time. In that way, stablecoins reinforce the dominance of the U.S. dollar as the global reserve currency at a time when that status is under threat by foreign adversaries like China and Russia.

Because stablecoins are powered by public blockchains, they are able to outperform existing payment rails that are slower, more expensive, and exclusive to incumbent financial institutions. In fact, the public nature of blockchains means they are more secure than proprietary infrastructure built and maintained by large institutions, since a successful cyberattack requires attacking thousands of computers running shared code rather than one single database. Blockchains are also more accessible, since they can be used by anyone with access to the internet. And they are more resilient, since their decentralized nature means they suffer virtually no outages compared to systems with single points of failure.

Stablecoins Are Actively Improving Cross-Border Transactions and Empowering Economically Disadvantaged Individuals Around the World

Although stablecoins have only existed for a short time, they have already shown a significant positive impact on the global stage. Stablecoins provide a meaningful alternative to the traditional payment system for disadvantaged individuals, particularly those who otherwise lack access to the U.S. dollar or who can only access inefficient payment systems that charge exorbitant fees and take days to process transfers.

Today, stablecoins are used by the United Nations Refugee Agency to distribute dollars to internally displaced persons and other war-affected people in Ukraine;[17] for cross-border remittances between family members working and living abroad;[18] by citizens in countries ravaged by inflation like Argentina, Turkey, and Zimbabwe;[19] and to fight for the health and safety of

---

[17] Michael Bodley, *Can Stablecoins Revolutionize Foreign Aid? The UN Thinks So.*, Blockworks (Dec. 16, 2022), https://blockworks.co/news/un-stablecoins-revolutionize-foreign-aid.

[18] Austin Adams et al., *On-chain Foreign Exchange and Cross-border Payments* (Jan. 18, 2023), https://papers.ssrn.com/sol3/papers.cfm?abstract_id=4328948.

[19] Sam Lyman, *Stablecoins as Statecraft: How Uncle Sam Could Replace Satoshi as the King of Digital Currency*, Fortune: Crypto (Feb. 26, 2023), https://fortune.com/crypto/2023/02/26/stablecoins-statecraft-uncle-sam-satoshi-digital-currency/.

people suffering under authoritarian regimes like that of Nicolás Maduro in Venezuela.[20]

Because stablecoins do not rely on intermediaries, they offer a viable payment method and value storage option for individuals living under authoritarian governments where access to U.S. dollars may be curtailed or restricted, and where local currencies often experience hyperinflation. For example, if a person is paid in an unstable national currency, such as the Venezuelan bolivar or Argentine peso, they can protect themselves by exchanging their inflationary currency for a U.S. dollar stablecoin that will not depreciate overnight and cannot easily be confiscated.

Examples of expanding access to financial services through stablecoins are plentiful. Leaf Global Fintech enables central African refugees without bank accounts to securely store, send, and receive digital cash without bank fees from low-tech feature phones.[21] Similarly, two licensed money transmitters, US-based FinClusive[22] and Mexico-based Pago Biccos,[23] have teamed up to help migrant day laborers safely and inexpensively send their U.S. earnings home to Mexico.[24] By converting their earnings into U.S. dollar stablecoins, these laborers avoid the risk of theft and assault that comes with carrying hard currency across the U.S. border. In addition, Circle and AirTM leveraged U.S. dollar stablecoins to bypass the repressive Maduro regime and distribute aid directly to front-line medical workers battling the coronavirus in Venezuela.[25] Stablecoins can enable similar gains in payment system

---

[20] Gideon Long, *Digital Scheme Pays Venezuela Health Workers from Frozen Funds*, Financial Times (Dec. 9, 2021), https://www.ft.com/content/2a271032-35b4-4969-a4bf-488d4e9e3d18.

[21] Nat Robinson & Tori Samples, *Leaf Wallet: Digital Financial Services for Refugees and Under-Resourced Communities*, UNICEF Innovation Fund (June 8, 2021), https://www.unicefinnovationfund.org/broadcast/updates/leaf-wallet-digital-financial-services-refugees-and-under-resourced-communities.

[22] FinClusive, https://finclusive.com/ (last visited Apr. 16, 2023).

[23] Pago Biccos, https://pagobiccos.com/ (last visited Apr. 16, 2023).

[24] *See ExpertEASE: FinClusive CEO Amit Sharma on Financial Compliance*, NGOSource (Sept. 14, 2022), https://www.ngosource.org/blog/expertease-finclusive-ceo-amit-sharma-on-financial-compliance; *Use Cases: Pago Biccos*, FinClusive, https://finclusive.com/use-cases#PagoBiccos (last visited Apr. 16, 2023).

[25] Nikhilesh De, *US Government Enlists USDC for 'Global Foreign Policy Objective' in Venezuela: Circle CEO*, CoinDesk (Nov. 20, 2020), https://www.circle.com/blog/circle-partners-with-bolivarian-republic-of-venezuela-and-airtm-to-deliver-aid-to-venezuelans-using-usdc.

competition, optionality, and cost reduction in the United States, where millions of households are on the margins of the banking system.[26]

U.S. Dollar Stablecoins Support the Role of the U.S. Dollar as Global Reserve Currency

U.S. dollar stablecoins can help ensure the primacy of the dollar and support the critical role that the U.S. financial system plays in the global economy. As explained by Christopher J. Waller, Governor of the Federal Reserve System ("Fed"): "stablecoins pegged to the U.S. dollar act as conduits for U.S. monetary policy and amplify policy actions. So, if anything, private stablecoins pegged to the dollar broaden the reach of U.S. monetary policy rather than diminish it."[27]

Indeed, the global reach of stablecoins makes it easier than ever for people all over the world to opt into the U.S. dollar as their currency of choice. As of March 2023, over 80 percent of global digital asset trading volume was denominated in U.S. dollar stablecoins.[28] With time and the benefit of regulatory clarity, stablecoins are likely to dominate markets unrelated to digital assets as well, amplifying U.S. economic and monetary policy around the world.

The United States Should Support Stablecoins Instead of Creating a CBDC

As technology allows for the digitization of money, the policy decisions that Congress must make will dramatically impact privacy, security, and the preservation of Americans' constitutional rights. The question of how best to implement digital cash in our society largely revolves around the choice between using U.S. dollar stablecoins or a central bank digital currency ("CBDC"), meaning a digital dollar issued by the Fed and made available to the general public.

---

[26] Dante Disparte, *Could Digital Currencies Make Being Poor Less Costly?*, Harv. Bus. Rev. (Aug. 5, 2020), https://hbr.org/2020/08/could-digital-currencies-make-being-poor-less-costly.

[27] Christopher J. Walker, Governor, Bd. of Governors of the Fed. Reserve Sys., Speech at the American Enterprise Institute: CBDC: A Solution in Search of a Problem? (Aug. 5, 2021) https://www.federalreserve.gov/newsevents/speech/waller20210805a.htm.

[28] *Share Trade Volume by Pair Denomination*, The Block (Apr. 14, 2023), https://www.theblock.co/data/crypto-markets/spot/share-of-trade-volume-by-pair-denomination.

Proponents of a CBDC may argue that, as a liability of the Fed, a U.S. CBDC would be the safest possible digital representation of the dollar. Yet, a CBDC is the wrong way to maintain U.S. dollar dominance in the digital era, for at least three reasons.

First, to strengthen the dollar's dominance as the global reserve currency, our main priority should be to spread dollars far and wide—to make them available to anyone and everyone around the world. Privately-issued stablecoins have already made a huge impact in global digital asset markets by adding to the competition in the payments landscape and serving as a faster, cheaper, and more flexible means of sending dollar-denominated payments internationally. Stablecoins have already achieved practically all of what a hypothetical CBDC might do. Rather than reinvent the wheel, the United States should support the growth of existing stablecoins.

Second, we should seek to maximize the contribution of our vibrant and experienced private sector, not sideline it in favor of a centrally-planned government project. While other nations like China might give their central governments total control over emerging industries and technologies, that is decidedly not the American way. As Randal Quarles, former Vice Chair for Supervision of the Fed, explained: "[a] global U.S. dollar stablecoin network could encourage use of the dollar by making cross-border payments faster and cheaper, and it potentially could be deployed much faster and with fewer downsides than a CBDC."[29]

Third, the fundamental right to privacy is a prized American civil liberty and an essential feature of a functioning free society that could be jeopardized if the United States were to create a CBDC. Challenges to Americans' rights to financial freedom and privacy have come to the forefront in recent years due to the increasing frequency of cybersecurity breaches and reliance by some companies on a business model of surveillance capitalism. This is an issue of constitutional import, given the Bill of Rights' guarantee of financial privacy. Thus, it is imperative that we separate the United States, which respects its citizens' autonomy and dignity, from countries like China, which has exploited technology to create a surveillance state.

---

[29] Randal K. Quarles, Vice Chair for Supervision, Bd. of Governors of the Fed. Reserve Sys., Speech at the 113th Annual Utah Bankers Association Convention: Parachute Pants and Central Bank Money (Jun. 28, 2020), https://www.federalreserve.gov/newsevents/speech/quarles20210628a.htm.

Importantly, neither the Fed nor the U.S. Department of the Treasury ("Treasury") can issue a CBDC without Congressional action.[30] The Fed acknowledged as much in a March 2023 House Financial Services Committee hearing and in a recent post on its website, stating, "The Federal Reserve . . . would only proceed with the issuance of a CBDC with an authorizing law. Testifying before the House Financial Services Committee in March 2023, Chair Powell said a central bank digital currency is, 'something we would certainly need Congressional approval for.'"[31]

The Fed's lack of authority stems from the Federal Reserve Act of 1913's limited grant of authority to issue one form of U.S. currency: "Federal reserve notes." The context surrounding the Act makes clear that this term includes only paper currency. The Act defines "Federal reserve notes" based on characteristics that don't apply to digital currency, such as requiring "a distinctive letter and serial numbers," providing for a process by which to cancel or destroy notes deemed "unfit for circulation," and setting forth details for the plates and dyes used to manufacture notes. These references make clear that the statute does not contemplate digital currency.[32]

Similarly, although the Treasury has the authority to mint and issue coins, the types of coins that it is authorized to mint are specifically defined by statute and do not include CBDCs.[33] Absent further action from Congress, the Treasury does not have the authority to issue a digital currency. For the reasons stated above, Congress should exercise extreme caution before granting such authority to either the Fed or the Treasury.

The SEC and CFTC Lack Authority to Comprehensively Regulate Stablecoins

Deciding how U.S. dollar stablecoins should be regulated is a major question that only Congress, not the federal agencies, can address. Some commentators may suggest that agencies like the SEC and CFTC already have authority to regulate stablecoins, thereby implying that Congress need not act. Yet, without

---

[30] Paige Paridon, *Legal Authority to Issue a U.S. Central Bank Digital Currency*, Bank Pol'y Inst. (Jun. 9, 2021), https://bpi.com/wp-content/uploads/2021/06/Legal-Authority-to-Issue-a-U.S.-Central-Bank-Digital-Currency.pdf.

[31] Board of Governors of the Federal Reserve System, *Is FedNow replacing cash? Is it a central bank digital currency?*, FAQs (April 2023), https://www.federalreserve.gov/faqs/is-fednow-replacing-cash-is-it-a-central-bank-digital-currency.htm.

[32] 12 U.S.C. § 411, *et seq.*

[33] 31 U.S.C. §§ 5103; 5111(a0(1); 5112(h).

further congressional authorization in the form of legislation, neither the SEC nor the CFTC has authority to comprehensively regulate stablecoins under current law.

The SEC would only have regulatory authority over stablecoins if they were "securities" under the federal securities laws. They are not. The two primary tests for analyzing whether stablecoins are securities are the *Howey*[34] and *Reves*[35] tests. The touchstone question for whether a financial instrument represents an "investment contract" under *Howey* is whether the instrument can be expected to return a profit to its holders. For stablecoins, the answer is decidedly "no." By definition, stablecoin holders expect stablecoins to maintain *stable* value, not to increase in value or yield profit in any way. Further, in *Reves*, the Supreme Court held that an instrument is not a security if it bears a "strong resemblance" to one of the types of "notes" that courts have determined are not securities, considering factors such as the motivations of the seller and buyer, and the reasonable expectation of the public. Because stablecoins hold no profit potential, they cannot be considered securities under this test either.

In the past, SEC Chair Gary Gensler has also suggested that a stablecoin is subject to regulation by the SEC if it "provides synthetic exposure to underlying securities."[36] However, where a stablecoin is backed in full or in large part by non-securities — cash, Treasury bills, or the like — then this definition does not fit. Finally, while the SEC has jurisdiction to regulate security-based swaps, stablecoins do not fit that category either. A swap is a financial contract in which two counterparties agree to exchange payments with each other as a result of such things as changes in a stock price, interest rate, or commodity price.[37] Stablecoins do not involve a swap of payment streams — neither the currency used to purchase the stablecoin nor the stablecoin itself have payment streams or other fluctuating measures of value to swap.

The CFTC also lacks general jurisdiction to regulate stablecoin markets. While stablecoins are likely considered commodities under the broad definitions of the Commodities Exchange Act, and the CFTC has broad

---

[34] *SEC v. W.J. Howey Co.*, 328 U.S. 293 (1946).

[35] *Reves v. Ernst & Young*, 494 U.S. 56, 65 (1990).

[36] Gary Gensler, Chair, U.S. Sec. and Exch. Comm'n, Prepared Remarks of Gary Gensler, Chair of the Securities and Exchange Commission, Before the American Bar Association Derivatives and Futures Law Committee Virtual Mid-Year Program (Jul. 21, 2021), https://www.sec.gov/news/speech/gensler-remarks-aba-derivatives-futures-law-committee-virtual-mid-year-program-072121.

[37] *See* 7 USC § 1a(47)(A) (defining "swap").

regulatory authority over commodity futures, derivatives, swaps, and options, its regulatory authority over spot trading in commodities markets is limited to fraud and price manipulation — and even then, only in certain circumstances.[38] Accordingly, absent fraud or manipulation, the CFTC lacks authority to regulate stablecoin markets as well.

The conclusion that the SEC and CFTC lack authority over stablecoins is justified not only as a matter of law, but also as a matter of good policy and common sense. The SEC and CFTC are financial markets regulators with specific remits, neither of which touches on payment systems. As Congress considers a proper regulator for stablecoins, it should look to the Fed and the OCC.

Congress Must Pass Stablecoin Legislation

Since the PWG published its report, Congress has made great strides toward well-tailored legislation that maximizes the benefits and mitigates the risks of stablecoins. These extensive efforts have received bipartisan, bicameral support. Last February, Rep. Josh Gottheimer released a discussion draft of the Stablecoin Innovation and Protection Act of 2022.[39] Last April, Sen. Patrick Toomey released a discussion draft of the Stablecoin TRUST Act of 2022.[40] Last fall, the blockchain industry was excited to hear about the progress that this Committee made on stablecoin legislation under the Committee's leadership. These recent efforts speak to how ripe stablecoins are for tailored legislation.

Effective stablecoin legislation must protect consumers and promote financial innovation. To achieve that goal, stablecoin legislation should account for the risks associated with these assets while also providing a clear path for stablecoin issuers to operate in the United States. Further, legislation should be technology-neutral and focus on the underlying activities and risks of a given stablecoin.

---

[38] *See* 7 U.S.C. § 9; 17 C.F.R. § 180.1; 17 C.F.R. § 180.2.

[39] Press Release, Rep. Josh Gottheimer, Release: Gottheimer Announces "Stablecoin Innovation and Protection Act," Critical New Cryptocurrency Legislation (Feb. 15, 2022), https://gottheimer.house.gov/posts/release-gottheimer-announces-stablecoin-innovation-and-protection-act-critical-new-cryptocurrency-legislation.

[40] Press Release, Sen. Comm. on Banking, Hous., and Urb. Aff. Minority Staff, Toomey Announces Legislation to Create Responsible Regulatory Framework for Stablecoins (Apr. 6, 2022), https://www.banking.senate.gov/newsroom/minority/toomey-announces-legislation-to-create-responsible-regulatory-framework-for-stablecoins.

Below, I outline five principles for your consideration that the Association believes are essential components of a balanced bill:

Legislation Should Focus on Custodial Stablecoins

Congress should apply tailored regulatory standards to custodial stablecoins, meaning those issued, maintained, and redeemed by a firm responsible for holding assets backing the stablecoins in a bank or other financial institution. Other types of stablecoins, like decentralized and algorithmic stablecoins, function in materially different ways that warrant further study and thoughtful analysis before they are ready to be addressed in legislation.

At present, over 90% of the market capitalization for all stablecoins comes from just five custodial stablecoins, all of which are denominated in U.S. dollars.[41] Moreover, custodial stablecoins present risks that are well-understood, and effective regulatory responses to mitigate those risks are likewise well-understood. On the other hand, the novel functionality of other stablecoin models present novel opportunities and risks, and their nascense means that effective policy and regulatory responses are under development. Thus, Congress should focus its efforts on establishing a legislative framework with proper standards for custodial stablecoin issuers.

Legislation Should Provide a Regulated Path for Both Banks and Non-Banks

Both insured depository institutions and non-bank firms should be allowed to issue stablecoins, subject to regulatory compliance obligations tailored for each category of issuer. Forcing all stablecoin issuers to obtain bank charters would severely restrict innovation without any attendant regulatory benefit, since stablecoins issued by properly-regulated non-bank firms will be equally safe and sound as those issued by banks.

Legislation Should Address the Quality of Stablecoin Reserves

Assets held by stablecoin issuers as backing for stablecoins should be limited to specified, high-quality, liquid assets that meet a minimum standard of safety and soundness. The federal regulator authorized to oversee stablecoin issuers should also be allowed to approve other assets at their discretion.

---

[41] *Top Stablecoin Tokens by Market Capitalization*, CoinMarketCap, https://coinmarketcap.com/view/stablecoin/ (last visited, Apr. 15, 2023).

Legislation Should Set Forth Operational Requirements to Protect Consumers

Stablecoin issuers should be subject to reasonable, risk-based operational requirements, such as making public disclosures regarding assets held as backing for stablecoins, segregating those assets from corporate funds, ensuring that those assets are bankruptcy-remote, implementing clear policies and procedures regarding issuance and redemption of stablecoins, and conducting routine audits or evaluations by registered public accounting firms.

Legislation Should Clearly Delineate Regulatory Authority on the Federal Level

At the federal level, stablecoins should be overseen by a prudential regulator such as the Fed or the OCC, regardless of whether there is a separate path for issuance by state-chartered and state-regulated entities. Stablecoins should also be exempt from overlapping federal regulation by the SEC or the CFTC, so as to provide regulatory clarity and clear delineation of responsibility between agencies.

Written Statement of Dante Alighieri Disparte, before the United States House Committee on Financial Services, Subcommittee on Digital Assets, Financial Technology and Inclusion "Understanding Stablecoins' Role in Payments and the Need for Legislation." Held on April 19, 2023 10 AM EST

Chairman Hill, Ranking Member Lynch, Members of the Subcommittee on Digital Assets, Financial Technology and Inclusion, it is my honor to submit my testimony to you today.

My name is Dante Disparte and I am the Chief Strategy Officer and Head of Global Policy for Circle, a leading global financial technology firm and the issuer of USD Coin, or USDC. USDC is a dollar digital currency supporting the extensibility of the U.S. Dollar in a competitive, always-on internet-based global economy. Indeed, as fears grow of de-dollarization or the rise of alternative payment systems that are non-conversant with U.S. values or broader norms in the rules-based financial system, Circle, USDC and dollar-denominated payment stablecoins can help to ensure the U.S. dollar remains the global currency of reference, including natively on the internet.

Over the course of our 10 years of activity in the U.S. and around the world, we have always aspired to a regulation-first approach based on trust, transparency, accountability and financial integrity. It has been 5 years since the first USDC was issued, which for the purposes of this hearing and proposed legislation, can be considered a dollar-denominated payment stablecoin. Today, USDC has supported more than $10 trillion in cumulative transactions on the public internet. USDC-enabled wallets support a global payment network in more than 190 countries, which is akin to a mobile money network like M-Pesa, but at world scale. More than 75% of all USDC in circulation are held in digital wallets and smart contracts rather than on digital asset exchanges, suggesting a strong correlation as a dollar-denominated store of value. Indeed, there is a Cambrian explosion of use cases and responsible innovation courtesy of the programmable, composale, trusted and open nature of USDC, with Circle's services built on and using open blockchain technology.

Rather than disrupting traditional financial systems or markets, we are seeing growing acceptance of USDC as a dollar settlement option among major financial services firms from Visa, to MoneyGram, WorldPay, among many others. A broader ecosystem of developers, businesses and people who rely on USDC and Circle's services for next generation payments and dollar settlement on the internet has promoted a wide range of use cases and developments. By every measure, courtesy of this early adoption of dollars as the currency of reference in digital asset markets, more than $132 billion of stablecoins in circulation reference the dollar, albeit to varying degrees of prudential regulatory standards. While some of these dollar-referenced stablecoins are starting to embrace sunlight and transparency, USDC was born in it. From the first issuance through to today, we have adopted macroprudential risk standards and transparency that is a hallmark of trust, even when compared to traditional financial services firms. As a result, a proliferation of enterprise use cases and adoption has followed.

Enterprise use cases for USDC run the gamut from treasury management to easing the exacting costs and slow speeds of cross border payments, which remain stubbornly high, inconveniently slow, with little meaningful competition. Indeed, one of the partnerships of which we are proudest shows the art of the possible with USDC and the advantages of open, interoperable payment systems. Last year, Circle, together with the Stellar Development Foundation and MoneyGram, partnered with the United Nations High Commissioner for Refugees (UNHCR) to enable USDC as a form of digital dollar cash assistance supporting war-displaced Ukrainian refugees.

This partnership enables UNHCR to dispatch a form of universally portable digital dollars directly to the mobile-based wallets of refugees. In turn, they can send, spend and save these digital dollars on their phones, notwithstanding the fact that much of their country and physical banking infrastructure has been destroyed in Russia's war of aggression. This form of near real time digital cash assistance also helps protect the personal safety of vulnerable communities, as such a basic activity of retrieving money from a bank in a war zone can imperil people's lives. Critically, this partnership also permits Ukrainian refugees to present their USDC at any MoneyGram location enabling them to freely convert from a payment stablecoin at the dollar exchange rate to the local currency, or to use USDC as a store of value or medium of exchange in its digitally native form.

This project marks a breakthrough and a new humanitarian blueprint for moving funds in a near-instant, transparent, corruption-resistant and auditable manner, which is an exponential improvement over the cumbersome and risky process of moving aid and disaster relief money. As this project shows, rather than disrupt traditional banking and finance, the availability of trusted dollar-based payment stablecoins can help extend the perimeter of the formal economy and the utility value of internet native dollars even in extreme conflict zones. This is as much a function of how USDC is designed at a technological level, as it is to how Circle is regulated and operates at a company level.

As the sole issuer of USDC, Circle has always operated under the highest prevailing regulatory standards for electronic stored value and money transmission in the U.S. While other countries regulate payments or electronic money (e-money) activity at a national level, the U.S. framework empowers state banking and money transmission supervisors to foster, develop and regulate the payments industry at the state level. Although this "sum of the parts" approach may be subject to potential operating and regulatory gaps, it has nonetheless produced an economic development model that has enabled companies to start up and scale across the U.S. Our states are not only the laboratories of U.S. democracy, and crucibles of economic development, they are also the laboratories of payment services innovation.

Rather than framing financial innovation and regulation as competing forces, Circle's operating experience over the last decade has prioritized public-private regulatory partnership and personhood. In short, financial innovation, inclusion and protecting the integrity of the financial system are not competing objectives. Today, we are comprehensively licensed as a state supervised money transmission and electronic stored value company in 48 states. We were the first company to receive a Bitlicense from the New York State Department of Financial Services (NYDFS) in 2015, and we have been and remain a registered Money Services Business (MSB) conforming with FinCEN's guidance on combating illicit financial activity. The net result is a company that went from a mere idea 10 years ago, to a business that has approximately 1,000 employees in 35 states and 12 countries, with both strong prospects and desires to become a U.S. listed company.

While there are blurred jurisdictional swimlanes among Federal prudential and markets regulators over whether digital assets fall into securities, commodities or payments and banking regimes, payment stablecoin legislation can build on already strong foundations that balance states' rights and risk-adjusted Federal oversight. For example, the dual banking system follows this model enabling state chartered banks to operate with a level playing field, while being held to certain aspects of Federal supervision. A comparable regime for bank and non-bank issuance of payment stablecoins can build on this federated approach, while creating a high bar for today's generation of payment stablecoin issuers and our future competitors. Indeed, the highest order objective in a competitive national and global payment system, is to pursue the widest degree of optionality and competition possible. There is no such thing as a one size fits all payments environment.

Establishing a similar approach with payment stablecoins and broader U.S. payments and financial market infrastructure innovations requires the provision of central bank services to regulated non-bank actors in the financial system. By this measure, the U.S. is an outlier among advanced economies in not having a national payment system, financial market infrastructure or equivalent electronic money frameworks offered at the Federal level. These developments can build on and complement the inherent value and competitiveness of state money transmission frameworks. Here too, Circle has played a part in helping strengthen and harmonize a model law with the Conference of State Bank Supervisors (CSBS), known as the Money Transmission Modernization Act.

It is also unhelpful that wider digital asset regulation in the U.S., including critical issues having to do with market structure, digital asset classifications, disclosure and consumer protection regimes, among others, labor under often insidious jurisdictional battles. All too often, regulation by enforcement is the go-to approach, when better disclosure, clearer market conduct and a more competitive playing field would help eschew the bad activity that caused so much harm in 2022. Indeed, regulators' protecting consumers and markets after losses are incurred, is like a pilot putting on the seat belt sign after the plane has crashed. Federal legislation for payment stablecoins would answer the President's Working Group on Financial Markets' (PWG) call for Congressional action, as much as it would answer the call among responsible, regulated firms in the U.S. for greater regulatory and legal clarity. This is essential to promote safe and sound competition for how Americans send, spend, save and secure their money in an increasingly technology dependent market. It will also ensure the U.S. remains a bellwether of financial innovation around the world.

The rest of the world is not waiting for the U.S. to issue a comprehensive regulatory approach to payment stablecoins and the broader digital assets market. Many global jurisdictions and financial centers have created comprehensive regulatory frameworks for fintech companies and digital asset firms, including clear treatment of payment stablecoins as payments and banking innovations. Most notable among these is the comprehensive European framework known as the Markets in Crypto-Assets (MiCA), which will be to digital assets what GDPR was to privacy. On its own this is not a bad development, especially as it creates a common regulatory framework in the third largest economic bloc in the world. If however, a yawning trans-Atlantic regulatory policy gap emerges, the world's most important economic relationship may find itself at odds with market and geopolitical realities, at a time when harmonization is needed.

If the U.S. does not lead at the national level - including by properly defining what is and what is not a payment stablecoin - then we can expect a future stable-in-name-only coin like Terra-Luna to emerge into the federal regulatory vacuum. Worst yet, offshore and potentially systemic activity continues to accrue to hyper-aggressive, large-scale and opaque actors with no demonstrable regulatory domicile or intention to compete on a level playing field. While crypto and digital asset markets may not be right for everyone, everyone's rights to participate in novel financial markets should be protected. This protection should include an end to perilous race to the bottom regulatory arbitrage and market conduct that violates the basic tenet of *same risk, same rules, technology neutral regulation.*

Against this backdrop there is a proverbial digital currency space race taking place with 114 central banks weighing the pros and cons of digitizing their national thrift. While these developments are not a zero-sum proposition where the U.S. will lose unless we fail to follow suit; the likeliest and most durable market outcomes, like the real space race, depend on the extent to which nations promote rules-based competition in and between their respective jurisdictions. Few things will do more for protecting, promoting and growing the role of the dollar in an always-on digital economy than payment stablecoin legislation. Legislation will also be a crucial linchpin in setting a foundation for rules-based competition, which in turn can help promote fungibility and wider exchange of comparably regulated and structured dollar-denominated payment stablecoins.

The reason blockchain-based digital currencies like USDC represent a breakthrough payments innovation is because they ride on open, interoperable and constantly upgradable technology infrastructure. As the largest payment stablecoin on the Ethereum blockchain, for example, USDC has become the payment stablecoin of reference supporting novel applications for programmable, composable digital dollars that do not take bank holidays. The use of constantly upgradable blockchains and open source technology in payments solves the insidious walled garden problem. This is a prevalent challenge even with modern payments companies that often charge exorbitant fees, suffer slow settlement times and are not interoperable with rival payment networks. It is the technological equivalent of a Gmail user not being able to send a message to a Hotmail account because technologies are not interoperable or incentives support anti-competitive market structures. Rather than relegating payments to competitive, non-conversant siloes, blockchains combined with USDC support open economic activity and competitive innovation in dollar-denominated payments.

When compared to virtually all other payment innovations to date, which have been about marginal improvements in debit and credit instructions and settlement speeds, payment stablecoins like USDC transmit a dollar-denominated form of electronic cash. Internet scale, near-instant dollar settlement, which will over time approximate the transactions per second of the world's largest payment systems, is a critical innovation that advances both U.S. economic competitiveness and national security interests in lockstep. This holds the promise to be a breakthrough in how people send, spend, save and secure their money in digital form to any internet connected device. Over time, provided national regulatory frameworks fall into place, a form of digital dollars can emerge enjoying legal certainty, internet-scale transmissibility, fundamental protections - including redemption rights at par even in the issuers' bankruptcy, privacy - rule of law and other critical features. The only way to achieve this is for Congress to enact comprehensive payment stablecoin legislation.

Just as the real space race was won when political leaders provided a national destination that marshaled U.S. ingenuity and spurred novel industries, the U.S. can also prevail in the digital currency space race. The time for payment stablecoin legislation is now.

Thank you for the opportunity to submit my testimony, I look forward to responding to the Committee's questions.

Payment Stablecoin Policy Principles

In the face of continued rapid growth as well as a broad crypto market correction, the time is now for U.S. policymakers to act. Delivering a bill to the White House that simultaneously addresses the clear risks that have emerged with stablecoins, while establishing clear rules of the road such that the U.S. dollar continues to be the leading digital currency of the internet can advance U.S. leadership and economic competitiveness.

In many ways, the broad crypto market correction vindicates policymakers and regulators who have been sounding alarm bells about excess risk and correlation with emerging crypto asset markets - even if fast growing algorithmic stablecoins were largely overlooked, despite warnings. Since 2019, much of this focus and concern has been placed on stablecoins, which is a catchall term denoting many variants of asset referenced cryptographic tokens purporting to afford economic stability, thus being usable as an efficient medium of exchange. At the same time, the crypto correction, amid broader economic turmoil and risk-off behavior in capital markets, also vindicates companies that have prioritized a regulation first approach, and worked to build deeper levels of trust, transparency and accountability when compared to other market actors.

For the past two decades, electronic money, payments and broader fintech innovations have been regulated in the U.S. under money services business and money transmission statutes. This is an approach the U.S. Department of the Treasury has embraced for crypto assets nearly ten years ago with the introduction of FinCEN's guidance for firms acting as a bridge between the existing banking system and digital assets. With digital currencies now being adopted globally as an internet-native medium of exchange, competition for the currency of the internet has now been amplified as a geopolitical and geoeconomic issue. Some are framing this as a digital currency space race, while others are arguing that the U.S. has the opportunity to lead the way, leveling the playing field amid intense international competition. As the Biden Administration's Executive Order works its way through a whole-of-government review, there is no greater testament to national unity of purpose than for Congress to act in a pro-innovation, bipartisan way on the President's Working Group on Financial Markets' (PWG) call to action on stablecoin policy.

In this spirit, the following policy principles reflect Circle's real-world experience operating the world's leading regulated dollar digital currency, USD Coin (USDC). USDC has safely powered more than $10 trillion in on-chain transactions and is available through a global network of thousands of digital wallets, exchanges and other products and services in more than 190 countries, lowering the fundamental cost of payments and financial services and establishing dollar payments utility as a native feature of the internet.

Circle's Payment Stablecoin Policy Principles

- To the right of lawful and consistent with democratic values, the use of money should be free, irrespective of its form factor.
- A dollar digital currency (or payment stablecoin or digital cash) is a digital bearer instrument entitling the holder to redemption at par for one U.S. dollar, even in the event of the issuer's bankruptcy.
- The presumption and preservation of privacy should be enshrined as a design principle in the issuance and circulation of dollar digital currencies.
- Transparency, accountability and harmonized risk disclosures are essential preconditions of market trust and consumer protection.
- The preservation of bank and non-bank dollar digital currency issuance promotes competition, a level playing field, and rules-based upgrades in the financial system. Bank-like risks should be addressed with scale-appropriate bank grade levels, including asset liability management, operational and enterprise risk management considerations.
- Dollar digital currency innovations are about optionality in the payments and banking system and not substitution. As such, their harmonized regulation and promotion should expand new forms of financial access through composable and programmable digital currency innovations, while promoting safe integration with existing systems of electronic money and financial markets infrastructure.
- The promotion of interoperability, fungibility and universal exchange of comparably regulated and reserved dollar digital currencies among

and between regulated intermediaries promotes competition, lowers barriers to entry and increases market choice. Stablecoin statutes should promote the development of supervisory, risk and operational frameworks for multiple issuers of the same stablecoin standard.

- The promotion of financial equity, inclusion and broader societal participation in lower cost payments, device-centric banking and trusted, always-on financial services can be a net benefit for historically marginalized communities. This must include a digital corollary to the Community Reinvestment Act (CRA), widening the net of participation to include community banks, minority depository institutions (MDIs) and credit unions in deposit taking, asset management and digital transformation efforts.
- The protection, application and collective defense of all applicable and appropriate financial integrity norms, including anti-money laundering (AML), countering the financing of terrorism (CFT), sanctions requirements and, know your customer (KYC) standards, should be universally applied. This should be done in ways that advance national and global security, while upholding democratic values and embracing new innovations in digital identity and credential verification that simultaneously preserve privacy while enhancing financial integrity.
- The application of safety, soundness and risk-adjusted prudential standards should be adopted, including in the strict adherence to cash and dollar-backed asset composition, maturity, weighting, liquidity and custody, including where appropriate, the promotion of direct custody at the Federal Reserve.
- Dollar digital currencies should be intermediated and responsive to monetary policy and its transmission, which is a sovereign activity that is conveyed through the intermediated, well-regulated and rules-based financial system designed to preserve global trust in the U.S. dollar. This includes applicable financial stability objectives, which should preclude dollar digital currency issuers from formulating monetary policy or calibration frameworks that may be in conflict with central banking and prudential regulatory norms.
- Dollar digital currencies provide different functionality from and can co-exist with central bank digital currencies (CBDCs). Policymaking should ensure an even playing field, robust competition and scalability, with careful consideration of technological and

operational risk, while preserving the two-tier banking and payment system.

- As a digital bearer instrument, dollar digital currencies should at all times remain backed 1:1 by equivalent dollar-backed high quality and liquid assets in the care, custody and control of well-regulated financial institutions and banks in a bankruptcy remote manner.
- Dollar digital currencies should promote responsible financial services innovation and trusted forms of always-on banking and payments through the use of open, internet-scale, constantly upgradable financial markets infrastructure. This combats technological obsolescence in financial infrastructure, improves cyber resilience and security and promotes domestic and global competitiveness through payment system optionality.
- Harmonizing national regulatory and policy frameworks for dollar digital currencies advances U.S. economic competitiveness, job creation and payment system optionality, while averting a harmful domestic "fintech constitutional crisis," and global regulatory arbitrage. With the passage of Europe's Markets in Crypto-Assets Framework (MiCA), which will be to crypto-assets what GDPR was to privacy, U.S. leadership is needed to avoid trans-Atlantic or global misalignment, while harmonizing standards for payment stablecoins.
- The promotion, development and standardization of digital identity and credential verification standards are critical companion solutions for more inclusive, privacy-preserving dollar digital currency innovations that advance in lockstep with financial integrity.
- Public private partnerships that employ dollar digital currencies, open financial markets infrastructure, digital wallets, decentralized identity standards and related services can advance policy through practice and the provision of digital public goods - while upgrading national, open technological infrastructure.
- The promotion of fair market practices and the adoption of a "stablecoin Glass-Steagall Act" can help to guard against manipulative market conduct and concentration that could erode trust, trigger systemic risks and imperil market participants and consumers to financial loss.
- Dollar digital currencies should be treated as cash or cash-equivalents under U.S. and globally accepted accounting principles to promote clarity for market participants and consistency across international

standard setting bodies. Such standardization will give households, firms and financial institutions confidence in integrating and using dollar digital currencies in everyday transactions.

Additional reference materials are offered to Committee members, including the following papers:

- A paper addressing common myths and misconceptions comparing today's generation of payment stablecoins to the era of wildcat banking in the U.S.
- A paper looking at comparative analysis between today's generation of payment stablecoins and a potential future central bank digital currency (CBDC).

Dante Disparte is the Chief Strategy Officer and Head of Global Policy for Circle, a leading global financial technology firm and the issuer of USDC. USDC has supported more than $10 trillion in cumulative transactions on the public internet and a global payment network in more than 190 countries. Prior to joining Circle, Dante served as a founding executive of the Diem Association (née Libra), leading public policy, communications, membership, and social impact.

Dante comes to Circle with two decades of experience as an entrepreneur, business leader and global risk expert, most recently as founder and Chairman of Risk Cooperative, a strategic risk advisory and insurance brokerage based in Washington, D.C. He is also a member of the World Economic Forum's Digital Currency Governance Consortium, helping drive global standards and regulatory harmonization for digital currencies. Dante served as an appointee on the Federal Emergency Management Agency's (FEMA) National Advisory Council, the United States' federal emergency response agency.

Dante is a frequent speaker and commentator on business and political issues shaping the world. His views on risk, economic competitiveness and security issues are regularly featured in leading media and publications, such as Harvard Business Review, BBC, Forbes, and Diplomatic Courier, where Dante serves on the editorial advisory board.

Dante is a graduate of Harvard Business School and holds an MSc. in Risk Management from the NYU Stern School of Business and a B.A. in International and Intercultural Studies from Goucher College. He is the co-author of "Global Risk Agility and Decision Making" (Macmillan, 2016) and was recognized as one of the 40 leaders under 40 by the Washington Business

Journal and in the inaugural Powermeter 100 list. Dante is also a life member of the Council on Foreign Relations and a member of The Economic Club of Washington, D.C. For access to Dante's upcoming speaking engagements and his 300+ published works, please visit www.dantedisparte.com.

Testimony of Delicia Reynolds Hand, Director, Financial Fairness, Consumer Reports, before the United States House Committee on Financial Services Committee

Good morning Chairman McHenry, Ranking Member Waters, Subcommittee Chairman Hill, Ranking Member Lynch, members of the Subcommittee and Committee.

Thank you for this invitation to testify. I'm pleased to participate in this important conversation about the overarching regulatory framework for stablecoins.

My name is Delicia Reynolds Hand, and I currently serve as the Director of Financial Fairness at Consumer Reports where I lead the organization's work in digital finance. There, I am evolving Consumer Reports' evaluation and ratings model to evaluate and rate digital financial products and services. In an equitable digital economy, digitized financial products let consumers spend, save, borrow, and invest safely in ways that respect their privacy and data, provide the benefits they expect, protect them from discriminatory and predatory practices, and help them achieve their financial goals.

Purveyors of digitized financial products and services promise all kinds of things - financial security, well-being, improved credit scores, the ability to manage daily expenses, the ability to leverage new forms of asset classes as investments without having to work through the complex landscape of financial intermediaries, all with a "simple" swipe or click. Whether digital financial products and services are living up to these promises is still an open question.

The marketplace of new digital products and financial asset types is vast and continually expanding. In 2019, there were approximately 5,800 new fintech startups in the United States. In 2021, this grew to approximately 11,000. As of February 2023, there were nearing 30K fintech start-ups, of which payments, cryptocurrency and blockchain technology startups represent a significant portion of this growth. From a consumer's perspective, this is a myriad of choices and promises for managing all things - basic financial transactions, payments, achieving financial security, and the American dream. It is confusing and there really is no meaningful choice in payments, for example, for consumers. Consumers pay by the means of payments requested; and one day potentially, in the mode of currency requested. Despite innovations meant to stabilize consumer digital asset transactions, there are no comprehensive frameworks or safeguards to ensure consumers are protected from potential risks and harm.

At Consumer Reports, we have begun evaluating these new digital financial products and services in order to demonstrate what these products and services actually do for consumers and how they rate alongside each other. Additionally, we hope to identify new norms and concrete best practices for industry and determine whether these products and services facilitate positive consumer outcomes, as some of them promise.

The convergence of new technologies and new forms of assets have made cryptocurrencies particularly appealing for consumers whom traditional finance has never appropriately served. For the most vulnerable consumers, often underserved or ignored by traditional finance; there is added complexity and risk; and yet there is faith and trust by some in the promise of digital assets and financial products and services which make cryptocurrencies accessible to consumers. Aligned with other statistics showing a similar trend, a 2022 Consumer Reports survey showed that African Americans owned cryptocurrencies at a higher rate than other ethnic groups.

Why? Because, these consumers have never been a priority of the traditional finance and banking system. These are consumers who continue to live in credit and intergenerational wealth deserts, exacerbated by bad business practices and government redlining. They have never had the benefit of financial advisors or adequate access to financial services, much less investment products. Thus, there is great allure of an asset class driven through payments and investment innovation, where power and governance is distributed outside of the very financial system which has largely ignored them. And these are the consumers who are targets of Super Bowl and other celebrity influencer ads, Cryptocurrency kiosks or ATMs at convenience stores and gas stations where consumers can easily and quickly convert fiat currency into cryptocurrency, and back.

Stablecoins and Consumers

The last couple of years have shown that even in the areas meant to usher in more stability, consumers can be caught in a vicious cycle of the boom and bust of crypto experimentation. There continues to be no uniform and meaningful regulatory framework in the U.S., potentially creating significant risks for the entire country. While these new technologies may hold some promise, the potential risks are significant, including an unlimited supply of tokens and coins serving as collateral for loans, rigid self-executing smart contracts, non-existent reserve requirements, lack of interoperability requirements, lack of meaningful disclosures, and the creation of debtor-creditor relationships. These risks are simply too big to place on unsuspecting consumers, especially if this entire ecosystem continues to be meaningfully and uniformly unregulated. This very complexity tied to the state of these technologies - crypto adolescence - makes it hard to assess risk and dangerous for the most vulnerable communities Stablecoins – a type of crypto-asset designed to maintain a stable value – have grown in popularity over recent years, alongside a wave of stablecoin companies which have entered the marketplace and facilitated consumer access to cryptocurrencies. Stablecoins are touted as an example of how cryptocurrencies can be used for payments and facilitate trade between fiat currency and other crypto-assets or between different crypto assets. In 2022 more than 75% of trading on large crypto exchanges involved a stablecoin on one or both sides of the trade.

Pegged to $1 USD, stablecoins are also purported to be a safer store of value in the crypto ecosystem. However, as we saw with the introduction of algorithmic stablecoins and the collapse of Terra and Celsius, stablecoins have also been volatile. Investors and consumers have lost their investments at the same time that globally financial institutions interests continue to grow and converge around the use of stablecoins to enhance or facilitate payments and other financial transactions.

Stablecoins and the Consumer Experience

Although stablecoins by design are meant to stabilize digital assets, we have seen in recent periods that reserves held by asset-backed stablecoins are subject to market, credit and liquidity risks. There are additional heightened risks due to unregistered, under regulated or unregulated issuers and service providers, opacity and complexity of the crypto ecosystem, potential conflicts of interest between issuers and consumers, and a lack of recourse for lost or stolen crypto-assets. If there is continued growth in the use of stablecoins, these could also become systemic risks as more consumers and the institutions they bank at continue to lose income and future financial security. And, with the billions of dollars in losses still being tabulated coming out of 2022's collapses of Terra Luna, Celsius and FTX, it is a public policy disaster to permit crypto currencies without comprehensive regulatory oversight and leave consumers at risk in this wild, wild west environment of caveat emptor or buyer beware. A comprehensive stablecoin framework that engages prudential, market and consumer protection regulators along with state banking and state securities regulators, is a critical first step to eliminate regulatory gaps and prevent regulatory arbitrage. As long as there are consumers in the cryptocurrency marketplace, there should be the strongest comprehensive oversight.

Common Sense, Consumer First, Comprehensive Regulation

Consumer Reports urges this committee to build on the work from last Congress and to continue to work in a bipartisan manner to develop common sense legislation to achieve effective regulation of stablecoins. This is especially important for responsible innovation, financial stability, and financial inclusion. Appropriate regulation, supervision and oversight need to be implemented before stablecoins become a risk to financial stability and the smooth functioning of payment systems.

It is clear, however, that the draft bill published in advance of this hearing is very close to the bill which was published in September of last year, under the last Congress. It appears that this committee has failed to take the critically important step to integrate into the bill key learnings from the continued volatility we saw at the end of last year with the collapse of FTX and recently with the collapse of Silicon Valley Bank and Signature Bank. As the country continues to tabulate the growing costs of these losses, lawmakers should aim to create a regulatory framework for stablecoin payments that reflects what we've learned from these events.

As drafted the bill introduces some important prudential standards into the regulation of the issuance and trading of payment stablecoins. But given the continued instability and the broader ecosystem, anything but the most comprehensive regulatory oversight that, at the very least, parallels existing guardrails in consumer protections in the prudential system, will be insufficient.

Inadequate Regulatory Process and Potential for Regulatory Arbitrage

In banking, before granting a charter, the chartering regulator must determine that the applicant bank has a reasonable chance for success and will operate in a safe and sound manner. This is an important check in our banking system which requires that even state chartered institutions obtain federal approval. There are no equivalent requirements for federal regulator review to allow meaningful assessment of surety in this bill. By not allowing the Federal Reserve Board authority to reject state licenses, this creates a regulatory gap which could drive a race to the bottom instead of a race to the top. In consumer finance, fiat currency payments are now 24/7 and borderless, which makes payments easier for consumers. These are lessons we have failed to learn from the past. On these basic matters for stablecoin payments, keeping with the tradition of congressional application of the Commerce Clause, the law should be the same across all 50 states.

For example, while this bill outlines an application process for becoming a stablecoin payment issuer for depository institutions and non-depository institutions, the bill could go further to include specific key requirements that parallel the requirements for traditional banking. Starting a new de novo bank is a long organization process, requiring permission from several regulatory authorities. While there are some equivalent requirements to provide information about the organizers, the business plan, senior management team, capital adequacy, and their plan to promote diversity and inclusion, there is no requirement for entities to outline their risk management infrastructure, and other relevant factors.

Second, while the bill does outline a role for federal oversight, the bill does not require entities that become stablecoin issuers to be insured depository institutions (IDIs). While the bill does require that the parent companies of bank subsidiaries authorized as stablecoin issuers be IDIs, it provides no such requirement for non-bank issuers. Instead, the bill attempts to make it clear that issuers shall not represent stablecoins as insured deposits. Allowing deposit-like instruments to not only be uninsured, but issued by banks who insure other deposits, will inevitably create confusion for customers, especially during periods of financial distress, and may inevitably provide less protection for consumers that choose to purchase stablecoins that do not offer such insurance.

Last, in creating the regulatory framework for stablecoin payments, the administrative process outlined is insufficient and would hamstring regulators and prevent meaningful regulation of this space. Specifically, it requires collective interagency rulemaking for which the first set of rules need to be issued within 180 days of this bill becoming law. Interagency rulemaking can often be a long and complicated process, and especially so in newer areas of authority. Additional time or the ability of individual FIRREA regulators to promulgate rulemaking jointly or independently would increase the likelihood of these entities receiving meaningful regulation. Additionally, given the high risk nature of this space, there should be a clear role for the FSOC.

Meaningful Payment Requirements and Consumer Protections

While this bill sets up a regime to approve issuers of payment stablecoins, it does not outline how payment activities conducted or facilitated by the issuers or their coins will have adequate consumer protections. Currently, most blockchain technologies are built without the capacity to reverse transactions, as many are append-only digital ledgers. But, being able to prevent, cancel, replace, or override a transaction is a critical function necessary to ensure payment system operators are able to conduct chargebacks or facilitate disputes over payments. Additionally, the bill does not include stablecoins in the rules under the Electronic Funds Transfer Act.

Additionally, stablecoin payment regulation should be technology neutral to promote interoperability and to ensure stablecoin arrangements share common features with the traditional financial system and are not walled off into each institution's specific system. They should be issued on interoperable technology protocols to prevent market concentration and potentially restrict data collection. This bill lacks any language which would require this and would be an impediment to consumer access. Consumers who have come to rely on interoperability in fiat currency payment systems, should have the same benefits in stablecoin payments.

Related, we would like to see the language associated with custodial wallets improved to provide strong oversight of custodial wallets. Language in the current bill does not cover all assets held by custodial wallets - a key point of interaction that consumers have with stablecoins. While custodial wallets may help consumers keep track of their keys, this has created a legal gray area that should be clarified. The law should prevent a debtor-creditor relationship from being formed and this should be clear in required disclosures.

Further, this bill's consumer and investor protections should be improved, specifically to give stronger protections than continued reliance on outdated check the box notice and disclosure regimes like Graham-Leach Bliley Act (GLBA), require more than monthly looks into an issuer's reserve portfolio and provide stronger bankruptcy protections for consumers. The bill lays out protections for holders of stablecoins in the event of an issuer becoming insolvent. But other parts of the bill appear to undermine those protections. For example, additional language in the bill allows stablecoin issuers to co-mingle funds received by coin holders in omnibus accounts to withdraw or use those funds to cover various administrative costs. In the event of issuer insolvency, a bankruptcy court could reasonably view, and the Court in Celsius already has held, that those commingled funds and such use by the company as grounds for giving the company and its creditors priority access to those funds, rather than stablecoin holders, the rightful owners.

Some additional key improvements we would like to see

1. Redemptions. While a process to allow redemptions is required, there is no specific timeframe established or comparable right to redeem at par or at some minimum threshold. At minimum, there should be a 24 hour redemption requirement. We want consumers to be able to access their funds within a calendar day, and not just one business day, especially if a redemption were to occur after the close of business on a Friday.
2. Increased activity limitations. While the bill does restrict risky activities such as pledging, rehypothecating, or reusing reserve and custody assets, it does not clarify the position of consumers when a stablecoin payment provider becomes bankrupt. A consumer's use with any stablecoin issuer or provider must not create a debtor-creditor relationship.
3. There should be no exception to the prohibition of certain convicted individuals to participate in stablecoin payments.
4. This bill, while outlining a clear role for the Federal Reserve Board over stablecoin payment issues, the FRB's authority would come second to that of the prudential regulators and consumer protection regulators.

Lack of Affirmative, Explicit Recognition of SEC authority

Perhaps one of the most notable things missing from this bill is the absence of any explicit recognition, consultation, or authority for the SEC, given the agency's active role in this space and the number of interventions it has brought on behalf of consumers. This is most unfortunate as the bill goes further than the last Congress to outline consultation with the states, a role for FinCEN and recognizes even the CFPB's authority, the lack of any role for the SEC is conspicuously absent from the bill.

Many stablecoins function and have been marketed as investment products like swaps or function like money market funds (MMFs). The bill contains a provision suggesting that the legislation shall not infringe upon the authority of other regulators to assert jurisdiction over stablecoins, but we believe that such language is insufficient protection for other agencies' regulatory authority. This bill needs more explicit clarity on how and when the SEC can and should regulate stablecoins. When these products mirror traditional finance products like swaps and MMFs and are traded on secondary markets, to assert jurisdiction over an issuer, asset or related party, the SEC would have to first establish jurisdiction in court, then seek enforcement action. Regulation by enforcement is expensive, inefficient, and is the antithesis of promoting good governance and capital formation. Not accounting for the SEC and market regulatory aspects of stablecoins is bad for consumers and will create additional regulatory uncertainties.

As it goes so far as to outline other engagement with other agencies, this bill would be enhanced by inserting a new consultation provision. Section "102 (d) (2) (E)" - Consultation with SEC, regarding "registration, disclosure and investor protection."

I urge the Committee to resume bipartisan efforts to ensure that the legacy of the country's first attempt to outline comprehensive oversight of stablecoin payments, is as robust and consumer first as possible. If not, this effort will not be a punctuated shift into more clarity, certainty and stability during this period of volatility; it will instead be a predictable pause before the next even bigger boom and bust.

Thank you again for the opportunity to testify today.

Statement of Adrienne A. Harris, Superintendent New York State Department of Financial Services, before the Subcommittee on Digital Assets, Financial Technology, and Inclusion, United States House of Representatives, April 19, 2023

Good morning, Chairman McHenry, Ranking Member Waters, Subcommittee Chairman Hill, Subcommittee Ranking Member Lynch, and members of the Subcommittee on Digital Assets, Financial Technology, and Inclusion. I am Adrienne Harris, Superintendent of New York's Department of Financial Services (DFS or the Department). Thank you for inviting me to today's hearing.

Strengthening the nation's regulatory oversight of virtual currency is critical to protecting consumers and ensuring the safety and soundness of institutions. I look forward to sharing with you DFS's expertise in the space as a prudential regulator of virtual currency since 2015. New York's virtual currency regulatory framework is the most comprehensive in the country, built on the model of full-scope banking supervision (including, *e.g.*, capitalization requirements, transaction monitoring and reporting obligations, and consumer protection requirements), but tailored for the unique considerations of the industry. It has served well to protect New York consumers, keep virtual currency entities safe and sound, and hold bad actors to account. I look forward to sharing with you some key features of the DFS framework and to offering continued assistance as you and your teams work to develop an appropriate framework for virtual currency regulation on a national level. State and federal regulators each have unique strengths that must be harnessed in developing a comprehensive regulatory framework for virtual currencies.

Before I speak to the specifics about how DFS regulates stablecoin issuers, I'd like to spend a moment to share with you how the Department's overall virtual currency framework is constructed. The Department has a wide range of tools to regulate the virtual currency industry, including licensing, supervision, examination, and enforcement.

Unlike states that license virtual currency entities as money transmitters, New York has two distinct licensing and chartering regimes for entities engaging primarily in virtual currency activities—the BitLicense and the limited purpose trust company (LPTC) charter—which allow for different types of activity and operate with guardrails tailored to the specific risks that virtual currency creates.

The BitLicense regulation[42], which was enacted in 2015 under the New York Financial Services Law, enables companies that can pass New York's rigorous licensing standards to engage in a wide variety of virtual currency activities—subject to additional DFS approvals— including storing, holding or maintaining virtual currency on behalf of others; buying and selling virtual currencies; or performing exchange services on behalf of customers.

Importantly, for a BitLicensee to engage with the fiat or traditional money transmission space, even in service of a virtual currency business activity, a separate money transmission license also is required. This provides the Department the ability to review and supervise against the unique risks of these distinct activities.

LPTCs, regulated under the New York Banking Law, are held to the same virtual currency-specific standards as BitLicensees but have additional powers and therefore additional supervisory expectations arising under the Banking Law. Specifically, an LPTC may act as a fiduciary, while a BitLicensee does not have fiduciary powers.[43]

Approval for a license or charter requires that companies meet the standards of DFS's comprehensive assessment of controls regarding financial crimes, cybersecurity, capitalization, financial/accounting, character and fitness of controlling parties, operational risk, consumer disclosures, and more.

In addition, when an entity is approved to be licensed or chartered, DFS creates a detailed supervisory agreement that is tailored to the specific risks presented by the company's business model. Licensed and chartered entities also are subject to ongoing supervision and are regularly examined for compliance with broadly applicable virtual currency regulations and other rules, as well as with their supervisory agreements. Supervisory agreements are updated on an as-needed basis to take account of changing business models, market conditions, or other relevant considerations. Licensed companies also must get approval from the Department for material changes of business, including for new product offerings and stablecoin issuance.

DFS also regularly issues guidance to regulated entities to make transparent more specific regulatory expectations and guardrails. In such a fast-moving industry, these pieces of guidance are critical to respond in a timely manner to market developments.

---

[42] 23 NYCRR Part 200.

[43] An LPTC also is permitted to engage in money transmission without having to separately obtain a money transmission license.

The Department also regularly examines our virtual currency entities, including to assess that the institutions have virtual currency-specific controls in place to protect consumers, that are appropriately tailored to the risks presented by the entity's business model.

The Department supplements such examinations through proactive supervision. Staff assigned evaluate each entity against regulatory requirements and bespoke supervisory agreements. Upon identification of supervisory gaps or deficiencies, the Department can require remedial actions[44] to swiftly address issues.

In the year and a half since my arrival, DFS also has strengthened this responsive oversight by acquiring technologies, onboarding specialized experts, and enhancing training to support more real-time supervisory awareness of our entities. For example, the Department now has a trained team in place who can review wallet addresses and transaction hashes associated with DFS-regulated entities and their counterparties to identify potential illicit finance activity.

If through our supervision we find that a regulated entity is not in compliance with our rules, our supervisory team can quickly refer cases to DFS's enforcement division to investigate and take appropriate enforcement actions[45] to ensure that companies pay penalties for violations, remediate issues, and where applicable, return lost funds to customers.

The core provisions of the DFS regulatory and supervisory framework, which is frequently cited by domestic and foreign regulators as the gold standard, are robust capital and financial standards, strong consumer protections, sophisticated cybersecurity requirements, and strong anti-money laundering provisions.

Virtual currency entities also are subject to custody and capital requirements designed to industry-specific risks necessary for sound, prudential regulation. For example, entities must hold virtual currency of the same type and amount, on a one-to-one basis, as that owed or obligated to a consumer. This is distinct from traditional banking based on a fractional reserve system, which enables entities to maintain only a portion of assets deposited by consumers and lend or use the rest for their own business.

---

[44] *Notice Regarding Paxos-Issued BUSD.* New York Department of Financial Services. https://www.dfs.ny.gov/consumers/alerts/Paxos_and_Binance.

[45] New York Department of Financial Services. (2023, January 4). *Superintendent Adrienne A. Harris Announces $100 Million Settlement with Coinbase, Inc. after DFS Investigation Finds Significant Failings in the Company's Compliance Program* [Press release]. https://www.dfs.ny.gov/reports_and_publications/press_releases/pr202301041.

The Department further underpinned these regulatory requirements with additional guidance in January 2023 reiterating expectations for sound custody and disclosure practices, and the paramount importance of the equitable and beneficial interest in the asset always remaining with the customer. Entities must have in place policies, processes, and procedures to appropriately segregate customer funds and provide appropriate disclosures.

In addition to requirements related to holding of customer assets, DFS-regulated virtual currency entities must have capital on hand to mitigate risk associated with cyber events, market volatility, or other exogenous events. The required capital amount is calculated based on specific risks presented by each entity's business model and other safety and soundness factors, such as custody (cold storage and hot wallets); transmitted assets (volume and value); and projected wind-down costs. Once the capital amount is initially determined with the Department, entities must maintain at least 110% of that amount at all times. Entities must submit reports to evidence they are meeting the minimum required amount against changes to the entity's business. If an entity falls below the 110% threshold at any time, they must notify DFS immediately.

DFS's virtual currency regulation also includes specific consumer protection requirements, including for advertising and marketing practices, proper disclosures, transaction receipts, and fraud prevention. Entities also are required to have policies, processes, and procedures to resolve complaints in a fair and timely manner.[46]

All virtual currency entities regulated by DFS are subject to our cybersecurity regulation,[47] as are our traditional banking institutions and insurance companies. Furthermore, our virtual currency regulation includes specific provisions to ensure individuals and their data are protected from the rise of hacks—a particularly salient concern with respect to virtual currency.

Lastly, from the development of the BitLicense regime and in the time since, the Department has prioritized addressing the inherently high risk that virtual currency business activity presents with respect to illicit transactions. These safeguards include requirements for annual risk assessments and independent testing, and annual certifications of compliance with transaction monitoring and filtering programs through the Department's Part 504

[46] 23 CRRNY § 200.20(a).

[47] DFS's cybersecurity regulation has become the model for other state and federal regulators since it was enacted in 2017. Recently, the Department has proposed amendments to our existing framework, taking into account new and evolving cybersecurity threats with the most effective controls and best practices.

certification requirements.[48] For example, in April 2022, the Department produced guidance to emphasize to all virtual currency business entities the importance of blockchain analytics to effective policies, processes, and procedures, including, for example, those relating to customer due diligence, transaction monitoring, and sanctions screening. The Department uses such tools itself as part of supervision.

The issuance of stablecoins is just one of many business activities in which a DFS-regulated entity might engage. Employing DFS's robust virtual currency regulatory framework described above, we use additional regulations, guidance, and company-specific supervisory agreements to tailor our oversight to the nuances of specific products and services. Our regulation and oversight of stablecoins is a prime example of how we develop specific guardrails for novel activity. DFS was the first agency to provide regulatory clarity for these products, which has helped protect New York consumers and provided the industry needed confidence and direction to create a strong, resilient market for these businesses in the state.

There are many different kinds of stablecoins, including fiat-backed, commodity-backed, and algorithmic.[49] As noted above, in addition to licensing entities to do business in New York, DFS also must approve separately each product a company seeks to offer, including the issuance of any stablecoins. The Department has not approved the issuance of any algorithmic stablecoins, which have very different characteristics in terms of design, backing, and issuance. The collapse of the algorithmic stablecoin, Terra, was well-reported in the news last year and had a ripple effect across the cryptocurrency ecosystem, ultimately leading to the bankruptcy of fintech firms Celsius and Voyager (neither of which was licensed or chartered in New York) and hedge funds such as Three Arrows Capital. However, the Department's strict coin listing requirements mitigated the impact of the Terra collapse to New Yorkers in a manner that cannot be said for any other jurisdictions because Terra had not been approved by DFS for custody or listing in New York State.

---

[48] 3 NYCRR § 504.3(a)(2).

[49] Algorithmic stablecoins attempt to maintain their peg by using algorithms that automatically adjust the circulating supply in response to market dynamics. The largest and most famous example of this was UST, which imploded in Summer 2022 and led to billions in losses across the cryptocurrency space. These algorithmic stablecoins in particular generally fail to meet the key defining characteristic of a stablecoin (stability) and should be viewed with upmost caution.

Currently, DFS regulates five fiat-backed stablecoins and one gold-backed stablecoin. In June 2022, DFS provided guidance related to the issuance of U.S. Dollar[50]-backed stablecoins (DFS Stablecoin Guidance)[51]. The DFS Stablecoin Guidance makes public the baseline requirements DFS expects from regulated entities, based on the work DFS has done in stablecoin supervision since 2018.

There are three key elements to the DFS Stablecoin Guidance: strict reserve requirements, confidence in redeemability, and transparency. Any stablecoin approved by the Department and issued by a DFS-regulated virtual currency entity must be one-to-one backed at all times by cash or cash equivalents held in custody with U.S. state- or federally-chartered depository institutions with deposits insured by the Federal Deposit Insurance Corporation and/or with asset custodians approved in advance by DFS. Entities must adopt clear, conspicuous policies which allow for "timely" redemption not more than two full business days after the issuer receives a redemption request (i.e., "T+2" conversion in response to redemption requests). Lastly, issuers are required to undergo monthly audits by an independent certified public accountant (CPA) and provide public bi-monthly attestations on the underlying reserves to provide the marketplace with the transparency needed to have confidence in their assets.

Beyond the DFS Stablecoin Guidance and individual supervisory agreements, the Department is actively augmenting regular reporting requirements to assess an entity's capital and liquidity. Stablecoin issuers are also required to report bi-weekly their bank partnership relationships, asset reserve mix, and flows related to minting and burning.

Together, these stablecoin-specific requirements, combined with the constellation of regulatory requirements unique to the Department, provide a level of transparency for existing and would-be issuers for how to responsibly build their business in a regulated environment.

Far from creating a disincentive to enter the market, strong regulation has drawn virtual currency companies to do business in New York. Crypto startups based in New York City have consistently raised more capital than companies in any other region of the country, including Silicon Valley and Miami. In

[50] The guidance on U.S. Dollar-backed stablecoins is noteworthy because DFS approves and regulates GMO-Z which issues GYEN—a stablecoin backed by the Japanese Yen. The industry guidance also does not reflect Paxos' gold-backed stablecoin. The guidance is attached here in the Appendix.

[51] The DFS Stablecoin Guidance is attached here in the Appendix.

2021, nearly half of that capital was raised by New York-based companies.[52] The Department continues to receive applications from a variety of companies which understand the critical need for a robust regulatory framework that is designed to ensure their safety and soundness and the protection of their customers. Further, other jurisdictions, regulators, and economic development agencies recognize the value of the DFS framework and are seeking to replicate it. From Illinois and California; to the United Kingdom, United Arab Emirates, and Singapore; DFS is engaged with regulators around the world seeking to build a regulatory framework that leverages DFS's expertise and experience.

Recent market events have demonstrated that DFS's regulatory framework is operating as intended. Now, more than ever, customers need to know that their assets are protected. In addition, industry needs clarity on how to develop innovative products in a responsible and compliant manner. Nonetheless, we are well aware of the significant risks virtual currency can pose to consumers and to the U.S. financial system, and we would welcome the opportunity for continued collaboration to help build a comprehensive and thoughtful state and federal framework that mirrors the mature and well-functioning regulatory system for more traditional financial institutions.

As members of this Committee contemplate federal legislation for stablecoins, I believe the best path forward is to build on the well-established dual banking regulatory system – where state and federal regulators share supervisory and regulatory authority. The dual banking system takes advantage of the comparative strengths of federal and state regulators. Federal regulators are able to comprehensively address macroprudential considerations and establish foundational consumer and market protections. Meanwhile, states can act more nimbly to respond to industry developments and support responsible innovation given their ability to modernize regulations more quickly and leverage their more immediate understanding of consumer needs.

Ultimately, we share the goal of establishing a national framework to protect consumers across the country without preempting the states' ability to regulate innovative financial services.

I am proud of the work DFS has done to develop a comprehensive supervisory framework and to foster a well-regulated virtual currency industry

---

[52] Bellusci, M. (2022, February 1). Global VC Funding for Blockchain Firms Surged to Record $25B in 2021: CB Insights. *Coindesk.* https://www.coindesk.com/business/2022/02/01/global-vc-funding-for-blockchain-firms-surged-to-record-25b-in-2021-cb-insights/ *citing:* CB Insights "2021 State of Blockchain Report."

in the state, and we would welcome further collaboration with you to take advantage of our lessons learned and develop a comprehensive national regulatory framework.

Thank you, and I look forward to your questions.

Crypto
Council for
Innovation

April 19, 2023

Patrick McHenry
Chairman
House Committee on Financial Services
2129 Rayburn House Office Building
Washington, DC 20515

Maxine Waters
Ranking Member
House Committee on Financial Services
4340 O'Neill House Office Building
Washington, DC 20515

French Hill
Chairman
Subcommittee on Digital Assets,
Financial Technology and Inclusion
1533 Longworth House Office Building
Washington, DC 20515

Stephen Lynch
Ranking Member
Subcommittee on Digital Assets,
Financial Technology and Inclusion
2109 Rayburn House Office Building
Washington, DC 20515

Dear Chairman McHenry, Ranking Member Waters, Chairman Hill, and Ranking Member Lynch:

The Crypto Council for Innovation (CCI) appreciates the opportunity to contribute to the important discussion taking place during today's hearing, and applauds efforts by the Committee to advance bipartisan legislation that provides a clear regulatory framework for stablecoins that fosters innovation while protecting consumers. CCI is a global alliance of industry leaders with a mission to communicate the benefits of crypto/Web3 and demonstrate its transformational promise. CCI members include some of the leading global companies and investors operating in the industry. They span the crypto ecosystem and share the goal of encouraging the responsible global regulation of crypto to unlock economic potential, improve lives, foster financial inclusion, protect national security, and disrupt illicit activity. CCI and its members stand ready and willing to work with the House Financial Services Committee and its members to support efforts to establish a clear legal framework for stablecoins here in the United States.

Stablecoins are digital assets with an added economic structure that aims to stabilize their price and purchasing power.[1] In other words, stablecoins seek to maintain a stable value to a reference asset, such as a sovereign currency like the USD. Importantly, there are a variety of models for stablecoins that involve different decisions around underlying collateral, governance, and more. Given the variance in designs, policy-making and regulation of stablecoins requires a nuanced approach. Moreover, it is important to understand the potential use cases, benefits, and risks provided by price-stable digital assets.

As the Financial Stability Board has highlighted, "stablecoins have the potential to bring efficiencies to payments, and to promote financial inclusion."[2] An emerging area of digital assets, they hold promise for a range of use cases including financial infrastructure improvements, new business models, humanitarian aid, and cross-border payments. Stablecoins are being used to solve many of the challenges associated with moving value across borders by enabling new peer-to-peer payment models and reducing burdensome costs and significant lag in the transfer of small amounts, as in the case of low-wage earners. As one example of the promise of this innovation, last December, the United Nations High Commission for Refugees announced a program through which it has coordinated with the Stellar Development Foundation, Circle Internet Financial, and MoneyGram to use Circle's stablecoin, USD Coin (USDC), to securely distribute humanitarian assistance payments to support refugees from the war in Ukraine.[3]

The Crypto Council welcomes the efforts of the House Financial Services Committee to explore avenues to establish clear rules of the road that foster innovation, provide critical protections for consumers and our financial system, and preserve the technological cutting edge of the United States.

Sincerely,

Sheila Warren
Chief Executive Officer
Crypto Council for Innovation

[1] https://papers.ssrn.com/sol3/papers.cfm?abstract_id=3633542

[2] https://www.fsb.org/work-of-the-fsb/financial-innovation-and-structural-change/crypto-assets-and-global-stablecoins/

[3] https://ukraine.un.org/en/211593-unhcr-launches-pilot-cash-based-intervention-using-blockchain-technology-humanitarian

eta ELECTRONIC TRANSACTIONS ASSOCIATION
1620 L Street NW, Suite 1020
Washington, DC 20036
202.828.2635
electran.org

April 19, 2023

The Honorable French Hill
Chairman
Subcommittee on Digital Assets,
Financial Technology, and Inclusion
Committee on Financial Services
Washington, DC 20515

The Honorable Stephen Lynch
Ranking Member
Subcommittee on Digital Assets,
Financial Technology, and Inclusion
Committee on Financial Services
Washington, DC 20515

Dear Chairman Hill and Ranking Member Lynch:

On behalf of the Electronic Transactions Association (ETA), we appreciate the opportunity to submit this statement for the record before the Subcommittee's hearing, "Understanding Stablecoins' Role in Payments and the Need for Legislation."

As the trade association that represents the breadth of the payments industry,[1] the Electronic Transactions Association (ETA) has deep expertise in payments technology, including the use of cryptocurrencies, blockchain, and other crypto-related technologies to facilitate payment transactions. At ETA, we are engaged in ongoing conversations within the industry and with policymakers about the promise and challenges of digital assets, and we believe there is a common set of principles against which any proposed governmental policies should be measured. In this regard, the payments industry has been a leader in developing industry best practices for mitigating risk and protecting the payments ecosystem.

As policymakers consider new laws and regulations for digital assets, they should carefully consider the following principles and ensure that any proposal best serves the needs of consumers and businesses, furthers financial inclusion, preserves and strengthens the financial system, minimizes fraud and money laundering, and ensures that consumers and businesses continue to have access to a robust and innovative array of secure banking and payment options.

1. **Properly Defining Digital Assets:** Developing appropriate and functional definitions of digital assets is a critical first step in ensuring clarity about the regulatory requirements that are applicable to the technology. Given that new technologies can be deployed in many ways, and that new use cases are constantly being developed, digital asset regulation should be based on the underlying activity or use case. ETA suggests policymakers should set principles-based guidelines for industry-led standards to meet. For example, stabilization mechanisms, consumer disclosures, methods for storing value, and redemption rights. This would permit flexibility over time to accommodate the technological capabilities of various stakeholders and satisfy consumer expectations. Adopting tailored definitions for specific activities and use cases will balance the need to appropriately regulate activity against the harms that might arise from sweeping definitions that inadvertently regulate other activities and use cases, while encouraging innovation that benefits consumers, businesses, and the economy.

2. **Ensuring Consumer Protection:** The public policy governing digital assets should include a framework of standards that appropriately safeguard the privacy and security of every transaction,

[1] ETA is the world's leading advocacy and trade association for the payments industry. Our members span the breadth of significant payments and fintech companies, from the largest incumbent players to the emerging disruptors in the U.S and in more than a dozen countries around the world. ETA members make commerce possible by processing more than $44 trillion in purchases worldwide and deploying payments innovation to merchants and consumers.

eta ELECTRONIC TRANSACTIONS ASSOCIATION
1620 L Street NW, Suite 1020
Washington, DC 20036
202.828.2635
electran.org

protect consumers' interests, and give consumers confidence to use the technology for in-person and online transactions. Policymakers should also ensure that consumers understand those protections and how they may differ from those offered by other payment methods. The ability to identify and reduce fraud is critical and should be part of the regulatory framework.

3. **Tailoring Regulations to the Risk Profile of the Participant/Activity:** Appropriate regulation involving digital assets is key to unlocking their potential while ensuring a properly functioning payments ecosystem and consumer protection. Entities engaging with digital assets should be subject to regulation that is tailored to the risks that they or the activity in which they are engaged poses to the payments ecosystem.

4. **Harmonizing With Existing Regulatory Frameworks:** The payments industry is heavily regulated, and the adoption of any new laws or regulations governing digital assets should be designed to fit within this established, robust, regulatory framework. This framework includes federal and state laws relevant to anti-money laundering, economic sanctions, and other anti-fraud and consumer protection requirements. New public policies for digital assets should complement and build upon not conflict with, existing laws and regulations as well as private sector rules and practices. Blockchain technology offers real time visibility and traceability that has proven immensely helpful for law enforcement, for example. These types of benefits should be harnessed into any legislation or regulation.

5. **Encouraging Responsible Innovation:** Continual investment in innovation is at the heart of past, present, and future improvements to the financial ecosystem. Development of new technologies and capabilities serve to strengthen cybersecurity and consumer protection, increase efficiencies, and expand access to financial services. As a technology, digital assets have the potential to further many of these developments and promote innovation and developments, including for financial access and inclusion. ETA urges policymakers to maintain technology neutral standards that does not unfairly disadvantage a new technology but apply principles adaptable as appropriate. Accordingly, any regulation involving digital assets should consider the technology's promise to improve existing capabilities while serving as a catalyst and platform for continued innovation.

We appreciate the opportunity to submit this letter for the record and the Committee's leadership on this topic. If you have any questions, please contact me or ETA's Executive Vice President, Scott Talbott, at stalbott@electran.org.

Sincerely,

Jeff Patchen
Director of Government Affairs
Electronic Transactions Association

AFR Americans for Financial Reform

HFSC Stablecoin Bill Discussion Draft
Criticisms
(Working Document)
April 18, 2023

Many people have lost trillions of dollars of value in the crypto crash over the past year, due in part to the collapse of at least one major stablecoin. Moves by policymakers that enable greater growth of this unstable asset class without adequate protections increase the scope and scale of the potential future risks these assets may pose to consumers and investors. And, regulators already have tools to exercise regulatory oversight over many digital assets, including stablecoins.

We believe the proposed legislation shared by the Committee falls far short of providing the protections and safeguards needed to address the risks posed by stablecoins for several reasons, including (but not limited to) the following:

- **State/Federal Regulatory Arbitrage**: The bill as drafted provides an optional pathway for stablecoin issuers to become regulated under federal law, but continues to give states the authority to regulate stablecoin issuers on their own.This means that issuers can more easily avoid federal oversight and seek out permissive, crypto-friendly regimes (such as Wyoming) that would provide issuers with a light-touch approval process, as well as access to payment systems (e.g., Fed Master Accounts, as below) without adequate supervision or regulation.
- **Lack of Deposit Insurance Requirements:** The bill does not require entities that become stablecoin issuers to be insured depository institutions. While the bill does require that the parent companies of bank subsidiaries authorized as stablecoin issuers be insured depository institutions (IDIs), it provides no such requirement for non-bank issuers. Instead, the bill attempts to make it clear that issuers shall not represent stablecoins as insured deposits. Allowing deposit-like instruments to not only be uninsured, but issued by banks who insure other deposits, will inevitably create confusion for customers, especially during periods of financial distress, and may inevitably provide less protection for consumers that choose to purchase stablecoins that do not offer such insurance.

- **Inadequate and confusing bankruptcy protections for consumers**: The bill lays out protections for holders of stablecoins in the event of an issuer becoming insolvent. But other parts of the bill appear to undermine those protections. For example, additional language in the bill allows stablecoin issuers to co-mingle funds received by coin holders in omnibus accounts to withdraw or use those funds to cover various administrative costs. In the event of issuer insolvency, a bankruptcy court could reasonably view those commingled funds and such use by the company as grounds for giving the company and its creditors priority access to those funds, rather than stablecoin holders.

- **Inadequate Evaluation Period and Process:** The time frame given in the bill for stablecoin issuers to submit applications to federal regulators, and for regulators to review and decide whether to approve such applications, is too short for regulators to conduct proper evaluations and does not provide adequate failsafe provisions, should regulators (or issuers) need more time to address concerns that arise during the evaluation.

  The evaluation criteria for issuers is also at times vague and/or subjective. For example, the bill requires federal regulators to evaluate stablecoins issuers in accordance with how the product provides a 'public benefit' and addresses the 'convenience and needs of the community to be served.' However, regulators have never established a test for what constitutes a 'public benefit', or how a product would meet the standard of 'serving the convenience and needs of the community', outside of the Community Reinvestment Act (CRA) - and this bill is silent with regard to the CRA. At best, this means it is uncertain how issuers would meet these criteria, and whether these evaluative standards are sufficient. At worst, it may mean that bank or non-bank entities might see value in organizing aspects of their business to fit the new stablecoin regime to take advantage of a permissive community benefit framework, in contrast to CRA requirements.

- **Over-reliance on Federal Reserve as regulator of last resort:** Though the bill identifies a number of federal regulatory agencies as potential regulators of stablecoin issuers (OCC, FDIC, others), in practice it appears that much of the regulatory oversight of stablecoin issuers will fall to the Federal Reserve. The Fed has a critical role to play in ensuring that digital assets, including stablecoins, do not present significant systemic risks to our financial system. But, arguably, the Fed is ill-equipped to conduct more direct oversight of commercial entities and this bill does not provide strong barriers of entry to a commercial stablecoin issuer. Thus, not only does it potentially create an ILC loophole 2.0, but also directs the Fed to enact a novel regulatory framework needed to regulate non-bank issuers. To put this in context, the Fed has not completed rulemaking for non-bank systemically financial institutions 12 years after Dodd-Frank.

- **Non-bank issuer pathway likely to lead to more lax oversight:** as alluded to in part above, the non-bank stablecoin issuer pathway in the bill would give non-bank entities greater access to national payment rails and systems and many of the privileges of banking institutions, without commensurate oversight and obligations; In particular, we fear the bill allows stablecoin issuers to use the non-bank issuer pathway to evade consolidated supervision, deposit insurance, and strict prudential standards and enforcement otherwise found in traditional regulatory regimes.

- **Lack of clarity re: safeguards against encroachment by non-financial companies:** Also as alluded to above, the bill also lacks sufficient clarity about how it would enable effective enforcement of the Bank Holding Company Act to prevent the co-mingling of commercial and banking activities. For example, the bill designates IDI-affiliated issuers as subject to Bank Holding Company Act, prohibits non-financial commercial companies from controlling non-bank entities, and requires that affiliates of that entity be financial in nature. But, there's no clear definition in this bill or elsewhere that articulates what 'financial in nature' might mean. And, there's less in the bill about how non-financial companies might act (and be regulated as) 'distributors' of stablecoins issued by non-bank entities – a marketing arrangement that has been a key feature of some prominent proposed stablecoin products, including Meta's (Facebook) proposal to distribute its Diem (previously Libra) coin in partnership with nominal issuers. This lack of clarity is a significant concern given the very real interest of tech and commercial companies in securing market share in the private payment space, despite obvious concerns that such encroachment would pose in terms of economic concentration and collusion.

- **Lack of specific payments- focused protections for consumers:** the bill sets up a regime to approve issuers of payment stablecoins, but does not speak to how payment activities conducted or facilitated by the issuers or their coins will have adequate consumer protections. As it stands, blockchain technologies lack the capacity to reverse transactions, a critical function necessary to ensure payment system operators are able to conduct chargebacks or facilitate disputes over payments. Additionally, the bill does not include stablecoins in the rules under the Electronic Funds Transfer Act.

- **Expanded Fed protections may increase systemic risk, requiring more Fed backstopping:** The bill gives federal reserve banks the discretion to provide a range of services typically reserved to solely IDIs, such as access to the discount window and master accounts--the key infrastructure to access the country's payment system. We are concerned this could lead to risky nonbanks (including nonbank stablecoin issuers) gaining access to many of the Fed's backstops (as there is already pressure on the Fed to expand master account access to nonbanks; this bill would likely increase that pressure), without the necessary oversight, thus increasing systemic risk throughout the financial system.

- Additionally, we are concerned that this may mean that even though the bill authors are seeking to 'protect' the banking system from the systemic risk posed by stablecoins (e.g., by not requiring all issuers to be IDIs; which we think may be counterproductive), the Fed may end up providing relief to stablecoin issuers in the event of hardship, through these systems, at the expense of the Fed and ultimately, taxpayers.

- **Lack of Affirmative, Explicit Recognition of SEC authority:** The bill contains a provision suggesting that the legislation shall not infringe upon the authority of other regulators to assert jurisdiction over stablecoins, but we believe that such language is insufficient protection for other agencies' regulatory authority. For example, if a bill such as this passed without giving more explicit clarity on how and when the SEC can and should regulate stablecoins when traded on secondary markets, to assert jurisdiction over an issuer, asset or related party, the SEC would have to first establish jurisdiction in court, then seek enforcement action.

bpi | BANK POLICY INSTITUTE

April 18, 2023

The Honorable Patrick McHenry
Chair
House Financial Services Committee
2129 Rayburn House Office Building
Washington, DC 20515

The Honorable Maxine Waters
Ranking Member
House Financial Services Committee
2129 Rayburn House Office Building
Washington, DC 20515

Dear Chairman McHenry and Ranking Member Waters,

The Bank Policy Institute (BPI) is writing to express views regarding the Committee's draft legislation on stablecoin issuers. Given the volatility of the crypto marketplace over the last year, BPI recognizes why Congress would wish to craft legislation to provide a regulatory framework that balances consumer protection and support for innovation in the financial sector. We thank the Committee for its attention to this important issue and engagement with key stakeholders throughout the process.

One provision of the bill, however, raises significant financial stability and other concerns: the inclusion of a provision that would allow nonbank stablecoin issuers access to accounts at the Federal Reserve.

Fed account access would increase systemic risk by allowing nonbank stablecoin issuers to (i) obtain Federal Reserve accounts and thereby back their respective stablecoins with central bank money and (ii) access the payments system without the strong regulatory and supervisory safeguards that currently apply to banks.

The Federal Reserve Act defines the institutions that are legally eligible for Fed accounts, and the Federal Reserve Board and Reserve Banks administer a review process for considering applications for master accounts that increases in rigor based on the applicant's insured status and federal oversight, if any. The applicant is also subject to assessment of potential risks it could pose to the payments and financial systems. The Board's recent decision to deny Custodia Bank – an uninsured, Wyoming-chartered Special Purpose Depository Institution – membership to the Federal Reserve highlights the dangers here. The Board's 86-page order describes a litany of risks inherent in Custodia's proposed activities, including its plan to offer a stablecoin product.[1] In its review, the Board said that a stablecoin issued by Custodia Bank backed by a Fed master account "could complicate the Federal Reserve's ability to manage the size of its balance sheet and overall conditions in the federal funds market."[2] The Board ultimately concluded that Custodia's proposed business model that "would focus almost exclusively on the crypto-asset sector and would aim to create further connections between traditional financial intermediaries and the crypto asset

---

[1] Federal Reserve System. (January 27, 2023). *Custodia Bank, Inc Cheyenne, Wyoming Order Denying Application for Membership.* https://www.federalreserve.gov/newsevents/pressreleases/files/orders20230324a1.pdf.
[2] Federal Reserve System. (January 27, 2023). *Custodia Bank, Inc Cheyenne, Wyoming Order Denying Application for Membership.* https://www.federalreserve.gov/newsevents/pressreleases/files/orders20230324a1.pdf (page 76).

1300 Eye St. NW, Suite 1100 West, Washington, DC 20005 | www.bpi.com | @bankpolicy | 202.289.4322

bpi | BANK POLICY INSTITUTE

ecosystem[3]" is inconsistent with the purposes of the Federal Reserve Act "[g]iven the speculative and volatile nature of the crypto-asset ecosystem."[4]

The Board's decision reflects our concern that allowing stablecoin issuers the benefits of Federal Reserve membership would expose other depository institutions to potential risks by allowing institutions not subject to comprehensive consolidated regulation and supervision access to the payments system.[5] Indeed, in light of the collapse of FTX and a long list of other crypto firms, the case for linking the crypto universe, of which stablecoins are a necessary part, to the Federal Reserve appears to have diminished significantly.

In addition to the significant financial stability and monetary policy risks of this provision, the draft legislation would also present significant illicit finance risks, if not properly addressed via robust safeguards. To effectively combat criminal activity, it is essential that stablecoin issuers be held to the same BSA/AML/sanctions requirements and standards as insured depository institutions. Currently, stablecoin issuers are state-licensed and generally regulated as money transmitters and are money service businesses for purposes of the Bank Secrecy Act, and therefore subject to FinCEN regulation; however, stablecoin issuers should be federally regulated and, more importantly, federally supervised to the same extent as banks in order to ensure compliance and avoid regulatory arbitrage.

While the bill would treat stablecoin issuers as "financial institutions" for purposes of the Bank Secrecy Act, this would leave important regulatory gaps. For example, it appears that the holders of stablecoins would not be "customers" and thus not subject to the "know your customer," customer due diligence, and customer identification obligations that apply to banks. Similarly, the bill does not clearly provide for ongoing federal supervision and examination of stablecoin issuers for BSA/AML purposes, which is an important aspect of the United States' framework to detect and combat illicit activity and actors.

As the Committee moves forward, any legislation must prioritize the safety, soundness, and resiliency of bank and nonbank stablecoin issuers, the protection of consumers, the preservation of U.S. financial stability and the prevention of financial crimes and illicit finance. We support the inclusion of text that clarifies the authority of FDIC-insured institutions to continue to issue and receive tokenized deposits and look forward to continuing to engage with the Committee as the stablecoin legislation is refined further to promote a safe, healthy, and competitive U.S. financial system.

Sincerely,

Edward Hill
Senior Vice President & Head of Government Affairs
Bank Policy Institute

---

[3] Federal Reserve System. (January 27, 2023). *Custodia Bank, Inc Cheyenne, Wyoming Order Denying Application for Membership.* https://www.federalreserve.gov/newsevents/pressreleases/files/orders20230324a1.pdf (page 7).
[4] Federal Reserve System. (January 27, 2023). *Custodia Bank, Inc Cheyenne, Wyoming Order Denying Application for Membership.* https://www.federalreserve.gov/newsevents/pressreleases/files/orders20230324a1.pdf (page 86).
[5] Federal Reserve System. (January 27, 2023). *Custodia Bank, Inc Cheyenne, Wyoming Order Denying Application for Membership.* https://www.federalreserve.gov/newsevents/pressreleases/files/orders20230324a1.pdf (page 73).

Credit Union National Association
CUNA

Jim Nussle
President & CEO

Phone: 202-508-6745
jnussle@cuna.coop

99 M Street SE
Suite 300
Washington, DC 20003-3799

April 19, 2023

The Honorable French Hill
Chairman
Subcommittee on Digital Assets, Financial Technology, and Inclusion
Committee on Financial Services
United States House of Representatives
Washington, DC 20515

The Honorable Stephen Lynch
Ranking Member
Subcommittee on Digital Assets, Financial Technology, and Inclusion
Committee on Financial Services
United States House of Representatives
Washington, DC 20515

Dear Chairman Hill and Ranking Member Lynch,

On behalf of America's credit unions, I am writing regarding your hearing entitled, "Understanding Stablecoins' Role in Payments and the Need for Legislation." CUNA represents America's credit unions and their more than 135 million members.

We thank the Committee for exploring this important issue as digital assets and the platforms that the underlying blocking technology has created are showing signs of creating major disruptions in the delivery of financial services. The continued operation of these financial platforms has created an unregulated financial sector that could have major repercussions to the United States economy.

As you know, our member credit unions are highly regulated in their operation and credit union members are protected by a plethora of consumer protection laws. The digital assets sector currently operates in a largely decentralized environment outside of the traditional financial safeguards and generally without financial intermediaries where the role of stabilizer and protector generally rest. In fact, like fintech, once one wades through the novel technology, the fundamental innovation of cryptocurrency is the elimination of the financial intermediary. Unfortunately, when there is no financial intermediary, the functions they provide are also lost.

Digital ledger technology (DLT) underpins digital currency and allows many industries to innovate. Nonetheless, we see no reason why innovation should change the government's role in overseeing an industry that uses DLT. The fundamental issue with DLT, as applied to the delivery of financial services, is that it disintermediates financial services providers—the very place where the government regulates the provision of financial services. Eliminating or weakening the backbone of the U.S. and world economies will have consequences and we think that these consequences should be understood before further harm occurs.

The Presidential Working Group on Financial Markets (PWG) recognized these risks and rightly directed Congress to promptly enact legislation to subject payment stablecoins to a federal prudential regulatory framework. This legislation should direct that insured depository institutions, that are subject to stringent regulations and oversight, and their subsidiaries serve as the sole issuers and conduit for payment stablecoins to ensure the safety, security, and continuity of the market. Moreover, there must be parity amongst all depository institution charters—both bank and credit union—as approved stablecoin issuers. We appreciate that the Committee's proposed legislation takes this into account and we ask the committee to continue to include credit unions as an equal part of the solution as legislation moves forward.

The risks to the financial system must also be considered as payment stablecoins gain legitimacy. Payment stablecoins holdings would not be liabilities of the financial institution and would be unable to be utilized for the lending and investment operations of the institution, thus reducing the credit supply, increasing the cost of credit, and causing a slow-down of the economy. This deposit substitution risk and its cascading effects would be compounded by the money supply multiplier effect. When financial institutions have lower liquidity levels and are unable to led at their current rate, the money supply reserve multiplier decreases, thus limiting the overall benefit to the economy. Financial institutions play a key role in the creation of money through their intermediate role between savers and borrowers. Decreased lending power by financial institutions would be particularly acute for community financial institutions like credit unions that are not-for-profit financial institutions and rely on deposit accounts to accumulate necessary capital to support their members.

For the reasons stated above, we think Congress should take their cue from the PWG and protect consumers and the financial system by subjecting payment stablecoins to a regulatory framework that limits stablecoin activity to insured depository institutions and their subsidiaries.

On behalf of America's credit unions and their more than 135 million members, thank you for holding this hearing and considering our views.

Sincerely,

Jim Nussle
President & CEO

ICBA
INDEPENDENT COMMUNITY BANKERS *of* AMERICA®

April 19, 2023

The Honorable Patrick McHenry
Chairman
Committee on Financial Services
U.S. House of Representatives
Washington, D.C. 20515

The Honorable Maxine Waters
Ranking Member
Committee on Financial Services
U.S. House of Representatives
Washington, D.C. 20515

Re: Community Bank Perspective on Stablecoin Legislation

Dear Chairman McHenry and Ranking Member Waters:

On behalf of the Independent Community Bankers of America and the nearly 50,000 community bank locations we represent, I write to offer the community bank perspective on draft stablecoins legislation before the Financial Services Committee. Community banks have a strong interest in ensuring that digital assets such as stablecoins do not create systemic, investor, or consumer risk and that resulting risks created by non-banks operating in this manner do not spillover into the traditional banking system. We appreciate the committee's engagement with key stakeholders throughout this process.

We believe legislation is needed to address the emerging systemic risk created by a proliferation of unregulated stablecoins. ICBA supports the draft legislation's goal of establishing a clear federal regulatory framework that addresses the gaps in the existing authority of financial regulators and its attempt to bring unregulated stablecoins into the regulatory perimeter. Currently, stablecoin arrangements are not subject to comprehensive consolidated supervision, which allows for risks to multiply and creates an unequal playing field with highly regulated banks. It is critical that stablecoin arrangements be subject to comprehensive federal prudential oversight and examination.

We would also like to thank the committee for its cautious approach to a Central Bank Digital Currency (CBDC). A U.S. CBDC would introduce significant privacy and cybersecurity risks to the nation's monetary system and obstruct bank deposit taking and lending, thus threatening the stability of the U.S. banking system. ICBA supports payments innovation and efforts to increase financial inclusion, but we do not think a CBDC is the best way to achieve those objectives. We urge Congress to keep these significant risks in mind while considering whether to authorize the creation of a CBDC.

The Nation's Voice for Community Banks.®

WASHINGTON, DC
1615 L Street NW
Suite 900
Washington, DC 20036

SAUK CENTRE, MN
518 Lincoln Road
P.O. Box 267
Sauk Centre, MN 56378

866-843-4222
www.icba.org

While we support these goals, we look forward to working with you to address some community bank concerns as this important process moves forward.

Specific Concerns Raised by the Discussion Draft

Access to Federal Reserve Programs

- Highly regulated depository institutions are given access to the Fed deposit account, as well as discount window and borrowing privileges, because they are subject to rigorous and comprehensive federal supervision and examination. Granting this access to nonbank payment stablecoin issuers, which are not subject to the same stringent regulatory oversight, would create significant systemic risk.
- Central bank reserves should not be used to back nonbank stablecoins. This change could lead to credit disintermediation by effectively creating a "pass-through CBDC," or a CBDC equivalent mediated by nonbank stablecoins. This concern was flagged in a January 2022 Federal Reserve paper.
- Nonbank stablecoin issuers should not be granted a privilege that is not available to money market mutual funds, which are structurally similar to stablecoins.

In practice, the Federal Reserve would not have effective "discretion" over application approval

- While the discussion draft grants the Federal Reserve discretion over approval of stablecoin issuers and issuer access to master accounts and other services, in practice, the Fed would be under extraordinary pressure to approve applications. Access to these privileges would be viewed as a directive from Congress, placing the burden on the Federal Reserve to demonstrate that an applicant does not qualify. Approval of one application, would create a precedent for the approval of additional applications. Denied applicants would seek relief from the courts and from Congress.

Permissive licensing of stablecoin issuers

The discussion draft would create three pathways to becoming a stablecoin issuer:

- **Insured depository institutions.** These highly regulated and supervised institutions offer a reasonable path for stablecoin issuance.
- **Nonbank applicants directly to the Federal Reserve**.
    - Federal Reserve review would be undermined because applications would be deemed approved if a decision is not rendered within 90 days. Placing a clock on application review is without precedent in financial regulation. Given the stakes for systemic safety, applications must be subject to rigorous review. The predictable outcome is

WASHINGTON, DC
1615 L Street NW
Suite 900
Washington, DC 20036

SAUK CENTRE, MN
518 Lincoln Road
P.O. Box 267
Sauk Centre, MN 56378

866-843-4222
www.icba.org

"deemed" approval of numerous, high-risk, nonbank applicants, and increased risk to the financial system.
    - The draft legislation also lacks needed detail on capital levels, supervision, and examination requirements for nonbank stablecoin issuers.

- **Nonbank state qualified payment stablecoin issuers**. The discussion draft would empower states to qualify stablecoin issuers in competition with the Federal Reserve. This would result in a non-uniform and even contradictory 50-state regime.
    - Moreover, the Federal Reserve would be forced to rely on examination reports made by state agencies. The Federal Reserve would be denied direct access to critical information needed to assess the safety and soundness of state-qualified stablecoin issuers. Inconsistent oversight would leave consumers vulnerable. Banks must comply with federal regulations governing all aspects of their operations, putting them at a competitive disadvantage to state-qualified, nonbank issuers.

Nonbank stablecoin issuers would have a significant regulatory competitive advantage and would effectively crowd out bank issuers

- For a bank subsidiary, stablecoin issuance would be likely considered a high-risk activity subject to burdensome requirements such as Bank Secrecy Act compliance, liquidity and risk-based capital requirements, and stress testing.
- The difficulty of obtaining regulatory approval and subsequent additional regulatory burden would effectively sideline banks. The draft should clarify that all well-capitalized and highly rated insured depository institutions will be considered qualified to establish a subsidiary to issue stablecoins.
- We recognize that the discussion draft attempts to apply the same regulatory regime to all stablecoin issuers, bank or nonbank. But this isn't the full story. Banks would remain at a significant competitive regulatory disadvantage. Nonbanks would dominate stablecoin issuance, creating a riskier financial system.

Recommendations for Stablecoin Legislation

ICBA encourages policymakers to harmonize regulations to ensure strong, clear, and consistent oversight of all stablecoin issuers.

- Any regulatory regime applied to stablecoins should be comparable to regulations applicable to traditional, functionally similar payments products and services offered by the banking system.
- The scope of regulation should include capital adequacy and reserves; activity restrictions; due diligence; information security and privacy; business resiliency; ownership and control of data; anti-money laundering and anti-terrorist financing; reporting and maintenance of

WASHINGTON, DC
1615 L Street NW
Suite 900
Washington, DC 20036

SAUK CENTRE, MN
518 Lincoln Road
P.O. Box 267
Sauk Centre, MN 56378

866-843-4222
www.icba.org

books and records; consumer protections; safeguarding customer information; vendor and third-party management; and ongoing examination.

- A more comprehensive, coordinated regulatory approach by banking and market regulators, including the Securities and Exchange Commission and the Commodity Futures Trading Commission, could help address risks, dispel confusion in the marketplace, and prompt more community banks to explore digital asset products and services to address customer needs. Stablecoin companies are not subject to comprehensive consolidated supervision, which allows for risks to multiply and creates an unequal playing field with banks.
- The harmonization of regulations would not only address risk—the additional clarity would level the playing field and create opportunities for more community banks to consider offering digital products and services, including stablecoin. Without such information, many banks may choose not to engage in digital asset activities.
- Collaboration can also help to ensure that the development of digital assets will not harm the integrity of the U.S. financial system by disintermediating community banks.
- Stablecoins must be brought within the regulatory perimeter. Appropriate federal oversight is needed to close regulatory gaps and mitigate the risk of regulatory arbitrage regardless of how these digital assets are classified by policy makers. The regulatory framework should address risks posed by any entity within a stablecoin arrangement that participates in the creation, transfer, or storage of stablecoins. Unregulated entities should not be permitted to issue stablecoins.
- A consistent federal regulatory framework for stablecoins should balance their benefits and risks and preserve the separation of banking and commerce.

We urge you to carefully consider the concerns expressed above and look forward to further discussions of the details of this important bill.

Sincerely,

/s/

Rebeca Romero Rainey
President & CEO

The Nation's Voice for Community Banks.®

WASHINGTON, DC
1615 L Street NW
Suite 900
Washington, DC 20036

SAUK CENTRE, MN
518 Lincoln Road
P.O. Box 267
Sauk Centre, MN 56378

866-843-4222
www.icba.org

NAFCU
3138 10th Street North
Arlington, VA 22201-2149
703.522.4770 | 800.336.4644
f: 703.524.1082
nafcu@nafcu.org | nafcu.org
National Association of Federally-Insured Credit Unions

April 18, 2023

The Honorable French Hill
Chairman
Committee on Financial Services
Subcommittee on Digital Assets,
Financial Technology, and Inclusion
Unite States House of Representatives
Washington, DC 20515

The Honorable Stephen Lynch
Ranking Member
Committee on Financial Services
Subcommittee on Digital Assets,
Financial Technology, and Inclusion
United States House of Representatives
Washington, DC 20515

Re: Tomorrow's Hearing: "Understanding Stablecoins' Role in Payments and the Need for Legislation"

Dear Chairman Hill and Ranking Member Lynch:

I write to you today on behalf of the National Association of Federally-Insured Credit Unions (NAFCU) to share our thoughts on issues of importance to credit unions ahead of tomorrow's hearing on the role of stablecoins in the payments ecosystem. NAFCU advocates for all federally-insured not-for profit credit unions that, in turn, serve over 135 million consumers with personal and small business financial service products.

NAFCU appreciates the continued work of the Subcommittee in examining the integration of digital assets into traditional financial products, including the creation of stablecoins – digital assets pegged to the value of another asset. Recent years have seen increased interest in cryptocurrencies and stablecoins, with prices reaching new highs as well as experiencing pullbacks. Notwithstanding these fluctuations, distributed ledger technology and other technologies that support a broad ecosystem of digital assets offer an array of potential operational efficiencies. For example, the ability to facilitate payment transactions that support smart contracts, either through use of stablecoins or other digital assets, may help members with specific business needs and potentially reduce credit unions' operational costs. Most importantly, digital asset technologies can be designed with strong auditability features, which can enhance regulatory compliance and reduce instances of human error, fraud, and other misconduct. However, the absence of a clear regulatory environment and appropriate supervisory framework poses risks to the adoption of these otherwise promising technologies.

In November of 2021, the President's Working Group on Financial Markets (PWG) issued a stablecoin report making several recommendations, including a proposed federal regulatory regime for stablecoins. While the report called for Congressional action and urged a new law that stablecoins may only be issued by insured depository institutions (IDIs), it unfortunately did not use a definition of IDI that included credit unions. This was a failing of the report.

The Honorable French Hill
The Honorable Stephen Lynch
April 18, 2023
Page 2 of 2

However, the draft legislation noticed for this hearing is a step in the right direction. NAFCU appreciates that the draft uses the Federal Reserve definition of an IDI instead of other definitions that exclude credit unions. Establishing barriers to credit union engagement with digital assets would also undercut many of the financial inclusion benefits that may be realized through related technologies given that the credit union industry has a long history of prioritizing the needs of underserved and low-income communities. NAFCU also supports enforcement and examination being left up to existing regulators – in the case of credit unions, the National Credit Union Administration (NCUA) – as well as establishing a basic framework for oversight of non-depository stablecoin issuers. We look forward to engaging with you on this proposal as it moves through the legislative process.

We thank you for the opportunity to share our thoughts and look forward to continuing to work with you on including emerging technologies into financial services. Should you have any questions or require any additional information, please contact me or Lewis Plush, NAFCU's Senior Associate Director of Legislative Affairs, at (703) 258-4981 or lplush@nafcu.org.

Sincerely,

Brad Thaler

Brad Thaler
Vice President of Legislative Affairs

cc: Members of the Subcommittee on Digital Assets, Financial Technology, and Inclusion

PUBLIC CITIZEN 50
People • Power • Progress YEARS

April 17, 2023

Char Patrick McHenry
Ranking Member Maxine Waters
Honorable Members of the Committee
U.S. House Committee on Financial Services
2129 Rayburn House Office Building
Washington, D.C. 20515

Dear Chair McHenry, Ranking Member Waters and Members of the Committee,

On behalf of more than 500,000 members and supporters of Public Citizen, we offer the following comments on the stablecoin legislation slated for consideration before the committee April 19, 2023.

Prevailing cryptocurrencies gyrate wildly in price often in a single day. In the last year, Bitcoin traded as high as $60,000 per token and as low as $16,000.[1] These swings undermine the case for digital assets as a means of exchange: A customer who believed that Bitcoin would rise in value would not rationally use one for a purchase on that day since they would be over-paying. They would only use the coin if they thought the price would fall. Conversely, a vendor who believed Bitcoin would fall would not accept the coin, since it would be an underpayment, and would only accept the token if they believed the price would rise. In other words, a fluctuating price stifles the use of Bitcoin as a vehicle of market exchange.

Stablecoins promised to answer the problem of volatility in pricing by pegging each token to a specific value, such as the U.S. dollar. However, many sponsors failed to fully back these tokens. The New York Attorney General fined Tether and Bitfinex for such failures.[2] Celsius promised high yields to those who purchased its stablecoin, but allegedly paid those yields with newer investors' money, a basic Ponzi scheme. Its bankruptcy filing noted it owed $4.7 billion to some 1.7 million investors, and only had $167 million in assets.[3] Voyager allegedly claimed its stablecoin was backed by FDIC insurance, according to

---

[1] *Bitcoin*, COINDESK (website accessed June 11, 2021) https://www.coindesk.com/price/bitcoin
[2] *Attorney General James Ends Virtual Currency Trading Platform Bitfinex's Illegal Activities in New York* NY ATTORNEY GENERAL, (Feb. 23, 2021) https://ag.ny.gov/press-release/2021/attorney-general-james-ends-virtual-currency-trading-platform-bitfinexs-illegal
[3] MacKenzie Sigalos, *Homeless, Suicidal, Down To Last $1,000: Celsius Investors Beg Bankruptcy Judge For Help* CNBC (Aug. 2, 2022) https://www.cnbc.com/2022/08/02/celsius-investors-owed-4point7-billion-beg-judge-to-recover-life-savings.html

the federal agencies.[4] Voyager declared bankruptcy.[5] FTX is bankrupt, and its founders have either pleaded guilty to fraud, or are under indictment.[6] [7]

Public Citizen believes any stablecoin bill should contain the following:

- Assets backed on a 1-1 basis.
- The assets must be safe and highly liquid, restricted to U.S. Treasury securities.
- The sponsor must maintain capital of 5 percent. (Sponsors must maintain assets that are 5 percent greater than the value of outstanding stablecoins.)
- Sponsors may not be affiliated with any commercial firm, or that is not a bank. (This means that firms such as Facebook or WalMart could be sponsors.)
- Sponsors must disclose their climate footprint.
- Sponsors must register with the Securities and Exchange Commission (SEC).
- Registration must include:
    - A list of any criminal conviction, deferred prosecution agreement, and pending criminal proceeding in any jurisdiction against all of the following: (i) The applicant; (ii) Any executive officer of the applicant; (iii) Any responsible individual of the applicant; (iv) Any person that has control over the applicant; (v) Any person over which the applicant has control.
    - A list of any litigation, arbitration, or administrative proceeding in any jurisdiction in which the applicant or an executive officer or a responsible individual of the applicant has been a party for the 10 years before the application is submitted determined to be material in accordance with generally accepted accounting principles and, to the extent the applicant would be required to disclose the litigation, arbitration, or administrative proceeding in the applicant's audited financial statements, reports to equity owners and similar statements or reports.
    - A list of any bankruptcy or receivership proceeding in any jurisdiction for the 10 years before the application is submitted in which any of the following was a debtor: (i) The applicant; (ii) An executive officer of the applicant; (iii) A responsible individual of the applicant; (iv) A person that has control over the applicant; (v) A person over which the applicant has control.
    - A set of fingerprints for each executive officer and responsible individual of the applicant.

- Sponsors must publicly disclose monthly their assets, liabilities, capital, income, and expenses of the licensee, and an independent audit of this financial data quarterly.

---

[4] FDIC, Federal Reserve, Letter to Voyager Digital, FEDERAL RESERVE *July 28, 2022) https://www.federalreserve.gov/newsevents/pressreleases/files/bcreg20220728a1.pdf
[5] Rohan Goswami, *Voyager CEO Made Millions In Stock Sales In 2021 When Price Was Near Peak* CNBC (Aug. 3, 2022) https://www.cnbc.com/2022/08/03/voyager-ceo-made-millions-in-stock-sales-in-2021.html
[6] Vicky Ge Huang, *FTX Tapped Into Customer Accounts to Fund Risky Bets, Setting Up Its Downfall* WALL STREET JOURNAL, (Nov. 11, 2022), https://www.wsj.com/articles/ftx-tapped-into-customer-accounts-to-fund-risky-bets-setting-up-its-downfall-11668093732
[7] Phil Helsel, *An FTX Co-Founder and The Former CEO At Alameda Research Plead Guilty To Fraud* NBC News Dec 21, 2022) https://www.nbcnews.com/business/business-news/ftx-co-founder-former-ceo-alameda-research-plead-guilty-fraud-rcna62891

- Sponsors shall maintain a surety bond or trust account in United States dollars in a form and amount as determined by the SEC for the protection of those who engage in digital financial asset business activity with the registrant.
- Banks that hold stablecoins must post 1250 percent risk capital, as described by the Basel Committee.[8]
- Penalties for infraction of any of these terms shall be one percent of the outstanding value of the stablecoin on the first infraction, and termination of the stablecoin on the second.

The bill the committee now considers lacks many of these features.

The bill allows that the reserve may include repurchase agreements. Instead of a fully audited reserve, the bill only requires management attestation as to its value. The bill requires a monthly disclosure of the composition of the portfolio, which is good, but an unaudited monthly statement invites dishonesty. Further, this bill requires no surety bond.

Instead of a robust examination of the integrity of the stablecoin sponsor, the bill establishes a 45-day review period. The application is automatically approved if the regulator has not already approved it. Firms with problem stablecoins "may" be prevented from sponsoring another one. Certainly, a prohibition on a second stablecoin should be mandatory.

There is no requirement for additional capital backing the stablecoins. Compounding this problem, the bill opens the Federal Reserve's Discount Window for the stablecoins, to be used when the stablecoin's sponsor runs into trouble.

While the bill does limit stablecoin affiliates to those of a "financial" nature (meaning that Facebook or WalMart would be barred), it would allow the likes of mutual fund giant Fidelity to compete and promote this wasteful product. Further, the bill allows the use of contractors. These could be foreign entities where US supervision could be frustrated.

We support the bill's prohibition of FDIC insurance for stablecoins, and the requirement that stablecoin sponsors make that clear to customers.

Penalties amount to $1 million, instead of one percent of the outstanding value of the stablecoin on the first infraction, and termination of the stablecoin on the second.

Finally, the bill requires no disclosure of climate footprint.

Improving the Payment System

Cryptocurrency promised to improve the payment system. We welcome efforts to make the payment system more efficient and less costly for consumers and businesses alike.

[8] Basel Committee on Banking Supervision, *Prudential Treatment Of Cryptoasset Exposures,* BANK OF INTERNATIONAL SETTLEMENTS (Sept. 10, 2021) https://www.bis.org/bcbs/publ/d519.pdf

Many U.S. residents are underbanked. More than six percent of American households, or some 33 million citizens are without a traditional bank account. Some do not trust banks, while others lack the funds that financial institutions require to open and maintain an account.[9]

Even for those lucky people with deposit accounts, the payment system is slow. Overdraft fees can be substantial. Checks and credit card payments can take two days or more to clear, meaning that vendors are without these funds during that time. It is also costly. Checks and particularly wire transfers can include substantial fees. Banks charge interchange fees for credit cards, a substantial burden for retailers.[10] And it is complex, with thousands of banks with idiosyncratic ledger systems communicating with one another and the Federal Reserve.

We note the apparent success of the Pix payment system in Brazil, sponsored by the Central Bank of Brazil.[11] This uses QR codes (or two-dimensional bar codes, formally known as a quick response code) that appear in the customers' cell phones. After a year of operation, this electronic system, free of fees to customers, represented some 6 percent of electronic commerce in the country.[12] During the pandemic, adoption of Pix led to a 73 percent decline in the unbanked population.[13] The Brazilian Central Bank requires Brazilian banks to participate. Banks reportedly discovered that while they lost some revenue from fees, they saved money from the reduced use of checks.[14]

The 28 countries of the European Union, along with several others, are experimenting with Single Euro Payments Area, an electronic transfer system that promises transaction completion within 10 seconds. (European regulators, however, do not require banks to participate.[15])

At the same time, Public Citizen does support exploration of a Central Bank Digital Currency (CBDC). This federal digital coin, in one form dubbed a FedAccount, holds the promise to address some of the problems with the payment system reviewed above. Currently, depository institutions maintain accounts with the Federal Reserve.

Conceived by Lev Menand of Columbia Law School in June 2018, the CBDC would be a Federal Reserve account. It would be available to "any U.S. resident or business in digital wallets operated by the Federal Reserve, the Post Office, or one of the country's several thousand community banks," he

---

[9] Mehrsa Baradaran, *How the Other Half Banks*, HARVARD UNIVERSITY PRESS (2015) https://www.hup.harvard.edu/catalog.php?isbn=9780674983960

[10] Aaron Klein, *A Few Small Banks Have Become Overdraft Giants*, BROOKINGS INST. (Mar. 1, 2021) https://www.brookings.edu/opinions/a-few-small-banks-have-become-overdraft-giants/

[11] *Pix*, CENTRAL BANK OF BRAZIL (website accessed July 18, 2022) https://www.bcb.gov.br/en/financialstability/pix_en

[12] *The Pix Revolution in Brazil*, EBANK (website accessed July 18, 2022) https://business.ebanx.com/hubfs/ABM/APMs/Pix/English/PIX-Revolution-EBANX-EN.pdf?utm_medium=email&_hsenc=p2ANqtz-9rbll_fY1tYx3FDsbh-srIZgbL8Xm3IC1j2G5w_c2Zc8YqlVgzOSnCMB8XLdkCn06suim1TD9pQ8gw1s4SdfcW3iIy1Q&_hsmi=206763316&utm_content=206763316&utm_source=hs_automation&hsCtaTracking=5529a87a-3179-4fcd-94eb-bf706937d921%7Cf2d4b972-00a6-4aed-a46a-3d880e2cf259

[13] *A Year of PIX in Brazil: What Does the Future of Real-Time Fraud Look Like?* ACI WORLDWIDE (Dec. 10, 2021) https://www.aciworldwide.com/blog/a-year-of-pix-in-brazil-what-does-the-future-of-real-time-fraud-look-like

[14] Maxnaun Gutierrez, *Why Pix is the Revolution of Consumer Experience in Brazil* PAYMENTS JOURNAL (Feb. 24, 2021) https://www.paymentsjournal.com/why-pix-is-the-revolution-of-consumer-experience-in-brazil/

[15] Andrew Singer, *Brazil's PIX Payments System Has the Same Spirit, but Not a Blockchain Structure* COINTELEGRAPH (Feb 28, 2020) https://cointelegraph.com/news/brazils-pix-payments-system-has-the-same-spirit-but-not-a-blockchain-structure

explains.[16] "The digital wallets would charge no fees and have no minimum balances. They would come with debit cards, direct deposit, and bill pay. They would have customer service, privacy safeguards, and fraud protection—if for example one lost their password. And these accounts would earn interest at the same rate that the Fed pays to banks."

Lack of profitability for the banks represents one of the reasons that banks fail to service roughly six percent of the population. The FedAccount would be available regardless of any balance and would be streamlined with immediate clearing. There would be no fees. With such an account, delivery of federal payments such as Covid relief or other government benefits, would be immediate.

Noting though that before such a system is implemented, important questions must be answered. For example, many bank account holders are subject to garnishments because of unpaid debt. Debt collectors would have a simple way to garnish funds through the CBDC. That also means the Federal Reserve would need to engage with debt collectors in addition to individual Federal Reserve account holders. There may be political issues. For example, the CARES Act might have more effectively delivered needed rescue funds to needy Americans via a FedAccount system. However, some of the individuals who received relief may have been subject to garnishment, meaning the Federal Reserve would be in a position of deciding whether, in times of extraordinary need, it would protect or release these funds.

We attach a letter submitted to the Department of Treasury in response to its request for comment on digital assets.

In conclusion, we appreciate the committee's efforts to address cryptocurrencies. But we believe that cryptocurrency has failed to prove its worth and instead has demonstrated that it's sponsors often scam consumers, provide a vehicle for money laundering, drug trafficking and other misconduct; and exacerbates climate change. Stablecoins exist and the committee should enact strong protections. But it would be better if this so-called innovation withered away.

For questions, please contact Bartlett Naylor at bnaylor@citizen.org.

Sincerely,

Public Citizen

[16] Lev Menand, *Testimony*, U.S. SENATE BANKING COMMITTEE (June 9, 2021) https://www.banking.senate.gov/imo/media/doc/Menand%20Testimony%206-9-21.pdf

PUBLIC CITIZEN 50
People · Power · Progress YEARS

August 8, 2022

Departmental Offices
Department of the Treasury
1500 Pennsylvania Ave., NW
Washington D.C. 20220

Re: Ensuring Responsible Development of Digital Assets; Request for Comment per Executive Order 14067

Dear Officers,

On behalf of more than 500,000 members and supporters of Public Citizen we offer the following comments in response to the Treasury Department's effort for "Ensuring Responsible Development of Digital Assets."[17] We applaud the Biden administration's principal policy objectives with respect to digital assets. We look forward to Treasury's scrutiny of the risks posed by digital assets to consumers, investors, financial institutions, democratic principles, and the climate. We also encourage Treasury to consider carefully the purported benefits of digital assets, particularly cryptocurrencies, which are often overstated.

In this request of comment, the Treasury asks: "What explains the level of current adoption of digital assets? Please identify key trends and reasons why digital assets have gained popularity and increased adoption in recent years."[18]

Indeed, the popularity of cryptocurrency has exploded in recent years. From adoption of the first cryptocurrency, Bitcoin, which was introduced in 2008[19] and could initially be purchased for pennies, the market capitalization of all cryptocurrencies peaked in 2022 at $3 trillion, before falling back to around $1 trillion during the latest so-called "crypto winter."[20]

The crypto boom came with a proliferation of projects trying to draw in new investors with exited promises of riches, democratized finance, and transformational technologies. No doubt, real problems

---

[17] Department of the Treasury, *Ensuring Responsible Development of Digital Assets,* FEDERAL REGISTER (July 8, 2022) https://www.govinfo.gov/content/pkg/FR-2022-07-08/pdf/2022-14588.pdf
[18] Id
[19] Satoshi Nakamoto, *Bitcoin: A Peer-to-Peer Electronic Cash System*, (2008) https://bitcoin.org/bitcoin.pdf
[20] Emily Flitter, How Wall Street Escaped the Crypto Meltdown, New York Times (July 5, 2022) https://www.nytimes.com/2022/07/05/business/economy/wall-st-cryptocurrency-prices.html

make the current U.S. payment system inefficient and expensive. Many understandably hold major banks in low regard. For many, the current economy truly is rigged against them.

But as the recent crypto crash is reinforcing, most of these projects are thinly veiled Ponzi schemes that use huge quantities of energy with few actual benefits or protections for retail investors or users and have grown only in the cracks created by regulatory inattentiveness. The failures of Celsius (now in bankruptcy), Luna and TerraUSD attest to the false claims and Ponzi characteristics of this market.[21]

Initially, advocates argued cryptocurrency would make the payment system faster and cheaper. But more than a decade later, few vendors accept cryptocurrency. Generally, cryptocurrency has failed in its initial promise of a decentralized, efficient, less costly, and more equitable financial system especially for those with less access to traditional banking. This failure follows more than a decade of efforts by thousands of experts exploring the potential of blockchain and Bitcoin, which was described in the 2008 white paper by the pseudonymous Satoshi Nakamoto as an alternative payment system.[22] Instead, cryptocurrencies have served mainly as a source of speculation, a vehicle for funding illegal activity including tax evasion, and a massive use of energy that exacerbates climate change.

Most immediately, the prevailing cryptocurrencies are gyrating wildly in price often in a single day. In the last year, Bitcoin traded as high as $60,000 per token and as low as $19,000.[23] These swings undermine the case for digital assets as a means of exchange: A customer who believed that Bitcoin would rise in value would not rationally use one for a purchase on that day since they would be over-paying. They would only use the coin if they thought the price would fall. Conversely, a vendor who believed Bitcoin would fall would not accept the coin, since it would be an underpayment, and would only accept the token if they believed the price would rise. In other words, a fluctuating price stifles the use of Bitcoin as a vehicle of market exchange.

Stablecoins promised to answer the problem of volatility in pricing by pegging each token to a specific value, such as the U.S. dollar. However, many sponsors failed to fully back these tokens. The New York Attorney General fined Tether and Bitfinex for such failures.[24] Celsius promised high yields to those who purchased its stablecoin, but allegedly paid those yields with newer investors' money, a basic Ponzi scheme. Its bankruptcy filing noted it owed $4.7 billion to some 1.7 million investors, and only had $167 million in assets.[25] Voyager allegedly claimed its stablecoin was backed by FDIC insurance, according to the federal agencies.[26] Voyager declared bankruptcy.[27]

---

[21] Wayne Duggan, *What Is Celsius? Why Is It Crashing the Crypto Market?* FORBES (July 18, 2022) https://www.forbes.com/advisor/investing/cryptocurrency/what-is-celsius/
[22] Satoshi Nakamoto, *Bitcoin: A Peer-to-Peer Electronic Cash System*, (2008) https://bitcoin.org/bitcoin.pdf
[23] *Bitcoin,* COINDESK (website accessed June 11, 2021) https://www.coindesk.com/price/bitcoin
[24] *Attorney General James Ends Virtual Currency Trading Platform Bitfinex's Illegal Activities in New York* NY ATTORNEY GENERAL, (Feb. 23, 2021) https://ag.ny.gov/press-release/2021/attorney-general-james-ends-virtual-currency-trading-platform-bitfinexs-illegal
[25] MacKenzie Sigalos, *Homeless, Suicidal, Down To Last $1,000: Celsius Investors Beg Bankruptcy Judge For Help* CNBC (Aug. 2, 2022) https://www.cnbc.com/2022/08/02/celsius-investors-owed-4point7-billion-beg-judge-to-recover-life-savings.html
[26] FDIC, Federal Reserve, Letter to Voyager Digital, FEDERAL RESERVE *July 28, 2022) https://www.federalreserve.gov/newsevents/pressreleases/files/bcreg20220728a1.pdf
[27] Rohan Goswami, *Voyager CEO Made Millions In Stock Sales In 2021 When Price Was Near Peak* CNBC (Aug. 3, 2022) https://www.cnbc.com/2022/08/03/voyager-ceo-made-millions-in-stock-sales-in-2021.html

Second, the promise of cost-free transactions has also proven illusory. The cost of transactions for Bitcoin are substantial and vary greatly. In the last year, they have reached $300 for each transaction.[28] This is hardly democratizing finance. Related to this, the same population that lacks a bank account, and who are most sensitive to financial fees, may also lack the technology to interact with digital currencies.

Third, investment scams involving cryptocurrencies abound. During a recent five-month period, the Federal Trade Commission reported 7,000 cryptocurrency scams covering some $80 million in reported losses. That is 12 times the number of scams reported during the same period a year earlier, with a 1000 percent greater estimated loss.[29] One review found some malicious actors created digital coins that can be purchased but not sold. Others promise enormous returns that proved untrue. [30]

Fourth, the number of cryptocurrencies is staggering, and growing. In 2021, there were more than 10,000 different cryptocurrencies.[31] In the summer of 2022, that number nearly doubled to 19,000, according to one estimate.[32] Commodity Futures Trading Commission Chair Rostin Behnam testified before Congress that "there are now hundreds of thousands of unique digital assets in circulation."[33] That is a greater than the number of banks in the United States. Dogecoin, the 10th largest cryptocurrency by value, was created as a "joke," according to its founders.[34] Even if one or a few cryptocurrencies are adopted as common tender, it is inconceivable that the number accepted would be greater than 10, or 100, and certainly not 19,000. Thus, their utility as a tender for goods and services seems limited, at best.

A few retailers have experimented with accepting Bitcoin for payment, but many have stopped.[35] Facebook (now called Meta) applied its prodigious muscle to launch a digital currency. In a test of remittances, however, the blockchain validation costs proved exorbitant.[36] [37]

Fifth, the claim that cryptocurrency cannot be stolen has proven untrue. While it may not be as vulnerable to street theft as cash, or to cyber criminals hacking a bank account, a cyber-criminal might be able to hack into a personal computer where Bitcoin codes are kept. In 2021, a ransom paid in digital assets by Colonial Pipeline to hackers that took over their system (which led to a temporary decline in gasoline

---

[28] *Bitcoin Average Cost Per Transaction,* YCHARTS (website accessed June 11, 2021) https://ycharts.com/indicators/bitcoin_average_cost_per_transaction

[29] Emma Fletcher, *Cryptocurrency Buzz Drives Record Investment Scam Losses,* FEDERAL TRADE COMMISSION (May 17, 2021) https://www.ftc.gov/news-events/blogs/data-spotlight/2021/05/cryptocurrency-buzz-drives-record-investment-scam-losses

[30] Alexis Goldstein, *Testimony,* HOUSE FINANCIAL SERVICES COMMITTEE (June 20, 2021) https://financialservices.house.gov/uploadedfiles/hhrg-117-ba09-wstate-goldsteina-20210630-u1.pdf

[31] *Understanding the Different Types of Cryptocurrencies,* SOFI LEARN (Jan. 15, 2021) https://www.sofi.com/learn/content/understanding-the-different-types-of-cryptocurrency/

[32] Arjun Kharpal, Crypto Firms Say Thousand
s Of Digital Currencies Will Collapse, Compare Market To Early Dotcom Days, CNBC (June 3, 2022) https://www.cnbc.com/2022/06/03/crypto-firms-say-thousands-of-digital-currencies-will-collapse.html

[33] Rostin Benham, *Testimony,* SENATE AGRICULTURE COMMITTEE (Feb. 9, 2022) https://www.cftc.gov/PressRoom/SpeechesTestimony/opabehnam20

[34] Avi Salzman, *Dogecoin Was Started as a Joke,* BARRON'S (May 5, 2021) https://www.barrons.com/articles/dogecoin-started-as-a-joke-now-its-too-important-to-laugh-off-51620229273

[35] Steve Fiorillo, *How to Use Bitcoin for Purchases,* THE STREET (April 18, 2018) https://www.thestreet.com/investing/what-can-you-buy-with-bitcoin-14556706

[36] Alexis Goldstein, Stablecoins: How Do They Work, How Are They Used, and What Are Their Risks? HOUSE FINANCIAL SERVICES COMMITTEE (Dec. 14, 2021) https://www.banking.senate.gov/imo/media/doc/Goldstein%20Testimony%2012-14-21.pdf

[37] Open Markets Institute, *Letter to Federal Regulators,* OPEN MARKETS INSTITUTE (Nov. 23, 2021) , https://downloads.regulations.gov/CFPB-2021-0017-0089/attachment_2.pdf

supplies on the East Coast), was traced and recovered by the FBI. "Crypto experts say it is at times easier to track than hard currencies such as U.S. dollars," according to one observer.[38]

Many experts question the value of cryptocurrency. Berkshire Hathaway CEO Warren Buffett recently called cryptocurrency "rat poison squared." His associate Charlie Munger labeled trading in this market as "dementia."[39] Investor Mark Cuban said he'd prefer bananas to Bitcoin, "Because at least as food, bananas have intrinsic value."[40] Bill Gates says cryptocurrencies are "100% based on greater fool theory," or reliance on a rational assumption of one speculator finding another speculator willing to pay a higher price.[41] JPMorgan CEO Jamie Dimon said he'd fire any employee he found investing in Bitcoin. European Central Bank President Christine Lagarde says cryptocurrency is worth "nothing."[42] Other skeptics include Allianz economist Mohamad El-Erian, economist Paul Krugman, and Oaktree Capital Management founder Howard Marks.[43] Nassim Taleb, who once considered Bitcoin promising, now says its ultimate worth is "zero."[44]

Finally, many experts question the utility of the underlying blockchain technology. In June 2022, 1,500 computer scientists, software engineers, and technologists sent an open letter urging Washington policy makers to "take a critical, skeptical approach toward industry claims that crypto assets (sometimes called cryptocurrencies, crypto tokens, or web3) are an innovative technology that is unreservedly good." The experts take direct issue with blockchain, which they argue, "by its very design . . . is poorly suited for just about every purpose currently touted as a present or potential source of public benefit." Further, they write, blockchain technologies facilitate few, if any, real economy uses."[45] Among the signatories are employees of IBM, Netscape, Google, Microsoft, Apple, MIT, Meta, Columbia, eBay and Amazon-- looking only to those signatories whose first name begins with "A."

Some legitimate use cases for public blockchains may exist. The U.S. government and private sector are evaluating the suitability of blockchain technologies for a variety of industries outside of creating tokens for digital currency. For example, the U.S. Department of Energy just concluded a $3 million, two-year blockchain for Optimized Security and Energy Management as part of its power grid modernization initiative.[46] Blockchain has been identified as having potential advantages to manage the allocation and distribution of Renewable Electricity Credits (RECs) produced by clean energy project managers. Four

---

[38] James Uberti, *How the FBI Got Colonial Pipeline's Money Back*, WALL STREET JOURNAL (June 11, 2021) https://www.wsj.com/articles/how-the-fbi-got-colonial-pipelines-ransom-money-back-11623403981
[39] James Royal, *Warren Buffet Says to Avoid these Two Types of Hot Investments,* BANKRATE (May 6, 2019) https://www.bankrate.com/investing/warren-buffett-says-avoid-these-hot-investments/
[40] Taylor Locke, *Mark Cuban: Bitcoin Is 'More Religion Than Solution' And Won't Help In 'Doomsday Scenarios,* CNBC (Dec. 17, 2020) https://www.cnbc.com/2020/12/17/mark-cuban-bitcoin-is-a-store-of-value-that-is-more-religion.html
[41] Ryan Browne, *Bill Gates Says Crypto And NFTs Are '100% Based On Greater Fool Theory,* ' CNBC (June 14, 2022) https://www.cnbc.com/2022/06/15/bill-gates-says-crypto-and-nfts-are-based-on-greater-fool-theory.html
[42] Ryan Browne, *Christine Lagarde Says Crypto Is Worth Nothing* CNBC (May 23, 2022) https://www.cnbc.com/2022/05/23/ecb-chief-christine-lagarde-crypto-is-worth-nothing.html
[43] Trisha Phillips, *Bill Gates and Other Powerful People Who Hate (or Love) Bitcoin,* SHOWBIZ CHEATSHEET (MAY 25, 2018) https://www.cheatsheet.com/money-career/powerful-people-love-or-hate-bitcoin.html/
[44] Tanaya Macheel, *Black Swan' Author Nassim Taleb Says Bitcoin Is Worth Zero And Fails As A Currency And A Hedge* CNBC (July 13, 2021) https://www.cnbc.com/2021/07/13/black-swan-author-nassim-taleb-says-bitcoin-is-worth-zero.html
[45] *Letter in Support of Responsible FinTech Policy,* (June 1, 2022) https://concerned.tech/
[46] National Energy Technology Laboratory, *Blockchain for Optimized Security and Energy Management,* NATIONAL ENERGY TECHNOLOGY LABORATORY (website visited July 25, 2022) https://netl.doe.gov/BLOSEM

automakers and IBM formed the Mobility Open Blockchain Initiative to share information on how to use the blockchain to allow electric vehicle owners to sell their automobile's stored energy into the grid; help manage transportation congestion; vehicle emissions testing; and supply-chain management. Law firms and real estate transactions are using contract automation technology based on the blockchain to utilize "smart contracts" that replace multiple (and often time-consuming and expensive) counterparties.

If cryptocurrency does not seem useful as a currency, why did the market capitalization reach $3 trillion? We believe, simply, perhaps obviously, that those who buy cryptocurrency hope to make money—they are speculators. (We leave aside for now those using cryptocurrency for illicit activities.) Presumably, most investors who might purchase stock in a jet manufacturer or pharmaceutical firm may have little personal expertise in aerospace technology or biochemistry. Similarly, few who purchase cryptocurrencies are likely familiar with Merkle Trees, nonces, or other technical features of blockchain. But these speculators can see that some who purchase stock in a jet maker have made money, and that's been the case with cryptocurrency as well.

The sad reality is that about 46 million Americans now own Bitcoin alone.[47] Why do so many people invest in Bitcoin and other cryptocurrencies? We assume, as with a stock or other traditional asset, these speculators believe the price will rise and that they will profit. To date, that has been the case. Bitcoin's market capitalization has occasionally exceeded four times that of JP Morgan Chase.[48] Speculators who purchased at lower prices are, indeed, sitting on a profit. Bitcoin sold for $1,000 in 2017, before peaking at $60,000 in 2021.[49] Would-be speculators saw these winnings and likely were attracted to the arena.

Bolstering the stories of success, mainstream institutions and public influencers are affirming the legitimacy of cryptocurrencies as investments. Well known brokers, including large firms catering to small investors such as Schwab, now offer cryptocurrencies. [50] Wells Fargo offers the product to is elite clients.[51] Fidelity Investments announced it would provide cryptocurrency options for sponsors of 401(k) plans.[52] Cryptocurrencies legitimized by large institutions naturally invites otherwise rational people to consider allocating at least some of their portfolio to this sector.

Cryptocurrency sponsors have spent extravagantly on advertising, relying conspicuously on influencers. Crypto.com spent $15 million in advertising in November 2021.[53] CoinDesk reportedly mounted a $100 million advertising campaign in 2021.[54]

---

[47] *About 46 Million Americans Own Bitcoin,* NASDAQ (May 14, 2021) https://www.nasdaq.com/articles/about-46-million-americans-now-own-bitcoin-2021-05-14

[48] *JP Morgan,* YCHARTS (website accessed June 11, 2021) https://ycharts.com/companies/JPM/market_cap

[49] James Royal, *Best online brokers for buying and selling cryptocurrency in June 2021,* BANKRATE *(June 1, 2021) https://www.bankrate.com/investing/best-online-brokers-cryptocurrency-trading/*

[50] James Royal, *Best online brokers for buying and selling cryptocurrency in June 2021,* BANKRATE *(June 1, 2021) https://www.bankrate.com/investing/best-online-brokers-cryptocurrency-trading/*

[51] *Wells Fargo: US Bank Set to Offer Crypto to Rich Clients*, BBC (May 19, 2021) https://www.bbc.com/news/business-57147386

[52]Rob Wile, *Fidelity Lets Companies Offer Bitcoin In A 401(K), But Financial Advisers Warn It's A Risky Bet* NBC (May 22, 2022) https://www.nbcnews.com/business/consumer/bitcoin-401k-fidelity-financial-advisers-warn-risk-cryptocurrencies-rcna29099

[53] Jet Encela, *Crypto Companies Slash Ad Spending By 90% Amid Market Jitters*, BITCONIST (website visited July 15, 2022) https://bitcoinist.com/crypto-companies-slash-ad-spending/

[54] Jamie Crawley, *Crypto.com Looks to Cash In on Bull Market With $100M Advertising Campaign*, COINDESK (Oct. 2021) https://www.coindesk.com/business/2021/10/28/cryptocom-looks-to-cash-in-on-bull-market-with-100m-advertising-campaign/

For those who believe there is little future as a currency, and that blockchain holds little promise, speculation may be based on the "greater fool" theory.[55] Such sponsors are effectively promoting a Ponzi scheme, with new investors paying a higher price than previous investors. (A sponsor is an individual or firm that creates and promotes the cryptocurrency. Bitcoin has no sponsor.)

Some cryptocurrency sponsors may be exploiting this "greater fool" theory with those who believe they've been shut out of the traditional financial system. We are especially dismayed by reports that of the U.S. individuals who own cryptocurrencies, 40 percent of people of color. According to one report, the average cryptocurrency trader is under 40 (mean age is 38) and does not have a college degree (55 percent). Forty-one percent are women. More than one-third (35 percent) have household incomes under $60k annually.[56] After centuries of exploitation of people of color, after nefarious bankers targeted Black borrowers with abusive mortgages leading to the 2008 financial crisis,[57] it is tragic that predatory cryptocurrency sponsors may have targeted the Black community with this Ponzi scheme. Derrick Hamilton of the New School noted, that crypto has a "low barrier to entry with a promise of high returns. , , , [The industry] preys on people's desire to make something of themselves."[58]

Digital asset markets are rife with scams and other manipulative financial practices. Several federal regulators, including the Consumer Financial Protection Bureau (CFPB), Securities and Exchange Commission (SEC), and Federal Trade Commission (FTC), among others, have issued regular alerts warning consumers and investors about the prevalence of scams, hacks and manipulative activities found within the digital asset markets, and have collected data to back up these warnings. Numerous media articles, academic studies and even industry reports have documented the large sums of money lost through these scams and exploitative practices. For example, a recent study by crypto analytics firm Chainanalysis found there were $14 billion in losses in 2021 alone due to malfeasance, and that there had been a 79% increase in crypto related crime during that same year.[59]

These scam-related losses may be the tip of the iceberg; a Better Business Bureau report profiling crypto schemes noted that the FTC claims that only about 5% of fraud victims end up reporting their losses or victimization.[60] Tellingly, the FTC has also historically found that Black and Hispanic or Latino Americans are more likely than white Americans to be victims of scams or fraud and are more likely to under-report such experiences as well.[61] This suggests that, even as digital assets are being promoted (via sophisticated marketing campaigns) as vehicles for financial inclusion for communities traditionally

---

[55] Nolan Whitcomb, *The Greater Fool Theory*, OXFORD BUSINESS REVIEW (Dec. 30, 2020) https://oxfordbusinessreview.org/the-greater-fool-theory/

[56] *More Than One in Ten Americans Surveyed Invest in Cryptocurrencies* University of Chicago (July 22, 2021) https://www.norc.org/NewsEventsPublications/PressReleases/Pages/more-than-one-in-ten-americans-surveyed-invest-in-cryptocurrencies.aspx

[57] Ylan Q. Mui *Ex-Loan Officer Claims Wells Fargo Targeted Black Communities For Shoddy Loans*, WASHINGTON POST (June 12, 2012) https://www.washingtonpost.com/business/economy/former-wells-fargo-loan-officer-testifies-in-baltimore-mortgage-lawsuit/2012/06/12/gJQA6EGtXV_story.html

[58] William Pierre-Louis Jr, *Why Crypto is not the Solution to Financial Inclusion*, AMERICANS FOR FINANCIAL REFORM (website accessed July 18, 2022) https://ourfinancialsecurity.org/2022/07/blog-why-crypto-is-not-the-solution-to-financial-inclusion/

[59] *The Chainalysius Crypto Crime Report*, CHAINALYSIS (website accessed July 22, 2022) https://go.chainalysis.com/2022-Crypto-Crime-Report.html

[60] Better Business Bureau, *Cryptocurrency Scams Study*, BETTER BUSINESS BUREAU (website accessed July 22, 2022) https://www.bbb.org/all/scamstudies/cryptocurrency_scams/cryptocurrency_scams_study

[61] Federal Trade Commission, *Combating Fraud in African America & Latino Communities*, FEDERAL TRADE COMMISSION (June 15, 2016) https://www.ftc.gov/system/files/documents/reports/combating-fraud-african-american-latino-communities-ftcs-comprehensive-strategic-plan-federal-trade/160615fraudreport.pdf

excluded from or exploited by traditional financial actors, these same communities may be bearing the brunt of the losses generated by fraud and scams.

Cryptocurrencies also serve as a medium of payment for illicit activities. One study found that "approximately one-quarter of Bitcoin users are involved in illegal activity" and that an estimated $76 billion in illegal activity per year involve Bitcoin (46% of Bitcoin transactions)," which is close to the scale of the U.S. and European markets for illegal drugs."[62] Many avoid paying taxes on cryptocurrency profits.[63]

Regulatory Options

The Treasury should advise the various financial regulatory agencies to remedy negative impacts that happen in the crypto ecosystem through fraud, financial crisis, energy consumption, waste, and carbon emissions.

Regulators must prevent crypto firms from engaging in fraud on their customers and must not allow crypto infrastructure to be used to perpetuate fraud. *Caveat emptor* is not an appropriate guiding principle for firms with access to retail investors. The people who digitally mint and promote the coins need to be liable for fraudulent statements, fraudulent transactions, rug pulls, abandoned projects, and self-dealing.[64] (In a "rug pull" predators lure investors into a project, then abandon the project and take the money.) We welcome announcements of greater staffing at the Securities and Exchange Commission (SEC) and urge the Federal Trade Commission (FTC) to increase its enforcement efforts as well. We also welcome the enforcement efforts of the Commodity Futures Trading Commission (CFTC). This agency polices fraud, false reporting, and manipulation over commodity cash markets in interstate commerce. Since 2014, the CFTC has brought 50 enforcement actions involving digital assets. In 2021, it brought 20 enforcement actions alleging digital asset-related misconduct.[65] Authorities are prosecuting "rug pulls" in several non-fungible token (NFT) cases. [66] [67] In one rug pull case, the durable wire fraud law proved reliable in arresting two suspects.[68] The FTC signaled it will better scrutinize "gatekeepers," where rug pulls are

---

[62] Sean Foley, et al, *Sex Drugs and Bitcoin*, THE REVIEW OF FINANCIAL ECONOMICS, (May 2019) https://academic.oup.com/rfs/article/32/5/1798/5427781

[63] Greg Iacurci, *Cryptocurrency Poses A Significant Risk Of Tax Evasion* CNBC (May 31, 2021) https://www.cnbc.com/2021/05/31/cryptocurrency-poses-a-significant-risk-of-tax-evasion.html

[64] *SEC Signals Ramp-Up in Crypto Enforcement by Nearly Doubling Its Crypto Assets Cyber Unit Staff* BAKERHOSTETLER (May 5, 2022) https://www.bakerlaw.com/SEC-Signals-Ramp-Up-in-Crypto-Enforcement-by-Nearly-Doubling-Its-Crypto-Assets-Cyber-Unit-Staff

[65] Rostin Benham, *Address*, BROOKINGS INSTITUTION, (July 25, 2022) https://www.cftc.gov/PressRoom/SpeechesTestimony/opabehnam24

[66] Kevin Roose, *What are NFTs?* NEW YORK TIMES (website visited July 21, 2022) https://www.nytimes.com/interactive/2022/03/18/technology/nft-guide.html

[67] *FYI on NFTs: Consumer Protection and Privacy Considerations* WILSON SONSINI (March 9, 2022) https://www.jdsupra.com/legalnews/fyi-on-nfts-consumer-protection-and-5976517/

[68] U.S. Attorney's Office, *Two Defendants Charged In Non-Fungible Token ("NFT") Fraud And Money Laundering Scheme* DEPARTMENT OF JUSTICE (March 24, 2022) https://www.justice.gov/usao-sdny/pr/two-defendants-charged-non-fungible-token-nft-fraud-and-money-laundering-scheme-0

prominent. [69]We welcome the Department of Justice's decision to establish a National Cryptocurrency Enforcement Team.[70]

The SEC should regulate cryptocurrency as a security. The SEC defines a security with the Howey Test. The Howey Test consists of four prongs, all of which must be satisfied for the SEC to classify a transaction as a security. The four elements are as follows: [1] An investment of money [2] in a common enterprise [3] with expectations of a profit [4] to be derived from the efforts of others.[71] (The "effort of others" derives from the promotion by the sponsor.) Given that sponsored cryptocurrencies satisfy all of these elements, they should be regulated by the SEC. And, in fact, in a recent case of alleged insider trading, the SEC declared several cryptocurrencies as "unregistered securities." [72]

Once cryptocurrencies status as securities is clarified, the SEC's climate disclosure rule, if adopted, could provide a comprehensive, verified view of the emissions generated by digital assets and trading, especially if the rule requires registrants to disclose the emissions released in their value chain, also known as Scope 3 emissions. Along with the immediate benefits to investors, such disclosures would also provide important inputs to systemic financial risk monitoring conducted by the Office of Financial Research and the Financial Stability Oversight Council, which has highlighted both climate and digital assets as emerging risk areas. To realize these benefits, it's important that the SEC clarify the reach of its proposed Scope 3 reporting requirement, which currently only requires disclosure if those emissions are "material." Ideally, the SEC would recognize the importance of Scope 3 emissions disclosure for all companies. But, at a minimum, it should clarify that for large firms that own or trade significant quantities of cryptocurrency, their Scope 3 emissions would be material and subject to disclosure for the reasons discussed above. Due to their importance, those emissions should also be subject to the level of assurance required for Scope 1 and 2 emissions.

Stablecoins should be regulated along the lines established recently by the European Markets in Crypto Assets (MiCA).[73] When implemented, European authorities will require stablecoin sponsors to hold liquid assets on a 1-1 basis with the tokens and provide for refunds with no charge. (Because stablecoin transactions require decentralized "miners" for verification, and they are paid in that stablecoin, then stablecoin sponsorship may be inherently unprofitable.[74]) Sponsors will also need to disclose their climate footprint. Crypto asset service providers must register with the European Securities and Markets Authority. We believe U.S. stablecoin sponsors should publish audits of their reserve monthly. Exchanges need margin requirements and stress tests; stablecoins need a liquid assets requirement and money market mutual fund-style protections to prevent runs and death spirals; banks and other traditional financial

[69] Lina Khan, *Vision and Priorities for the FTC*, FEDERAL TRADE COMMISSION (Sept 22, 2021) https://www.ftc.gov/system/files/documents/public_statements/1596664/agency_priorities_memo_from_chair_lina_m_khan_9-22-21.pdf

[70] Department of Justice, *Justice Department Announces First Director of National Cryptocurrency Enforcement Team* DEPARTMENT OF JUSTICE (Feb. 17, 2022) https://www.justice.gov/opa/pr/justice-department-announces-first-director-national-cryptocurrency-enforcement-team

[71] *Framework for "Investment Contract" Analysis of Digital Assets* SEC (website accessed August 3, 2022) https://www.sec.gov/corpfin/framework-investment-contract-analysis-digital-assets

[72] Press Release, *SEC Charges Former Coinbase Manager, Two Others in Crypto Asset Insider Trading Action* SECURITIES AND EXCHANGE COMMISSION (July 21, 2022) https://www.sec.gov/news/press-release/2022-127

[73] European Council *Digital finance: agreement reached on European crypto-assets regulation (MiCA)* EUROPEAN COUNCIL (June 30, 2022) https://www.consilium.europa.eu/en/press/press-releases/2022/06/30/digital-finance-agreement-reached-on-european-crypto-assets-regulation-mica/

[74] *The Stablecoin Cryptocurrency System* JDSUPRA (Dec. 1, 2020) https://www.jdsupra.com/legalnews/part-2-the-stablecoin-cryptocurrency-78223/

institutions must hold adequate capital to reflect the riskiness and volatility of crypto assets. Banks that hold crypto should post 1250 percent risk capital, as described by the Basel Committee.[75]

The Financial Stability Oversight Council (FSOC) should use its authority (under Dodd-Frank Section 120) to recommend that primary financial regulatory agencies move quickly to address these issues.

Regulators must look at the impacts of crypto operations and financial footprint on groups who have been excluded from financial markets because of racial discrimination. Crypto purportedly permits access to the financial system for those groups, but those claims rarely amount to more than marketing.

The Department of Labor (DOL) should instruct fiduciaries that crypto is not a responsible investment. We welcome DOL guidance that notes that "Fiduciaries may not shift responsibility to plan participants to identify and avoid imprudent investment options, but rather must evaluate the designated investment alternatives made available to participants and take appropriate measures to ensure that they are prudent." The DOL notes a U.S. Supreme Court explanation that "even in a defined-contribution plan where participants choose their investments, plan fiduciaries are required to conduct their own independent evaluation to determine which investments may be prudently included in the plan's menu of options." The failure to remove imprudent investment options is a breach of duty, the DOL states.[76]

Regulators must account for the energy and emissions impacts of crypto, particularly given the lack of underlying economic value of the assets. Both the direct emissions from mining and the broader effects of a mining ecosystem can have serious consequences for energy prices, the environment, and the climate. Crypto firms must adopt practices and protocols that mitigate these impacts in line with science-based targets for emissions and waste reduction.

Crypto's anonymity must not enable avoidance of legal obligations or illicit behavior. Regulators must make crypto firms comply with Know Your Customer rules, not facilitate sanctions avoidance, and issue tax docs for sale of coins (including swaps into other cryptocurrencies). Agencies must better ensure that gains from the sales of cryptocurrencies are properly taxed, including an increased focus on this issue by enforcement officials at the IRS. We support greatly increased funding to the agency to help tackle this type of enforcement.

In addition to cryptocurrencies, other digital assets such as NFTs may require no additional regulation. We are astounded at some of the prices, such as the $69 million paid for a digital collage called "Everyday: the First 5000 Days," by an illustrator known as Beeple.[77] The bidding, conducted by Christies, started at $100, suggesting that this expert auction house itself had no accurate understanding of what the market value might be. The purchaser owns this digital asset, but not the copyright. Anyone can enjoy the identical digital image as the purchaser by searching for it on the internet. We are aware that

---

[75] Basel Committee on Banking Supervision, *Prudential Treatment Of Cryptoasset Exposures,* BANK OF INTERNATIONAL SETTLEMENTS (Sept. 10, 2021) https://www.bis.org/bcbs/publ/d519.pdf

[76] Department of Labor, *401(k) Plan Investments in "Cryptocurrencies* (March 10, 2022) https://www.dol.gov/agencies/ebsa/employers-and-advisers/plan-administration-and-compliance/compliance-assistance-releases/2022-01

[77] Abram Brown, *Beeple NFT Sells for $69 million*, FORBES (March 11, 2021) https://www.forbes.com/sites/abrambrown/2021/03/11/beeple-art-sells-for-693-million-becoming-most-expensive-nft-ever/?sh=402d6d0c24

NFT promotions may involve scams to exploit a consumer's digital wallet. But these take place outside the question of whether NFT have value that any reasonable investor would assign. [78]

Improving the Payment System

As noted, the cryptocurrency promised to improve the payment system. We welcome efforts to broadly make the payment system more efficient and less costly for consumers and businesses alike.

Many U.S. residents are underbanked. More than six percent of American households, or some 33 million citizens are without a traditional bank account. Some do not trust banks, while others lack the funds that financial institutions require to open and maintain an account.[79]

Even for those lucky people with deposit accounts, the payment system is slow. Overdraft fees can be substantial. Checks and credit card payments can take two days or more to clear, meaning that vendors are without these funds during that time. It is also costly. Checks and particularly wire transfers can include substantial fees. Banks charge interchange fees for credit cards, a substantial burden for retailers.[80] And it is complex, with thousands of banks with idiosyncratic ledger systems communicating with one another and the Federal Reserve.

We note the apparent success of the Pix payment system in Brazil, sponsored by the Central Bank of Brazil.[81] This uses QR codes (or two-dimensional bar codes, formally known as a quick response code) that appear in the customers' cell phones. After a year of operation, this electronic system, free of fees to customers, represented some 6 percent of electronic commerce in the country.[82] During the pandemic, adoption of Pix led to a 73 percent decline in the unbanked population.[83] The Brazilian Central Bank requires Brazilian banks to participate. Banks reportedly discovered that while they lost some revenue from fees, they saved money from the reduced use of checks.[84]

---

[78] Amanda Hetler, *Eight Ways to Avoid NFT Scams,* TECHTARGET (May 26, 2022) https://www.techtarget.com/whatis/feature/8-ways-to-avoid-NFT-scams

[79] Mehrsa Baradaran, *How the Other Half Banks*, HARVARD UNIVERSITY PRESS (2015) https://www.hup.harvard.edu/catalog.php?isbn=9780674983960

[80] Aaron Klein, *A Few Small Banks Have Become Overdraft Giants*, BROOKINGS INST. (Mar. 1, 2021) https://www.brookings.edu/opinions/a-few-small-banks-have-become-overdraft-giants/

[81] *Pix*, CENTRAL BANK OF BRAZIL (website accessed July 18, 2022) https://www.bcb.gov.br/en/financialstability/pix_en

[82] *The Pix Revolution in Brazil*, EBANK (website accessed July 18, 2022) https://business.ebanx.com/hubfs/ABM/APMs/Pix/English/PIX-Revolution-EBANX-EN.pdf?utm_medium=email&_hsenc=p2ANqtz-9rbIl_fY1tYx3FDsbh-srIZgbL8Xm3IC1j2G5w_c2Zc8YqlVgzOSnCMB8XLdkCn06suim1TD9pQ8gw1s4SdfcW3iIylQ&_hsmi=206763316&utm_content=206763316&utm_source=hs_automation&hsCtaTracking=5529a87a-3179-4fcd-94eb-bf706937d921%7Cf2d4b972-00a6-4aed-a46a-3d880e2cf259

[83] *A Year of PIX in Brazil: What Does the Future of Real-Time Fraud Look Like?* ACI WORLDWIDE (Dec. 10, 2021) https://www.aciworldwide.com/blog/a-year-of-pix-in-brazil-what-does-the-future-of-real-time-fraud-look-like

[84] Maxnaun Gutierrez, *Why Pix is the Revolution of Consumer Experience in Brazil* PAYMENTS JOURNAL (Feb. 24, 2021) https://www.paymentsjournal.com/why-pix-is-the-revolution-of-consumer-experience-in-brazil/

The 28 countries of the European Union, along with several others, are experimenting with Single Euro Payments Area, an electronic transfer system that promises transaction completion within 10 seconds. (European regulators, however, do not require banks to participate.[85])

At the same time, Public Citizen does support exploration of a Central Bank Digital Currency (CBDC). This federal digital coin, in one form dubbed a FedAccount, holds the promise to address some of the problems with the payment system reviewed above. Currently, depository institutions maintain accounts with the Federal Reserve.

Conceived by Lev Menand of Columbia Law School in June 2018, the CBDC would be a Federal Reserve account. It would be available to "any U.S. resident or business in digital wallets operated by the Federal Reserve, the Post Office, or one of the country's several thousand community banks," he explains.[86] "The digital wallets would charge no fees and have no minimum balances. They would come with debit cards, direct deposit, and bill pay. They would have customer service, privacy safeguards, and fraud protection—if for example one lost their password. And these accounts would earn interest at the same rate that the Fed pays to banks."

Lack of profitability for the banks represents one of the reasons that banks fail to service roughly six percent of the population. The FedAccount would be available regardless of any balance and would be streamlined with immediate clearing. There would be no fees. With such an account, delivery of federal payments such as Covid relief or other government benefits, would be immediate.

Noting though that before such a system is implemented, important questions must be answered. For example, many bank account holders are subject to garnishments because of unpaid debt. Debt collectors would have a simple way to garnish funds through the CBDC. That also means the Federal Reserve would need to engage with debt collectors in addition to individual Federal Reserve account holders. There may be political issues. For example, the CARES Act might have more effectively delivered needed rescue funds to needy Americans via a FedAccount system. However, some of the individuals who received relief may have been subject to garnishment, meaning the Federal Reserve would be in a position of deciding whether, in times of extraordinary need, it would protect or release these funds.

Conclusion

From a non-existent market in 2008 to a recent market capitalization of $3 trillion, cryptocurrency has mushroomed to the point where it now threatens to become a source of systemic risk. If regulators worried that more forceful intervention in this giant Ponzi scheme might concuss through broader markets, such concerns should be allayed by the recent collapse, where the market value has now declined by about $2 trillion in a matter of months. If erasing two thirds of market capitalization has not caused tremors, we believe the final $1 trillion will not either.

We urge the Treasury to recommend to agencies a robust regulatory scheme without fear of sparking systemic risk, and with support from consumer protection advocates when it comes to protections for consumers contemplating an investment in assets without true value.

---

[85] Andrew Singer, *Brazil's PIX Payments System Has the Same Spirit, but Not a Blockchain Structure* COINTELEGRAPH (Feb 28, 2020) https://cointelegraph.com/news/brazils-pix-payments-system-has-the-same-spirit-but-not-a-blockchain-structure

[86] Lev Menand, *Testimony*, U.S. SENATE BANKING COMMITTEE (June 9, 2021) https://www.banking.senate.gov/imo/media/doc/Menand%20Testimony%206-9-21.pdf

For questions, please contact Yevgeny Shrago at ysharago@citizen.org, Tyson Slocum at tslcocum@citizen.org, Alan Zibel at azibel@citizen.org, and/or Bartlett Naylor at bnaylor@citizen.org.

Sincerely,

Public Citizen

Questions for the Record from Ranking Member Maxine Waters
Subcommittee Hearing, entitled "Understanding Stablecoins' Role in Payments and the Need for Legislation"
Wednesday, April 19, 2023 at 10am

The Honorable Adrienne A. Harris

1. Which of the following options best describes your self-identified race? (you may choose more than one)
   a. White or Caucasian
   b. Black or African American
   c. Hispanic/Latinx
   d. Asian
   e. Middle Eastern/North African
   f. Choose not to answer
2. Which of the following options best describes your gender identity?
   a. Woman
   b. Man
   c. Non-binary
   d. Transgender Man
   e. Transgender Woman
   f. Choose not to answer
   g. Prefer to self-describe (please specify)

The Honorable Patrick McHenry
Chairman
U.S. House Financial Services Committee
2129 Rayburn House Office Building
Washington, DC 20515

The Honorable Maxine Waters
Ranking Member
U.S. House Financial Services Committee
4340 O'Neill House Office Building
Washington, DC 20515

The Honorable French Hill
Chair
Subcommittee on Digital Assets
U.S. House Financial Services Committee
2129 Rayburn House Office Building
Washington, DC 20515

The Honorable Stephen Lynch
Ranking Member
Subcommittee on Digital Assets
U.S. House Financial Services Committee
4340 O'Neill House Office Building
Washington, DC 20515

April 18, 2023

Dear Chairman McHenry, Ranking Member Waters, Subcommittee Chair Hill and Ranking Subcommittee Member Lynch,

We, the undersigned organizations, write to express our concerns about the grave risks stablecoins pose to households and to our financial system and urge the Committee to take the utmost care to not advance legislation that will increase these risks by expanding the reach of stablecoins without providing adequate protections.

Unfortunately, the draft bill up for discussion this week - H.R.____, a bill to provide requirements for payment stablecoin issuers, research on a digital dollar, and for other purposes - which attempts to provide a regulatory framework for stablecoins fails to provide adequate protections for consumers, investors and financial markets, and may in fact amplify the risks posed by stablecoins. We oppose the introduction and markup of this bill.

Stablecoins, despite their name, have proven anything but stable. There are ongoing questions regarding the degree to which their issuers hold enough stable reserves as collateral in order to redeem their customers should they choose to withdraw their funds. What's more, the fragility of stablecoins and how their vulnerabilities can amplify market instability was on full display during the market crash last spring, where the collapse of the Terra stablecoin and its ecosystem, along with other factors, helped to spur roughly $2 trillion in investor losses in a mere few weeks.

In addition to these concerns, there are other risks and harms to consider. Stablecoins have yet to be proven as a truly effective means of payment. Instead, stablecoins are primarily used to facilitate speculative cryptocurrency trading, lending or various types of decentralized finance. The underlying blockchain technology used to generate these coins is also prone to hacks and theft. A large share of issued stablecoins rely on energy intensive verification methods that generate negative environmental impacts. And as of now, blockchain 'payment' systems are generally incapable of reversing erroneous or fraudulent transactions, given the inability to delete data from the chain. The Committee should thoroughly consider the possibility that stablecoin legislation intended to transform stablecoins into a mainstream, reliable mode of payment might instead further fuel the mining and trading of cryptocurrencies in an environment rife with pump-and-dump scams, lack of consumer protections, extreme volatility, and cybersecurity risks.

While federal financial regulators already possess considerable authority to effectively police stablecoins, these powers could be supplemented for some regulators. At the same time, the Committee should be careful not to materially undermine existing regulatory protections, or create new regulatory loopholes for both stablecoins, but potentially other assets.

Any stablecoin legislation pursued by Congress must adequately address the risks associated with stablecoins, many of which are similar to the risks posed by banks, including, but not limited to: run risk, credit risk, operational risks, and liquidity risk, as discussed in the President's Working Group report on stablecoins. Furthermore, legislation must also address concentration and anti-competitive effects, as stablecoins issuers continue to rapidly grow and eventually seek to benefit from economies of scale through mergers and acquisitions. Such legislation should also actively affirm consumer and investor protections and the roles of regulators in protecting said investors and consumers, and lastly, should make it clear that rigorous standards should be applied to oversight of stablecoins across sectors, rather than relying primarily on the discretion of any one regulatory agency.

Because the use or theorized uses of stablecoins spans the gamut of financial sector activities (e.g., banking, consumer finance, investments, etc.), crafting legislation that would adequately address the risks associated with all these activities is a complex and difficult endeavor that requires time and careful consideration. Additionally, any new legislation in this arena must be careful not to materially undermine the SEC's regulatory oversight beyond stablecoins.

The bill introduced this week falls short of the elements listed above in many respects. For example:

- The bill provides an overly permissive regulatory approach to stablecoins, allowing issuers to seek primarily state regulatory oversight in lieu of meaningful federal oversight, even as state oversight often falls short of what is needed to manage the systemic risks these assets pose.
- The bill has a streamlined approach to federal oversight and authorization of stablecoin issuers that provides insufficient time or fail safes to adequately evaluate issuers' applications for approval or for proposed mergers and acquisitions that involve stablecoin issuers or associated entities.
- The non-bank stablecoin issuer pathway in the bill would give non-bank entities greater access to national payment rails and systems and many of the privileges of banking institutions, without commensurate oversight and obligations to comply with consumer protection laws.

- In particular, we fear the bill allows stablecoins issuers to use the non-bank issuer pathway to evade effective consolidated supervision, deposit insurance, consumer protection, and strict prudential standards and enforcement otherwise found in traditional regulatory regimes.
- The bill also lacks sufficient clarity about how it would enable effective enforcement of the Bank Holding Company Act to prevent the co-mingling of commercial and banking activities, despite containing provisions attempting to address such activities. This is a significant concern given the very real interest of tech and commercial companies in securing market share in the private payment space, despite obvious concerns that such encroachment would pose in terms of economic concentration and collusion.
- The bill lacks language that explicitly affirms other regulators' authority, in particular the SEC and the CFPB, to regulate stablecoins when traded on secondary markets. The bill's current language saying this stablecoin regime shall not infringe upon other regulators' authority is insufficient, and if enacted as written would likely hamstring the SEC and other regulators' rulemaking and enforcement abilities.

We strongly urge the Committee to withdraw this bill. In the meantime, we urge the Committee to encourage the regulators to use the tools currently at their disposal; any legislation you choose to pursue in the future should supplement existing authority for regulators through rigorous protection of consumers and investors and additional efforts to protect against systemic threats to our financial system and economy.

We would be happy to speak further and at length with Members of your Committee and staff on these guiding principles and our opposition to this bill in more detail.

Sincerely,

(Signatories as of Wednesday, April 18, 2023, 3 p.m., ET)

Action on Race and the Economy (ACRE)

Americans for Financial Reform (AFR)

Center for LGBTQ Economic Advancement & Research (CLEAR)

Center for Responsible Lending

Demand Progress

National Fair Housing Alliance

National Community Reinvestment Coalition (NCRC)

National Consumer Law Center (NCLC)

Public Citizen
Revolving Door Project

Texas Appleseed

U.S. PIRG

Virginia Citizens Consumer Council

20/20 Vision

Chapter 3

Putting the "Stable" in "Stablecoins": How Legislation Will Help Stablecoins Achieve Their Promise*

Committee on Financial Services

U.S. House of Representatives, Subcommittee on Digital Assets, Financial Technology, and Inclusion, Committee on Financial Services

Washington, D.C.

The subcommittee met, pursuant to notice, at 9:02 a.m., in room 2128, Rayburn House Office Building, Hon. French Hill [chairman of the subcommittee] presiding.

Members present: Representatives Hill, Davidson, Rose, Steil, Timmons, Flood, Houchin; Lynch, Foster, Gottheimer, Torres, Sherman, Green, Casten, and Nickel.

Ex officio present: Representative Waters.

Chairman HILL. The Subcommittee on Digital Assets, Financial Technology, and Inclusion will come to order.

Without objection, the Chair is authorized to declare a recess of the subcommittee at any time.

Today's hearing is entitled, "Putting the 'Stable' in 'Stablecoins': How Legislation Will Help Stablecoins Achieve Their Purpose."

---

* This is an edited, reformatted and augmented version of Hearing Before the Subcommittee on Digital Assets, Financial Technology, and Inclusion of the Committee on Financial Services, U.S. House of Representatives, One Hundred Eighteenth Congress, First Session; Serial No. 118–25, dated May 18, 2023.

In: Stablecoins
Editor: Olivier Bullock
ISBN: 979-8-89113-502-4

The Chair notes that votes are expected at 10:10, and it is only one vote, so we will adjourn for that vote, and then come back and continue our work.

I will now recognize myself for 4 minutes to give an opening statement.

I want to thank all of you for joining our second stablecoin hearing in the new Subcommittee on Digital Assets, Financial Technology, and Inclusion. And although this is only the second stablecoin hearing for the subcommittee, Member-level conversations have been going on since 2021, and the committee has worked significantly with our Members on both sides of the aisle and with the President's Working Group on Financial Markets' report on stablecoins. Both sides of the aisle have discussed key guideposts for an effective regulatory framework for payment stablecoins, which were incorporated into the stablecoin proposal in the last Congress, and into the two proposals that were noticed for today's hearing.

For example, Treasury Under Secretary Liang made it clear that any regulatory framework for stablecoins must have strict requirements in place around reserves and capital to guard against potential runs, so we included those requirements in both of the proposals. The Under Secretary also made it clear that disclosures and attestations are critical for creating enhanced transparency among stablecoin issuers, and those were included as well. To echo the Under Secretary, and the title of today's hearing, we want stablecoins to be used as a payment mechanism, which they really are not today. And also, the only way we can do that is by passing the appropriate regulatory framework legislation.

In 2022, we made extensive progress on bipartisan stablecoin legislation, and we have continued to build on those efforts by taking feedback from members and stakeholders, and the legislation noticed today reflects that feedback. There are clearly many areas where Members have different views, and you can see that from the two proposals. But from my seat as chairman of this subcommittee, I remain convinced that Members on both sides of the aisle are actively working in good faith to find agreement on these key points. We also agree on the basic protections that must be included in any stablecoin legislation—consumer investor protection—which is at the heart of our bill.

So, I want to be clear that while we notice two different legislative proposals today, we are not starting from scratch. To do so would have ignored all of the effort that has been made and the common ground that was found during the negotiations on the previous proposal. In fact, Ranking Member Waters' proposal is substantially similar to the September draft that we noticed at the April hearing, apart from three key changes. Not only that, but Republicans made the exact same change in our proposal as well for one of those. So, while there is still work to be done, and we should use today's hearing to discuss those key areas, I want to emphasize that the similarities between the two proposals are strong, and that we are not that far apart.

Without action from Congress, however, offshore and opaque projects will continue to thrive, and stablecoin issuers will not feel confident to seek opportunities in the United States, and to echo the hearing title, stablecoins will not be stable. Thus, opposing legislation is not a vote in favor of consumer protection. Rather it is a vote for putting consumers at risk by allowing a regulatory environment that pushes stablecoins further away from appropriate U.S. regulatory oversight. We have the power to reverse this trend and cement the U.S. as the leading place for safe payments innovation.

I look forward to the discussion today. I look forward to hearing our witnesses' views on the two proposals, and to ultimately bringing legal clarity and consumer protection to the stablecoin eco-system.

And with that, I now recognize the ranking member of the sub-committee, Mr. Lynch of Massachusetts, for 4 minutes.

Mr. LYNCH. Thank you, Mr. Chairman, for holding this hearing as we consider legislative options for regulating stablecoins. I want to welcome all of the witnesses, and thank you for attending to help this subcommittee with its work.

Last Congress, this committee came close to reaching a bipartisan agreement led by then-Chair Waters. While the bill was far from perfect, we had come to an agreement on some key issues on stablecoins. Since then, however, much of the digital assets space— including many stablecoin companies—has collapsed. The recent bank failures have also taught us some important lessons. It is clear that we need to ensure that future legislation addresses the cracks that have deepened.

It appears that we have shifted further apart from a bipartisan agreement and are now considering two different pieces of proposed legislation. One is led by the Chair of the Subcommittee, Chairman Hill, and the other by Ranking Member Waters of the full Financial Services Committee. Ranking Member Waters' bill and Mr. Hill's bill each address different issues with stablecoins, taking various approaches. My hope is that we can use this hearing to further discussion and to find some alignment.

My concern with stablecoins remains the same as the last time we held the hearing on this topic: stablecoin issuers claiming their products are pegged to reserve assets and used for the purpose of payments when we know that is not correct. Eighty percent of stablecoin volume is dedicated to facilitating the trading of cryptocurrencies and are instead used as speculative instruments. I also continue to worry that the stablecoins contain structural fragilities that make them vulnerable to runs and pose risks to monetary policy, national security, and financial stability. As we consider the recent bank failures and threats to economic stability, we need to ensure that any proposal provides adequate safeguards to our financial system.

I do acknowledge and appreciate that my Republican colleagues have attempted to address some of those issues that we raised last time, such as disallowing non-bank issuer access to Federal Reserve services, including master accounts and access to the discount window. However, I still have concerns about custody, the lack of acknowledgement of the SEC as primary regulator, a lack of adequate consumer protection, and the removal of exploration of a central bank digital currency (CBDC).

Ranking Member Waters' bill gets us a step closer to addressing some of those newer issues that have emerged. For example, Ms. Waters' bill includes specific rules that require issuers to protect assets they hold in custody from customers and restricts the commingling of customer and company assets.

There are still a number of outstanding questions and issues I would like to address. We need to reach an agreement on the role of the States and of Federal regulators. I have concerns about giving sole authority to States, because it risks the possibility of States engaging in a race to the bottom, and crypto companies seeking out jurisdictions with the weakest regulation, which has been their practice.

I am going to take all 5 minutes, Mr. Chairman.

Chairman HILL. Sure.

Mr. LYNCH. Yes. This also creates a moral hazard for States wishing to attract crypto businesses. I believe it is also important that all regulators weigh in and have a specific role. We should ensure that there is alignment between the Administration and financial regulators, and there needs to be a specific role for the SEC and for the Consumer Financial Protection Bureau (CFPB). While I understand there is some agreement to allow non-bank companies to issue stablecoins, I continue to have major concerns about access to deposit insurance.

We must consider the lessons we have learned in recent months regarding bank runs and losses. I must also reiterate the need to separate digital assets from our banking system to avoid the risk of exposure to our banking core. I am confident that through discussions and input from regulators, advocates, and banking experts, we can find alignment to address many of the issues I have mentioned. Mr. Chairman, I yield back the balance of my time.

Chairman HILL. The ranking member yields back.

We now welcome the testimony of our witnesses. First, Mr. Matt Homer. Mr. Homer is the managing member of The Department of XYZ, an early-stage venture capital firm focusing on blockchain. He is also the former executive deputy superintendent for research and innovation at the New York State Department of Financial Services.

Second, Mr. Robert Morgan. Mr. Morgan is the CEO of the USDF Consortium, an association of insured depository institutions working to build a blockchain network to support interoperable bank minute tokenized deposits.

Third, Mr. David Portilla. Mr. Portilla is a partner at Davis Polk & Wardwell, where he specializes in a range of policy matters related to financial institutions.

Fourth, Ms. Fennie Wang. Ms. Wang is the founder and CEO of Humanity Cash, which helped launch the community stablecoin in Berkshire County, Massachusetts.

And finally, Ms. Delicia Reynolds Hand. Ms. Hand is the director of financial fairness at Consumer Reports.

We thank each of you for taking the time to join us today. Each of you will be recognized for 5 minutes to give an oral presentation of your testimony. And without objection, each of your written statements will be made a part of the record.

Mr. Homer, you are now recognized for 5 minutes.

Statement of Matthew Homer, Managing Member, the Department of Xyz, and Former Executive Deputy Superintendent for Research & Innovation, New York State Department of Financial Services (NYDFS)

Mr. HOMER. Good morning, Subcommittee Chairman Hill, Sub-committee Ranking Member Lynch, and members of the sub-committee, and thank you for the opportunity to participate in this hearing. My name is Matt Homer. I was previously the executive deputy superintendent for research and innovation at the New York State Department of Financial Services (NYDFS), where my responsibilities included overseeing the Department's licensing supervision and examination of digital asset-related companies. Earlier in my career, I was a Federal bank regulator in the FDIC's Division of Depositor and Consumer Protection. And today, I am an investor advisor to startup companies, and the managing member of The Department of XYZ, a venture capital firm that invests in early-stage companies building the next generation of financial systems.

I first became familiar with stablecoins through my experience regulating these products at the NYDFS. As this committee is aware from prior testimony, New York State was one of the first jurisdictions in the world to regulate the digital asset space generally, as well as stablecoins specifically. My experience as a regulator taught me that fiat-backed stablecoins represent an important but incremental improvement in the concept of money. In some ways, stablecoins are not so different from the stored-value products many people already use and are familiar with, such as gift cards or prepaid cards.

The question of how to effectively regulate stablecoins has a more clear and straightforward answer than one may find in considering how to regulate other parts of the digital asset ecosystem. New York's experience shows that it is possible to effectively regulate stablecoins using common sense and time-tested regulatory practices.

For example, New York's regulatory framework for stablecoins includes three major prongs: first, reserve requirements to ensure the assets backing stablecoins are held on a segregated basis on behalf of customers, are fully reserved on a one-to-one basis, and are comprised of cash deposits or other cash equivalents; second, redemption rights, ensuring that stablecoin users have the right to redeem their stablecoins on a one-to-one basis for U.S. dollars in a timely manner; and third, public transparency requirements, including monthly attestations from independent CPAs. The stablecoin issuers covered by these standards are also subject to robust supervision and examinations.

I believe there are eight important principles that should guide legislation on this topic and help payment stablecoins achieve their promise. I will discuss three of these for which my background offers unique insight.

First, stablecoin legislation and implementing regulation should recognize the dual banking system as an inherent feature of the American economy that benefits consumers, innovators, and markets. The parallel system of State and Federal regulations supports economic growth by providing innovators and founders optionality that can reduce barriers to launching new products on a small scale, before rolling them out at a national scale. It benefits consumers by providing access to financial services tailored to local needs, and protects them because States are able to move more quickly to fill regulatory gaps.

Finally, it benefits markets by encouraging healthy competition. The legislative drafts I have seen preserve this dynamic. It would establish a Federal floor in the form of a national standard, but would allow States to license and supervise stablecoin issuers and set even tougher rules within their own jurisdictions.

Second, stablecoin legislation should promote competition and the competitiveness of the U.S. system. The stablecoin market so far has trended toward oligopoly. Today, two issuers alone make up over 80 percent of the market for U.S. dollar-denominated stablecoins. Legislation should promote competition by providing pathways for new players to enter the space and challenge incumbents. One idea would be to create a safe harbor for new entrants to test new products or services at limited scale, and with limited customers, before requiring comprehensive regulation, in order to expand to the general public at greater scale.

I would also like to touch on competitiveness as a distinct concept from competition. It is in the American interest to ensure that issuers of U.S. dollar-backed stablecoins remain in the U.S. so that we can regulate stablecoins on our own terms. One way to promote this objective would be to add competitiveness to the official mandates of Federal regulators and to the set of criteria to be used by Federal regulators when considering whether to license a stablecoin issuer.

Third, regulatory capabilities need to keep pace with developments in the market. One of the aspects of regulating digital assets that most intrigued me when I was at NYDFS is the possibility of supervising the space more effectively using digital tools and technologies. For example, I previously mentioned monthly attestations of stablecoin reserves, but we could conceivably move towards more real-time or near real-time dashboards that provide insight into the backing assets of a stablecoin, or even into the financial condition of the entire issuing firm at any given moment in time.

I want to thank you again for the opportunity to be here, and I look forward to your questions.

[The prepared statement of Mr. Homer can be found on page 41 of the appendix.]

Chairman HILL. The gentleman yields back.

Mr. Morgan, you are now recognized for 5 minutes.

Statement of Robert Morgan, CEO, USDF Consortium

Mr. MORGAN. Chairman Hill, Ranking Member Lynch, and members of the subcommittee, thank you for the opportunity to join you to represent the USDF Consortium and our member banks. My name is Rob Morgan, and I am the

CEO of the USDF Consortium, which represents a group of community, mid-sized, and regional banks that have come together to build blockchain infrastructure for the responsible delivery of traditional banking services.

Today's hearing comes at a critical moment. Distributed ledgers hold tremendous promise to improve financial services by offering faster, cheaper, and more-efficient products that can help promote financial inclusion, drive growth in our communities, and support the role of the U.S. dollar as the global reserve currency. To date, most blockchain innovation has occurred outside of the regulated banking sector, in novel cryptocurrency markets. These markets have provided testing grounds that have proven the efficiency and stability that blockchain technology can deliver.

However, financial services only deliver value when they facilitate real-world activity, such as helping small businesses invest and grow, or helping families purchase a home. To leverage blockchain for real-world transactions, you first need a trusted form of digital money that exists natively on blockchain. This is what led to the rise of stablecoins and has driven the policy discussion around the creation of a central bank digital currency (CBDC). The debate on how to digitize the dollar is too often pitched as a binary choice between these two options. We believe there is a third path that leverages the way money already exists in our economy.

The U.S. dollar is already largely digital and exists primarily in the form of bank deposits. Today, bank deposits represent 73 percent of money in our economy. At its core, blockchain is a ledger technology. Banks have long relied on ledgers to record value and facilitate transactions. Over the years, this technology has evolved from paper-based ledgers, to on-premise servers, and now the cloud. We believe that blockchain is the next evolution in ledger technology. By recording a traditional bank deposit on blockchain, we can bring many of the benefits of stablecoins to the real economy while maintaining the numerous benefits and protections that our two-tier banking system provides today.

Unlike stablecoins, tokenized deposits are not designed to connect the broader crypto ecosystem to the real world. Tokenized deposits are backend technology designed to improve the delivery of traditional banking services. They will not trade on exchanges, and in many cases will not be held directly by the public. Like all bank deposits, they are a liability of an insured depository institution.

Bank deposits are a cornerstone of our monetary and financial systems that support the dominance of the U.S. dollar around the world. They play a critical role in supporting a bank's ability to lend into the communities they serve, driving economic growth, and promoting social mobility. The value of bank deposits is supported by stringent regulation and proactive oversight, which includes capital and liquidity requirements as well as technology risk man- agement designed to control for the risks associated with deposit taking.

Tokenizing deposits facilitates the creation of a real-time blockchain-based payments infrastructure that can significantly improve the delivery of banking services. It can facilitate faster, cheaper payments, programmable payments, and atomic settlement. We can only realize these benefits when innovation is delivered responsibly and regulatory guidelines are clear, certain, and consistently applied.

Legislation like that being discussed today is an important step to ensuring stablecoins are delivered responsibly and that consumers remain protected. It is important that these efforts do not inhibit the adoption of blockchain for other applications like tokenized deposits. To that end, we were pleased to see that the draft legislation makes the critical distinction between stablecoins and tokenized deposits, and that it affirms a bank's ability to leverage blockchain for traditional banking applications.

Unfortunately, there is not currently a clear regulatory path for banks to adopt blockchain. Today, banks require formal regulatory approval for any such project. We would encourage Congress to work with the banking agencies to ensure there is a clear and credible path for banks to adopt blockchain technology. Competition breeds innovation, and we believe there is a role for many forms of money, both novel and traditional. We look forward to working with Congress to ensure there is an appropriate regulatory framework for novel assets like stablecoins, and to ensure there is regulatory clarity for banks to adopt new technologies that benefit the customers and communities that they serve.

Thank you for the opportunity to testify today. I would be happy to answer any questions you may have.

[The prepared statement of Mr. Morgan can be found on page 49 of the appendix.]

Chairman HILL. Thank you, sir.

Mr. Portilla, you are now recognized for 5 minutes for your oral presentation.

Statement of David L. Portilla, Partner, Davis Polk & Wardwell LLP

Mr. PORTILLA. Thank you, Chairman Hill, Ranking Member Lynch, and members of the subcommittee. It is a pleasure to have the opportunity to speak before you today. I commend all of your diligent efforts and the progress that has been made to develop stablecoin legislation. I believe a bipartisan substantive consensus should be achievable.

These types of financial products are special because they pose well-known risks, such as the risk of a run, that is, request for redemption and loss that cannot be met due to a mismatch in the liquidity of reserve assets. We can and should proactively mitigate these risks by establishing a regulatory framework now before the risks grow larger and scale makes that change more difficult.

I cannot say with certainty whether stablecoins represent a part of the future of payments, yet I feel quite confident that the current legal framework is ill-suited to comprehensively regulate payment stablecoins. Correspondingly, legislation that enables fit-forpurpose regulation would help foster an environment where this technology can develop and scale.

Some of the potential that payment stablecoins offer include the programmability of money and additional means for mobile-based, real-time payments for consumers, and the creation of an additional payments infrastructure in which further innovation can occur. If realized, all of these developments may amplify the potential for building a more efficient, competitive, and resilient payment system.

Legislation should establish privileges and responsibilities along a spectrum. Greater privileges from the government should be coupled with more-stringent regulatory oversight; a more-tailored regulatory approach, on the other hand, should be coupled with appropriately-calibrated privileges from the government.

The remainder of my remarks will focus on what I believe are the key outstanding issues that should be addressed in any legislation.

One, who should be permitted to issue payment stablecoins? Nonbanks should be permitted to issue payment stablecoins. Within a banking organization, it makes the most sense for a stablecoin to be issued by a non-bank entity within the corporate group. The reason is that the common conception of a payment stablecoin business, the issuance and redemption of an instrument backed by a discrete pool of high-quality liquid assets, is distinct from the traditional banking business model.

Two, who should regulate payment stablecoins? Federal regulation of stablecoin issuers would offer more uniform, consistent rules, where a State regulation could promote more diversity and innovation in regulation and supervision. The answer to this question need not be binary. Many of the legislative proposals released by Members of Congress to date have followed the model of our dual banking system. that is, they would establish a framework in which stablecoin issuers could be regulated either directly at the Federal level, or primarily at the State level with an overlay of Federal oversight. There are many options, including providing Federal regulation as a backup to State regulation, or an approach that toggles based on the scale of an issuer.

Three, should non-bank payments stablecoin issuers be provided access to the Federal Reserve's payment system or discount window? Granting non-bank payment stablecoin issuers access to master accounts could help them provide more-efficient services to their customers. Perhaps legislation could grant non-bank stablecoin issuers access to Federal Reserve Bank services, but limiting those services in both scale and scope, or access to Federal Reserve Bank services could be available as an option or based on the scale of an issuer.

Four, to what extent, if at all, should payment stablecoins be subject to, "deposit insurance?" Whether some form of insurance is ultimately needed for stablecoins may turn on the nature of the reserves that backed them, and relatedly, the degree to which consumers expect their stablecoins to be redeemable on demand at par.

Five, what insolvency standard should be applicable to payment stablecoins? To the extent payment stablecoins are designed or perceived to be effectively free of credit risk, it would be prudent to provide stablecoin holders with structural priority over an issuer's other creditors. In addition, customers should know that the companies that help them hold stablecoins do so in a safe way. Existing Federal and State laws provide standards for custodians and should be useful in this context.

Six, what other legal regimes should apply to payment stablecoins and related products and services? Well, I focused primarily on prudential issues. Payment stablecoins and related products also present other common regulatory concerns such as those related to consumer protection and illicit finance. All of these considerations should be thoughtfully explored, but this does not mean that the securities laws should apply to payment stablecoins nor does it mean that we should be vexed to paralysis in trying to answer questions that, frankly, permeate traditional finance, such as how to regulate any service provider that is adjacent to a regulated firm. Ultimately, consumers in our financial system more broadly will be best-served by focusing on the issues I outlined, where I believe we can find common ground.

Thank you.

[The prepared statement of Mr. Portilla can be found on page 59 of the appendix.]

Chairman HILL. Thank you, sir.

Ms. Wang, you are recognized for 5 minutes for your oral presentation.

Statement of Fennie Wang, Founder and CEO, Humanity Cash

Ms. WANG. Good morning. Thank you, Chairman McHenry, Chairman Hill, and Ranking Members Lynch and Waters for giving me this opportunity to testify.

People like me rarely have this opportunity. I do not represent a large corporation or an industry organization. I am an independent lawyer and entrepreneur working with grassroots organizations. While in my past life, I have worked for a Wall Street bank and Wall Street law firms, the work I do now is a labor of love, working with community organizations to design local currencies that make money work harder for local communities. Indeed, my company is called, "Humanity Cash," because we want to make money personal again.

During the pandemic, I studied the history of community currencies, which are not legal tender, but they complement national currencies as a local medium of exchange to ensure more money circulates and stays within local communities. In the United States, where we enjoy the world's reserve currency, one downside is that the U.S. dollar sometimes works minimally for local communities, with most of that money benefiting big banks and large corporations. Therefore, the goal of a local currency may be to promote patronage of small businesses and local banks, which recirculate deposits back into the local economy in the form of productive loans, creating a money multiplier effect. This is the model of a local currency in The Berkshires, Massachusetts.

During the pandemic, small businesses were under and continue to be under pressure. The pandemic also accelerated the shift towards contactless payments, which means that more money is leaking out of local economies. Even if you shop locally, if you pay with a credit card, the local economy loses out on the money multi- plier effect of that dollar being put to work by local banks, as well as the 3- to 4-percent transaction fees that are taken off the top. I saw this as an opportunity to address a real-world problem for which blockchain was suited. By digitizing a local currency, we can better compete with credit cards, and reduce transaction fees, while ensuring that the underlying dollar reserves remain deposited and, therefore, invested in the local economy via local banks.

During the process of designing and launching additional local currency, I interviewed small business owners, community bankers, and ordinary citizens, whether in The Berkshires or across the United States, from Puerto Rico to Hawaii to Indiana. The people I have met are not interested in crypto as a speculative investment, and neither is anyone in this room. We are all deeply passionate about making money work for our communities—that, "we," includes a concrete mixer driver, a retired accountant, community organizers who support Black-owned businesses, and a small business owner who produces Massachusetts-made ukuleles.

As grassroots entrepreneurs and community innovators, we need risk-appropriate regulations that will not be cost-prohibitive, while providing guardrails to protect us from bad actors. Chairman McHenry's stablecoin proposal strikes a good balance between these two needs. Importantly, it provides space for local initiatives in innovation through State regulators in a clear roadmap for implementation. This proposal also provides the groundwork for community financial institutions as well as non-bank institutions, such as Economic Development Organizations, to staunch the flight of deposits from local communities.

Payment stablecoins enable higher-quality deposits, as we can transact amongst each other without needing to withdraw the underlying dollars. The urgency of keeping deposits local is more important than ever in light of the regional banking crisis. The community banks we work with in Massachusetts recirculate 70 cents of every dollar back into the local economy, compared to just 20 cents for large banks.

Long term, blockchain technology can replace outdated banking and payments infrastructure, which is currently limiting the ability of smaller banks to innovate and compete effectively against big banks and fintechs. With the right policies, starting with the stablecoin proposals, we can enable our financial system to be more competitive and more responsive to local economies, a benefit that ordinary Americans deeply desire. Thank you.

[The prepared statement of Ms. Wang can be found on page 67 of the appendix.]

Chairman HILL. Ms. Reynolds Hand, you are now recognized for 5 minutes for your oral presentation.

Statement of Delicia Reynolds Hand, Director, Financial Fairness, Consumer Reports

Ms. HAND. Thank you. Good morning, Chairman McHenry, Ranking Member Waters, Subcommittee Chairman Hill, Sub-committee Ranking Member Lynch, and members of the sub-committee, and thank you for this invitation to testify. My name is Delicia Reynolds Hand, and I serve as the director of financial fairness at Consumer Reports, where I lead the organization's work in digital finance. At Consumer Reports, we examine what fintech products and services actually do for consumers and how they rate alongside each other. Do they actually live up to what they promise?

As I testified recently, the convergence of new technologies and new forms of assets have made cryptocurrencies particularly appealing for consumers whom traditional finance has never appropriately served. In a volatile and stressed economic environment, consumers and investors are at an even greater risk in the absence of rules and noncompliance with regulations to protect them and prevent the misuse or exploitation of these assets. Since the last conversation on stablecoins, Europe has succeeded in bringing crypto assets, crypto asset issuers, and crypto assets service providers under a regulatory framework, and today, we have two bills under consideration. I hope we can land in a good place for consumers.

Consumer Reports urges this committee to work together to achieve effective and comprehensive regulation of stablecoins. This is especially important for responsible innovation, financial stability, and financial inclusion. Appropriate regulation, supervision, and oversight needs to be implemented before stablecoins become a greater risk to financial stability, safety, and soundness, and the smooth functioning of payment system.

To be clear, this space will be regulated, and new frameworks will be developed. The question is, whether the development will be driven by crisis or collaboration? We support updates to the committee draft which include Federal regulatory review to ensure the safety and soundness of stablecoin issuers. And we encourage the adoption of provisions in the bill granting the Federal Reserve Board authority to reject State licenses. Not including these provisions creates regulatory arbitrage, which could drive a race to the bottom instead of a race to the top. These are lessons we have failed to learn from the past. Keeping with the tradition of congressional implication of the commerce clause, the law should be the same across all 50 States.

The committee draft could also go further to include specific key requirements which parallel requirements for traditional banking. While both drafts retain some equivalent requirements to provide information about the organizers, senior management teams, and capital adequacy, we urge the committee to also retain requirements to promote diversity and inclusion in the compromise bill. We support the addition of requirements for Federal regulators to issue rules related to risk management infrastructure.

Second, while the committee bill outlines a role for Federal oversight, it does not require entities that become stablecoin issuers to be insured depository institutions. The compromise bill, however, makes it clear that issuers shall not represent stablecoins as insured depositors. We would encourage adoption of this language. We are most concerned about the removal of key text in the committee draft, maintaining separation of banking and commerce, prohibiting non-financial commercial businesses like Facebook or Walmart from owning a payment stablecoin issuer. Additionally, we would encourage the adoption of stronger consumer protections. The bill sets up a regime to prove issuers of payment stablecoins, but it doesn't outline adequate consumer protections for payment activities conducted or facilitated by issuers or their coins. We urge the committee to move forward with the provisions in the compromise bill that require stablecoin payment regulation to additionally be technology-neutral, to promote interoperability and to ensure stablecoin arrangements share common features with the traditional financial system.

We also request that the committee adopt language associated with strong oversight of custodial wallets, as the committee draft does not cover all assets held by custodial wallets. We do not need another Lehman Brothers. And in the event of another insolvency, a bankruptcy court could reasonably view, as they have in Celsius, that commingled funds are grounds for giving the company and its creditors priority access to those funds rather than stablecoin holders, the rightful owners. Lastly, we urge explicit clarification on how and when the SEC can and should regulate in this space.

Thank you again for the opportunity to testify.

[The prepared statement of Ms. Hand can be found on page 36 of the appendix.]

Chairman HILL. Thank you for your testimony. And we appreciate all of the testimony from our witnesses. We will now turn to Member questions.

The Chair recognizes himself for 5 minutes.

Mr. Homer, those were interesting comments you made about validation of the reserves for a stablecoin, and you referenced the ability to do that on an intraday basis versus the way the bill is drafted. Is that technology readily available for a stablecoin issuer to provide an intraday valuation of their reserves and transparency on that?

Mr. HOMER. Thank you for the question, and, yes, the technology is available. I think there will be two aspects of it. One is the number of stablecoins that you have issued, which is available publicly through the blockchain, and then, the second aspect of it would be technology to show that the backing assets match that on a one- to-one basis. And both of those things can be accomplished,

Chairman HILL. Right. And that would obviously be backed up by the attestation and monthly financial reporting, and then audits. Yes. Thank you. That is a good comment you made.

In our last hearing, we heard testimony from NYDFS Superintendent Harris on the role of State regulators. She described how State regulators can regulate payments, stablecoin issuers, and how a regulatory regime could be built on a well-established dual banking system that we have in our country. I think it is important as we work through the drafts that we strike the right balance there. I think it is a key, effectively, a difference between these two drafts, and the one that we are going to try to figure out between both sides of the aisle as we work through this. And naturally, it is an area that the Federal Reserve cares a lot about since they would be the primary regulator for federally-qualified nonbanks. And in our Republican draft, we have the Comptroller of the Currency as the primary Federal regulator for national trusts.

Our September bill, from last fall, the Maxine Waters-Patrick McHenry bill, would require a State-chartered issuer also registered with the Fed.

Mr. Homer, striking a balance there, what is your view on making sure we get that balance right?

Mr. HOMER. Yes. As you pointed out, I think that balance is very important to get right for a number of reasons, most importantly, that we want a competitive marketplace. I have been a Federal regulator, and I have been a State regulator, and I think both regulatory systems are important to the stability of our financial system. But I will say with certainty that State regulators are much closer to the ground. They know their local constituents much better. They are much more able to effectively calibrate a regulatory environment that meets local requirements. The State pathway is important, because if you are someone who is starting a financial services company, that is where you go to get licensed or chartered for the first time.

Chairman HILL. But you know the ranking member's concerns about a race to the bottom, right? You have been a State regulator and an FDIC employee. Can we strike that balance with the way we have approached it in the Republican bill, do you think?

Mr. HOMER. I think so. I think in both of these bills, there is a strong Federal floor. I would argue that a race to the bottom is not possible.

Chairman HILL. Okay. Good. Thank you.

Let me turn to you, Mr. Portilla, on the issue of the OCC charters. The Comptroller of the Currency had two digital asset firms that they had given conditional approval to act as a trust. And those conditional approvals now have lapsed, like so many things, around our lack of a regulatory framework, adding to the frustration here. The Republicans on the subcommittee sent a letter to the Agency pointing out its inconsistent approach in reviewing national trust bank charter applications. Could you discuss the benefits of allowing the OCC to serve as the primary regulator for any stablecoin issuers that receive an OCC national trust charter, please?

Mr. PORTILLA. Yes. Thank you for the question. I think the main benefit of having the OCC serve as the primary Federal regulator for a stablecoin issuer that has a national trust charter is that you avoid multiple Federal regulators of the same entity. And in addition, the OCC is at heart a supervisor and an examiner of banks and trust companies, and so they are well-qualified to do that.

Chairman HILL. That is helpful. Let me yield back the balance of my time, and call on my friend from Massachusetts, the ranking member of the subcommittee, Mr. Lynch, for his 5 minutes of questions.

Mr. LYNCH. Thank you, Mr. Chairman. Mr. Homer, how many stablecoins are registered in New York State?

Mr. HOMER. There are, I believe, currently three companies that have been chartered to issue—

Mr. LYNCH. How many stablecoins are there? Mr. HOMER. I believe it is five.

Mr. LYNCH. No, no. How many stablecoins are in existence right now?

Mr. HOMER. There are probably— Mr. LYNCH. 20,000, I think, yes.

Mr. HOMER. That would claim they are stablecoins.

Mr. LYNCH. Yes. So, 5 out of 20,000 are registered in New York. I think that is evidence of a race to the bottom right there, where stablecoins are trying to and crypto companies are trying to go to the areas with the least amount of regulation. I also worry, and I know you have done extensive work in New York. We had Ms. Harris in yesterday, and I know people have done a lot of good work in New York around this issue.

But the practice—a race to the bottom is not possible. A race to the bottom is the practice, is the custom of this industry, to go offshore and seek areas of least regulation. I compliment the State of New York for the work that they have done. However, my feeling is that if we directed this to the 50 States and the Territories, perhaps that practice would continue, and cryptocurrencies would seek out those areas, those jurisdictions that offer the best opportunity for them to maximize their profit and avoid cumbersome and costly regulation and disclosure. That is what I worry about here, that we are not engaged in that type of practice where New York would be penalized for having a robust regulatory system. They would run elsewhere. There are other States that are in the game here. We all know who they are, that are offering themselves as safe havens, that offer us some real concerns.

But anyway, I do appreciate you all being here and helping us. This is a learning process, and we are all trying to understand this in a better way so that we can craft this legislation and come to a meeting of the minds. I deeply respect the chairman, Mr. Hill, and I know he is a good man, and we are trying to get to a good situation on this. But, Ms. Reynolds Hand, back in February of this year, the Fed Board of Governors offered guidance on member banks regarding the use of digital assets within the Federal banking ecosystem, and they said they are offering this guidance because of rampant fraud.

The rule that they promulgated covered two directives. One was to presumptively prohibit holding crypto assets out of safety and soundness concerns, and the rule also noted significant risks associated with the cryptocurrency sector, including fraud, legal ambiguity and volatility. They also said—and this really got me—that in the absence of a fundamental use case, the value of most crypto assets is driven largely by sentiment and future expectations, and not by cash flows from providing goods or services outside the crypto asset ecosystem.

So in light of so many of these stablecoins breaking the buck, becoming de-pegged, wreaking havoc for those who hold this because of the inability of depositors and investors to get their money back in redemption, is this something that we want to tie to a traditional financial system and give access to the Federal Reserve discount window or access to Federal Reserve services?

Ms. HAND. I would say we certainly shouldn't start there, with so much volatility and disruption occurring. We shouldn't open up the Federal purse, frankly, until industries are proven to be safe and we cut down on rampant fraud and other abuses. We should start first with clear rules of the road and strong protections for consumers. Then, once proven, we should add the additional programs in which companies are interested.

Mr. LYNCH. That is great. Thank you. Mr. Chairman, I yield back.

Chairman HILL. The ranking member yields back.

I now recognize Mr. Davidson of Ohio, who is the vice chairman of this subcommittee, and the chairman of our Housing and Insurance Subcommittee, for 5 minutes.

Mr. DAVIDSON. I thank the chairman. Thanks for our witnesses, and, frankly, for the colleagues who are here to help make good policy. I will try to stay calm and measured in my responses here. But the whole point that we are trying to do is provide a clear legal framework for the entire country so that no one State can game the system or, frankly, so that people aren't driven offshore, out of our capital markets and our regulatory framework. Often, they are fleeing our markets to find certainty, so it would be great if we would provide some. I have been working on this for a long time, as have many of you.

Speaking of efforts, people say, oh, there is a lack of stability, that a lot of the same people are working to create a lack of stability.

Mr. Homer, this year it has become fairly apparent to many people in a bipartisan way that the traditional banking industry has started taking a hostile position with digital asset companies in thespace in which they operate. When Silicon Valley Bank failed, some people pointed to digital asset companies, one of which was a stablecoin issue, and said they held too much of their capital at one bank, Silicon Valley Bank. When Signature Bank failed, people claimed that maybe it had something to do with digital assets.

Barney Frank, a former chairman of this committee, said it didn't have anything to do with that. The director of the New York State Department of Financial Services, who was there for the whole thing, said it didn't have anything to do with digital assets. So, where are they going to go for banking? Could you speak to the harm that comes with deep banking, the industry, and the damage, and, frankly, the lack of stability that it has caused?

Mr. HOMER. Yes. Thank you for the question. I think it is something that has been a challenge, and it has become much more difficult for companies in the space to find banking services, even for the most basic of services, to find an account for payroll, for example. I think, unfortunately, what that will lead to is people looking for alternatives that are, in some instances, offshore.

Mr. DAVIDSON. If you can't deposit your cash in America, you are probably going to deposit your cash somewhere, right?

Mr. HOMER. Right.

Mr. DAVIDSON. So then, they will point to that and say, see, they are offshore. Well, you drove them there, on purpose, I might add. Let me just address this. Could a stablecoin go to zero, a regulated stablecoin that is backed by high-quality liquid assets, or, frankly, commodities, physical custody of commodities, would that really go to zero?

Mr. HOMER. Under this proposal, it would be very difficult to foresee a scenario.

Mr. DAVIDSON. There would have to be complete fraud. They didn't have the assets, right? Could somebody in that case, where you had full custody of the assets that you say you have, whether they are level-one, high-quality assets or physical custody of a commodity that backs it, could it possibly go to less than the value unless there was actual fraud?

Mr. HOMER. It would be very difficult.

Mr. DAVIDSON. I think that is the case, and that is the whole goal of the regulatory regime we are trying to put in place here with stablecoins. As we confront the debt ceiling and the fact that this town spends way more money than we collect in revenue for a long, long period of time, we are spending more money than anyone will even lend us, there seems to be a shortage of demand for Treasuries, given that the most frequent backing for a stablecoin so that it really is fully backed is Treasuries.

Mr. Portilla, could you talk about the important linkage that stablecoins would create for demand for U.S. dollar-denominated Treasuries?

Mr. PORTILLA. Right, yes. Thank you for the question. I think you are right. If stablecoins are required to hold their reserves and high-quality liquid assets, which of course includes short-term Treasuries, there would inherently be increased demand for those assets from those issuers. So, I think that is right.

Mr. DAVIDSON. Yes. I think it could actually help us solve a number of problems. And then the last thing in terms of the payment space, frankly, for a lot of people, is they look at a stablecoin as in many ways superior to a fiat currency, because while the fiat currency is backed by the full faith and credit of the United States, and we could just print more money, you have a hard time guaranteeing that it will buy the same amount of goods. But in the case of a stablecoin, it is fully backed and could be backed by physical custody of assets as well.

My time has expired. I hope we land on something in a completely bipartisan way and that we can get this done. I yield back.

Chairman HILL. I thank the gentleman. Mr. Foster, who is the ranking member on our Financial Institutions and Monetary Policy Subcommittee, is now recognized for 5 minutes.

Mr. FOSTER. Thank you. Mr. Homer, you mentioned real-time monitoring of reserve balances versus tokens issued. Wouldn't it be actually easiest and safest to simply require as part of the minting process that digital attestation for the Federal Reserve, that the amount of deposit in the relevant account at the Fed exceeds the amount of tokens that are proposed to be in circulation following any proposed minting operation? So basically, that any proposed minting operation would not be cryptographically valid until it was accompanied by a Fed attestation that the assets are actually there on reserve. Do you understand where I am going? It seems like this is a very unburdensome operation to require for both the Fed and the issuer.

Mr. HOMER. I think they could be complementary. If we are thinking about trust in the market and how do we produce trust, I think real-time dashboards could assist with that. But of course, attestations from a regulator or required by a regulator are important and probably not in addition to that. I don't think they are mutually exclusive.

Mr. FOSTER. I am worried about the sort of abuses that we saw with flash loans and things where even, for a fraction of a second, you can have weird things happening, and all of a sudden, a giant fraud has taken place, whereas if you would have simply said the minting is not valid until the Federal Reserve says, yes, they are there, before, during, and after the minting operation, you have some excess buffer of reserves. It seems like that should be an absolutely solid way of guaranteeing.

Also, that approach, it seems to me, really eliminates all of the worries about monetary effects, because there is a one-to-one ratio in which you emphasize fraudulent issuance, runs on stablecoins, and that would all just disappear if we adopted that approach. So, I think there is a lot to be said for it.

Ms. Wang, in your testimony regarding Humanity Cash projects, I see that you have kind of independently discovered and implemented the two principles that I believe must be included to have the controlled privacy and security that will be needed to avoid fraudulent and criminal use of stablecoins.

First, in your testimony you state that the use of a blockchain ledger can also cost-effectively and in transparency meet part of the public reporting requirements under the proposed stablecoin bill. For example, you can show in real time that the number of tokens on a chain compared to the U.S. dollar reserve balances is what we have just been talking about.

But second, I was very pleased to see that you have also attached what amounts to be automobile license plates on each digital wallet, something that I have been advocating in this committee for quite some time.

Then, in your testimony, you state that at the point of wallet creation, we collect information regarding username and contact information associated with each wallet, not available to the public on a public ledger to preserve user confidentiality, and then go on to explain why it would be to the advantage of that system.

So, let us spend a moment looking through the privacy implications of this to see if it is a comfortable place to land. For example, if a person uses Humanity Cash to buy a secret gift for their secret lover with no criminal activity involved, can they expect that it will remain anonymous and secret?

Ms. WANG. Yes. The blockchain itself doesn't show any personal identifying information, but we can also design systems that preserve the balance between preserving your privacy versus law enforcement needs. One of the other areas that I have done work on is around digital identity. You can, for example, have the DMV or a bank issue a digital token that represents like KYC credential, right? So, your identity

Mr. FOSTER. Yes. The so-called mobile ID or digital driver's license?

Ms. WANG. Right. And a wallet can hold that digital identity token to signal that it has been checked, and then, you are going to have safe transactions without needing to actually know who that person is, unless there was a compliance reason to reveal the underlying information.

Mr. FOSTER. I know that. I am a huge fan of mobile ID as well. Now, on the other hand, if there is a ransomware attack, say attempting to use Humanity Cash as a payment and someone's screen locks up and says that in order to decrypt your computer files, we want you to transfer this much Humanity Cash to this wallet, then I presume you can go to some judge somewhere, prove a crime has been committed, and de-anonymize the owner of that wallet. How does that take place? What is the mechanism for control of de-anonymization?

Ms. WANG. In our specific case, I think the chances of that are pretty low because you would only be able to suspend it—

Mr. FOSTER. I understand, but we are talking about systems at a scale.

Ms. WANG. Right, but at a systems level, there will be ways to prevent that. Instead, you would know exactly where the money has been transferred. But you can freeze, for example, compromised tokens and so they would no longer be transactable after the point of attack. And then, you still have the underlying real- world assets, the deposits in the bank, and all of that remains safe, so we can then—

Mr. FOSTER. Thank you. I think my time is up. Your project may be small, but I think you have seen the future pretty clearly.

Ms. WANG. Thank you.

Chairman HILL. Thank you, Dr. Foster. We now turn to the gentleman from Tennessee, Mr. Rose, for 5 minutes.

Mr. ROSE. Thank you, Chairman Hill and Ranking Member Lynch, for holding this hearing, and thank you to all of our witnesses for your time today. I would like to also thank the chairman for noticing Ranking Member Waters' stablecoin draft to this hearing to give us the opportunity to discuss some of the bad policies that it includes. For instance, it would require each stablecoin issuer to disclose so-called diversity statistics, which have nothing to do with the financial stability of the issuer. Additionally, the Waters draft proposes to push forward with a study on a central bank digital currency, which has been called the single greatest assault to financial privacy since the creation of the Bank Secrecy Act.

Since my time is limited, I want to dive directly into my questions. Mr. Morgan, the U.S. dollar is the world's reserve currency, accepted all around the world because it is backed by the full faith and credit of the U.S. Government. In that sense, it is the original utility token. I see the value in U.S.-based stablecoins to facilitate payments. So, Mr. Morgan, if we are going to use blockchain technology and crypto rails to facilitate payments, is it essential to have a less-volatile asset, like a U.S.-backed stablecoin, than, say, Bitcoin or an Ethereum-based token?

Mr. MORGAN. Congressman, thank you for the question. We think that stable asset is a critical piece of facilitating real-world value. In particular, we believe tokenized deposits are one path to do that. Today, bank deposits are 73 percent of money in the U.S. economy. Stablecoins are separate and apart from that, but we believe that competition from well-regulated parties for the form of that money can only benefit the economy.

Mr. ROSE. Thank you.

Mr. Portilla, the McHenry bill does not include a requirement for a report on financial inclusion, which was included as part of an earlier draft. It also does not require regulators to consider financial inclusion when evaluating a stablecoin issuer's application, which is also required in the earlier draft. Mr. Portilla, does information pertaining to diversity and financial inclusion have any bearing on whether the stablecoin issuer is capable of operating a stablecoin in a safe and sound manner?

Mr. PORTILLA. Yes. Thank you for the question as well. No, I think the safety and soundness factors in the proposed legislation, both of the proposed pieces of legislation, are different than what you might call the community benefit or the financial inclusion standards. I think the financial inclusion or community benefit standards are not going towards safety and soundness. They are addressing other policy goals.

I think those are borrowed from our banking laws, where those factors are required to be considered under the banking statutes for mergers and acquisitions, for example, for different reasons. For example, classic banking is taking deposits and making mortgage loans, and Congress in the past has worried about banks making decisions about whom they are lending to. To me, that is not relevant to the business of a stablecoin. They are not making those types of decisions. So, I think there is a question of if that is the right piece of the banking statutes to draw from for stablecoin legislation.

Mr. ROSE. Thank you. I agree.

Mr. Morgan, tokenized deposits have a role to play in utilizing the benefits of the blockchain in our payment systems. Can you address the benefits of tokenized deposits and how they differ from traditional stablecoins?

Mr. MORGAN. Congressman, thank you for the question. We believe that this is a critical distinction. Unlike stablecoins, tokenized deposits are not designed to connect that broader crypto ecosystem to the real world. Tokenized deposits will not trade on exchanges, and in most cases, will not be held by the general public. They are simply backend infrastructure that can bring the innovations associated with blockchain technology into the traditional banking space.

Mr. ROSE. Thank you.

Mr. Homer, how do we ensure that stablecoin issuers work with their regulator to utilize an appropriate amount of on-balance sheet liquidity and concentration limits to offset the risk of withdrawals in a stress scenario based on their risk profiles?

Mr. HOMER. Thank you, Congressman, for the question. It is a great question, and it really speaks to the importance of a prudential supervisor being the primary regulator of stablecoins. And that is the balance the stablecoin issuers have to strike, a balance between stability and liquidity, and prudential supervisors have an important role to play there in helping them think through scenario planning to get that right.

Mr. ROSE. Thank you. I see my time is expiring, so I yield back.

Chairman HILL. The gentleman yields back. The gentleman from California, Mr. Sherman, is recognized for 5 minutes.

Mr. SHERMAN. I am here to channel Nancy Reagan. Just say no to crypto and to so-called stablecoins, the biggest oxymoron in the American language. Mr. Rose points out that the other way to go here is with the digital dollar, and the reason he opposes that is he wants to have financial privacy. That is right. If you want to be a drug dealer, you need financial privacy. If you want to evade our sanctions laws, you need financial privacy. But the big market is the tax evaders. The IRS has testified that we have a trillion dollars of uncollected taxes, chiefly from billionaires, in this country. That means they have to hide $3 trillion of income every year. That is the big market for this.

I first got involved in crypto because it blows a giant hole in what has been the most effective element of national power, and that is our ability to impose sanctions. We differed on the Iran nuclear deal, but we were able to order every country in the world to not buy Iranian oil in excess of the amount we specified for that country because of the role of the U.S. dollar. Some would say that got us a great nuclear deal, some would say it should have gotten us a better nuclear deal, but if this works, we are not going to have that power anymore. You can build a couple more aircraft carrier groups at great expense, but it isn't going to give you the power that we had at that time.

My concern is what happens if this works as a payment system. It is designed to compete with the U.S. dollar. I think Mr. Davidson had it right. Here in Congress, we spend money like we are Democrats, we impose taxes like we are Republicans, and we have a fiscal deficit that would make Argentina blush. If we didn't have the U.S. dollar playing the role that it does, our economy would be worse than that of Argentina, so if this works, it is a problem. We have people here concerned with either helping billionaires make money or maybe helping consumers not get ripped off. All of the billionaires make the money, but we don't have anybody on our panel concerned with the power of the United States through its U.S. dollar.

Now, we have the McHenry bill, which allows you to go to any one of the 50 States and make them your regulator. So, you supposedly have one-to-one backing for your money, but you pick your auditor out of any one of the 50, so it certainly gives you the opportunity to have less oversight, and eventually not to have support. Mr. Davidson points out that the inflation means that the dollar is worth less. That doesn't mean these stablecoins preserve value because these stablecoins are tied to the value of the U.S. dollar. They are never worth more than one-to-one. They can be worth less if you have fraud and you invite fraud by saying, go to the State that has the least-effective audits.

Finally, there is the use of private wallets. Now, those who talk about fiat currencies will say, hey, I have a private wallet. You can't conveniently put a million dollars in this. The Federal Government doesn't regulate it, but how much money can you put in it? In contrast, we are going to have a stablecoin system that is like an iceberg. Some will be above the water and will see it, but then you will have private wallets below the water that will be a lot more efficient for tax evaders, drug dealers, and sanctions evaders.

I can't believe I still have an additional 40 seconds.

I will also point out that this stablecoin is not some hip new thing. It is as hip as John Quincy Adams. We already had this in the 1820s. Banks would issue their own currency, similar to what Ms. Wang was talking about. I want to add one more thing, and that is, we already have money market funds. They work much better than stablecoin as a payment system now, and we can make them much better than they are now. You can tie them to a debit card. The only problem is they have Know Your Customer (KYC) rules, and that means they are not good for tax evaders and sanction evaders. I yield back.

Chairman HILL. The gentleman yields back, and the Chair reminds all Members that there is no loss of prestige by yielding back in less than 5 minutes.

The Chair now recognizes the gentleman from Wisconsin, Mr. Steil, for 5 minutes.

Mr. STEIL. Thank you very much, Mr. Chairman. Thanks for holding today's hearing. I think it is a really important topic.

Mr. Homer, one of the things I think a lot about is how we make sure that the development of these products isn't overseas, but rather, in the United States. A lot of times, I think about the cha lenges that I have with Big Tech, but if I look at all of the challenges that I have with Big Tech, I think I can't even fathom to wrap my head around the challenges that we would face if, instead of having U.S.-domiciled companies at the forefront, if all of our Big Tech companies were like TikTok and were developed outside the United States, the challenges that we would face or the infancy in some ways of this technological revolution.

I want to make sure it remains and is developed here in the United States with our values rather than internationally, as well as the jobs and value that will come from that. And so, as I look at that, do you believe that the proposed McHenry legislation will provide innovators with the certainty they will need to invest here in the United States?

Mr. HOMER. I do, and I can—

Mr. STEIL. No, no, no. That is good. Okay. Straightforward answer then. Singapore has enacted a regulatory framework for stablecoins, so let's examine Singapore's experience as we craft our own framework here in the

United States. Is there anything specifically we can learn from the Singapore experience?

Mr. HOMER. Sure. I think one thing that is important now is that stablecoins will happen regardless of whether we want them to happen or not. The U.S. dollar dominates stablecoins. There is nothing stopping offshore entities from doing this already. We should have it done in the U.S. so we can regulate it on our own terms.

We can learn a lot from stablecoin frameworks being proposed in other countries like Singapore and the European Union. In some ways, they mirror much of what is reflected in this proposal regarding reserve requirements. I think one feature that is different that you see in other markets is a tiering. Under this proposal, someone who issues $5 of stablecoins is regulated in the same way as someone who issues $5 billion worth of stablecoins, and in other country's proposals, we see a tiering in terms of regulatory requirements.

Mr. STEIL. That is helpful. Thank you very much. Let me stay with you, Mr. Homer, but let me shift gears somewhat dramatically. The SEC recently issued a, "Wells notice," to Paxos that alleges the stablecoin, BUSD, is a security. We all know one of the key prongs to the Howey test is that there will be an expectation of profit. Could a purchaser of a stablecoin have an expectation of profit?

Mr. HOMER. It is hard to understand how a user of a stablecoin could have an expectation of profit.

Mr. STEIL. So, you would agree that stablecoins are not securities, based on your answer, correct?

Mr. HOMER. Correct.

Mr. STEIL. Thank you. I think that is important for the record. Let me shift gears, if I can, to you, Mr. Portilla. I am assuming you have had an opportunity to review the ranking member's alternative proposal ahead of this hearing?

Mr. PORTILLA. I have.

Mr. STEIL. Did you review the section of the legislation entitled, "Risk Management for Contracted Services," which requires Federal regulation of payment stablecoin issuers, affiliates, and subsidiaries?

Mr. PORTILLA. I did.

Mr. STEIL. And would you agree that the legislation requires an entity without an existing Federal regulator to be regulated by the Federal Reserve?

Mr. PORTILLA. That is correct.

Mr. STEIL. So is it fair to say that entities that may not issue stablecoins, but instead engaged in other market activities, would end up being regulated by the Fed?

Mr. PORTILLA. Correct, if they provide the services in that section.

Mr. STEIL. And you agree that this is outside the scope of the Fed's normal regulatory activities?

Mr. PORTILLA. It would be a new responsibility for them, right.

Mr. STEIL. Is this even in the Fed's area of expertise?

Mr. PORTILLA. I don't want to speak for them, but to my knowledge, no.

Mr. STEIL. It appears to me to be a bit of a question as to why we would look for the Fed to engage in a regulatory oversight role that is outside their area of expertise, so I appreciate your feedback. I think it is broadly problematic. I think it would further cause market confusion and potentially conflict with other regulators. I appreciate your time.

Mr. Chairman, since you noted I could yield back time with no disgrace, I will yield back to the Chair. Thank you.

Chairman HILL. The gentleman from Wisconsin yields back in a most gracious manner.

The Chair now recognizes the ranking member of the Full Committee, Ms. Waters, for 5 minutes.

Ms. WATERS. Thank you very much, Mr. Chairman. Mrs. Reynolds Hand, the Democratic compromise draft that I posted for today's hearing includes several critical provisions that are missing from the Republican draft. One of them would give the Federal Reserve Board the option to decline any registration of a State-approved stablecoin issuer. This aligns bank and non-bank stablecoins issuers with the current process we have for State-chartered banks and would ensure a strong Federal floor for registration. This means that stablecoin issuers could not engage in regulatory arbitrage. Can you elaborate on the importance of giving a Federal agency, like the Fed, a role to approve payment stablecoins before they are issued?

Ms. HAND. Thank you for the opportunity, Ranking Member Waters. In this country, there is a strong role for Federal regulators in approving all banks, the backbone of consumer finance, and the cryptocurrency and the Fed overlap when banks hold cryptocurrency as an asset on their balance sheets. And in the last couple of years, we have seen that when the traditional banking system and decentralized finance (DeFi) begin to intersect, it can create significant questions and structural issues. For example, although stablecoins may peg their value to the same real-world asset, stabilization mechanisms vary greatly.

This is one of the reasons payment stablecoins can impact the monetary system, and why we need a role for the Fed in the same way that there is the role for Federal regulators to approve State- chartered banks. There has to be a role for the Fed to review applications and reject them if they don't meet certain requirements.

Ms. WATERS. Thank you. That is an important issue that we are dealing with, with stablecoins. Let me move on. One of the most-devastating impacts of the FTX collapse resulted from the intentional lack of customer asset segregation. The assets of FTX's customers were used to fund personal loans for senior FTX staff, and funneled into FTX founder, Sam Bankman-Fried's, trading from Alameda Research. Customer funds were commingled with the firm funds. When the exchange collapsed, commingled customer assets largely vanished, and to this day are difficult to recover. Some are unlikely to be recovered at all. However, this is a different experience compared to FTX's Japanese customers, who were largely made whole because Japan passed strong regulations against the commingling of funds. Unfortunately, only a few months after the FTX collapse, the Republican stablecoin draft allows for the creation of stablecoins but has no oversight of the wallets where they would hold them.

Can you describe the importance of customer protections, like the complete segregation of customer assets by issuers, exchanges, wallet providers, and other entities? What are the dangers presented by firms commingling customer assets with the firm's own assets?

Ms. HAND. Briefly, custodial structures help protect consumer funds, and it is important because if a firm goes bankrupt, then consumers need to have a clear pathway to be able to recover their funds. And as we saw in the court rulings in Celsius, there is a clear gray area there, and we need clear rules of the road, particularly around custodial wallets. We need a segregation of consumer funds in these instances.

Ms. WATERS. So, commingling is a serious issue. Again, we have seen it with FTX, and we should be aware of that, and that is one of the issues we have to resolve in this legislation. Thank you, and I yield back the balance of my time.

Chairman HILL. The gentlewoman yields back. The gentleman from Illinois, Mr. Casten, is recognized for 5 minutes.

Mr. CASTEN. Thank you, Mr. Chairman. Mr. Homer, I want to just run through some hypotheticals with you as I think about some of the mechanics of this bill. If I am a broker-dealer of conventional equities, am I legally allowed to unilaterally halt trades on a volatile security, or do I need to have the regulator's approval for that?

Mr. HOMER. I don't have the answer to that question right now.

Mr. CASTEN. It is a, "yes." I hope you would agree that we would not want to give broker-dealers that power, give them the conflicts of interest. I asked the question, because from March 10th to March 12th, Coinbase made a unilateral decision. Coinbase was registered as a broker-dealer, and made a unilateral decision to pause USDC conversions after Circle disclosed that they had $3.3 billion in exposure to Silicon Valley Bank and they lost their peg. So, exchanges that are registered as broker-dealers in the crypto space, is there something unique about crypto? Should they have authorities that we do not give to other broker-dealers because of the conflicts of interest? It is not a super-complicated question.

Mr. HOMER. I think that anyone who is registered as a broker-dealer should experience a consistent set of regulatory requirements.

Mr. CASTEN. Okay. That is great, because the implication of that is that cryptocurrency exchanges should comply with securities laws and be registered with the SEC.

Second question. Mr. Homer, I was trying to read your background, and I don't know how long you have been at this firm, but you are the managing member of a venture capital fund. Is that right?

Mr. HOMER. That is correct.

Mr. CASTEN. And does your fund invest in crypto firms?

Mr. HOMER. In companies, yes. Not in tokens.

Mr. CASTEN. Okay. Do you receive or buy cryptocurrency tokens in connections with those investments?

Mr. HOMER. We have not.

Mr. CASTEN. Would you be open to that possibility with the right deal and the structure?

Mr. HOMER. I would not preclude it.

Mr. CASTEN. Okay. So if you did, once your contractual lockout ends, however long that is, you are then allowed to sell those tokens to the public immediately, right?

Mr. HOMER. It depends on how it is structured, but in your scenario, it sounds like yes.

Mr. CASTEN. I am just saying, legally; I am not saying how you might structure it. I am just saying, just as a venture fund, when your lockout period is over, you can sell that back, because if you were subject to SEC registration, those would first have to comply with Section 5 of the Securities Act and be registered with the Commission, right?

Mr. HOMER. I am guessing the answer is yes.

Mr. CASTEN. And furthermore, if you are getting paid in these crypto tokens, you don't have to comply with Section 12(a)(1), which would allow individuals who might feel that they had been defrauded, to sue you if there was something that they thought was a fraudulent conveyance or something else, right?

Mr. HOMER. I am following.

Mr. CASTEN. I raise all this because this lack of regulation in the crypto space—and I am not saying anything about you personally; it is just that you are the only venture capital guy up here—allows crypto startups to bypass regulations so that you could exit your position quicker even if it is defrauding investors. I am not saying that is your intent, but I am saying there are a whole lot of problems here with this lack of regulation, and I, frankly, don't think that either of these bills go far enough to address that.

The next piece is, do non-bank stablecoin issuers have a fiduciary obligation to meet customer demands for redemption?

Mr. HOMER. Yes, they would.

Mr. CASTEN. Okay. When Circle saw that SVB was going under, they tried to pull the $3.3 billion out. They were meeting their obligations to their customers, right?

Mr. HOMER. Yes.

Mr. CASTEN. Okay. Now in the case of SVB, $3.3 billion wasn't going to make a difference in the overall troubles that they were facing. But it is really easy to imagine that money being in a smaller bank or stablecoin succeeding the way we are talking about, and it all of a sudden being a massively destabilizing event on our fiscal system if you have this obligation to pull, right?

Mr. HOMER. Yes. This is why I think prudential supervision is important and prudential supervisors are the best set of regulators.

Mr. CASTEN. No, I think there is a different issue here. There is a good case for blockchain. There is a good case for Web3. There is a good case for distributed ledger. Why are we creating a currency within that mix that has access to our financial system? If you want to buy this pen for three magic ponies, we can do that. That is a barter transaction. Why are we connecting this to our financial system?

And Ms. Reynolds Hand, I guess I will just end with you, if you have any final thoughts on what risks we expose ourselves to?

Chairman HILL. The gentleman's time has expired. I am just sensitive to it since we have votes on the Floor, and I want to get to Mr. Green. So, I yield to Mr. Green for 5 minutes, and at the end of Mr. Green's questioning, the hearing will be adjourned.

Mr. GREEN. Thank you, Mr. Chairman. And I thank the witnesses for appearing. Let me just start by indicating to you that I am very much concerned about the stability of our currency. There is a war for currency supremacy. This war for currency supremacy is one that involves countries that don't always have our best interests at heart, and our reserve currency is preeminent. It is something that we treasure, but opposition in the world is dependent, to a certain extent, on the validity of our currency. People trust us because of the validity of our currency. They invest in our country and our Treasury because of the validity of our currency. So, my concern emanates from this belief that we must proceed with caution. And as we proceed with caution, we must keep in mind that the system we have, has some flaws, but it isn't bad, it isn't the worst system in the world, and I want to be very careful about how we do things to impact a system that is fairly efficacious. It seems to be something that others would love to have. In fact, they try to create it on a daily basis.

Here is my concern for you non-bank financial companies. Non-bank financial companies can issue stablecoins. What kind of power are we giving to non-bank financial companies when they can issue stablecoins? In a sense, someone might say they are issuing currency of a sort.

Why don't we just start with you, Ms. Reynolds Hand? Could you kindly comment on what we will be doing when we do this?

Ms. HAND. Congressman, I completely share your concern. I was on the Hill as a staffer during the last financial crisis, and since then, we have continued to see the proliferation of non-bank financial services, i.e., fintech, explode and eclipse, in some parts, the traditional banking system. And that is a primary reason why we do need some clear rules of the road. Unfortunately, via the mobile phones that consumers walk around with, consumers now have access to these digital assets, but they severely lack protections. And that is the only reason why there is a need for legislation and clear rules of the road in this space, but I do share your concern about how we proceed forward.

We have a strong financial system. We have some solid principles around which that system is based, and yet, because there are clear vagaries and gaps in terms of regulation and rules, new entrants are always entering the space and engaging with consumers without adequate protections.

Mr. GREEN. Thank you.

Ms. Wang, just an additional predicate before you respond. Our fiat currency is the envy of the world. Everybody wants the dollar. If we allow circumstances to continue unabated without the legislation, what can happen? Give me your opinions as to how this can metamorphose into something.

Ms. WANG. Thank you, Congressman, for the question. I think, on a global level, countries want to de-dollarize. They want to have the dollar be less influential in international trade. So if there are competing stablecoin legislations elsewhere, they are going to promote their own national currency and de-emphasize dollar-denominated stablecoins, so having this bill would allow us to stay competitive.

And as you said, the U.S. dollar is the reserve currency. I believe that, and I understand the concerns you have, but don't paint all of us with the same brush, because there are those of us who may be non-bank financial institutions, but we are community organizations. We are grassroots organizations. We support the work of local community banks. And we are doing that work to ensure that the U.S. dollar works harder, and by allowing us an opportunity to also—

Mr. GREEN. Let me recede. The chairman has been very generous. Thank you, Mr. Chairman. Mr. Chairman, I am a supporter of Ms. Waters' bill, and I am going to do what I can to help us to have a good piece of legislation.

Chairman HILL. I thank the gentleman from Texas. And I thank our witnesses, and I appreciate your patience. We have two votes on the House Floor. We have other Members who do have some questions. It won't be that many. We ask your indulgence. And the committee will stand in recess until after votes.

[recess]

Mr. TIMMONS. [presiding]. The committee will come to order. I now recognize myself for 5 minutes.

My colleagues across the aisle have asserted that all stablecoin issuers must register with Federal regulators before conducting business, including those that are regulated on the State level.

Mr. Homer, although stablecoin issuers that go through the State pathway are not also required to register with the Federal Reserve under the McHenry proposal, would there still be a significant role for the Federal Reserve to play, and what would that role be under the McHenry proposal?

Mr. HOMER. Thank you for the question, Congressman. There would be a significant role for the Federal Reserve to play in that scenario, namely, in two ways, the first being backstop supervision. The Federal Reserve would have access to the books and records of the companies that are regulated by the States and would have the ability to step in if they felt they were not being properly regulated, and also would be able to take enforcement actions.

Mr. TIMMONS. Thank you for that. Both proposals noticed to this hearing establish a list of factors that Federal regulators must utilize when considering an application for a given stablecoin issuer. Again, Mr. Homer, would you discuss the factors in the McHenry proposal and how they provide the bounds for what the banking regulators may and may not consider?

Mr. HOMER. Yes. Thank you for the question. The factors include the financial requirements, including reserve assets, etc. It includes character and fitness of management and includes an analysis of risks and benefits.

Mr. TIMMONS. And what are the consequences of including more open-ended or subjective factors, as contemplated in the Waters proposal?

Mr. HOMER. There are tradeoffs associated with doing that. For companies/applicants in the space, it makes it more difficult to understand your requirements and to put together a complete application, and for regulators, it would give them significant discretion to reject applications based on a potentially unlimited set of reasons.

Mr. TIMMONS. And if our objective is to provide certainty and a framework from which the market can operate, would the McHenry or the Waters proposal accomplish that objective?

Mr. HOMER. Yes. I think that the first noticed proposal would provide greater certainty.

Mr. TIMMONS. Thank you. One risk identified in the President's Working Group report on stablecoins was a lack of transparency. Mr. Portilla, would you describe how the draft legislation attached to this hearing could help provide transparency and how that transparency will in turn give consumers confidence in stablecoins?

Mr. PORTILLA. Yes, for sure. Thank you for the question. I think both of the proposals noticed for the hearing include provisions that would enhance transparency for stablecoin issuers. In particular, there is a requirement to disclose the issuers' redemption policy, to establish procedures for timely redemption, to publish the monthly composition of the reserve assets, and to provide attestations of the accuracy of the report of those disclosures to the relevant regulators. And there are, in fact, criminal penalties associated with false attestations, which should provide significant incentive for management to make sure those attestations are correct and provide accountability for when they are not.

Mr. TIMMONS. Thank you for that. Some claim that the State regulatory framework under Chairman McHenry's legislation will be insufficient to address anti-money laundering and financial crime issues with stablecoins.

First of all, the bill requires all stablecoin issuers to be treated as financial institutions for purposes of the Bank Secrecy Act, which levels a number of requirements including registering with the Financial Crimes Enforcement Network (FinCEN) and submitting suspicious activity reports (SARs). States may add additional enhanced requirements under their framework.

Mr. Homer, again, can you describe how the New York DFS considers anti-money laundering compliance when determining whether to approve the application of a stablecoin?

Mr. HOMER. Yes. Thank you for the question, Congressman. It is one of the most significant factors. New York is a leading regulator in the space, but it is not an easy regulator, and it is still very challenging for companies to get approval in New York, and rightfully so. This risk area is one of the most-significant areas, I would say, where it takes companies a while to really adequately meet those requirements. The requirements in New York are incrediblyrobust, and look at the policies and procedures a company has related to this issue, including ensuring that adequate KYC is being done at the time of issuance and at the time of redemption of stablecoins.

Mr. TIMMONS. Thank you for that. I yield back.

And the Chair now recognizes Representative Nickel from North Carolina for 5 minutes.

Mr. NICKEL. Thank you so much, and I want to thank Chairman Hill and Ranking Member Lynch for holding today's hearing, and thanks so much to our witnesses for being with us here today. I am hopeful that we can come to a bipartisan agreement on stablecoin legislation as the status quo is both risky for consumers and stifling for innovation. We also have the opportunity with stablecoins to reinforce the dominance of the U.S. dollar as the global reserve currency, all while making it stronger, more accessible, and more competitive.

We are already seeing challenges to the dollar's influence with the share of dollars in global currency reserves decreasing from 66 percent to 58 percent since 2015. If the dollar were to lose its status, there would be negative impacts across our economy, in addition to national security concerns. The dollar is the asset underlying 98 percent of stablecoin transactions. If stablecoin use increases, the dollar will only get stronger. By passing bipartisan stablecoin legislation to provide regulatory clarity and improve the infrastructure on which the U.S. dollar travels, we can ensure it remains the global reserve currency.

Mr. Homer, I would like to start with you. Can you please describe the role of stablecoins in supporting U.S. dollar-dominance?

Mr. HOMER. Thank you for the question, Congressman. I believe stablecoins are the most significant way in which the U.S. Government can ensure continued dollar dominance in a digital era. We are seeing a transformation of money from analog to digitized, and we are moving toward a digital native era which stablecoins represent, and we see that in the form of users in other countries wanting to hold U.S. dollar-denominated stablecoins. If we want to maintain our ability to engage in economic statecraft and use tools like sanctions, having stablecoins be issued from the U.S. is essential to that objective.

Mr. NICKEL. And you kind of touched on this in your answer here, but I would like to hear more about the national security implications of the dollar losing its status as the global reserve currency. How would this impact the effectiveness of our sanctions, having stablecoin legislation?

Mr. HOMER. Yes. Sanctions tools are only effective to the extent to which payment instruments or payment systems are denominated in dollars or involve U.S. leadership. And if significant stablecoin issuance were to happen outside of the U.S., it would lessen our ability to use sanctions tools in the future.

Mr. NICKEL. I think we are really close on a lot of the different forms of legislation that I am seeing, but I am concerned about the Federal Reserve Board having a very broad veto authority to decline registrations by State-regulated issuers of stablecoins. Are there certain scenarios where you think the Fed should have this veto? How can we narrow this to keep a strong Federal floor while also preserving North Carolina's ability to regulate stablecoins in our dual banking system? Mr. Homer?

Mr. HOMER. I think we can look at some of what has happened in other countries, places like the EU or even Singapore, where there is a tiered approach, where issuers who are below a certain threshold can be subject to subnational regulation or a different regulatory regime. But once you have reached a systemic or significantly-important level, then I certainly think enhanced oversight would make sense.

Mr. NICKEL. Thank you so much, and I yield back.

Mr. FLOOD. [presiding]. The gentleman yields back. And I now recognize myself for 5 minutes. First of all, I want to thank all of the witnesses who are here today.

My number-one concern on stablecoins is ensuring that there is a robust State pathway for stablecoin issuers. Much like the dual banking system, there should be an opportunity for stablecoin issuers to be regulated at both the State and the Federal level. This is important for a few reasons. First, it makes it possible for States like Nebraska to come up with our own regulatory frameworks for stablecoins. Over time, States will learn from each other and adopt best practices from their neighbors, reaching consensus on common issues and, ultimately, better regulation across-the-board.

The problem with only Federal regulation is that it doesn't undergo that natural iterative process. Instead, you have this topdown approach that might be more difficult to change over time, and that is not a system that fosters innovation. And it is hard to argue that America's financial system built on this two-tier Federal and State approach to regulation of banks hasn't yielded great results for the United States. In the case of stablecoins, we are talking about something that we may very well have to revisit periodically as blockchain technology and its use cases continue to develop. It is much better to have several State regulators working in this area than just one or two Federal regulators, who may require an act of Congress to make technical changes.

Additionally, it creates opportunities for States to develop specialization. Regulators can establish a reputation as knowledgeable on a particular set of issues. Such a reputation can then become a reason for a business to locate in that State. My hope was to develop precisely that kind of environment in Nebraska when, as a State senator, I wrote and passed the Nebraska Financial Innovation Act.

Ms. Wang, in your testimony, you compared the State regulatory pathway for stablecoins to the, "laboratories of democracy," that Constitutional scholars write about. Can you elaborate on this point and on the importance of allowing States to write some of their own rules?

Ms. WANG. I think that the State regulatory pathway is absolutely critical for grassroots innovation, without which we would not be able to have true bottom up diversity and inclusion of our financial system. These grassroots innovators are for the community, of the community, and by the community, and we should be allowed to experiment and to fail safely.

Under Chairman McHenry's proposal, we would already be required to meet the minimum Federal guidelines for issuance under Section 4, backstopped by the Federal Reserve Board in the event of exigent circumstances. In my view, there is no constitutional reason to preempt State regulation in the case where not all stablecoins may necessarily implicate interstate commerce.

Mr. FLOOD. Thank you for that.

Mr. Homer, one of the claims we hear occasionally, and we heard it today about a State pathway for stablecoin issuers, is that it could lead to a so-called race to the bottom. As a former New York State Department of Financial Services executive deputy superintendent, would you mind just responding to that claim?

Mr. HOMER. Yes. I think under the proposal, it would be very hard to imagine a race to the bottom. A Federal standard is established, which is basically the New York standard. New York best practices that have been tried and tested and proven would be established as a Federal floor.

Mr. FLOOD. I would like to close by speaking just a little bit on the two drafts noticed for this hearing. I am glad that Ranking Member Waters and the Democrats have come forward with a stablecoin proposal. I am hopeful that we can take serious steps on this and lead because the United States needs to lead here, not just for our country, but for the world.

However, when I look at Ranking Member Waters' bill, the State pathway includes the following provisions: number one, State-issued stablecoins must register with the Federal Reserve, and the Fed is responsible for creating registration requirements; number two, the Federal Reserve is directly responsible for regulating and examining the State issuer; and number three, the Federal Reserve may, if it chooses, enter into a memorandum of understanding where it could delegate some of the regulatory enforcement obligations to the State regulator if they so choose.

To summarize, the Federal Reserve would be in charge of processing applications, regulation, examination, and enforcement. That is the whole ballgame. The Federal Reserve would be responsible for all of the nuts and bolts of regulating and overseeing State issuers, and they would delegate some of their responsibilities only if they so choose. To be frank, that is just not a State pathway in any meaningful sense. And my number-one focus as a member of this subcommittee is to maintain a State pathway, an opportunity for all of these laboratories in our democracy, all of the different States to be able to participate in a true two-tier system.

With that, I yield back. And I now recognize Mr. Torres.

Mr. TORRES. Thank you, Mr. Chairman. There has been a suggestion that State regulators cannot be trusted to regulate State-licensed stablecoins without parental supervision from the Federal Reserve. If State regulators can be trusted to regulate State-chartered banks, then why can they not be trusted to have analogous authority with respect to stablecoins? Regulating fractionally-reserved banks that take on credit risk strikes me as far more complicated than regulating a fully-reserved stablecoin that takes on no credit risk at all.

So, Mr. Homer, can you explain to me why there should be a strong State option for fractional reserve banking but no strong State option for stablecoin issuance? Imagine you are ChatGPT, and I am a 5-year-old. Please explain the logic that underlies that criticism.

Mr. HOMER. It is really hard to make a rational argument for that. I think, as you point out, fully-reserved stablecoins and other forms of non-bank companies don't hold the same type of risk as fractional companies. And States like New York have really been the primary chartering entities or regulators for non-bank companies in the history of the United States.

Mr. TORRES. So, it certainly should be possible to set a Federal floor that prevents regulatory arbitrage that prevents a race to the bottom without subordinating State regulators, like DFS, to the Federal Reserve?

Mr. HOMER. Absolutely.

Mr. TORRES. Okay. And let's be crystal clear, State regulators, like DFS, have been more effective at crypto regulation than the Federal Government. The SVB collapse happened under the watch of the Federal Reserve. The FTX Ponzi scheme happened under the watch of the Federal Government. Federal regulators, like the SEC, spent more time targeting Kim Kardashian than Sam Bankman-Fried. So, the evidence is crystal clear that we have been poorly served by the SEC's regulatory ambulance chasing. As far as the lessons learned from FTX, those lessons should inform the development of a Federal framework for regulating stablecoins. A lesson learned, stablecoins should be fully reserved, and those reserves should consist of 100 percent cash or cash equivalents. Raise your hand if you agree.

[Hands raised.]

Mr. TORRES. I imagine all of you agree. Lesson learned, stablecoin reserves should be verified not only by self-attestation, but also by a third-party audit. Please raise your hand if you agree.

[Hands raised.]

Mr. TORRES. Customers should have the right to immediately redeem a stablecoin on a one-to-one basis. Please raise your hand if you agree.

[Hands raised.]

Mr. TORRES. And stablecoin issuers should be prohibited from lending, leveraging, or commingling customer funds. Please raise your hand if you agree.

[Hands raised.]

Mr. TORRES. A federally-licensed stablecoin issuer should have a single Federal regulator. Too many cooks in the kitchen creates regulatory confusion and duplication. If a stablecoin is a currency regulated by the Federal Reserve or trust regulated by the OCC, it should not simultaneously be a security regulated by the SEC. Do you agree with that, Mr. Homer?

Mr. HOMER. I do.

Mr. TORRES. There is a common misconception that crypto threatens the status of the dollar as the world's reserve currency, but the experience of stablecoins has shown the exact opposite. The fact that most stablecoins are pegged to the dollar reinforces rather than challenges the reserve status of the U.S. dollar.

Mr. Homer, you actually referenced competition. My understanding is that, in the realm of financial technology, China has largely been now competing with the United States. The only fintech battleground on which the United States has been now competing, China has been the domain of digital currency, stablecoins. Dollar stablecoins have been far more successful than China's failed attempt at a CBDC. Is that a fair assessment?

Mr. HOMER. It is a fair assessment, and it is because that is what people throughout the world want. People want U.S. dollar-denominated stablecoins.

Mr. TORRES. And a common refrain heard from critics of crypto in Congress is that crypto has no use case. But it seems to me that blockchain enables real-time transactions, stablecoin tokenizes the dollar, and the ability of a tokenized dollar to move at the speed of the blockchain creates a better, cheaper, and faster payment system, which would include the potential for better, cheaper, and faster remittances for the lowest-income Americans. Is that a fair assessment?

Mr. HOMER. A very fair assessment, and we are already seeing that happen.

Mr. TORRES. Would anyone else like to comment on the use cases of stablecoins?

[No response.]

Mr. TORRES. The enthusiasm is overwhelming, I know. The 8 seconds you have, okay. Other than that, I yield back.

Mr. FLOOD. The gentleman yields back. I would like to thank all of our witnesses for their testimony today.

The Chair notes that some Members may have additional questions for this panel, which they may wish to submit in writing. Without objection, the hearing record will remain open for 5 legislative days for Members to submit written questions to these witnesses and to place their responses in the record.

Also, without objection, Members will have 5 legislative days to submit extraneous materials to the Chair for inclusion in the record.

With that, this hearing is adjourned.

[Whereupon, at 11:18 a.m., the hearing was adjourned.]

Appendix

Testimony of Delicia Reynolds Hand, Director, Financial Fairness, Consumer Reports Before the United States House Committee on Financial Services, Subcommittee on Digital Assets, Financial Technology and Inclusion

""'Putting the 'Stable' in 'Stablecoins:' How Legislation Will Help Stablecoins Achieve Their Promise.'""

Thursday, May 18, 2023
Rayburn House Office Building Washington, DC

Good morning Chairman McHenry, Ranking Member Waters, Subcommittee Chairman Hill, Ranking Member Lynch, members of the Subcommittee and Committee.

Thank you for this invitation to testify. I'm pleased to be back to participate in this important conversation about the overarching regulatory framework for stablecoins.

My name is Delicia Reynolds Hand, and I currently serve as the Director of Financial Fairness at Consumer Reports where I lead the organization's work in digital finance. There, I am evolving Consumer Reports' evaluation and ratings model to evaluate and rate digital financial products and services. In an equitable digital economy, digitized financial products let consumers spend, save, borrow, and invest safely in ways that respect their privacy and data, provide the benefits they expect, protect them from discriminatory and predatory practices, and help them achieve their financial goals.

At Consumer Reports, we are beginning to demonstrate what fintech products and services actually do for consumers and how they rate alongside each other. Additionally, we are beginning to identify new norms and concrete best practices for industry and determine whether these products and services facilitate positive consumer outcomes, as some of them promise.

As I previously testified on April 19, 2023, the convergence of new technologies and new forms of assets have made cryptocurrencies particularly appealing for consumers whom traditional finance has never appropriately served. For the most vulnerable consumers, often underserved or ignored by traditional finance; there is added complexity and risk; and yet some put their faith and trust in the promise of digital assets and financial products and services which make cryptocurrencies accessible to consumers. However, in a 2022 Consumer Reports nationally representative survey of 3,208 U.S. adults, we found and reported that African Americans were significantly more likely than other racial/ethnic groups to say they had owned crypto in the past but don't anymore. In a volatile and stressed economic environment, consumers and investors are at an even greater risk in the absence of rules, and the non-compliance with regulations, to protect them and prevent the misuse or exploitation of these assets.

Stablecoins and Consumers

Even in the areas meant to usher in more stability, consumers can be caught in a vicious cycle of the boom and bust of crypto experimentation. Since this subcommittee's last conversation on stablecoins, Europe has succeeded in bringing crypto-assets, crypto-assets issuers and crypto-asset service providers under a regulatory framework. And, today we have two bills under consideration; one of which has stripped out important safeguarding principles and consumer protections. We must avoid repeating history in an area so volatile and potentially disruptive, with high and rising interest rates, workers losing jobs to emerging technologies, markets are collapsing; and U.S. companies race to the bottom and chase the lowest common denominator oversight in states and overseas markets as the places from which to drive innovation in a regulatory light environment. We need the strongest federal rules to ensure a solid foundation upon which companies and consumers can safely and reliably participate in digital assets and in the digital marketplace.

There continues to be no uniform and meaningful regulatory framework governing stablecoins in the U.S., potentially creating significant risks for the entire country. While these new technologies may hold some promise, the potential risks are significant, including an unlimited supply of tokens and coins serving as collateral for loans, rigid self-executing smart contracts, non-existent and unaudited reserve requirements, lack of interoperability requirements, inadequate disclosures, conflicts of interest and self-dealing, and the creation of debtor-creditor relationships. These risks are simply too big to place on unsuspecting consumers, especially if this entire ecosystem continues to be uniformly unregulated prudentially, and non-compliant with market regulations. This very complexity tied to the state of these technologies - crypto adolescence - given asymmetry of information, makes it hard to assess risk particularly for the most vulnerable communities.

Common Sense, Consumer First, Comprehensive Regulation

Consumer Reports urges this committee to bridge the gap and to continue to work in a bipartisan manner to develop common sense legislation to achieve effective and comprehensive regulation of stablecoins. This is especially important for responsible innovation, financial stability, and financial inclusion. Appropriate regulation, supervision and oversight needs to be implemented before stablecoins become a greater risk to financial stability, safety and soundness, and the smooth functioning of payment systems.

The presence of two draft bills published in advance of this hearing signals that instead of one conversation, we are potentially going down divergent paths. To be clear, this space will be regulated and frameworks will be developed. The question is whether the development of oversight will be driven by a crisis, or collaboration.

There are alas two bills; one of which seems to be a compromise on many issues. The other of which seems to have pared back prior areas of agreement. Both, as drafted, will introduce some important prudential standards into the regulation of the issuance and trading of payment stablecoins. But, as previously emphasized, anything but the most comprehensive will be insufficient and put consumers and investors at risk.

Strong Regulatory Process and Federal Oversight Are Needed

Consumer Reports supports the updates to the committee drafts which include federal regulatory review to ensure the safety and soundness of stablecoin issuers. While the committee draft would allow federal regulators to bring an enforcement action following the failure of a state regulator to do so, we encourage the adoption of provisions in the compromise bill granting the Federal Reserve Board authority to reject state licenses. Not including these provisions creates regulatory arbitrage which could drive a race to the bottom instead of a race to the top. In consumer finance, fiat currency payments are now 24/7 and borderless, which makes payments easier for consumers. These are lessons we have failed to learn from the past. On these basic matters for stablecoin payments, keeping with the tradition of congressional application of the Commerce Clause, the law should be the same across all 50 states.

For example, while the committee bill outlines an application process for becoming a stablecoin payment issuer for depository institutions and non-depository institutions, the bill could go further to include specific key requirements that parallel the requirements for traditional banking. Starting a new de novo bank is a long organization process, requiring permission from several regulatory authorities. While both drafts retained some equivalent requirements to provide information about the organizers, senior management team, and capital adequacy, we urge the committee to retain requirements to promote diversity and inclusion found in the compromise bill. We support the addition of requirements for federal regulators to issue rules related to risk management infrastructure.

Second, while the committee bill does outline a role for federal oversight, it does not require entities that become stablecoin issuers to be insured depository institutions (IDIs). While the bill does require that the parent companies of bank subsidiaries authorized as stablecoin issuers be IDIs, it provides no such requirement for non-bank issuers. By contrast, the compromise bill draft attempts to make it clear that issuers shall not represent stablecoins as insured deposits while the committee draft does not even require this disclosure. Allowing deposit-like instruments to not only be uninsured, but issued by banks that insure other deposits, will inevitably create confusion for customers, especially during periods of financial distress, and will inevitably provide less protection for consumers that choose to buy, sell, or hold stablecoins that do not offer such insurance.

Last, in creating the regulatory framework for stablecoin payments, the administrative process outlined is insufficient and would hamstring regulators and prevent meaningful regulation of this space. Specifically, it requires collective interagency rulemaking for which the first set of rules need to be issued within 180 days of this bill becoming law. Interagency rulemaking can often be a long and complicated process, and especially so in newer areas of authority. Additional time or the ability of individual FIRREA regulators to promulgate rulemaking jointly or independently would increase the likelihood of these entities receiving meaningful regulation.

Additionally, given the high risk nature of this space, there should be a clear role for the FSOC.

Strong Consumer Protections Needed

While this bill sets up a regime to approve issuers of payment stablecoins, it does not outline adequate consumer protections for payment activities conducted or facilitated by the issuers or their coins. Currently, most blockchain technologies are deliberately designed and built without the capacity to reverse transactions, as many are append-only digital ledgers. But, being able to prevent, cancel, replace, or override a transaction is a critical function necessary to ensure payment system operators are able to prevent fraud, conduct chargebacks, or facilitate disputes over payments. Additionally, the bill does not include stablecoins in the rules under the Electronic Funds Transfer Act.

We urge the committee to move forward with the provisions in the compromise bill that require stablecoin payment regulation to be technology neutral to promote interoperability and to ensure stablecoin arrangements share common features with the traditional financial system and are not walled off into each institution's specific system. They should be issued on interoperable technology protocols to prevent market concentration and potentially restrict data collection.

The lack of interoperability would be an impediment to consumer access. Consumers who have come to rely on interoperability in fiat currency payment systems, should have the same benefits in stablecoin payments.

Related, we request that the committee adopt language associated with strong oversight of custodial wallets. The committee draft does not cover all assets held by custodial wallets - a key point of interaction that consumers have with stablecoins. While custodial wallets may help consumers keep track of their keys, this has created a legal gray area that must be clarified.

The law must prevent a debtor-creditor relationship from being formed and this should be clear in required disclosures.

Further, this bill's consumer and investor protections should be improved, specifically to give stronger protections than continued reliance on outdated check the box notice and disclosure regimes like Gramm-Leach-Bliley Act (GLBA), require more than monthly looks into an issuer's reserve portfolio, and provide stronger bankruptcy protections for consumers. The bill lays out protections for holders of stablecoins in the event of an issuer becoming insolvent. But other parts of the bill appear to undermine those protections. For example, the committee should include clarifying language that requires stablecoin issuers account for the full segregation of customer assets when co-mingling client assets received by coin holders in omnibus accounts to withdraw or use those funds to cover various administrative costs. This is not a new idea.

Under the Dodd-Frank Act, Congress mandated LSOC, that is legal segregation with operational commingling, to protect swaps customers. Protections must apply to both customer positions and any other customer assets, and is needed to reduce risk to other customers. We do not need another Lehman Brothers. Otherwise, without these protections, in the event of issuer insolvency, a bankruptcy court could reasonably view, and the Court in Celsius already has held, that those commingled funds are grounds for giving the company and its creditors priority access to those funds, rather than stablecoin holders, the rightful owners.

We encourage the committee to move forward with language in the compromise bill that imposes a timeline to allow consumers to redeem their stablecoins and other customer assets within 24 hours of notifying the stablecoin provider. We suggest adding clarifying language to specify that consumers should be able to redeem to be able to access their funds within a calendar day, and not just one business day, especially if a redemption were to occur after the close of business on a Friday, or holiday weekend.

Some additional key improvements we would like to see

1) Increased activity limitations. While the bill does restrict risky activities such as pledging, rehypothecation, or reusing reserve and custody assets, it does not clarify the position of consumers when a stablecoin payment provider becomes bankrupt. A consumer's use with any stablecoin issuer or provider must not create a debtor-creditor relationship.
2) There should be no exception to the prohibition of certain convicted individuals to participate in stablecoin payments. The committee draft being considered removed the prohibitions altogether.
3) This bill should make clear that the Federal Reserve Board's authority over stablecoin payment issuers would come second to that of the prudential regulators and consumer protection regulators.

Explicit Recognition of SEC Authority Is Needed

Given the agency's active role and number of interventions brought on behalf of consumers, we are pleased to see that the compromise bill retains provisions that the SEC is not limited in its authority by the bill to regulate stablecoins but there is no further clarity. The compromise bill also requires theSEC to be consulted in a study of endogenously collateralized stablecoins, which are stablecoins backed by other crypto such as bitcoin or ether.

Many stablecoins function and have been marketed as investment products like swaps or function like money market funds (MMFs). The compromise bill contains a provision suggesting that the legislation shall not infringe upon the authority of other regulators to assert jurisdiction over stablecoins, but we believe that such language is insufficient protection for other agencies' regulatory authority. This bill needs to explicitly clarify on how and when the SEC, as a market regulator, can and should regulate stablecoins. When these products mirror traditional finance products or services - like swaps and MMFs - and are traded on secondary markets, to assert jurisdiction over an issuer, asset or related party, the SEC would have to first establish jurisdiction in court, then seek enforcement action. Regulation by enforcement is expensive, inefficient, and is the antithesis of promoting good governance and capital formation. Not accounting for the SEC and market regulatory aspects of stablecoins is bad for consumers and will create additional regulatory uncertainties.

I urge the Committee to resume bipartisan efforts to achieve robust and comprehensive oversight of stablecoin to ensure consumers and investors are adequately protected.

Thank you again for the opportunity to testify today.

Written Testimony of Matthew Homer, Managing Member of the Department of XYZ, Former Executive Deputy Superintendent for Research & Innovation, New York State Department of Financial Services Before the United States House of Representatives Committee on Financial Services Subcommittee on Digital Assets, Financial Technology and Inclusion in a Hearing Entitled Putting the "Stable" in "Stablecoins": How Legislation Will Help Stablecoins Achieve Their Promise

Heldon May 18, 2023

Good morning, Chairman McHenry, Ranking Member Waters, Subcommittee Chairman Hill, Subcommittee Ranking Member Lynch, and members of the Subcommittee on Digital Assets, Financial Technology, and Inclusion.

Thank you for the opportunity to participate in this hearing. It is an honor to offer my testimony on payment stablecoins, the role they play in the ongoing evolution of financial services from analog to digital, and principles to consider as you contemplate how best to regulate the space. Money and payments form the basic plumbing of our modern economy, so there is an obvious national interest in getting this right.

My name is Matt Homer. I was previously the Executive Deputy Superintendent for Research & Innovation at the New York State Department of Financial Services (NYDFS), where my responsibilities included overseeing the Department's licensing, supervision and examination of digital asset related companies. Earlier in my career, I was a federal bank regulator in the FDIC's Division of Depositor and Consumer Protection. Today, I am an investor and advisor to startup companies and the Managing Member of the Department of XYZ, a venture capital firm that invests in early stage companies building the next generation of financial systems. We help founders in the space build in a compliant manner.

I first became familiar with stablecoins through my experiences regulating these products at the NYDFS. As this Committee is aware through previous testimony, New York State was one of the first jurisdictions in the world to regulate the digital asset space generally, as well as stablecoins specifically, and as such it has confronted many of the same issues this Committee is exploring. Our work on stablecoins included evaluating the suitability of these instruments to be issued by regulated entities as new products, which ultimately led the Department to publish stablecoin guidance in June 2022, following my tenure. I believe New York's approach provides a useful model for others to consider.[1]

My experience as a regulator taught me that fiat-backed stablecoins represent an important but incremental improvement in the concept of money. They may also represent the first major real-world asset to be tokenized in a market that is moving in the direction of many different types of real-world assets becoming tokenized, meaning a right of ownership or entitlement being recorded on a public blockchain. In some ways, stablecoins are not so different from the stored value products many people already use and are familiar with, such as gift cards or prepaid cards. The question of how to effectively regulate

---

[1] https://www.dfs.ny.gov/industry_guidance/industry_letters/il20220608_issuance stable coins.

stablecoins has a more clear and straightforward answer than one may find in considering how to regulate other parts of the digital asset ecosystem. Because of this, and because stablecoins are an entry point into the broader digital asset ecosystem, they represent a logical starting point for a federal framework to regulate the industry overall.

New York's experience shows that it is possible to effectively regulate stablecoins using common-sense and time-tested regulatory practices. For example, New York's regulatory framework for stablecoins includes three major prongs: (1) reserve requirements, to ensure the assets backing stablecoins are held on a segregated basis on behalf of customers, are fully reserved on a one-to-one basis, and are comprised of cash deposits and/or other cash equivalents; (2) redemption rights ensuring that stablecoin users have the right to redeem their stablecoins on a one-to-one basis for US Dollars in a timely manner; and (3) public transparency requirements including monthly attestations from independent CPAs certifying the value of reserves, their composition, the quantity of outstanding stablecoins, and whether the reserve is adequate to fully back the number of outstanding stablecoins. The stablecoin issuers covered by these standards are required to hold a license or charter, subjecting them to robust bank-like supervision and examinations from NYDFS to ensure they operate in a safe and sound manner. It is encouraging to see these requirements and practices generally reflected in the legislative drafts that have been circulated on this topic thus far.

As stablecoins increasingly come to represent an improved payment system, a number of real-world use cases are coming into focus. For example:

- Stablecoins as a store of value for individuals living in economies with high or volatile rates of inflation who prefer to hold their savings in US Dollars;
- Stablecoins for peer-to-peer payments for cross-border remittances, shopping, and other expenses; and
- Stablecoins for business payments for employees, vendors, and suppliers, including cross border.

Based on my experiences regulating stablecoins, as well as my more recent work with early-stage companies and founders in the broader digital asset space, I believe there are eight important principles that should guide federal legislation on this topic and which will help payment stablecoins achieve their promise. I will discuss three of these for which my background offers unique insights, and touch upon the remaining five later in my testimony.

First, stablecoin legislation should recognize the dual banking system as an inherent feature of the American economy that benefits consumers, innovators, and markets. The dual banking system refers to the parallel regimes under which state and federal banking regulation co-exist. In the case of insured depository institutions, a bank may receive a national charter from the OCC or be chartered by a single state. When chartered by a state, the bank will also have a primary federal supervisor, either the FDIC or one of the Federal Reserve banks.

Non-depository institutions are not always subject to federal supervision, but are often supervised by multiple states if they intend to operate in more than one jurisdiction. Of course, all firms offering consumer financial products and services are subject to the federal consumer laws and the jurisdiction of the Consumer Financial Protection Bureau – regardless of the provenance of their license or charter. The parallel system of state and federal regulation supports economic growth by providing innovators and founders optionality that can reduce barriers to launching new products on a small scale before rolling them out at national scale. It benefits consumers by providing access to financial services tailored to local needs and protects them because states are able to move more quickly to fill regulatory gaps. Finally, it benefits markets by encouraging healthy competition.

The legislative draft I have seen preserves this dynamic, which has been so important in making the American financial system an engine of innovation and experimentation. It also provides a model for what digital-era dual regulation could look like, not only for stablecoins but other products and services as well. Importantly, it would establish a federal floor in the form of a national standard, but would allow states to license and supervise stablecoin issuers and set even tougher rules within their own jurisdiction. A federal baseline of standards and backup supervision means consumers can expect a consistent set of foundational protections regardless of where a stablecoin issuer has received their license or charter. It also avoids a race to the bottom whereby some states could seek to attract issuers by offering the lightest possible touch.

Second, stablecoin legislation and implementing regulation should promote competition in the market and the competitiveness of the US system. I'll start with competition. The stablecoin market has so far trended toward oligopoly. Today, two issuers alone make up over 80% of the market for US

Dollar-denominated stablecoins.[2] Legislation should promote competition by providing pathways for new players to enter the space and challenge incumbents. This could help address the risks typically associated with oligopolistic markets, including rent-seeking and systemic risks that emerge when activities are concentrated into only a few hands. In an environment where we are seeing community and regional banks consolidating or being acquired by mega-banks, it would be wise to think proactively about opportunities to promote a competitive system from scratch when it comes to novel developments in the industry. One idea would be to create a safe harbor for new entrants to test new products or services at limited scale and with limited customers before requiring comprehensive regulation in order to expand to the general public at greater scale.

I'd also like to touch on competitiveness as a distinct concept from competition. Here I am referring to the desirability of the US as the preferred jurisdiction from which to launch stablecoins. The stablecoin market will continue to evolve and grow globally, regardless of what approach our government chooses to take. Dollar-denominated stablecoins can be issued offshore, backed by US Dollars held in offshore bank accounts, from jurisdictions with lower regulatory barriers to entry. Therefore, it is in the American interest to ensure that issuers of US Dollar-backed stablecoins remain in the US so we can regulate stablecoins on our own terms. One way to promote this objective would be to add competitiveness to: (1) the official mandates of federal regulators as it relates to stablecoins; and also to (2) the set of criteria to be used by federal regulators when considering whether to license a stablecoin issuer. For example, regulators could be required to consider the risks associated with not granting a license, including the possibility that the same stablecoins could be issued offshore and therefore expose consumers to greater risks than if they were issued from the US.

Third, regulatory capabilities need to keep pace with developments in the market. One of the aspects of regulating digital assets that most intrigued me when I worked at NYDFS was the possibility of supervising the space more effectively using digital tools and technologies.[3] The digital nature of firms in this space provides an opportunity to further evolve the capabilities of regulators and create incentives for the market to self-correct through transparent public data. For example, I previously mentioned monthly attestations of stablecoin reserves, but we could conceivably move toward

---

[2] https://www.theblock.co/data/decentralized-finance/stablecoins.

[3] https:/www.dfs.ny.gov/system/files/documents/2021/11/2021_techsprintlessons_learned. pdf.

real-time or near-real-time dashboards that provide insight into the assets backing a stablecoin, or into the financial condition of the issuing firm, at any given moment in time. Such data could even be made publicly available, encouraging a race to the top among stablecoin issuers wanting to show they are the safest and most secure. This type of regulatory transformation would require new skill sets and new types of collaborations. One tool that some regulators have been using is the "techsprint," in which regulators invite industry technologists and other experts to co-create new digitally-native supervision tools. Efforts like this could be helpful for standing up technologies and data-collection methods to allow regulators to monitor stablecoins and supervise their issuers.[4]

I'd like to now more briefly highlight five other principles that are just as important as the preceding three.

Fourth, legislation and regulation should provide predictability, reliability, and protection for users. The drafted legislation goes a long way toward achieving this, and it mirrors many of the best practices that have been tested in New York.

Fifth, legislation and regulation should provide oversight and accountability for issuers. Here too the draft legislation provides opportunities for meaningful oversight of issuers, including through a backstop of federal regulators in the case of entities authorized at the state level. This will hold sub-national regulators accountable to standards of effective supervision in order to discourage market participants from engaging in regulatory arbitrage.

Sixth, legislation and regulation should ensure transparent and accountable government. The public should have confidence in our regulatory system, and this can be achieved through greater transparency and public engagement, such as by requiring that any regulations be developed through public notice and comment.

Seventh, legislation and regulation should establish national consistency. As already mentioned, this proposal would achieve this through a national floor, while also preserving the dual banking system.

And eighth, legislation and regulation should promote national security and advance the influence of the US Dollar. Compliance with rules related to the detection of illicit finance and money-laundering should be required. And the spread of US Dollar-backed stablecoins should be embraced as an

[4] https://www.jbs.cam.ac.uk/faculty-research/centres/alternative-finance/publications/early-lessons-on-regulatory-innovation-to-enable-inclusive-fintech/.

important means of maintaining and growing the influence of the US Dollar as the world's reserve currency.

Thank you again for the opportunity to be here. I look forward to your questions.

Testimony
of the USDF Consortium for the hearing entitled
Putting the "Stable" in "Stablecoins": How Legislation Will Help Stablecoins Achieve Their Promise of the Subcommittee on Digital Assets, Financial Technology and Inclusion of the House Committee on Financial Services

May 18, 2023

Introduction

Chairman Hill and Ranking Member Lynch, the USDF Consortium5 welcomes the opportunity to testify at this hearing entitled "Putting the 'Stable' in 'Stablecoins': How Legislation Will Help Stablecoins Achieve Their Promise."

Today's hearing comes at a critical moment. Distributed ledgers leveraging blockchain technology hold tremendous promise to improve financial services, offering faster, cheaper, and more efficient products that can help promote financial inclusion, drive growth in our communities, and support the role of the U.S. Dollar as the global reserve currency.

To date, most blockchain innovation has occurred outside of the regulated banking sector in novel cryptocurrency markets. These markets have provided testing grounds that have proven the efficiency and stability blockchain technology can deliver. However, financial services only deliver value when they facilitate real-world activity such as helping small businesses invest and grow or helping families purchase homes.

To leverage blockchain for real-world transactions, you first need a trusted form of digital money that exists natively on blockchain. This need is

[5] The USDF Consortium is a membership-based association of insured depository institutions. Our mission is to build a network of banks to further the adoption and interoperability of a bank-minted tokenized deposit (USDF™). We believe that blockchain technology can make payments more efficient and improve traditional banking, expanding access to safe and affordable financial services.

what led to the rise of stablecoins and has driven the policy discussion around the creation of a central bank digital currency (CBDC). However, the debate on how to "digitize the dollar" is too often pitched as a binary choice between these two options.

We believe there is a third option that leverages the way money already exists in our economy. While we tend to think of paper money, the reality is that most money in the U.S. is already digital and exists in the form of bank deposits. Today, bank deposits represent 73% of money in our economy.6

At the end of the day, blockchain is a ledger technology. Banks have long relied on ledgers to record value and facilitate transactions. Over the years, this technology has evolved from paper-based ledgers, to on-premises servers, to cloud infrastructure.

We believe blockchain is the next evolution in ledger technology. By recording a traditional bank deposit on blockchain, we can bring many of the benefits of stablecoins to the real economy while maintaining the numerous benefits and protections that our two-tier banking system provides today.

Unlike stablecoins, these tokenized deposits are not designed to connect the broader crypto ecosystem to the real world. Tokenized deposits are back-end technology designed to improve the delivery of traditional banking services. Tokenized deposits will not trade on exchanges, and in the case of USDF, will not be held directly by the public. Like all bank deposits, they are a liability of an insured depository institution.

Bank deposits are a cornerstone of our monetary and financial systems that support the dominance of the U.S. Dollar around the world. They play a critical role in supporting banks' ability to lend into the communities that they serve. Today these loans are an important funding source powering $2.5 trillion in residential mortgages, $2.5 trillion in business lending, and $2 trillion in consumer lending.7 These loans are a critical driver of economic growth and social mobility.

Banks are subject to stringent regulation and proactive oversight. This includes bank capital and liquidity requirements as well as technology risk management regulation designed to control for the prudential and operational risks associated with deposit taking. Tokenized deposits also maintain the privacy protections associated with our two-tier banking system today.

---

[6] Money as measured by M1 (Federal Reserve H.6).

[7] FDIC Quarterly Banking Profile 4Q 2022. https://www.fdic.gov/analysis/quarterly-banking-profile/index.html.

Tokenizing deposits facilitates the creation of a real-time blockchain-based payments infrastructure that can significantly improve the delivery of traditional banking services. The use of blockchain infrastructure facilitates:

- Faster, cheaper payments, ensuring that consumers and businesses can have real- time access to their funds.
- Programmable payments, allowing for the automation of complex transaction flows that can reduce fraud and improve transparency.
- Atomic settlement, leveraging blockchain to record other traditional banking assets can break down silos between systems making it easier to buy and sell these assets.This added liquidity allows for new funding options that can lower the cost of credit, expanding access to affordable financial products.

We can only realize these benefits when innovation is delivered responsibly and regulatory guidelines are clear, certain, and consistently applied. Legislation like that being discussed today is an important step to ensuring stablecoins are delivered responsibly and that consumers remain protected.

It is important that these efforts do not inhibit the adoption of blockchain for other applications in traditional banking like tokenized deposits. To that end, we are pleased to see that the draft legislation makes the critical distinction between stablecoins and tokenized deposits, and that it affirms banks' ability to leverage blockchain for traditional banking applications.

Unfortunately, there is not currently a clear regulatory path for banks to adopt blockchain- based solutions. As highly regulated institutions, any new offering by banks is subject to scrutiny, but blockchain initiatives are held to a higher standard. Although they have clear authority to do so, any bank wishing to undertake a blockchain project must receive formal regulatory approval. This process does not exist when utilizing other technologies. We encourage Congress to work with the banking agencies to ensure that there is a clear and credible path for banks to adopt blockchain technology.

Competition breeds innovation and we believe there is a role for many forms of money, both novel and traditional. We look forward to working with Congress to ensure that there is an appropriate regulatory framework for novel assets like stablecoins and to provide regulatory clarity for banks to adopt new technologies.

Policymakers Should Distinguish Blockchain from Cryptocurrencies

Blockchain technology is flexible infrastructure that can support a variety of applications. Despite this, it is most commonly associated with novel assets like cryptocurrencies. It is important to clearly distinguish blockchain infrastructure from crypto assets as policymakers consider appropriate regulation for these novel technologies and assets. By analogy, we do not regulate the internet, but instead regulate the numerous industries that leverage the internet to deliver their services. Similarly, a one-size-fits-all approach to blockchain that seeks to address the risks that have emerged from novel crypto markets may limit its use in other industries.

Policymakers are right to focus on the risks that have emerged from these novel crypto markets. Blockchain facilitated the creation of new financial services products that fall outside the perimeter of existing regulatory and supervisory structures. Many of these services resemble traditional financial services products but are not supervised for the same risks because they are offered by new kinds of businesses that do not fit under traditional licensing and supervisory regimes. Despite this, the risks presented by the use of blockchain are rarely novel. In many cases, existing banking regulation is well suited to manage these risks.

At its core, blockchain is a ledger technology that can facilitate a wide range of activities, each presenting a different risk profile. The risks associated with delivering a novel asset in an unregulated market are very different from the risks associated with a regulated financial institution offering a traditional product, like deposits.

In banking, we believe that blockchain technology can provide efficiencies that lower the cost of offering financial services, allowing banks to reach more Americans with safe, affordable, and inclusive products. Blockchain is not a silver bullet, but it has a unique ability to break down silos, facilitating real-time collaboration between financial institutions. In particular, we believe that blockchain can facilitate the following activities:

- *Faster, cheaper, safer payments.* As a shared system of record, blockchain can facilitatethe near real-time transfer of value. USDF leverages a proof-of-authority model where trust is already established, eliminating the need for participants to undertake costly computing exercises to create skin in the game. This allows for rapid transactions at minimal cost. We believe this can be particularly valuable in supporting business-to- business transactions, which are still largely paper based today.

- *Programmable payments.* Blockchain can integrate smart contracts, enabling banks toautomate the execution of complex payments based on real-world conditions. For example, smart contracts could be used to automate the payments process associatedwith buying a home. Today, a buyer sends money to escrow, and an escrow agent calls individual banks and confirms wires to all of the various parties that participated in thetransaction. With a smart contract, we can deliver each payment to the right party theminute a contract is signed.
- *Atomic settlement.* Blockchain adds additional value when used as a system of recordfor other traditional banking assets (like loans). Today, banking infrastructure is a system of siloed proprietary databases. These silos create friction when a transaction requires moving assets in multiple systems at the same time. A buyer will not release funds until they are sure the asset has moved in a separate system of record.

Blockchain allows for both payments and assets to be recorded on the same system of record. This allows a buyer to trade their dollars for an asset in real time without settlement risk because the transfer of money and the purchased asset move in the same block.

Incorporating atomic settlement into traditional banking assets makes it easier to buy and sell those assets. By making these assets more liquid, we add new funding options that lower the cost of credit, expanding access to affordable financial products.

Blockchain also has potential to ensure the continued competitiveness of community banks. A key force driving industry consolidation is the large, fixed cost of technology investments. Large institutions have better ability to spread these investments over a large customer base. As shared infrastructure, blockchain changes this equation, promoting a focus on the value of individual customer relationships. This is similar to cloud technology, which helped level the playing field for small businesses by offering flexible and scalable infrastructure.

Bank Deposits Should Play a Central Role in The Creation of Any Digital Dollar

Financial innovation adds value only when it helps facilitate real-world economic activity like buying capital goods, hiring employees, or purchasing a home. Before blockchain can make a positive impact on the real world, we need a safe, reliable, and trusted form of payment that exists natively on chain. This has led to demand for blockchain native "cash equivalents" that can be used as a means of payment and a store of value.

This demand led to the development of stablecoins and has driven a policy dialogue on whether the U.S. should issue a CBDC. While we believe there is room for many forms of digital money in a modern economy, commercial bank money (i.e., bank deposits) plays a critical role as the dominant form of money in our economy today.

Despite the recent turmoil, bank deposits are subject to a strong and tested regulatory regime and play a prominent role in supporting the availability of credit. These benefits are why bank deposits make up 73% of money in the U.S. economy today. We believe they will continue to play a dominant role as money is developed natively on blockchain.

The existing U.S. monetary and financial system provides numerous benefits to consumers and the broader economy, and supports the important role that the U.S. dollar plays around the world today. Tokenized deposits (sometimes referred to as deposit tokens or dollar tokens) allow us to bring the benefits of bank deposits on-chain by creating a representation of an existing bank deposit on blockchain. Tokenized deposits can take many forms; some might be held by the customers of the bank while others may only be used by financial institutions to create blockchain-native payments rails. In the initial implementation of USDF, no customers will engage directly with the blockchain just as they do not engage directly with existing payments rails today.

In a recent speech Sir Jon Cunliffe, Deputy Director for Financial Stability at the Bank of England, notes that tokenized bank deposits "might offer some or all of the functionality and efficiency claimed for stablecoins, allowing bank deposits to compete better with non-bank payment coins."[8] Given the important role that bank deposits play in our economy today, we believe it is

[8] Bank of England. "The Shape of Things to Come: Innovation in Payments and Money – Speech by Sir John Cunliffe," April 18, 2023. https://www.bankofengland.co.uk/speech/2023/april/jon-cunliffe-keynote-speech-at- the-innovate-finance-global-summit.

critical that bank deposits are able to compete with novel forms of tokenized money.

Tokenized deposits have the following features which make them an attractive form of money in a digitized economy:

Banking Regulation Ensures That Deposits Are Safe

Bank deposits are backed by robust capital and are subject to a regulatory regime that ensures liquidity and solvency. For banks, the implementation of blockchain technology does not fundamentally change the nature of banking or how regulation controls for the risks associated with it. Banks are heavily supervised to ensure they deliver the numerous consumer protections associated with digital payments.

Moreover, the bank regulatory structure is designed to maintain important broader public policy objectives. For example, under the Community Reinvestment Act and other laws, banks have long demonstrated their unique ability to support underserved communities. These laws are directly tied to bank deposits.

Bank Deposits Support Credit Creation

Banks play a critical role in our economy, engaging in maturity transformation. Banks take short-term assets in the form of deposits and use those funds to extend long-term assets in the form of loans.

When a bank makes a loan, it creates new money in the form of a deposit in the borrower's account that did not previously exist. That deposit in turn can be used to power additional lending. The amount of deposits that can be used to support additional lending is determined by the capital the bank must hold to support new loans. Today, the core capital (leverage) ratio for FDIC-insured institutions is near 8.7%.[9] This system, called fractional reserve banking, means that a $1 deposit can power more than $10 of lending. These loans allow businesses to invest in new employees or capital goods that create jobs and drive economic growth.

The New York Federal Reserve staff reinforced the importance of this in a post, in which they argued in favor of tokenized bank deposits. The post notes, "In this post, we argue that if DLT [distributed ledger technology] platforms are the transfer mechanism of the future, then it seems worthwhile

---

[9] FDIC Quarterly Banking Profile, FDIC QBP Graph Book, https://www.fdic.gov/analysis/quarterly-banking-profile/graph-book/2022mar/QRE GCAP.html.

to find the best possible money that can be used on that transfer mechanism. We suggest that tokenized deposits might be a fruitful avenue to pursue."[10]

The only scalable way to bring traditional financial assets on-chain is to leverage the banking system to support that by tokenizing existing bank deposits.

Bank Deposits Maintain Privacy

There exists an inherent tension between the need to protect the privacy of those conducting transactions with the need for the transparency necessary to combat illicit finance.

Policymakers have the difficult task of determining the appropriate balance of these competing concerns.

Today, this careful balance is maintained through the two-tier banking system. Banks are trusted custodians of their customers' most sensitive data and are subject to enhanced regulatory requirements to designed to protect the privacy of financial data such as the Gramm-Leach-Bliley Act.

Banks also have an affirmative responsibility to combat illicit finance. The Bank Secrecy Act requires banks to implement a risk-based program to prevent money laundering and the financing of terrorism.

In certain instances, banks are required to share data with the government through the filing of Suspicious Activity Reports, Currency Transaction Reports, or similar programs. The instances where banks are required to share this data with the government is subject to important legal guardrails designed to protect privacy.

Congress Should Ensure There Is a Clear, Credible Path for Well-Regulated Institutions to Offer Responsible Products

As policymakers work to unlock the potential of blockchain they should focus on an approach that promotes innovation while maintaining critical protections. Banking regulation already provides a robust regulatory structure for the delivery of digital money. Congress should ensure that applicable protections are applied in novel markets while taking care that any legislation

[10] Federal Reserve Bank of New York, The Future of Payments Is Not Stablecoins (Feb. 7, 2022), https://libertystreeteconomics.newyorkfed.org/2022/02/the-future-of-payments-is-not-stablecoins/.

does not inhibit the adoption of blockchain for other applications that are already well- regulated.

The Draft Legislation Is an Important First Step Towards Creating an Appropriate Regulatory Structure for Stablecoins

The legislation being discussed today is an important first step towards creating regulatory clarity that addresses the risks demonstrated by recent stablecoin failures. We offer the following feedback on the draft legislation and stand ready to work with Congress to advance policies that can promote responsible innovation:

1) A consistent theme of the legislation is ensuring that stablecoin issuers fully reserve against the stablecoins that have been issued. We believe this is a prudent step to ensure that stablecoins remain backed by high-quality assets.
2) The definition of "payments stablecoin" used in draft legislation is quite broad. Despite clarifications in the recent draft to distinguish tokenized deposits, there is a risk of capturing bank deposits recorded on blockchain. Banks are subject to stringent capital and liquidity standards that allow them to use deposits to fund loans. If banks are required to fully reserve against tokenized deposits, it would limit banks' ability to lend into the communities they serve.

   We were pleased to see clarifications in the text that recognize the critical distinction between stablecoins and tokenized deposits. We support language that ensures any legislation does not impede banks authority to engage in permissible activities including:

   - accepting or receiving deposits and issuing digital assets that represent deposits;
   - utilizing a distributed ledger for the books and records of the insured depository institution and to affect intrabank transfers; and
   - providing custodial services for payments stablecoins, private keys of payments stablecoins, or reserves backing payments stablecoins.

   We would respectfully urge Congress to strengthen this language by amending the definition of "payments stablecoin" to make explicit that the activities mentioned above would not be considered a payments stablecoin.

3) We also appreciate the clarification that any assets held in custody should not be recorded as a liability on a bank's balance sheet and should not be subject to additional capital charges.

Congress Should Urge the Banking Agencies to Create a Clear Path for the Approval of Blockchain- Based Activities

Banks are often slower to adopt new technologies than other industries. This is not for a lack of interest or skill but due largely to the fact that banks are so heavily regulated. Technology companies can bring nascent technologies directly to customers, iterating daily and fixing bugs after releases are made. Before releasing new products, banks must perform countless rounds of testing and ensure that their approach is aligned with regulatory expectations.

While caution is warranted given the important role that banks play, the standard for approval for blockchain-based activities is putting banks at a competitive disadvantage. Currently, banks must obtain formal approvals from their regulators prior to offering any blockchain product, a standard that does not exist for any other technology.[11] To date, no clear set of expectations has been determined for regulatory approval and few approvals have been given.

Since creating these policies, the federal banking agencies have been careful to highlight that banks are "neither prohibited nor discouraged from providing banking services to customers of any specific class or type," but have put out a series of statements, rules and reports highlighting the risks when banks engage in crypto-related activates.

- Joint Statement on Crypto-Asset Risks to Banking Organizations (1/3/23): Highlights safety and soundness risks of holding cryptocurrencies or dealing with crypto clients.[12]

[11] The OCC's Interpretive Letter 1179 requires OCC-regulated banks to obtain supervisory non-objection prior to engaging in any permissible crypto-related activity. OCC Interpretive Letter 1179 (Nov. 18, 2021), https://www.occ.gov/topics/charters-and-licensing/interpretations-and-actions/2021/int1179.pdf. The FDIC's FIL-16-2022 requires banks to notify the FDIC for supervisory feedback prior to engaging in any crypto-related activities. FDIC FIL-16-2022 (Apr. 7, 2022), https://www.fdic.gov/news/financial-institution-letters/2022/fil22016.html. The Federal Reserve similarly requires all its regulated banks to notify the Federal Reserve for supervisory feedback prior to engaging in any crypto-related activities. Federal Reserve SR 22-6 (Aug. 16, 2022), https:// www.federalreserve.gov/supervisionreg/srletters/SR2206.htm.

[12] Federal Reserve, FDIC and OCC, Joint Statement on Crypto-Asset Risks to Banking Organizations (Jan. 3, 2023), https://www.federalreserve.gov/newsevents/pressreleases/files/bcreg20230103a1.pdf.

- Federal Reserve Policy Statement and Final Rule (1/27/23, 2/7/23): The Federal Reserveissued a policy statement,[13] which was later published as a final rule,[1410] clarifying that banks cannot hold crypto as principal. The Federal Reserve highlights that banks may beable to issue dollar tokens but that they do not believe banks can meet their obligationson a public, permissionless, or decentralized blockchain.
- The Administration's Roadmap to Mitigate Cryptocurrencies' Risks (1/27/23): The National Economic Council released a statement highlighting its plan to reduce cryptorisk. In the statement, the Council discourages policy that would allow "mainstream institutions" to dive headlong into crypto.[15]
- Joint Statement on Liquidity Risks to Banking Organizations Resulting from Crypto-Asset Market Vulnerabilities (2/23/23): Highlights heightened liquidity risks for deposits from crypto platforms involving customer funds or stablecoin reserves.[16]

These statements focus primarily on the risks associated with the broader crypto markets, but few address the use of blockchain for traditional banking. Despite this, the statements could beinterpreted by the banking industry to set a tone that discourages banks from exploring these technologies.

We recommend that Congress engage to ensure that there is a clear path for regulated entitieslike banks to bring responsible blockchain innovation to market.

Conclusion

Blockchain technology holds tremendous potential to improve financial services. When delivered responsibly, it has the potential to promote financial inclusion and help ensure that the United States remains a global leader.

[13] Federal Reserve, Policy Statement on Section 9(13) of the Federal Reserve Act (Jan. 23, 2023), https://www.federalreserve.gov/newsevents/pressreleases/files/bcreg20230127a1.pdf.

[14] 88 Fed. Reg. 7,848 (Feb. 7, 2023), https://www.govinfo.gov/content/pkg/FR-2023-02-07/pdf/2023-02192.pdf.

[15] National Economic Council, The Administration's Roadmap to Mitigate Cryptocurrencies' Risks (Jan. 27, 2023), https://www.whitehouse.gov/nec/briefing-room/2023/01/27/the-administrations-roadmap-to-mitigate- cryptocurrencies-risks/.

[16] Federal Reserve, FDIC and OCC, Joint Statement on Liquidity Risks to Banking Organizations Resulting fromCrypto-Asset Market Vulnerabilities (Feb. 23, 2023), https://www.federal reserve.gov/newsevents/pressreleases/files/bcreg20230223a1.pdf.

Recent bank failures do not lessen this potential. We believe the bank regulatory structure is well-equipped to manage the risks associated with this novel technology and that tokenized deposits are the best way to realize these benefits.

The USDF Consortium was created as a venue for banks to collaborate as they design blockchain infrastructure that will power the future of financial services. We are committed to delivering these innovations responsibly, ensuring that our customers receive the world-class safety and protections inherent in U.S. banking regulation. We are committed to working with Congress to help ensure an appropriate regulatory framework to enable this critical innovation.

Written Statement of David L. Portilla Before the United States House of Representatives Financial Services Committee, Subcommittee on Digital Assets, Financial Technology and Inclusion

Putting the 'Stable' in 'Stablecoins:' How Legislation Will Help Stablecoins Achieve Their Promise

May 18, 2023

David L. Portilla

I am a partner in the law firm of Davis Polk & Wardwell LLP in New York City, where I began my legal career in 2006. As a member of the firm's financial institutions group, I advise banking organizations and nonbank financial institutions on a range of M&A, regulation, policy, enforcement and governance matters – including the full gamut of the prudential regulatory framework. My practice includes a focus on the intersection of financial services laws with innovation and the future of banking and payments, including with respect to stablecoins.

I served as a senior policy advisor to the Treasury Department's Financial Stability Oversight Council office at its launch following the enactment of the Dodd-Frank Wall Street Reform and Consumer Protection Act. I graduated with a degree in literature from Rutgers College and received my law degree from Rutgers Law School.

Today I am presenting my own views, and not those of my firm or any client of the firm.

Chairman Hill, Ranking Member Lynch, Chairman McHenry, Ranking Member Waters and members of the Subcommittee, thank you for the privilege to speak before you today.

Questions about the future of money have rightfully captured significant attention from Congress and other policymakers. As technological advances continue to push the boundaries of how we store, spend and conceptualize money, our regulatory framework also should evolve.

Among the innovations that have garnered attention and market share are products known as stablecoins. These digitally native "coins" are designed to maintain a stable value relative to a reference asset, typically the U.S. dollar.

As with other forms of money resulting from earlier innovations, stablecoins present both risks and opportunities for the financial system and for consumers. In November 2021, the President's Working Group (PWG) on Financial Markets, together with the FDIC and OCC, published their examination of a class of stablecoins referred to as "payment stablecoins" (PWG Report).[17] The PWG Report identified prudential risks associated with payment stablecoin arrangements, such as: run risks; payment system risks; and competitive and financial stability risks. The report also noted various investor protection and illicit finance risks that may be implicated by stablecoin activities. The report recommended that Congress act promptly to pass legislation regulating payment stablecoins.

Following the release of the PWG Report, many legislative proposals have been introduced to regulate payment stablecoins. I commend Chairman McHenry, Chairman Hill, Ranking Member Waters and the other Republican and Democratic members of this Subcommittee for their diligent efforts and the progress that has been made. I believe a bipartisan substantive consensus on payment stablecoin legislation should be achievable.[18]

---

[17] PRESIDENT'S WORKING GRP. ON FIN. MARKETS, THE FED. DEPOSIT INS. CORP., AND THE OFF. OF THE COMPTROLLER OF THE CURRENCY, REPORT ON STABLECOINS 2 (Nov. 2021), https://home.treasury.gov/system/files/136/StableCoinReport_Nov1_508.pdf (defining "payment stablecoins" as "those stablecoins that are designed to maintain a stable value relative to a fiat currency and, therefore, have the potential to be used as a widespread means of payment"). References to "stablecoins" throughout this written statement are intended to refer to "payment stablecoins" unless otherwise noted.

[18] For a discussion of the outlook for stablecoin legislation, as well as the broader context for crypto asset legislation, see Daniel E. Newman & Justin Levine, The 2023 Outlook for Crypto Legislation: What's In and What's Missing from Current Proposals, 31, 4 MKT.

Why Stablecoin Legislation Is Important

Stablecoins represent the latest form of a class of financial products that have long been recognized as "special"[19] and worthy of regulation: products that are (1) payable on demand at par, by their terms or by virtue of market expectations, and (2) readily transferable to third parties.[20]

These types of financial products are special because they pose well-known risks. Chief among them is the risk of a run – that is, requests for redemption en masse that cannot be met due to a mismatch in the liquidity of reserve assets. The ramifications of such a run, along with the potential need for government support, necessarily become more pronounced as stablecoins scale. We can – and should – proactively mitigate these risks by establishing a regulatory framework now, before these risks grow larger and scale makes change more difficult. Importantly, some form of appropriately calibrated prudential regulation can minimize the risk of needing to provide government support to stablecoin issuers during a period of stress.[21]

SOLUTIONS, (Dec. 2022), https://www.davispolk.com/sites/default/files/2023-01/52887102_1.pdf.

[19] I have written about what makes stablecoins special previously. See David L. Portilla & Will C. Giles, The Stablecoins Debate, HARVARD LAW SCHOOL FORUM ON CORPORATE GOVERNANCE (Oct. 24, 2021), https://corpgov.law.harvard.edu/2021/10/24/the-stablecoins-debate/#6b (using E. Gerald Corrigan's 1982 paper, "Are Banks Special?" as a framework for evaluating proper stablecoin regulation); E. Gerald Corrigan, ANNUAL REPORT 1982: ARE BANKS SPECIAL?, FED. RESERVE BANK OF MINNEAPOLIS, https://fraser.stlouisfed.org/title/annual-report- federal-reserve-bank-minneapolis-473/annual-report-1982-18309.

[20] Academics often have focused on deposit taking when analyzing stablecoins. See, e.g., Gary B. Gorton & Jeffery Zhang, Taming Wildcat Stablecoins, 90 U. CHICAGO L.R. (Sept. 30, 2021), https://papers.ssrn.com/sol3/papers.cfm?abstract_id=3888752; Howell E. Jackson & Morgan Ricks, Locating Stablecoins within the Regulatory Perimeter, HARVARD LAW SCHOOL FORUM ON CORPORATE GOVERNANCE (Aug. 5, 2021), https://corpgov.law.harvard.edu/2021/08/05/locating-stablecoins-within-the-regulatory-perimeter/. Others have focused on transforming such shorter-term obligations into longer-term assets like commercial paper. See Bill Nelson, Liquidity Transformation Always Finds That Path of Least Regulation, BPI (Sept. 23, 2021), https://bpi.com/liquidity-transformation-always-finds-that-path-of-least- regulation/.

[21] As a useful analogy, *see* Report of the President's Working Group on Financial Markets, MONEY MARKET FUND REFORM OPTIONS, (Oct. 2010), https://home.treasury.gov/system/files/ 136/archive-documents/10.21-PWG-Report-Final.pdf, (introducing bank-like regulation of MMFs); Report of the President's Working Group on Financial Markets, OVERVIEW OF RECENT EVENTS AND POTENTIAL REFORM OPTIONS FOR MONEY MARKET FUNDS, (Dec. 2020), https://home.treasury.gov/system/files/136/PWG-MMF-report-final-Dec-2020.pdf (examining COVID- 19-related disruptions to short-term funding markets and suggesting prudential-based measures to improve market stability).

This is not to say stablecoins pose precisely the same risks as other products that feature similar characteristics, such as bank deposits. A stablecoin issuer that fully backs outstanding coins with high-quality liquid assets is subject to a meaningfully lower risk of debilitating runs than a deposit-taking bank that uses a fractional reserve model.[22] And stablecoins that operate on decentralized, public networks may present different types of illicit finance risks compared to products that exist purely on traditional payment rails or on private permissioned networks; however, even on public networks, technological solutions to address illicit finance concerns may be available.[23]

I cannot say with certainty whether stablecoins represent part of the future of payments. Yet I feel quite confident that the current legal framework is ill-suited to comprehensively regulate payment stablecoins. Correspondingly, legislation that enables fit-for-purpose payment stablecoin regulation would help foster an environment where this technology can develop and scale. Some of the potential that payment stablecoins offer include: the programmability of money (e.g., increased automation of transactions); an additional means for mobile-based, real-time payments for consumers; and an additional payments infrastructure on which further innovation can occur. If realized, all of these developments may amplify the potential for building a more efficient, competitive and resilient payment system.[24]

---

[22] That said, even high-quality liquid assets, such as three-month Treasury bills, can experience stress during market crises. At the beginning of the COVID-19 pandemic, for example, the five-day moving average bid-ask spread for three-month Treasury bills widened from one basis point to nearly eight basis points. See Dep't. of the Treasury, Bd. of Governors of the Fed. Reserve System, Fed. Reserve Bank of New York, Sec. and Exch. Comm'n, Commodity Futures Trading Comm'n, RECENT DISRUPTIONS AND POTENTIAL REFORMS IN THE U.S. TREASURY MARKET: A STAFF PROGRESS REPORT 15 (Nov. 8, 2021), https://home.treasury.gov/system/files/136/IAWG-Treasury- Report.pdf. This episode demonstrates that caution should be given to assuming some level of maturity mismatch is immune to run risk.

[23] Technological innovations related to blockchain tracing and whitelisting capabilities may offer a viable approach to mitigate these risks. *See, e.g.*, Forge Societe Generale Grp., *EUR CoinVertible (EURCV) Stablecoin White Paper* 18 (Apr. 2023), https://www.sgforge.com/wp-content/uploads/2023/04/SGF_Coinvertible_White-Paper-v1.0.pdf ("[O]nly addresses that are whitelisted by SG-FORGE will be eligible to receive our stablecoins. Such whitelisting process based on the CAST Framework means that SG-FORGE has performed compliance controls (KYC, AML-CFT, sanctions and embargoes) according to Societe Generale Group policies, and has duly onboarded the owner of such address.").

[24] For a discussion of the potential benefits of payment stablecoins and the role regulation can play, *see generally Stablecoins: How Do They Work, How Are They Used, and What Are Their Risks?*: *Hearing Before the S. Comm. On Banking, Housing and Urban Affairs*, 117th Cong. (Dec. 14, 2021) (statement of Jai Massari, Partner, Davis Polk & Wardwell LLP), https://www.banking.senate.gov/imo/media/doc/Massari%20Testimony%2012-14-211.pdf.

Key Issues for Stablecoin Legislation

The remainder of my remarks will focus on what I believe are the key issues that should be addressed in any payment stablecoin legislation.[25] A common theme in my testimony today is that a one-size-fits-all approach is neither necessary nor prudent. I believe payment stablecoin legislation should establish privileges and responsibilities for stablecoin issuers along a spectrum. As a general principle, greater privileges from the government should be coupled with more stringent regulatory and supervisory oversight; a more tailored regulatory approach, on the other hand, should be coupled with appropriately calibrated privileges from the government.

1) Who should be permitted to issue payment stablecoins?

A threshold question relating to the regulation of stablecoins is, quite simply, who should be allowed to issue them? The PWG Report, for example, recommended that stablecoin issuers be limited to insured depository institutions.[26] Since its release, many domestic and international regulatory bodies appear to have shifted away from this recommendation.[27] Indeed, Treasury Under Secretary for Domestic Finance Nellie Liang, a lead contributor to the PWG Report, subsequently acknowledged that an appropriate regulatory structure for nonbank stablecoin issuers could "plausibly address concerns about stablecoin runs and payment system risk."[28]

---

[25] The issues I discuss in my testimony are not exhaustive, and many other important questions remain. For example, even if payment stablecoin legislation is enacted, there would still be questions around other types of stablecoins, such as the various categories of decentralized and algorithmic stablecoins. It is also not entirely clear how the regulation of payment stablecoins might interact with the potential for a future in which central bank digital currencies (CBDCs) or tokenized demand deposits issued by banks, also known as deposit coins, become mainstream.

[26] PWG Report, *supra* note 1 at 2.

[27] See, e.g., FIN. STABILITY OVERSIGHT COUNCIL, REPORT ON DIGITAL ASSET FINANCIAL STABILITY RISKS AND REGULATION (Oct. 2022), https://home.treasury.gov/system/files/261/FSOC-Digital-Assets-Report-2022.pdf; FIN. STABILITY BD., REVIEW OF THE FSB HIGH-LEVEL RECOMMENDATIONS OF THE REGULATION, SUPERVISION AND OVERSIGHT OF "GLOBAL STABLECOIN" ARRANGEMENTS (Oct. 11, 2022), https://www.fsb.org/wp-content/uploads/P111022-4.pdf.

[28] Under Secretary for Domestic Finance Nellie Liang, Remarks at King's College London's Global Banking and Finance Conference (July 5, 2022), https://home.treasury.gov/news/press-releases/jy0850. Under Secretary Liang did, however, caution that bank stablecoin issuance and nonbank stablecoin issuance might have "different implications for financial stability." *Id.*

In addition, many of the legislative proposals released to date have contemplated a dual approach, whereby nonbanks would be permitted to issue stablecoins provided they comply with varying degrees of prudential regulation.[29] These approaches make sense, given that the common conception of a payment stablecoin business (that is, issuance and redemption of an instrument backed by a discrete pool of high-quality liquid assets) is distinct from the business of fractional reserve banking.[30]

Because payment stablecoins typically hold a limited range of reserve assets, the regulatory framework should be designed to address the specific characteristics of this business model and the risk tradeoffs it presents. This principle is true whether the stablecoin issuer is a nonbank entity lacking any affiliation with a banking organization, or a subsidiary or affiliate of a banking organization. For example, the existing minimum, non-risk sensitive leverage capital ratios that apply to banks would likely need to be modified to reduce the potential negative capital implications arising from a direct or indirect subsidiary of a bank or bank holding company issuing stablecoins.[31]

2) Who should regulate payment stablecoins?

The next question that naturally follows is one of jurisdiction: who should be the primary regulator of payment stablecoin issuers? Should stablecoin issuers be regulated at the federal or state level?

---

[29] *See, e.g.*, Sam Sutton, Eleanor Mueller, *McHenry's scaled-back stablecoin plan would give states flexibility,* POLITICOPRO (Apr. 2023), https://subscriber.politicopro.com/article/2023/04/mchenry-scales-back-stablecoin-plan-gives-states-flexibility-00093539?source=email (publishing revised discussion draft of stablecoin bill reportedly being developed by Rep. McHenry); Discussion Draft, S. __ 118th Cong. (2022), https://docs.house.gov/meetings/BA/BA21/20230419/115753/BILLS-118pih-Toproviderequirementsforpaymentstablecoinissuersresearchonadigitaldollarandforotherpurposes.pdf (discussion draft of stablecoin bill posted for Apr.19, 2023 House Financial Services Committee hearing); Lummis-Gillibrand Responsible Financial Innovation Act, S. 4356, 117th Cong. (2022); Stablecoin Transparency of Reserves and Uniform Safe Transactions Act of 2022, S. 3970 117th Cong. (2022); Gottheimer Stablecoin Innovation and Protection Act of 2022, S. __ 117th Cong. (2022).

[30] In contrast, an insured depository institution could (and should be permitted to) issue tokenized deposits.

[31] *See* DAVIS POLK & WARDWELL LLP, *U.S. Regulators Speak on Stablecoin and Crypto Regulation* (Nov. 12, 2021), https://www.davispolk.com/insights/client-update/us-regulators-speak-stablecoin-and-crypto-regulation#:~:text=The%20PWG%20Report%20on%20Stablecoins&text=The%20Report%20announces%20no%20immediate,issuers%20 and%20custodial%20wallet%20providers (explaining challenges for stablecoins associated with the minimum leverage capital ratios that apply to banks today). *Cf.* Economic Growth, Regulatory Relief, and Consumer Protection Act, S. 2155, 115th Cong. (2018) (tailoring the supplementary leverage ratio for custodial banks).

Federal regulation of stablecoin issuers would offer more uniform, consistent rules, whereas state regulation could promote more diversity and innovation in regulation and supervision. Today, for example, the most detailed publicly available prudential guidance and standards regarding stablecoins and related topics have been issued by a state regulator.[32] But the answer to this question need not be binary. Many of the legislative proposals released by Congress to date have followed the model of our dual-banking system. That is, they would establish a framework in which stablecoin issuers could be regulated either (1) directly at the federal level, or (2) primarily at the state level, with an overlay of federal oversight. Options include providing federal regulation as a backup to state regulation or an approach that toggles based on the scale of an issuer. In all cases, the roles of federal and state regulators should be clear to avoid overlap, confusion and inefficiency.

3) Should nonbank payment stablecoin issuers be provided access to the Federal Reserve's payment system or discount window?

The question of who should be entitled to have a master account has emerged as a key policy question for the U.S. financial system. A master account at one of the twelve Federal Reserve Banks is necessary for an institution to have direct access to the Federal Reserve's payment systems, as well as to settle transactions in central bank money.[33] Technological changes in the payments landscape have driven a number of fintech and crypto asset-based companies to seek access to these services.

Granting nonbank payment stablecoin issuers access to master accounts could help them provide more efficient services to their customers. It also carries monetary policy and political implications. Here, again, multiple options are possible. Perhaps legislation could grant nonbank stablecoin issuers with access to Federal Reserve Bank services, but limit those services in both scale and scope. For instance, the absolute or relative amount of reserves that a nonbank stablecoin issuer may invest in central bank deposits

---

[32] See N.Y. DEP'T OF FIN. SERV., GUIDANCE ON THE ISSUANCE OF U.S. DOLLAR-BACKED STABLECOINS (June 8, 2022), https://www.dfs.ny.gov/industry_guidance/industry_letters/il20220608_issuance_stablecoins; N.Y DEP'T OF FIN. SERV., GUIDANCE ON CUSTODIAL STRUCTURES FOR CUSTOMER PROTECTION IN THE EVENT OF INSOLVENCY (Jan. 23, 2023), https://www.dfs.ny.gov/industry_guidance/industry_letters/il20230123_guidance_custodial_structures.

[33] A master account is also a necessary, but not sufficient, condition for an institution to have access to the Federal Reserve's discount window.

could be limited by the Federal Reserve.[34] Or perhaps issuers could be granted access to the discount window, but only at certain times and in limited amounts. Other options include making access to Federal Reserve Bank services available at the option, or based on the scale, of an issuer. In all events, it seems that if a firm is granted access to Federal Reserve Bank services, regulation and supervision should correspond to the level of such access (including with respect to issues such as limitations on affiliations with commercial companies).

4) To what extent (if at all) should payment stablecoins be subject to "deposit" insurance?

Banks offer economic and societal value, in the form of increased money supply and credit, by engaging in the business of maturity and liquidity transformation.[35] But this business model is inherently susceptible to run risk.[36] Deposit insurance was introduced in the U.S. in the 1930s in an effort to mitigate this risk.

A similar form of insurance for payment stablecoins could also help mitigate run risks by making available aspects of the federal safety net to stablecoin issuers. The availability of deposit insurance would thus affect whether other bank-like requirements should be considered. For example, insured banks are subject to extensive capital, liquidity and risk management requirements, as well as activities restrictions, in part to prevent them from externalizing risks through the federal safety net.

Whether some form of insurance is ultimately needed for stablecoins may turn on the nature of the reserves that back them and, relatedly, the degree to which consumers expect their stablecoins to be redeemable on demand at par. As noted previously, a stablecoin issuer that fully backs its coins with high-

---

[34] Similarly, the amount of interest on reserve balances could be limited or capped at a certain amount.

[35] E.g., Kenneth J. Arrow, *The Organization of Economic Activity: Issues Pertinent to the Choice of Market versus Non-market Allocation*, in JOINT ECONOMIC COMMITTEE OF THE CONGRESS OF THE UNITED STATES, THE ANALYSIS AND EVALUATION OF PUBLIC EXPENDITURES: THE PPB SYSTEM 48 (1969) ("The creation of money is in many respects an example of a public good.").

[36] *See, e.g.*, Douglas W. Diamond & Philip H. Dybvig, *Bank Runs, Deposit Insurance, and Liquidity*, 91 J. POL. ECON. 401 (1983) ("It is precisely the 'transformation' of illiquid assets into liquid assets that is responsible both for the liquidity service provided by banks and for their susceptibility to runs.").

quality liquid assets likely poses a meaningfully lower risk of becoming subject to a run than a bank.[37]

5) What insolvency standards should be applicable to payment stablecoins?

Recent high-profile bankruptcies of crypto asset-related companies have brought questions related to the treatment of customer assets in the event of an intermediary's insolvency into stark focus. To the extent payment stablecoins are designed or perceived to be effectively free of credit risk, it would be prudent to provide stablecoin holders with structural priority over an issuer's other creditors. Other important considerations include rehypothecation limits and recordkeeping requirements. In addition, a company that holds stablecoins for customers should be subject to standards to help ensure that a customer's stablecoins are not commingled with the assets of the company and, therefore, to help ensure that the customer's stablecoins would be available to the customer in the event of an insolvency of the company. Existing federal and state laws provide standards for custodians and should be useful in this context. In any case, clear rules and plain-language disclosure and terms are important to provide customers and creditors confidence that their claims will be resolved in a predictable and timely manner.

6) What other legal regimes should apply to payment stablecoins and related products and services?

While I have focused primarily on prudential issues, payment stablecoins and related products, such as wallet and other custodial providers, also present other common regulatory concerns, such as those related to consumer protection and illicit finance. All of these considerations should be thoughtfully explored.

But this does not mean that payment stablecoins should be shoehorned into regulatory frameworks that were crafted for entirely different products. Nor does it mean that we should be vexed to paralysis in trying to answer questions that, frankly, permeate traditional finance – such as how to regulate any service provider that is adjacent to a regulated firm.

Ultimately, consumers and our financial system more broadly will be best served by focusing on the above issues where I believe we can find common

---

[37] *But see supra* note 6.

ground to establish a regulatory framework that treats payment stablecoins as such – payment instruments that are subject primarily to prudential regulation and supervision, rather than, for example, as an investment asset subject to market and investment management regulation.

Thank you again for the opportunity to participate today. I look forward to addressing your questions.

Testimony of Fennie Wang Founder and CEO of Humanity Cash before the House Financial Services Committee, Subcommittee on Digital Assets, Financial Technology and Inclusion

Hearing titled: Putting the 'Stable' in 'Stablecoins:' How Legislation Will Help Stablecoins Achieve Their Promise

May 18, 2023

Humanity Cash Testimony to the House Financial Services Committee

Thank you Chairman McHenry, Chairman Hill, and Ranking Member Lynch and Ranking Member Waters for giving me this opportunity to testify. People like me rarely have this opportunity. I do not represent a large corporation or an industry organization. I am an independent lawyer and entrepreneur working on grassroots projects. My name is Fennie Wang and I run a small organization called Humanity Cash that works with community organizations to design local currencies that make money work harder for local communities. In my previous life, I worked as a research analyst on Wall Street, then a Wall Street lawyer before jumping into the deep end of digital currencies and start-ups. In that capacity, I have worked at a number of prominent projects, including stablecoins, where I developed my knowledge of the technology.

i. A brief introduction to existing stablecoins

Decentralized stablecoins are typically digital currency protocols that attempt to issue digital tokens with a price target of $1 USD (or some other real world fiat currency), and achieves that target price through mechanisms that are primarily executed through smart contracts on a blockchain. Within the universe of decentralized stablecoins, there are different designs and mechanics for achieving the price target with different financial risk profiles. For example, some are called algorithmic stablecoins, whereby the stablecoin protocol uses predefined rules or algorithms to adjust its supply in response to demand in order to keep the stablecoin at its price target. For example, if the stablecoin rises above the price target, the algorithm may increase the stablecoin's supply by minting new stablecoins and removing related collateral tokens from the market. When the stablecoin falls below the price target, the algorithm may reduce supply by burning stablecoins in exchange for inflating the related collateral tokens. Oftentimes with algorithmic stablecoins, the stablecoin's supply is moderated by its relationship with a second token of fluctuating value that functions like collateral. Importantly, the second token is also issued by the same protocol; therefore its value and market behavior are endogenous to the stablecoin protocol and highly correlated with market behaviors of the stablecoin. This is inherently risky, given the highly correlated nature of the two tokens.

In contrast, other types of decentralized stablecoins are collateralized by digital assets and other digital currencies whose value are exogenous to the stablecoin protocol itself. Under these models, in order to generate one stablecoin (with a target value of $1 USD), a user must deposit into a smart contract another digital currency of value as collateral e.g., $1.50 worth of ETH. These protocols typically require overcollateralization due to the volatile prices of the underlying assets used as collateral. The stablecoin is collectively backed by all collateral locked into the protocol, which is a collection of different digital currencies that are approved as collateral types. A complex governance system of the stablecoin protocol is required to ensure that the price target of $1 is met, given the varying market characteristics and price volatility of the underlying portfolio of collateral. Such a system may be considered, in some aspects, to be less risky than an algorithmic model, where there is no collateral whose value and market dynamics are exogenous and orthogonal to the value or dynamics of the stablecoin itself. However, crypto-collateralized stablecoins still have inherent price risks, as the price target of

$1 USD is inherently asymmetrical with the value and price movement of the underlying collateral.

The only way to fundamentally reduce the price risk is to have the underlying collateral of a stablecoin match the price target e.g., one stablecoin with a price of $1 USD is backed by one dollar (or dollar equivalent). These types of stablecoins are sometimes called centralized or custodial stablecoins because the peg mechanism is dependent on assets that are inherently off-chain and therefore not publicly verifiable in the same way that on-chain collateral may be verified. In short, the peg is dependent on the market's trust that the issuer of the stablecoin indeed has sufficient dollar assets to match the amount of stablecoins issued. Where that trust is established, primarily due to clear regulatory standards and market reputation for adhering to those standards, these types of dollar-backed stablecoins become go-to choices for transactions.

In all of the above examples, the predominant use case for the stablecoins is crypto-trading. For example, with crypto collateralized stablecoins, users are essentially borrowing against their collateral in order to generate additional liquidity in the form of stablecoins e.g., instead of having to sell ETH in order to buy another digital asset, a user can purchase the digital asset using a stablecoin that is issued against her ETH, and then when a profit is generated, she can return the stablecoin to retrieve her ETH collateral, capturing any upside value of her ETH. While a centralized dollar-backed stablecoin can be used for real world payments given its dollar reserves, these are still primarily traded on exchanges and most of its volume is still in the cryptomarkets where it is used as a dollar proxy for on-chain transactions.

However, with a clear regulatory framework, banks and other institutions will feel more confident in issuing stablecoins for payment use cases, which would have great public benefit by reducing the cost of transactions and increasing the speed of settlement. Currently, the U.S. lags behind many other countries in digital payments. For example, in the U.S. the predominant and cheapest form of payment transactions use a settlement network called the Automated Clearing House (ACH), which can take 5-6 business days for payments to fully clear. In contrast, in the European Union, the predominant payments network is the Single Euro Payments Area (SEPA), which can process payments in one business day. The difference of a few business days can make or break many small businesses that have tight working capital requirements. Therefore, laying the groundwork for regulated stablecoins for payment use cases would have enormous benefit to ordinary Americans and Main Street.

ii. A short primer on community currencies

During the pandemic, I resolved to use my knowledge of blockchain and stablecoins to build non-speculative applications that could improve the lives of ordinary Americans. To understandthe role that alternative currencies can play in a non-speculative way, I studied the history of community currencies in the United States and around the world, which have existed long before the advent of Bitcoin and blockchain.

A fundamental tension of all ecosystems — whether monetary systems or blockchain ecosystems— is the balance between efficiency and resiliency. A broadly used currency is highly efficient given its breadth, yet it may be at the expense of local economies that provide resilience in the broader economic ecosystem. For example, a community that relies more on local production of food may be less susceptible to COVID supply chain issues or knock-on consequences from geopolitical events like war. The core thrust of community currencies is to restore resiliency to the monetary ecosystem by focusing on the balance of trade within localized economies, particularly those situated within a larger monetary regime. Community currencies are not legal tender, but they complement national currencies as a local medium of exchange to ensure more money recirculates and stays within local communities.

In times of crisis, community currencies, sometimes called complementary currencies, can function as an alternative source of funding to facilitate local trade and productive activity when national currency is scarce in the case of severe recessions, or as a means to organize productive activity at the local level in the absence of productive capacity at a national level. For example, when the only bank in the town of Tenino, Washington closed during the Great Depression, the local government issued a wooden currency to continue the facilitation of trade.[38] This wooden currency is still in circulation today and was utilized in the town's COVID19 relief program, which distributed $300 a month to those with a demonstrated economic hardship to help them meet their basic needs. A similar approach was taken in post World War I Germany during the Weimar Republic with the creation of "notgeld," an emergency scrip that was issued to combat hyperinflation and stabilize the economy.[39]

In the absence of a deep crisis, the role of community currencies is to create more balance in the flow of funds within regions. This is the primary

---

[38] https://www.strongtowns.org/journal/2020/6/29/wooden-money.

[39] https://designobserver.com/feature/notgeld-emergency-money-in-inflationary-germany/39926.

space in which Humanity Cash operates. Our mission is to work with community banks, credit unions and community organizers to create locally responsive financial tools. With a broad currency, economic activity can easily flow out of a region to larger corporations headquartered elsewhere, sometimes even offshore. This dynamic is most visible on Main Street in the form of mom and pop shops that shut down because they cannot compete with big retailers.

Community currencies posit that when a currency (primarily functioning as a medium of exchange) is restricted to facilitating transactions in a particular community, this would stimulate local economic productivity. There is suggestive evidence that local currencies have a higher velocity of money than national currencies.[40] The velocity of money is a measure of how fast or how often the same dollar recirculates in the economy by facilitating multiple economic transactions. In other words, there is a multiplier effect. For every dollar injected into a community, it may create 3–4x the economic value.[41] The initial recipient, for example, may spend that dollar at the local grocer, who then spends the same dollar at the local bakery, whose owner then spends the same dollar at the local diner before that dollar exits the community.

In addition, a key design of some community currencies is to keep underlying dollar reserves with community banks, which are critical to creating a money multiplier effect in local economies, whereby the same dollar deposited at a local bank creates more than one dollar of economic value to the local economy. When a community currency is working right, the currency is being used to facilitate multiple trades locally, creating multiples of income on the initial local dollar injected into the economy, while the underlying U.S. dollar is being reinvested into the local economy via local banks, creating additional multiplier effects.

Community currencies show how payment stablecoins can help support community banks and credit unions that are critical for financial inclusion. In the US, almost half of our deposits are kept with just 10 banks.[42] That is more than $11 trillion with just 10 banks,[43] despite there being 4,750 community

---

[40] https://www.researchgate.net/figure/Figura-6-Fonte-De-la-Rosa-J-Stodder-J-On-velocity-in-several-complementary_ fig4_306315018.

[41] Id.

[42] https://www.statista.com/statistics/727546/market-share-of-leading-banks-usa-domestic-deposits/#:~:text=Bank%20of%20America%20held%20the,bank's%20share%20exceeded%20five%20percent.

[43] https://www.insiderintelligence.com/insights/largest-banks-us-list/.

banks[44] and 5,298 credit unions.[45] This trend is now dangerously accelerating with the current regional banking crisis. The number of community banks has declined by 50% since 2000 due to market consolidation and competition.[46] In total, we have lost more than two-thirds[47] of our community banks since 1984 due to financial consolidation, with disproportionate impact on minority-owned banks.[48] The results are consequential.

Community banks are critical providers of financing for the local economy. While community banks hold only 15% of the banking industry's total loans, they hold 30% of the industry's commercial real estate loans that finance multifamily housing, retail, hospitality and industrial projects, 36% of the industry's small business loans, and 31% of farm loans.[49] More dollars held by community banks means greater liquidity for local productive activity.

iii. Digital community currency experiment

In the summer of 2020, I discovered a community currency in Berkshire County, Massachusetts, which is collateralized by federal dollars held with local community banks and, at the height of its popularity, accepted at approximately 400 local stores. The goal is to promote patronage of small businesses and local banks, creating multiplier effects on both the demand side (stimulating transactions with local businesses) and the reserve side (keeping dollars with local banks to reinvest as local productive capital). The dollar backing and convertibility between the community currency and the underlying dollar reserves enabled small business owners to obtain liquidity to pay bills in USD if necessary, and provided a clear measure of the value of each local currency note. The local currency was originally in the form of paper notes that were exchanged for U.S. dollars on a 1:1 basis.

---

44 https://www.fdic.gov/resources/community-banking/cbi-study.html.

45 https://www.statista.com/topics/7633/credit-unions-in-the-us/#topicHeader wrapper.

46 https://www.abrigo.com/blog/community-bank-outlook-challenges-and-opportunities-in-2021-and-beyond/.

47 https://fred.stlouisfed.org/series/USNUM.

48 https://www.cnbc.com/2020/08/25/minority-entrepreneurs-at-tipping-point-as-black-owned-banks-dwindle.html.

49 https://www.fdic.gov/resources/community-banking/report/2020/2020-cbi-study-full.pdf.

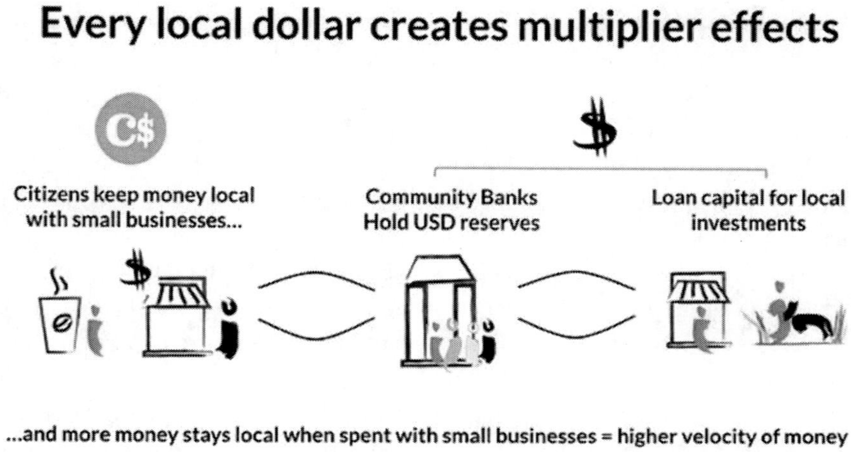

During the pandemic, small businesses were under, and continue to be under, pressure. Moreover, the pandemic accelerated the shift towards contactless payment. All else equal, this means more money is leaking out of local economies, just when they need it the most. I believed this was an opportunity to address a real world problem that blockchain was suited for – by digitizing a local currency, we can better compete with electronic payments and reduce transaction fees to the immediate benefit of small businesses, while ensuring that the underlying dollar reserves remained deposited, and therefore invested, in the local economy via local banks.

Humanity Cash transposed the Berkshires-based local currency model into digital form; instead of swapping federal dollars for paper notes at physical bank branches, we minted tokens in exchange for federal dollars electronically deposited with two local banks. On the asset side, the community banks can redeploy the deposits back to the local community; on the liability side, the digital tokens are exchanged within a closed loop of local businesses, creating a virtuous cycle.

An important distinction between the digital community currency we created versus other stablecoins is that by design the community currency cannot be traded on an exchange, as its purpose is to facilitate economic transactions within a region. As such, by design a community currency is a closed loop system, which also substantially reduces the risk of money laundering and other types of financial crime risks. Users could load up their digital wallets by linking a bank account, with the funds transferred to two participating local banks in the Berkshires, upon which the user would be credited an equivalent amount of digital tokens to be spent at nearly 90 participating local businesses. Those local businesses may choose to cash out if they needed the liquidity, but many business owners chose to reuse their tokens to support other local businesses and show solidarity. Because the use case profile is focused on bona fide economic activity in a local community, as opposed to trading or purely financial activities, the risk profile of a community currency is also substantially lower, with underlying deposits of higher quality.

Banks are allowed to loan out higher quality deposits, which creates the money multiplier effect in local economies.

Lessons learned from the digital community currency experiment

iv. While ordinary people may or may not care about blockchain or cryptocurrency, there is an appetite and desire to use digital currency if people believe that it will benefit and strengthen their local communities.

During the process of designing and launching the project in the Berkshires, I interviewed small business owners, community bankers and ordinary citizens. Whether in the Berkshires, or across the United States from Puerto Rico to Hawaii to Indiana, the people I've met are not interested in crypto as a speculative investment; they are deeply passionate about making money work for their communities. This includes a concrete mixer driver who spends 92 hours on the road each week, a retired accountant looking to give back, a small business owner who produces Massachusetts-made ukuleles, and community organizers who are experimenting with ways to use digital community currencies to support Black-owned businesses. There is a deep passion and appreciation for supporting local businesses, as well as trust in their community banks.

Community banks see stablecoins as an innovative deposit-gathering tool, and see blockchain technology as replacing core banking infrastructure in the next 10-15 years, enabling smaller banks to be more innovative and competitive, while continuing to serve their local communities.

The biggest shift in attitude came from the community bankers we worked with, who went from initially skeptical about participating in a digital currency-based project to very excited about how they might participate in the future of this new financial technology. The president of one of the banks noted that he understood that blockchain technology was the future, and they needed to get ahead of the curve in order to stay competitive. Participating in a community-based project was a low-risk way for them to learn about the technology, as they would not otherwise have the budget or bandwidth to engage in research and development work. Critically, they saw how participating in the program could enable smaller banks to be more innovative in the types of products they could offer.

We believe that with the right policies — starting with this stablecoin bill — alongside continued testing, education, and maturity of the technology, we have an existentially critical opportunity to staunch the flight of deposits from community banks and credit unions. Payment stablecoins enable higher quality deposits, as we can transact amongst each other without needing to withdraw the underlying dollars. The urgency of keeping deposits local is more important than ever. With the right policies that enable community organizations to safely experiment, the technology can mature to serve as a de-monopolizing force in our highly concentrated banking industry, by enabling community banks and credit unions to cost effectively deploy new products and services that better serve their communities.

v. Blockchain provided seamless and transparent ways to enable various aspects of legal compliance, including documentation of end users for pass-through insurance

In working with our external counsel and other stakeholders, consumer protection was of paramount importance. We were thoughtful in constructing the program such that the underlying deposits would qualify for FDIC pass-through insurance, which requires, in part, that there is a clear record of outstanding obligations and balances of end users. As a digital currency with transactions recorded in real-time on the blockchain, the blockchain functions as real-time record keeping of all wallets created and the real-time balances of each wallet. At the point of wallet creation, we collected information regarding user name and contact information associated with each wallet (not available to the public on a public ledger to preserve user confidentiality).

Therefore, we can seamlessly and cost-effectively meet the requirements of FDIC pass-through insurance by showing verifiable recordkeeping of outstanding users and their balances, which would serve as evidence of claims in the event of a bank bankruptcy.

The use of a blockchain ledger can also cost effectively and transparently meet part of the public reporting requirements under the proposed stablecoin bill. For example, you can show in real time the number of tokens on-chain, compared against the U.S. dollar reserve balances. With the right policy, starting with this bill, we can enable our financial system to be more competitive and less monopolistic, and more responsive to local economies, a benefit that ordinary Americans appreciate and deeply desire.

vi. Importance of the stablecoin bill

As grassroots entrepreneurs and community innovators, we need risk-appropriate regulations that will not be cost prohibitive, while providing guardrails to protect us from bad actors. The proposed stablecoin bill strikes a good balance between those two needs. Importantly, it provides space for local initiatives and innovation through state regulators, and a clear roadmap for implementation. State regulators are closer to the ground and better able to tailor and respond to the regulatory needs of local innovation. It would not make sense for local or community initiatives to be governed by a federal organization. Small projects that are trialing or piloting different aspects of community development work are more likely to qualify for state regulator sponsored sandboxes, providing those necessary guardrails while allowing ordinary citizens to learn by doing. Without an opportunity for grassroots work and community experiments, the technology will indeed remain within big banks and other large financial institutions.

The concern that state regulators would somehow be lax regulators does not take into account grassroots innovation and the principle of risk appropriate regulation, which the proposed stablecoin bill mandates. For example, grassroots projects like the one we did are closed loop (does not trade widely or on exchanges) and focused on bona fide local payments and economic transactions, as opposed to financial transactions where there is greater risk for large swings in deposit and withdrawal activity. Both of these factors substantially reduce risks to the consumer. State regulators are better positioned to provide appropriate oversight for these kinds of projects. If those early grassroots projects provide lessons that are then scaled up in subsequent projects, the regulatory requirements would also scale up in proportion, and where appropriate those stablecoin projects may become federally regulated, which the proposed stablecoin bill also provides for. This pathway provides smaller organizations that are critical to local economies with the time to safely make mistakes, pivot, or build on initial successes into larger, more viable projects, with the confidence necessary to secure additional funding to meet greater regulatory requirements. The avenue for state regulation in the proposed stablecoin bill, alongside federal regulation, is in line with our Constitution's history that supports states as "laboratories" of democracy. As Justice Brandeis wrote in 1932, "It is one of the happy incidents of the federal system that a single courageous State may, if its citizens choose, serve as a laboratory; and try novel social and economic experiments without risk to the rest of the country."[50] Indeed, both state and federal oversight of stablecoins can co-exist and support the other in developing a healthy financial ecosystem.

Enabling non-bank stablecoin issuers also falls within this tradition of local "laboratories." In the case of our project in the Berkshires, the local banks did not have the capacity to take on such a project as an issuer given their capacity restraints. However, enabling another community organization to function as the issuer allowed them to learn in a low-risk, low-resource environment. They will now have more confidence and knowledge going forward should they decide to issue their own stablecoins, or to work with other community organizations to do so.

For very small banks, they may never have the resources to take on stablecoin issuance. However, a local chamber of commerce or economic development agency could issue and market a stablecoin to support regional small businesses while keeping underlying reserves with community banks, therefore still locking in the money multiplier to the benefit of the local economy.

Finally, it is important to stress that the role of government is not to decide which projects are successful and useful. Indeed, many community-based and grassroots projects will fail or fail to achieve scale. What is important is that our government ensures that Americans have the ability to experiment and to fail safely. What has deeply moved me is speaking to ordinary Americans who feel both a deep passion for their communities and a sense of possibility that no matter how small they are, they have the ability to use new tools to help their communities become more self-sufficient and self-reliant. Though they deeply criticize the existing financial system, they are not cynical. They believe that even if they are not immediately successful, their work can help educate their communities and build upon lessons that can ultimately be successful in ensuring that our financial system works for everyone. This is the spirit that we must preserve and support. As one small business owner told me, she loves the concept of a community currency because it forces people to stop and acknowledge the human aspects of a financial transaction. Community currency this isn't merely another faceless financial transaction; it is an exchange between one neighbor to another.

---

[50] New State Ice Co. v. Liebmann, 285 U.S. 262, 311 (1932) (Brandeis, J., dissenting).

Statement for the Record
House Financial Services' Digital Asset Subcommittee
Hearing Putting the 'Stable' in 'Stablecoins':

How Legislation Will Help Stablecoins Achieve Their Promise

May 17, 2023

Dear Chair Hill, Ranking Member Lynch, and other members of the House Financial Services Committee,

We write to express our concerns about the grave risks stablecoins pose to households and to our financial system and urge the Committee to take the utmost care to not advance legislation that will increase these risks by expanding the reach of stablecoins without at a minimum providing adequate protections from these risks for consumers, investors and financial markets.

We are also concerned that both legislative proposals being considered during this hearing may fall short of this standard, to varying degrees. The following comments are shared to provide context for discussion regarding stablecoins, some key principles that should be fully addressed by any regulatory approach to stablecoins, and some initial concerns we have with these proposals.

Stablecoins, despite their name, have proven anything but stable. There are ongoing questions regarding the degree to which their issuers hold enough stable reserves as collateral in order to redeem their customers should they choose to withdraw their funds. What's more, the fragility of stablecoins and how their vulnerabilities can amplify market instability was on full display during the market crash that began last year with the collapse of the Terra stablecoin and its ecosystem, along with other factors, helped to spur roughly $2 trillion in investor losses in a mere few weeks.

In addition to these concerns, there are other risks and harms to consider. Stablecoins have yet to be proven as a truly effective means of payment. Instead, currently stablecoins are primarily used to facilitate speculative cryptocurrency trading, lending or various types of decentralized finance. The underlying blockchain technology used to generate these coins is also prone to hacks and theft. A large share of issued stablecoins rely on energy intensive verification methods that generate negative environmental impacts. And as of now, blockchain 'payment' systems are generally incapable of reversing erroneous or fraudulent transactions, given the inability to delete data from the chain. The Committee should thoroughly consider the possibility that stablecoin legislation intended to transform stablecoins into a mainstream, reliable mode of payment might instead further fuel the mining and trading of cryptocurrencies in an environment rife with pump-and-dump scams, extreme volatility, and cybersecurity risks.

At the outset, we believe regulators already possess considerable authority to effectively police stablecoins. Section 21(a)(2) of the Glass-Steagall Act prohibits commercial entities and other nonbanks from offering financial products and services that are functionally equivalent to deposits. The banking agencies and the Department of Justice can and should interpret this section to include stablecoins. This would then require stablecoin issuers to apply for a banking charter without an act of Congress. The SEC under its authority from the Exchange Act of 1934 has the ability to police the exchanges on which stablecoins are traded or used. The CFPB has authority to enforce the Electronic Funds Transfer Act and other statutes with respect to stablecoins as they are used for consumer finance broadly and for electronic transfer of funds more specifically. Finally, FSOC has some authority to designate stablecoins and their issuers as systemically important financial institutions and/or market utilities. Using this authority might bring stablecoin issuers under regulatory oversight without having to establish a wholly new regulatory framework that could create unforeseen risks or weaknesses in coverage.

If the Committee decides to move forward with legislation, it must adequately and comprehensively address the risks associated with stablecoins, many of which are similar to the risks posed by banks; including, but not limited to: run risk, credit risk, operational risks, and liquidity risk, as discussed in the President's Working Group report on stablecoins. Furthermore, legislation must also fully address concentration and anti-competitive effects as stablecoins issuers continue to rapidly grow and eventually seek to benefit from economies of scale through mergers and acquisitions. Such legislation should also actively affirm the roles of various regulators in protecting investors and consumers, and lastly, should make it clear that rigorous standards should be applied to oversight of stablecoins, rather than relying primarily on the discretion of any one regulatory agency.

The bill H.R., *To provide for the regulation of payment stablecoins, and for other purposes* (referred to by news reports as the "Republican" bill), fails to address many of these risks or principles. A few of our key concerns are as follows:

- No Explicit Custody Rules. The Republican bill lacks specific custody rules directing issuers how they will protect those assets they hold in custody for them. This could raise risks associated with the commingling of funds and complicate asset recovery for coin holders if and when an issuer became insolvent.
- The Republican bill appears to strip or diminish SEC authority over stablecoins if/when traded on secondary markets. The Republican bill does not acknowledge the current reality that most stablecoins are used to facilitate speculative investment or are traded on secondary markets – instances where the SEC has jurisdiction. Furthermore, the bill alters securities laws to specifically state that payment stablecoins are NOT securities – a change that would likely further erode securities regulator's authority over the investment and secondary trading activity.
- The Republican bill is silent on how specific payments focused protections, such as EFTA would apply. If payment stablecoins are supposed to be used as payments, rules such as Regulation E and EFTA should be applied to protect consumers using them – provisions that help reverse false or erroneous charges. Yet the bill does not affirm the application of these regulatory requirements, which either creates confusion or uncertainty or worse would allow stablecoin issuers to evade such requirements.
- The Republican bill appears largely silent on how and whether issuers would be directly subject to Community Reinvestment Act (CRA) obligations or Community Benefit Agreements. These are bedrock elements of the current banking regulatory regime, which ensure that banking entities don't abuse their privileges and extract wealth from or fail to meaningfully contribute to the economic health of the communities they operate in – in other words, help contribute to financial inclusion.

But, apart from a very brief mention of 'benefit to consumers' in the evaluation criteria that federal regulators would use to evaluate issuers and their applications, the Republican bill is silent on this topic, which raises concerns about whether approved issuers would be largely exempt from such requirements. This could negatively impact communities, and could also incentivize other financial institutions to migrate to the stablecoin model to avoid their obligations under the CRA and similar programs, depleting these funds, and communities, of important resources and support.

- The Republican bill appears virtually silent on Glass Steagall/Bank Holding Company Act concerns. This bill appears to have virtually no language that addresses concerns that large commercial non-financial entities might use this regulatory framework to become stablecoin issuers, despite longstanding concerns about such activity in terms of economic concentration, market risk and other issues. There is some language in the bill about "institution-affiliated parties" being subject similar oversight as the institutions (that is, issuers) are themselves, but that language appears weak and may primarily refer to individuals or persons associated with issuers, not with third parties, distribution partners or other types of entities that could exercise de facto control over issuers that are nominally regulated under this law.
- The Republican bill appears silent on rules, requirements and procedures related to mergers and acquisitions. This bill is virtually silent on this topic, raising concerns that the acquisition of an issuer by another company could increase risks and/or allow issuers and parents to bypass or elide meaningful oversight by federal or state regulators.

The one significant positive element of the Republican bill we are able to identify at this time is what it omits - namely, it does not have language giving non-bank stablecoin issuers access to Fed services such as master accounts or the discount window. Allowing such access would in our view create concerns about non-bank entities receiving access to banking services and privilege, without oversight and supervision equivalent to what banks are subject to - which could amplify the risk and impact should these non-bank issuers suffer failures. However, the other bill being considered by the committee today (discussed below) also omits this language.

H.R., To provide requirements for payment stablecoin issuers, research on a digital dollar, and for other purposes (referred to by news reports as the "Democratic" bill), does have language that in some cases, relative to the Republican bill, better addresses the principles and concerns mentioned above. However, in a number of key ways, the Democratic bill still may fall short of what we believe would be necessary to adequately protect consumers and investors from the risks and harms posed by stablecoins. In some cases, the

Democratic bill shares those shortcomings with the Republican bill; in others, language or elements are different but still raise concerns.

First, to note some relative improvements:

- Custody and Asset Segregation Rules: In contrast to the Republican bill, the Democratic bill has specific rules requiring issuers to protect those assets they hold in custody from customers, with some restrictions on commingling of customer and company assets.
- Fed veto of state issuers: Compared to the Republican bill, The Democratic bill gives the Fed, as one primary federal regulator of issuers, power to decline applications of state stablecoin issuers (filed at the state level) prior to the issuer going on the market. This provision does appear to give a bit more weight to federal oversight of state issuers, in ways that could somewhat offset concerns about regulatory arbitrage between state and federal regimes.

  It's unclear, however, how effective this would be in practice. The Fed has veto power but doesn't appear to have the ability to proactively and/or directly influence the evaluation of state issuers prior to actually reviewing completed applications (beyond some consultative powers). Thus, if that is the case, this power would not establish a 'floor' for federal oversight of state issuers, but more of a ceiling, which could limit its usefulness in ensuring issuers use the state application process to avoid more rigorous regulatory scrutiny.

- A moratorium on endogenously collateralized stablecoins: The bill would establish a moratorium on these types of stablecoins, more commonly known as 'algorithmic' stablecoins - and authorize a study of such coins for future consideration. These coins have consistently demonstrated fragility and instability that has resulted in harms to consumers - most famously with the collapse of Terra.

Second, we note concerns specific to the Democratic bill:

- Over reliance on the Fed as the regulator as the default regulator for federally approved issuers. The bill says the OCC, Fed and FDIC are the appropriate federal regulators. But it seems likely most non-bank issuers would seek or be qualified to apply with the Federal Reserve.

The Democratic bill gives the Fed more ways to exert oversight over issuers than the Republican bill, including state issuers, and provides more details on how the Fed might evaluate federally licensed issuers.

But we remain concerned that, while the Fed has an important role to play in overseeing the systemic risks posed by stablecoins, in several respects it is sometimes ill-suited to conduct more direct supervision and oversight (as we've learned from the SVB collapse). In particular, the lack of statutory specifics in the bill around how supervision and examination by the Fed would occur raises questions - how feasible is it for the Fed to suddenly develop new, robust rules in a timely fashion for yet another novel class of assets with unique risks, yet pose a very small part of the financial ecosystem?

- The State pathway for issuer registrations is too permissive, and lacks adequate federal oversight. The bill as drafted provides an optional pathway for stablecoin issuers to become regulated under federal law, but continues to give states the authority to regulate stablecoin issuers on their own - albeit with some federal power to decline state issuers.

  While it is possible the Fed might establish a regulatory framework that guards against regulatory arbitrage between federal and state pathways, we remain concerned that state issuers might use this framework more easily avoid meaningful federal oversight and seek out permissive, crypto-friendly regimes (such as Wyoming) that would provide issuers with a light-touch approval process.

- The bill's language regarding the Bank Holding Company (BHC) Act's application to non-bank issuers is vague and may not provide a sufficient firewall. While it is good to see language in the Democratic bill that speaks to and attempts to address BHC related issues, we remain concerned that language lacks sufficient clarity about how it would enable effective enforcement of the Bank Holding Company Act to prevent the co-mingling of commercial and banking activities.

  For example, the bill designates IDI-affiliated issuers as subject to Bank Holding Company Act, prohibits non-financial commercial companies from controlling non-bank entities, and requires that affiliates of that entity be financial in nature. But there's no clear definition in this bill or elsewhere that articulates what 'financial in nature' might mean. And there's less in the bill about how non-financial companies might act (and be regulated as) so-called 'distributors' of stablecoins issued by non-bank entities – a marketing arrangement that has been a key feature of some prominent proposed stablecoin products, including Meta's (Facebook) proposal to distribute its Diem (previously Libra) coin in partnership with nominal issuers.

This lack of clarity is a significant concern given the very real interest of tech and commercial companies in securing market share in the private payment space, despite obvious concerns that such encroachment would pose in terms of economic concentration and collusion.

- The bill's language regarding SEC or CFPB authority over stablecoins when traded or used as payments may be insufficient. Unlike the Republican bill, the Democratic bill does have a section stating that nothing in the bill shall infringe on the jurisdiction or authority of other regulators, including the SEC and CFPB, as appropriate. However, we are concerned that without additional explicit affirmation of how and when these regulators would have authority, this infringement language could be read too narrowly.

  For example, at a minimum, the SEC should have jurisdiction over stablecoins when traded on secondary markets. Yet, without mentioning such in this bill, stablecoin issuers could challenge the SEC's attempts to exert jurisdiction once the law is enacted, citing lack of statutory clarity beyond this statement.

  With respect to the CFPB, payment stablecoins are meant to be used as payments. As such, the consumer protection laws that the CFPB administers with respect to payment systems, such as the Electronic Funds Transfer Act, should apply. But there are no specific and/or explicit references to these and other key consumer protections relevant to payment systems in the bill. Without such explicit language, we're concerned the bill would enable issuers to evade or avoid such obligations, or might otherwise undermine the CFPB's role in protecting consumers from potential risks associated with these products.

- The bill lacks sufficient statutory language regarding how and whether issuers would meet standards comparable to Community Reinvestment Act obligations and Community Benefit Agreements. In contrast to the Republican bill which appears largely silent on these programs and requirements, the Democratic bill does appear to speak more directly to them. Specifically, the evaluation criteria the bill instructs federal regulators to use to evaluate applicants does provide some detail on how an issuer and its coin might contribute to a range of community benefits.

  However, the language used isn't standardized or fully consistent with what's already in use with respect to these programs. As such, the new language could create confusion or uncertainty and ultimately might allow issuers to avoid some or much of what normal depository institutions are required to do under these programs. This in turn could affect overall funds available for these programs, if and when financial institutions took advantage and moved their business to the less rigorous stablecoin regime.

  Lastly, we have a range of initial concerns with characteristics shared by both bills, including:

- Insufficient Audit Requirements for Issuer Reserves. Attestations are not the same as audits and are not adequate to provide real insight into the stability of a stablecoin issuer's reserve assets. There is ample literature that spells this out and demonstrates why relying on attestations is insufficient. Issuers should be subject to real, independent audits.
- Lack of Deposit Insurance Requirements for Issuers: The bill specifically states that stablecoins and their issuers are not insured deposits or deposit institutions. This is done in the name of differentiating stablecoin issuers as 'higher' risk, so that customers won't treat the coins they buy or use as such. But, given past misleading practices by crypto asset firms, and given that there are already risks with customers using non-bank payment platforms effectively as they would depository instruments, our concern is that by Allowing deposit-like instruments to not only be uninsured, but issued by banks who insure other deposits, will create confusion for

customers, especially during periods of financial distress, and inevitably provide less protection for consumers that choose to purchase stablecoins that do not offer such insurance.

Unfortunately, the list of concerns above is not exhaustive. We are continuing to evaluate these bills and consult experts and allies regarding both bills' treatment of a number of issues, including: consolidated supervision; operational risks associated with cybersecurity and blockchain technology; interoperability standards; the adequacy of the bankruptcy protection provisions described in the bills; the lack of coverage of state issuers under Graham-Leach-Bliley; the requirement that federal regulators 'tailor' their regulations, rules, and examination procedures to 'unique aspects of crypto assets; the significant restrictions placed on federal regulators to not duplicate information requests when conducting supervision or regulatory oversight; the wisdom of authorizing credit unions to become issuers and the NCUA as a federal regulator, despite significant concerns about whether either is suited to the task; and other issues.

Given the wide range of concerns listed above, and because the use or theorized uses of stablecoins spans the gamut of financial sector activities (e.g., banking, consumer finance, investments, etc.), crafting legislation that would adequately address the risks associated with all of these activities is a complex and difficult endeavor that requires time and careful consideration.

We strongly urge the Committee to first seek to empower the regulators to use the tools currently at their disposal to address present risks associated with stablecoins, and only proceed with legislation that rigorously protects consumers and investors and prevents stablecoins from posing systemic threats to our financial system and economy.

Rather than seek to get 'something on the books' with respect to regulatory oversight, Congress should seek to get it right, and seek first to do no harm to existing regulatory frameworks.

We would be happy to speak further and at length with Members of your Committee and staff on these guiding principles in more detail.

Thank you.

Mark Hays
Senior Policy Analyst Americans for Financial Reform
markhays@ourfinancialreform.org

Fact Sheet: "Un" Stablecoins and Risks to Investors, Consumers, and Economic Productivity

"History doesn't repeat itself, but it often rhymes"

The short history of stablecoins has been characterized by instability, bank-like runs, and the evaporation of tens of billions of dollars in investor losses. The use of the moniker "stablecoin" has become a misnomer in that these financial products are anything but stable. A more appropriate name would be "unstablecoins" considering how susceptible they are to bank-like runs and how often they depeg from their "stable" value.

Stablecoins are remarkably similar to money market funds – an industry that had to be bailed out by the federal government in 2008 and 2020 after experiencing bank-like runs. And despite industry fantasies and talking points touting stablecoins as an innovative and inclusive form of payment, stablecoins have not lived up to the hype as a payment mechanism outside the unregulated crypto ecosystem. In fact, more than 80 percent of the trade volume on major centralized exchanges involves stablecoins – demonstrating that their primary use case is simply trading activity for no purpose other than the pursuit of speculative profit.[51]

However, despite their instability and lack of prowess as a form of payment, policymakers have debated codifying these money market fund-like products as a payment mechanism. For the reasons stated below, regulators and policymakers should stop and consider the risks to investors, consumers, and the economy before legislating stablecoins into a form of payments.

The Myth of "Stable"Coins and Inherent Run Risk

Stablecoins are defined in President Biden's Executive Order as "a category of cryptocurrencies with mechanisms that are aimed at maintaining a stable value, such as by pegging the value of the coin to a specific currency, asset, or pool of assets or by algorithmically controlling supply in response to changes in demand in order to stabilize value."[52] The term "stablecoin" can refer to a

[51] *Share of Trade Volume by Paid Denomination*, THE BLOCK (last visited May 16, 2023), https://www.theblock.co/data/crypto-markets/spot/share-of-trade-volume-by-pair-denomination.

[52] Exec. Order No. 14,067, Ensuring Responsible Development of Digital Assets, 87 Fed. Reg. 14,143, 14,152 (Mar. 14, 2022).

number of different types of digital asset products, which all claim to maintain a stable value relative to a reference asset, often the U.S. dollar, but not exclusively. There are principally three different types of stablecoins:

- off-chain collateralized (fiat-based or commodity-based)
- on-chain collateralized (crypto-based)
- non-collateralized (algorithmic)

Despite stablecoins only having existed for a few years, all three types of stablecoins have exhibited bank-like run risk that is inherent in any financial product that is not guaranteed by a sovereign government. While each type of stablecoin presents differing degrees of run risk, they all present run risk, nonetheless. The President's Working Group on Financial Markets Report on Stablecoins identifies four specific ways confidence in stablecoins could be undermined and trigger bank-like runs:

1) use of reserve assets that could fall in price or become illiquid;
2) a failure to appropriately safeguard reserve assets;
3) a lack of clarity regarding the redemption rights of stablecoin holders; and
4) operational risks related to cybersecurity and the collecting, storing, and safeguarding ofdata.[53]

We have already witnessed that many of these risk factors have triggered runs on stablecoins within the past year alone. If stablecoins have proved anything over their short history, it is that they will experience bank-like runs and depeg. The questions regarding stablecoins have quickly become when will they depeg from their exchange rate, not if they will depeg, and what happens to token-holders in the aftermath.

Off-Chain Collateralized Stablecoins

Off-chain collateralized stablecoins are the most popular stablecoins. These stablecoins are designed to maintain a stable value in reference to a specific

[53] President's Working Group on Financial Markets, the Federal Deposit Insurance Corporation, and the Office ofthe Comptroller of the Currency, Report on Stablecoins 12 (November 2021).

asset, often the U.S. dollar, with a fixed one-to-one exchange rate by holding in reserves various forms of traditional financial products (e.g., cash, U.S. treasury securities, commercial bonds, etc.). But there is often little transparency into the reserves held by stablecoin issuers. And stablecoin issuers are vulnerable to runs if customers lose faith in their reserves. What is more, most stablecoin issuers are not subject to federal regulations and protections designed to instill faith in an issuer's reserves, such as deposit insurance and portfolio restrictions.[54] Issuers are also free to change the composition of their reserves or modify their disclosures without prior notice.[55]

Specifically, the two most prominent off-chain collateralized stablecoins, Tether ($82.8 billion) and USDC ($29.9 billion), make up about 80% of the market cap of all stablecoins.[56] Tether reportedly[57] holds a combination of cash and cash equivalents, corporate bonds, commodities, and other cryptocurrencies in reserves to maintain its peg to the U.S. Dollar. For its part, USDC reportedly holds a more conservative mix of assets in reserves that includes cash and cash equivalents. However, it is important to remember that cash equivalents can include short-term investment securities with maturity periods up to 90 days.

---

[54] Stablecoins: Legal Issues and Regulatory Options (Part I), Congressional Research Service, June 9, 2022,https://crsreports.congress.gov/product/pdf/LSB/LSB10753.

[55] Wilmarth, Arthur E. Jr., Comment Letter to the U.S. Treasury Department regarding the Risks of Stablecoins(2022), https://scholarship.law.gwu.edu/faculty_publications/1623.

[56] David Canellis, *Tether Nears 50% of Stablecoin Markets, Highest in 14 Months*, BLOCKWORKS (Feb. 13, 2023), https://blockworks.co/news/tether-stablecoin-market-half.

[57] Tether has been fined by the NYAG and CFTC for lying about its reserves in the past. *See* Press Release, Attorney General James Ends Virtual Currency Trading Platform Bitfinex's Illegal Activities in New York, NYAG (Feb.23, 2021) ("Tether's claims that its virtual currency was fully backed by U.S. dollars at all times was a lie"),https://ag.ny.gov/press-release/2021/attorney-general-james-ends-virtual-currency-trading-platform-bitfinexs-illegal; *See also* Press Release, CFTC Orders Tether and Bitfinex to Pay Fines Totaling $42.5 Million, CFTC (Oct.15, 2021) ("Tether has represented that the tether token is a stablecoin with its value pegged to fiat currency and 100% backed by corresponding fiat assets…However…Tether misrepresented to customers and the market that Tether maintained sufficient U.S. dollar reserves to back every USDT in circulation with the 'equivalent amountof corresponding fiat currency' held by Tether and 'safely deposited' in Tether's bank accounts. In fact Tetherreserves were not 'fully-backed' the majority of the time").

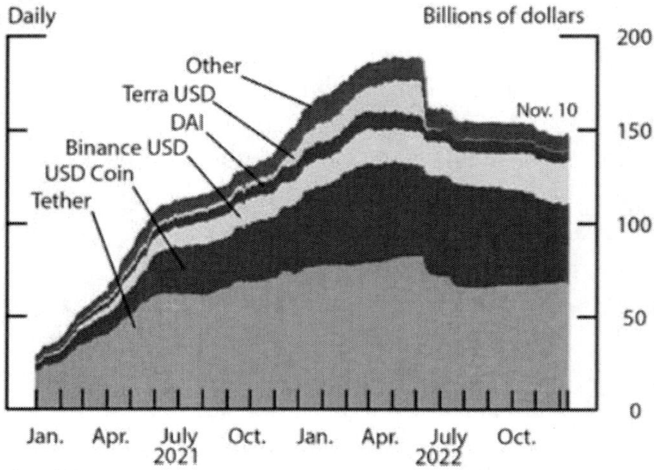

Source: Federal Reserve The Fed - The stable in stablecoins (federalreserve.gov).

Figure 1. Market cap by stablecoin.

Despite their market dominance, both stablecoins have experienced bank-like runs and depegged from their fixed exchange rate within the past 6 months. Tether, a stablecoin notorious for secrecy and misstatements about the status of their reserves, depegged in November 2022 after the failure of FTX. In the days after the collapse of FTX, Tether traded as low as 96 cents on the dollar.[58] As a point of reference, in 2008, the Federal Reserve felt compelled to intervene and rescue the money market fund industry as it confronted funds facing less dramatic deviations from the dollar. Similarly, USDC depegged in March 2023 after the failure of Silicon Valley Bank, which held $3 billion of USDC's reserves, dropping to as low as 85 cents on the dollar and experiencing $6 billion in redemptions.[59]

On-Chain Collateralized Stablecoins

On-chain collateralized stablecoins represent a much smaller subset of stablecoins in the market. Similar to off-chain collateralized stablecoins, on-

[58] Crystal Kim, *Tether's USDT stablecoin depegs from dollar for a brief window*, AXIOS (Nov. 10, 2022),https://www.axios.com/2022/11/10/tethers-usdt-stablecoin-depegs-from-dollar-for-a-brief-window.

[59] Olga Kharif, *Circle USDC Stablecoin Redemptions Rise to About $6 billion*, BLOOMBERG (Mar. 21, 2023),https://www.bloomberg.com/news/articles/2023-03-21/redemptions-rise-to-about-6-billion-from-circle-usdc- stablecoin?sref=mQvUqJZj.

chain collateralized stablecoins are designed to maintain a stable value in reference to a specific asset, often the U.S. dollar, with a fixed one-to- one exchange rate. However, instead of holding traditional financial products such as cash and bonds in reserves, they instead hold other cryptocurrencies in their reserves. So on-chain collateralized stablecoins introduce an additional weakness, as the collateral is another cryptocurrency whose value can fluctuate significantly relative to the U.S. Dollar.[60] The largest on-chain collateralized stablecoin is MakerDAO's DAI ($4.8 billion), which uses a system of smart contracts and user deposits of Ethereum in exchange for DAI stablecoin tokens. Despite the decentralized nature of DAI and the use of Ethereum as collateral for its stablecoins, the DAI stablecoin depegged in March 2023 after the collapse of Silicon Valley Bank to 88 cents on the dollar.[61]

Non-Collateralized Stablecoins

The most volatile and most dangerous of the three types of stablecoins are the non-collateralized stablecoins. Similar to off-chain and on-chain collateralized stablecoins, these stablecoins are designed to maintain a stable value in reference to a specific asset, often the U.S. dollar, with a fixed one-to-one exchange rate. However, instead of holding assets in reserves, non-collateralized stablecoins utilize complicated algorithms and smart contracts to maintain their peg to their reference assets.

While these stablecoins witnessed the most growth in the first half of 2022, they also witnessed the most dramatic collapses of all stablecoins. The most prominent collapse, which triggered the crypto carnage of 2022, was that of TerraUSD. At its height, TerraUSD was a $18 billion non- collateralized stablecoin that used a companion token, LUNA, to help it maintain a one-to-one peg with the U.S. dollar. However, this financial alchemy project blew up in a matter of days in May 2022. The crash in crypto markets that followed

---

[60] Garth Baughman, Francesca Carapella, Jacob Gerszten, and David Mills, The stable in stablecoins, FEDS Notes, Board of Governors of the Federal Reserve System (Dec. 16, 2022), https://www.federalreserve.gov/econres/notes/feds-notes/the-stable-in-stablecoins-20221216.html.

[61] Sam Reynolds, *DAI Depegs to Lifetime Lows as Stablecoin Rout Plagues Crypto*, COINDESK (Mar. 11, 2023), https://www.coindesk.com/markets/2023/03/11/dai-depegs-as-stablecoin-rout-plagues-crypto/.

Terra's collapse inflicted painful losses on millions of retail investors.[62] The $40 billion overnight collapse of both TerraUSD and LUNA caused widespread financial panic in the crypto ecosystem, spurring more than $300 billion in losses in the aftermath, including notably FTX.[63]

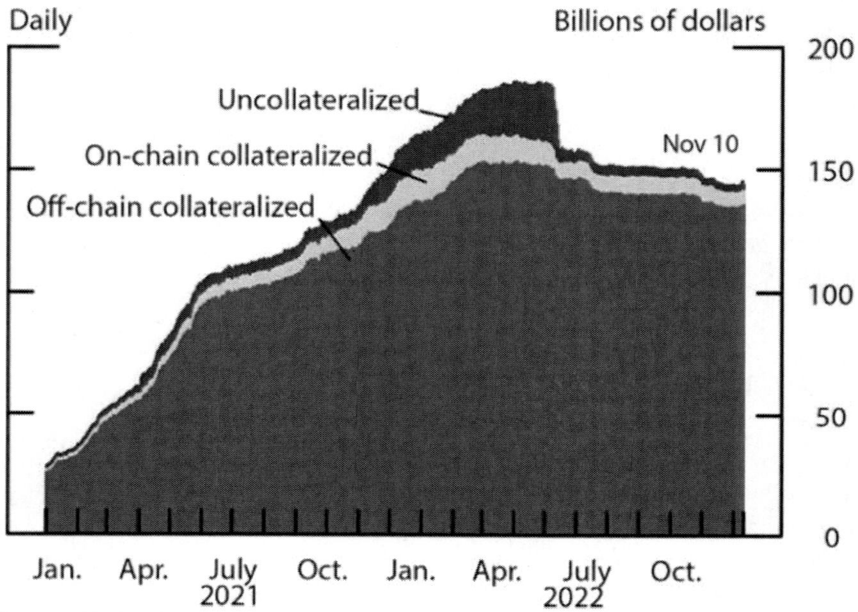

Source: Federal Reserve The Fed - The stable in stablecoins (federalreserve.gov).

Redeemability Risks

In addition to the risk of stablecoins due to their stabilization mechanism, stablecoins contain other features that add to their riskiness. For instance, investors should be able to redeem their stablecoins at any moment and at par value to the referenced, fixed exchange rate. However, stablecoin issuers often constrain investors' right of redemption and offer insufficient public disclosure about their redemption terms. Currently, the two most prominent

[62] Wilmarth, Arthur E. Jr., Comment Letter to the U.S. Treasury Department regarding the Risks of Stablecoins (2022), https://scholarship.law.gwu.edu/faculty_publications/1623.

[63] Elizabeth Napolitano, *The Fall of Celsius Network: A Timeline of the Crypto Lender's Descent Into Insolvency*, COINDESK (Jul 15, 2022), https://www.coindesk.com/markets/2022/07/15/the-fall-of-celsius-network-a-timeline-of-the-crypto-lenders-descent-into-insolvency/.

stablecoins issuers do not provide a direct right of redemption to investors because many of those investors purchase the stablecoin through unregulated cryptocurrency exchanges.[64] In other cases, holders of stablecoins also face limits or high minimum thresholds for redemptions.[65] This makes them unredeemable for the majority of ordinary retail users.[66] Investors must pay particularly close attention to the terms of service to ensure they understand their right of redemption, which is often mischaracterized by stablecoin issuers.

Money Market Funds by Another Name

Much like an off-chain collateralized stablecoin, a money market fund is a financial services product that invests in short-term corporate and government debt securities while offering investors a stable value of exchange. Created in the 1970s, money market funds purported to offer investors higher returns than bank deposit accounts, while at the same time offering the same security as a bank account. Because of their stable value and higher rate of return, investors came to expect they could benefit from the same on-demand liquidity and protection from losses that they already received through bank deposit accounts. However, money market funds are unlike bank deposit accounts, which are facilitated and supported by extensive regulations that ensure the safety and soundness of banks and explicitly protect depositors from losses—from capital requirements that ensure the financial health of banks to federally-backed, bank-funded deposit insurance that protects depositors from

[64] *See* Gary Gensler, Chairman, Sec. and Exch. Comm'n, Prepared Remarks of Gary Gensler on Crypto Markets at Penn Law Capital Markets Association Annual Conference (Apr. 4, 2022); *See, e.g.,* Circle Legal & Privacy (Lastupdated December 20, 2022) ("You may not redeem USDC with Circle unless and until you open a Circle Account.Eligibility for and requirements related to opening a Circle Account are set forth in the Circle Account User Agreement."), https://www.circle.com/en/legal/usdc-terms; *See, e.g.,* Tether Legal (Last updated September 2, 2022) ("In order to cause Tether Tokens to be issued or redeemed directly by Tether, you must be a verified customer of Tether. No exceptions will be made to this provision"), https://tether.to/en/legal/.

[65] *See* Tether Legal (Last updated September 2, 2022) ("Tether reserves the right to delay the redemption or withdrawal of Tether Tokens if such delay is necessitated by the illiquidity or unavailability or loss of any Reserves held by Tether to back the Tether Tokens"), https://tether.to/en/legal/.

[66] Mitsu Adachi et al., Stablecoins' role in crypto and beyond: functions, risks, and policy, European Central Bank, https://www.ecb.europa.eu/pub/financial-stability/macroprudential-bulletin/html/ecb.mpbu202207_2~836f682ed7.en.html#4%20Potential%20Risks%20to%20Financial%20Stabilit y%20Stemming%20from%20StableCoins.

losses should their banks fail. Money market funds do not have mandatory capital cushions, deposit insurance, or the other protections surrounding bank accounts. Thus, despite the purported stable value offered to investors by money market funds, in times of stress they have experienced bank-like runs requiring government bailouts.

During the Financial Crisis of 2008 and the COVID-19 panic in the markets in March 2020, money market funds "broke the buck" from their fixed exchange rates. During the week of September 15, 2008, investors withdrew approximately $310 billion (or 15 percent) of prime money market fund assets. This caused havoc in the short-term funding markets, triggering a vicious cycle of asset fire sales, depressed prices, redemption requests, more asset fire sales, and rapidly evaporating liquidity. Controlling the run required drastic government (and taxpayer) intervention: the Treasury, on September 19, 2008, established the Temporary Guarantee Program for Money Market Funds, and the Federal Reserve established a variety of facilities to support the credit markets frozen by the money market fund crisis.

Once again, in March 2020, the money market fund industry experienced financial stress and the corresponding contagion imperiled the markets broadly and forced government intervention. For the second time in just a dozen years, taxpayer money had to be put at risk to support a backstop of money market funds. The assets of prime money market funds dropped dramatically. For example, ICI data showed that prime money market fund assets overall dropped by $85.38 billion, or over 10%, just between March 4 and March 18, 2020. Some funds were faring much worse, with their assets falling by half as investors withdrew.[67] And many money market fund sponsors were being forced to backstop their money market funds with cash infusions to prevent them from "breaking the buck" as they sold assets to meet redemptions when all asset classes were falling in value. The situation became so grim that on Wednesday, March 18, 2020, the Federal Reserve established an emergency lending facility so that banks could buy more assets from prime funds, thus injecting desperately needed cash, preserving the ability of money market funds to honor redemptions, and supporting the commercial paper market upon which so many companies rely.[68] And, the $2 trillion rescue legislation passed in early 2020 renewed the Treasury Department's authority

---

[67] Paul Kiernan, Andrew Ackerman & Dave Michaels, *Why the Fed Had to Backstop Money Market Funds, Again*, WALL ST. J. (Mar. 21, 2020), https://www.wsj.com/articles/why-the-fedhad-to-backstop-money-market-funds- again-11584788401?mod=article_inline.

[68] James Politi, Federal Reserve sets up facility to make loans to banks, FIN. TIMES (Mar. 19, 2020), https://www.ft.com/content/0e6029be-6995-11ea-800d-da70cff6e4d3.

to guarantee the money market fund industry again. This put the full faith and credit of the United States behind a single financial product, just as the government—and the taxpayers—did in 2008.

One of the purported benefits of money market funds to investors is the higher rate of return than bank deposit accounts. A big distinction between money market funds and some of the most prominent stablecoins is that money market funds actually return interest to its investors. Investors in Tether and USDC receive none of the interest that the pooled assets collect. Instead, those assets go right to Tether and USDC's bottom line. Even a conservative investment portfolio of short-term U.S. Treasury bills can yield between 2-4%, which for an $80 billion investment portfolio can mean billions of dollars in profits that investors of stablecoins are forgoing. For example, Tether claimed to make $1.4 billion in net profit last quarter alone, all forgone interest income from its investors.[69] Compared to the $2.36 billion in net income Mastercard made last quarter, stablecoins are quickly catching up to major credit card companies in gouging their consumers.

The short history of stablecoins and the much longer history of money market funds have confirmed that these similarly designed products—offering instant liquidity to investors despite holding much longer duration assets—are susceptible to bank-like runs, especially during periods of financial stress. However, unlike bank deposit accounts, investor assets are not insured by the FDIC. Further, the recent volatility in the regional banking sector, specifically the runs on banks with high percentages of uninsured deposits, is further proof that any financial product will be subject to bank-like runs absent a federal guarantee. Stablecoins have already faced significant bank-like runs in their short history and have proven that during times of financial stress they are anything but "stable."

The Misguided Lure of Private Money

Since the announcement of Facebook's Project Libra in June 2019, which sought to create a blockchain-based stablecoin payment system, regulators and

[69] Tether, Tether's Latest Q1 2023 Assurance Report Shows Reserves Surplus At All-Time high of $2.44B, up $1.48B in Net Profit; New Categories for Additional Transparency Reveals Bitcoin and Gold Allocations, (May 10, 2023), https://tether.to/en/tethers-latest-q1-2023-assurance-report-shows-reserves-surplus-at-all-time-high-of- 244b-up-148b-in-net-profit-new-categories-for-additional-transparency-reveals-bitcoin-and-gold-allocations/.

policymakers have grappled with the idea of a blockchain-based stablecoin. In the midst of the announcement, governments around the world and policymakers in the U.S. expressed concern with the project on a bipartisan basis. For example, the Chairwoman of the House Financial Services Committee, Maxine Waters, said in a statement that "[r]egulators should see this as a wake-up call to get serious about privacy and national security concerns, cybersecurity risks, and trading risks that are posed by cryptocurrencies." Additionally, even then-President Donald J. Trump tweeted that "[i]f Facebook and other companies want to become a bank they must seek a new [b]anking [c]harter and become subject to all [b]anking [r]egulations." Facing extensive backlash, Facebook later abandoned its initiative to issue a private, global currency.

However, despite that announcement by Facebook and the severe backlash by governments around the world, the use of stablecoins have risen in prominence, although only as a means of facilitating trading in cryptocurrencies. Nevertheless, stablecoin advocates have advanced the theory that stablecoins could be an effective form of payment for a broader spectrum of assets. Now, regulators and policymakers are debating how to regulate stablecoins as "payment stablecoins" even though they are not currently used as a form of payment outside the incestuous world of crypto. Moreover, both regulators and policymakers have skipped the more important threshold question of whether or not it is desirable to have a form of currency controlled by a private company coexisting with the U.S. dollar, a sovereign currency controlled and issued by the U.S. government. For instance, banks use customer deposit funds to make loans to individuals in their community, spurring economic activity. Additionally, tying up safe and liquid assets in a stablecoin arrangement means they are not available for other uses, such as helping banks satisfy their regulatory requirements to maintain sufficient capital and liquidity. This could lead to disruptive shortages of safe and liquid assets.[70] Have regulators or policymakers explored the primary and secondary economic effects of a migration of customer funds out of banks and into digital wallets? What are the effects on bank lending to prospective homeowners to purchase their first house or the effects on small business lending for innovative entrepreneurs seeking to start their own business? These are

---

[70] Rod Garratt, Michael Lee, Antoine Martin, and Joseph Torregrossa, *The Future of Payments is Not Stablecoins*, Liberty Street Economics, Federal Reserve Bank of New York (Feb. 7, 2022), https://libertystreeteconomics.newyorkfed.org/2022/02/the-future-of-payments-is-not-stablecoins/.

important economic considerations being glossed over in this debate over how to regulate payment stablecoins.

There is a reason why privately issued currencies are not prominent in the U.S. economy and it isn't because they have never been attempted. Prior to enactment of the National Banking Act of 1863, private banks issued their own bank notes on a one-for-one basis with state bonds in a period known as the Free Banking Era.[71] However, these hyper-localized currencies required merchants to be wary when accepting bank notes for fear of counterfeiting.[72] The inefficient Free Banking Era was replaced when the National Bank Act required all notes to be backed by U.S. Treasury bonds and the taxation of all forms of private bank notes. Another example of private currencies in the U.S. was the use of company scrip in remote towns across the country. Scrip was a credit for wages and it was often used in remote towns where money supply was scarce and a single private enterprise such as a mining company was the central employer. Private companies used scrip as a credit to employees on their earned wages to spend at the local company-owned shops. It quickly became a trap employers used to exploit their workforces that was largely outlawed by the Supreme Court in 1918.

Regulators and policymakers should first debate whether or not private currencies as a form of payments, such as stablecoins, are in the best interest of the American people prior to codifying stablecoins as a form of payments. Private currencies have been tried in the U.S. before and abandoned because they were either too inefficient or because they were used by private enterprise to exploit their workers. Payment stablecoins appear to be repeating the mistakes of the past.

Better Banks | Better Businesses Better Jobs | Better Economic Growth Better Lives | Better Communities

Better Markets is a public interest 501(c)(3) non-profit based in Washington, DC that advocates for greater transparency, accountability, and oversight in the domestic and global capital and commodity markets, to protect the American Dream of homes, jobs, savings, education, a secure retirement, and a rising standard of living.

---

[71] Gary B. Gorton and Jeffrey Y. Zhang, *Taming Wildcat Stablecoins*, 90 UNIV. OF CHICAGO L. REV. at 25 (Forthcoming 2023).

[72] Gorton and Zhang at 29.

Better Markets fights for the economic security, opportunity, and prosperity of the American people by working to enact financial reform, to prevent another financial crash and the diversion of trillions of taxpayer dollars to bailing out the financial system.

By being a counterweight to Wall Street's biggest financial firms through the policymaking and rulemaking process, Better Markets is supporting pragmatic rules and a strong banking and financial system that enables stability, growth, and broad-based prosperity. Better Markets also fights to refocus finance on the real economy, empower the buyside and protect investors and consumers.

For press inquiries, please contact us at press@bettermarkets.com or (202) 618-6430.

NAFCU
3138 10th Street North
Arlington, VA 22201-2149
703.522.4770 | 800.336.4644
f: 703.524.1082
nafcu@nafcu.org | nafcu.org
National Association of Federally-Insured Credit Unions

May 17, 2023

The Honorable French Hill
Chairman
Committee on Financial Services
Subcommittee on Digital Assets,
Financial Technology, and Inclusion
United States House of Representatives
Washington, DC 20515

The Honorable Stephen Lynch
Ranking Member
Committee on Financial Services
Subcommittee on Digital Assets,
Financial Technology, and Inclusion
United States House of Representatives
Washington, DC 20515

Re: Tomorrow's Hearing: "Putting the 'Stable' in 'Stablecoins:' How Legislation Will Help Stablecoins Achieve Their Promise"

Dear Chairman Hill and Ranking Member Lynch:

I write to you today on behalf of the National Association of Federally-Insured Credit Unions (NAFCU) to share our thoughts on issues of importance to credit unions ahead of tomorrow's hearing on stablecoins. NAFCU advocates for all federally-insured not-for profit credit unions that, in turn, serve over 135 million consumers with personal and small business financial service products.

NAFCU appreciates the continued work of the Subcommittee in examining the integration of digital assets into traditional financial products, including the creation of stablecoins. As we have previously shared, we appreciate that both drafts of legislation noticed for this hearing use definitions of an insured depository institution (IDI) that include credit unions and definitions of federal banking regulators that include the National Credit Union Administration (NCUA). However, the Subcommittee must be careful not to unintentionally create an uneven playing field among credit unions, banks, and non-depository institutions by establishing chartering and enforcement provisions based solely on the Federal Deposit Insurance Act, with which the NCUA cannot strictly comply. The Subcommittee should also be cautious of granting bank-like chartering privileges to entities not offering insured deposits or engaged solely in stablecoin activities if doing so compromises safety and soundness. Along those lines, we have concern with the language found on the May 11th discussion draft noticed for this hearing that would seem to open the door for a special purpose "fintech" charter on page 24. We have concerns about this section and would urge better clarity before this draft moves forward.

To operate most efficiently, regulatory frameworks for stablecoins should acknowledge the NCUA's role as the primary financial regulator for credit unions. Establishing barriers to credit union engagement with digital assets would undercut many of the financial inclusion benefits that may be realized through related technologies. The credit union industry has a long history of prioritizing the needs of underserved and low-income communities and desires to continue this important work. While the bills generally recognize this, we have particular concern with language found in the May 11th discussion draft under subclause VIII on page 34 that clarifies supervisory and consumer protection requirements for functionally regulated custodians. This language appears to exclude credit unions because it cross-references a "primary financial regulatory agency" as described "under subparagraph (A), (B), or (C) of section 2(12) of the Dodd-Frank Wall Street Reform and Consumer Protection Act (12 U.S.C. 5301(12))" and this section of the Dodd-Frank Act does not explicitly reference the NCUA. We would urge you to amend this language before advancing this draft.

NAFCU also supports enforcement and examination being left up to existing regulators—in the case of credit unions, the NCUA—as well as establishing a basic framework for oversight of non-depository stablecoin issuers.

Finally, we would like to take this opportunity to reiterate our strong opposition to creating a Central Bank Digital Currency (CBDC). NAFCU believes that any advantages of a CBDC are outweighed by a multitude of risks, including those related to consumer privacy, financial stability, misallocation of Federal Reserve resources, and government intrusion into banking services traditionally provided by the private sector. Whatever benefits CBDC might hypothetically provide can be achieved more reliably and with less risk using existing financial sector infrastructure, including the Federal Reserve's soon-to-launch FedNow service. Furthermore, studies that consider the role of a CBDC in relation to other countries' use of digital currency—particularly China—tend to overlook critical issues around privacy and have not fully considered whether adoption of digital currency in foreign jurisdictions serves primarily a surveillance purpose. Given the strong position of the U.S. dollar today and public wariness of CBDC as a surveillance tool, near-term attention should be devoted instead to policy actions that can strengthen institutions like credit unions that stand ready to offer affordable and safe financial products and services to millions of Americans without fear of financial institutions acting as a government monitor.

Notwithstanding our concerns over a CBDC and our additional comments above, we are generally supportive of both legislative approaches for stablecoins that were noticed for this hearing. We believe that any study of CBDCs will confirm our concerns and further prove the need for stablecoins as a trusted means of real time settlements.

We thank you for the opportunity to share our thoughts and look forward to continuing to work with you on including emerging technologies into financial services. Should you have any questions or require any additional information, please contact me or Lewis Plush, NAFCU's Senior Associate Director of Legislative Affairs, at (703) 258-4981 or lplush@nafcu.org.

Sincerely,

Brad Thaler

Brad Thaler
Vice President of Legislative Affairs

cc: Members of the Subcommittee on Digital Assets, Financial Technology, and Inclusion

Questions for the Record from Ranking Member Maxine Waters
Subcommittee Hearing, entitled "Putting the 'Stable' in 'Stablecoins:' How Legislation Will Help Stablecoins Achieve Their Promise"
Thursday, May 18, 2023 9am

Ms. Fennie Wang

1. Which of the following options best describes your self-identified race? (you may choose more than one)
   a. White or Caucasian
   b. Black or African American
   c. Hispanic/Latinx
   d. Asian
   e. Middle Eastern/North African
   f. Choose not to answer
2. Which of the following options best describes your gender identity?
   a. Woman
   b. Man
   c. Non-binary
   d. Transgender Man
   e. Transgender Woman
   f. Choose not to answer
   g. Prefer to self-describe (please specify)

Mr. Matt Homer

1. Which of the following options best describes your self-identified race? (you may choose more than one)
   a. White or Caucasian
   b. Black or African American
   c. Hispanic/Latinx
   d. Asian
   e. Middle Eastern/North African
   f. Choose not to answer
   g. Prefer to self-describe (please specify)
2. Which of the following options best describes your gender identity?
   a. Woman
   b. Man
   c. Non-binary
   d. Transgender Man
   e. Transgender Woman
   f. Choose not to answer
   g. Prefer to self-describe (please specify)

Mr. David Portilla

3. Which of the following options best describes your self-identified race? (you may choose more than one)
   a. White or Caucasian
   b. Black or African American
   c. Hispanic/Latinx
   d. Asian
   e. Middle Eastern/North African
   f. Choose not to answer
4. Which of the following options best describes your gender identity?
   a. Woman
   b. Man
   c. Non-binary
   d. Transgender Man
   e. Transgender Woman
   f. Choose not to answer
   g. Prefer to self-describe (please specify)

Mr. Robert Morgan

3. Which of the following options best describes your self-identified race? (you may choose more than one)
    a. White or Caucasian
    b. Black or African American
    c. Hispanic/Latinx
    d. Asian
    e. Middle Eastern/North African
    f. Choose not to answer
    g. Prefer to self-describe (please specify)
4. Which of the following options best describes your gender identity?
    a. Woman
    b. Man
    c. Non-binary
    d. Transgender Man
    e. Transgender Woman
    f. Choose not to answer
    g. Prefer to self-describe (please specify)

Ms. Delicia Reynolds Hand

1. Which of the following options best describes your self-identified race? (you may choose more than one)
    a. White or Caucasian
    b. Black or African American
    c. Hispanic/Latinx
    d. Asian
    e. Middle Eastern/North African
    f. Choose not to answer
    g. Prefer to self-describe (please specify)
2. Which of the following options best describes your gender identity?
    a. Woman
    b. Man
    c. Non-binary
    d. Transgender Man
    e. Transgender Woman
    f. Choose not to answer
    g. Prefer to self-describe (please specify)

Statement for the Record of Steven L. Schwarcz, the Stanley A. Star Distinguished Professor of Law & Business, Duke University School of Law, for the May 18, 2023 Stablecoin Hearing, U.S. House of Representatives, Financial Services Committee, Digital Assets Subcommittee

INTRODUCTION

The principal challenge for digital, or electronic, currencies is facilitating day-to-day retail payments, in order to improve speed, reduce costs, and increase consumer financial access. Businesses already quickly and efficiently send large "wholesale" payments electronically through Fedwire, SWIFT, and other electronic wire-transfer systems.

The Federal Reserve could simply and cost-effectively utilize these existing wire-transfer systems to implement a retail central bank digital currency, or CBDC.[1] Although such a CBDC would require consumers to have bank accounts, consumers could use their ordinary commercial bank accounts.[2] Still, that could potentially limit financial access to the unbanked.

Stablecoins represent nongovernment-issued "currencies"[3] that are backed by—that is, exchangeable for—highly liquid assets (sometimes called "reference assets") that have intrinsic value.[4] Being cryptographically recorded, their transfer does not require the use of bank

[1] *See* Steven L. Schwarcz, *Regulating Digital Currencies: Towards an Analytical Framework*, 102 BOSTON UNIVERSITY LAW REVIEW 1037, 1051-55 (2022) (hereinafter, "*Regulating Digital Currencies*").
[2] *Id.*
[3] Stablecoins represent currencies insofar as they operate as a medium of exchange to facilitate the sale of goods and services and to otherwise make payments and satisfy debts. *Id.* at 1046. That function does not depend on a stablecoin being seen as "legal tender." *See* Steven L. Schwarcz, *Regulating Global Stablecoins: A Model-Law Strategy*, 75 VANDERBILT LAW REVIEW 1729, 1747-48 (2022) (hereinafter, "*Regulating Global Stablecoins*") (observing, among other things (*id.* at 1747 n.113), that the United States does not limit the medium of legal payment; rather, it allows any commercially reasonable and widely accepted medium to be used for payment).
[4] Stablecoins contrast sharply with bitcoin and other nongovernment-issued digital "currencies" that are *not* backed by reference assets. Those generic cryptocurrencies have unpredictably fluctuating values, which makes it difficult for consumers to use them on a daily basis as an alternative to cash; a successful retail currency should have a stable value. *Regulating Global Stablecoins*, *supra* note 3, at 1736-37.

accounts. (A CBDC could also be designed to be cryptographically recorded and thus not require the use of bank accounts.[5])

Not being government issued, stablecoins present complex and novel domestic and, when used for making international payments, cross-border regulatory challenges. This Statement for the Record focuses on the domestic regulation of stablecoins that are intended to be used as mediums of exchange. This Statement also concerns a Discussion Draft of a Bill to "provide for the [effectively, domestic] regulation of payment stablecoins, and for other purposes" (hereinafter, the "Bill").[6]

If interested, please note that I have separately analyzed in detail the possible cross-border regulation of stablecoins.[7]

OVERVIEW OF REGULATORY CHALLENGES

The principal challenges for the domestic regulation of stablecoins include protecting consumers and their privacy, protecting monetary integrity (including prohibiting money laundering and restricting the financing of terrorism and weapons proliferation that could threaten national security), protecting against breaches of cybersecurity and failures of operational resilience, and protecting against factors that could undermine financial stability or otherwise threaten the broader financial system.[8]

Of these challenges, the most fundamental to the nature of stablecoins is their underlying financial stability. Consumers could lose confidence in a stablecoin due to the issuer's inability

---

[5] *See Regulating Digital Currencies*, *supra* note 1, at 1051-55.
[6] Bill § 2(13)(A), at p. 4, lines 10-11. *Cf. supra* note 3 (observing that stablecoins would represent currencies if they operate as a medium of exchange).
[7] *See Regulating Global Stablecoins*, *supra* note 3.
[8] *See, e.g.*, PRESIDENT'S WORKING GRP. ON FIN. MKTS., FED. DEPOSIT INS. CORP. & OFF. OF THE COMPTROLLER OF THE CURRENCY, REPORT ON STABLECOINS 1, 3 (2021), https://home.treasury.gov/system/files/136/StableCoinReport_Nov1_508.pdf [https://perma.cc/2A79-AL95]; *Regulating Global Stablecoins*, *supra* note 3, at 1743-44.

to timely redeem the stablecoin for its underlying reference asset.[9] Consumer could even lose confidence due to doubt about that ability.[10] That loss of confidence could trigger a run on the issuer that resembles a classic bank run: the issuer may well be unable to obtain sufficient reference assets in time to satisfy correlated demands by stablecoin holders.[11]

I have separately proposed possible text for a model law to regulate stablecoins.[12] That text includes various ways to protect against the aforesaid run risk, including by collateralizing the redemption obligation by segregated investment-grade short-term money market instruments or by making stablecoins the equivalent of insured deposits.[13] That text also includes protections against the other above-referenced regulatory challenges.

The text of my model law is "generally consistent with the principles and recommendations advanced by the world's leading central banks [including the U.S. Federal Reserve] and multinational financial organizations [including the Bank for International Settlements (BIS) and the G20's Financial Stability Board]" for regulating stablecoins.[14] For that reason, I will reference the model law's text as applicable when analyzing the Bill, below.

Analysis of the Bill

The Bill protects against certain of the above identified regulatory challenges. I next address each such regulatory challenge. Thereafter, I provide some additional observations.

REGULATORY CHALLENGES

[9] *Regulating Global Stablecoins*, *supra* note 3, at 1758.
[10] *Id.*
[11] *Id.*
[12] *See* Appendix – Proposed Text for a Model Law, *Regulating Global Stablecoins*, *supra* note 3, at 1778-85.
[13] *Id.* at 1758-59 & 1782.
[14] *Id.* at 1778.

Protecting against factors that could undermine financial stability or otherwise threaten the broader financial system. Section 4(a)(1) of the Bill (at pp. 8-9) reasonably requires permitted stablecoin issuers to "maintain reserves backing the issuer's payment stablecoins outstanding on an at least one to one basis" with reasonably liquid assets. You may wish to analyze, however, whether 90-day maturity Treasury bills would enable an issuer to timely meet a run.

Section § 4(a)(3) of the Bill (at pp. 10-11) appropriately contemplates the possible issuance of capital, liquidity, and risk-management regulatory requirements. The "may not exceed what is sufficient" language is odd, though. Although that language may well be politically motivated, I'd have preferred "is sufficient." Also (and though I recognize the political backlash against creating moral hazard), I wonder whether some government entity should serve as a discretionary emergency liquidity provider, as I have separately proposed for consideration.[15]

The Bill also lacks a clear mechanism for the government to restrict stablecoin issuance and use in order to protect monetary policy.[16]

Protecting consumers. I did not see any consumer protection provisions in the Bill. That may well be because the U.S. Electronic Fund Transfer Act[17] already provides at least some protection.[18] Section 3.02 of my proposed model law provides possible comparative consumer-protection text.[19]

A question might arise whether the Bill should require segregation (and prohibition against commingling) of customer assets. I do not believe that would be relevant because stablecoin issuers would not, in their capacity as issuers, operate as exchanges or hold (in a

[15] *Cf. Regulating Global Stablecoins*, *supra* note 3, at 1761-62 & 1781.
[16] *Cf. id.* at 1767-68 & 1781 (discussing how to protect monetary policy).
[17] 15 U.S.C. § 1693.
[18] *Cf. Regulating Global Stablecoins*, *supra* note 3, at 1751 (discussing consumer protections for stablecoins).
[19] *Id.* at 1782.

custodial capacity or otherwise) or trade customer assets. The relevant segregation requirement regards collateral being used to satisfy the redemption obligation.[20]

Protecting privacy. I did not see any privacy protections in the Bill.[21] Section 3.03 of my proposed model law provides possible comparative privacy-protection text.[22]

Protecting monetary integrity. I did not see any provisions in the Bill prohibiting money laundering or restricting the financing of terrorism and weapons proliferation that could threaten national security. That may well be because the U.S. government already is committed to observe (and separately will be observing) the Financial Action Task Force's recommendations to implement these types of protections.[23] Section 3.05 of my proposed model law provides possible comparative text regarding anti-money-laundering and related protections.[24]

Protecting against breaches of cybersecurity and failures of operational resilience. I did not see these types of protections in the Bill.[25] Section 3.04 of my proposed model law provides possible comparative text regarding these types of protections.[26]

ADDITIONAL OBSERVATIONS

I support § 2(7) of the Bill (at p. 3), which allows nonbank entities to be approved by the primary Federal payment stablecoin regulator. Allowing "nonbanks to become stablecoin issuers" would "provide[] additional commercial flexibility for experimentation and innovation."[27]

[20] *See supra* note 13 and accompanying text.
[21] *Cf. Regulating Global Stablecoins*, *supra* note 3, at 1752 (discussing privacy protections for stablecoins).
[22] *Id.* at 1782-83.
[23] *Cf. id.* at 1753-54 (discussing monetary integrity protections for stablecoins).
[24] *Id.* at 1783-84.
[25] *Cf. id.* at 1755-58 & 1783 (discussing cybersecurity and operational resilience protections for stablecoins).
[26] *Id.* at 1783.
[27] *Id.* at 1749.

I am concerned that the "unsafe or unsound" standard of § 5(a)(4)(C) of the Bill (at p. 15, lines 12-15) is too weak to enable denial of an application to entities that lack integrity, reliability, or stability.[28] At the very least, that language of the Bill appears to invite litigation; an approved stablecoin issuer should have standards that exceed not merely being unsafe or unsound.

It is unclear why the Bill fails to cover the right to trade stablecoins or otherwise to engage in stablecoin-related services or other activities.[29]

Questions may arise regarding state approval of stablecoin issuers. I have not yet reviewed the interaction between the Bill's federal and state approval process sufficiently to express a view.[30]

There might be concern that the Bill does not explicitly address the ability of large commercial retailers to issue their own stablecoins. The Bill implicitly addresses that concern, however, by making it unlawful for any person other than a "permitted payment stablecoin issuer" to issue a payment stablecoin.[31]

There also might be concern that the Bill does not explicitly address algorithmic stablecoins. Algorithmic stablecoins are stablecoins that are backed by reference assets that are crypto-assets.[32] The Bill implicitly addresses that concern, however, by limiting the reference assets to specific high quality short-term assets that do not include crypto-assets.[33]

---

[28] *Cf. id.* (discussing the importance of a stablecoin issuer having integrity, reliability, and stability).

[29] *Cf. id.* at 1750 & 1779-80 (discussing regulating the right to trade stablecoins).

[30] I note, however, that giving the Federal Reserve Board the option to decline any state-approved issuer would (at least to that extent) reduce state regulatory autonomy.

[31] Bill § 3, at p. 8, lines 7-9.

[32] The required collateral reserves would then vary on a dynamic basis based on the changing market value of those crypto-assets.

[33] Bill § 4(a)(1)(A), at pp. 8-9, lines 16-24 & 1-3, respectively.

The following additional observations are more technical.

Sec. 3, p. 8, line 9 of the Bill: Should the phrase “use by any person in the United States” be expanded? For example, should non-permitted persons have the right to issue a stablecoin that is used by persons outside the United States to make payments within the United States?

Sec. 6(b)(5)(A), p. 27, line 18 of the Bill: Change "issued" to “issued or outstanding.”

Sec. 10, p. 35, lines 16-25 of the Bill: Is “insolvency” too limited? Also, in line 23, consider changing “from” to “by.” In lines 24-25, should stablecoin holders have priority over, for example, depositors? Also, should stablecoin holders have priority over state-law perfected secured creditors?

Respectfully submitted,

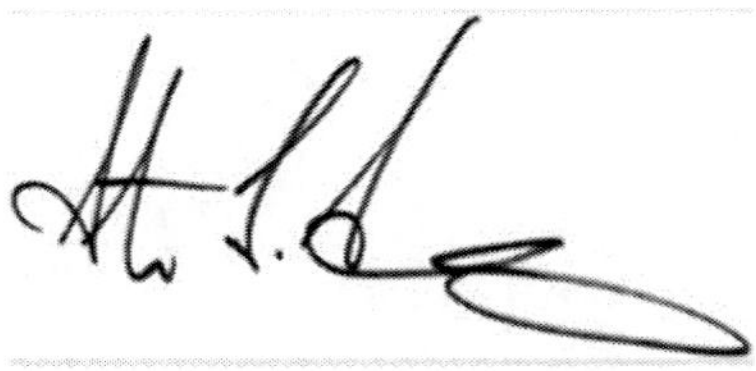

Index

R

S

T

U